THE ROMAN EMPIRE DIVIDED, 400–700

THE ROMAN EMPIRE DIVIDED, 400–700

John Moorhead

Longman

An imprint of **Pearson Education**

Harlow, England · London · New York · Reading, Massachusetts · San Francisco
Toronto · Don Mills, Ontario · Sydney · Tokyo · Singapore · Hong Kong · Seoul
Taipei · Cape Town · Madrid · Mexico City · Amsterdam · Munich · Paris · Milan

Pearson Education Limited

Head Office:
Edinburgh Gate
Harlow CM20 2JE
Tel: +44 (0)1279 623623
Fax: +44 (0)1279 431059

London Office:
128 Long Acre
London WC2E 9AN
Tel: +44 (0)20 7447 2000
Fax: +44 (0)20 7240 5771
Website: www.history-minds.com

First published in Great Britain in 2001

ISBN 0 582 25111 7

British Library Cataloguing in Publication Data
A CIP catalogue record for this book can be obtained from the British Library

Library of Congress Cataloging in Publication Data
A CIP catalogue record for this book can be obtained from the Library of Congress

10 9 8 7 6 5 4 3 2
06 05 04 03 02

Typeset in 11.5/14pt Garamond by Graphicraft Limited, Hong Kong
Printed and bound in Malaysia, LSP

The Publishers' policy is to use paper manufactured from sustainable forests.

CONTENTS

◆

Contents

The plates will be found in the middle of the book.

PREFACE

———◆———

It is a pleasure to thank those people and institutions without whose help this book would not have been written. I am grateful to the Australian Research Commission for a Large Grant which gave me time away from teaching, and to Andrew Maclennan, who commissioned it. The staff at Longman have been a model of efficiency and tact. I also thank the scholars, their identities unknown to me, who reported on a draft. While a book on the scale of this one must contain errors of fact and interpretation, they will be fewer because of their comments. Finally, if the readers of this book detect a certain authorial tone, the voice they hear will be mine, in conversation with students at the University of Queensland, for whose intriguing questions and sense of delighted surprise I am grateful beyond words.

John Moorhead
Feast of the Ascension, 2001

ABBREVIATIONS

———◆———

AA SS	*Acta Sanctorum*
CCSG	*Corpus Christianorum Series Graeca*
CCSL	*Corpus Christianorum Series Latina*
CIL	*Corpus Inscriptionum Latinarum*
CSCO	*Corpus Scriptorum Christianorum Orientalium*
Scr Ar	*Scriptores Arabici*
Scr Iber	*Scriptores Iberici*
CSEL	*Corpus Scriptorum Ecclesiasticorum Latinorum*
MGH	*Monumenta Germaniae Historica*
AA	*Auctores Antiquissimi*
Ep.	*Epistulae*
Leg nat Germ	*Leges nationum Germanicarum*
SRLI	*Scriptores Rerum Langobardicarum et Italicarum*
SRM	*Scriptores Rerum Merovingicarum*
PG	*Patrologia Graeca*
PL	*Patrologia Latina*
PLS	*Patrologia Latina Supplementum*
PLRE	*Prosopography of the Later Roman Empire*, vol. 1, Cambridge, 1971; vol. 2, 1980; vol. 3, 1992.
PO	*Patrologia Orientalis*
SChr	*Sources Chrétiennes*

INTRODUCTION

◆

Writing as he did in the first century BC, when the power of Rome was expanding more rapidly than at any other time, optimism as to the future of the Romans came easily to the poet Vergil. He represented Jupiter, the father of the gods, as saying: 'To them I set no limits in space or time. I have given them dominion without end' (*Aeneid*, 1.277f). Our purpose in this book is to examine the different ways in which, from the beginning of the fifth century of the Christian era to the beginning of the eighth, this prophecy proved false.

During these three centuries, the part of the world that forms the subject of this book experienced the greatest political changes in its recorded history. When they began, the borders of the Roman Empire seemed to stand firm. But before long, Germanic groups came to control the western parts of the Empire, while somewhat later Slavs and other peoples occupied most of the Balkans, and in the seventh and early eighth centuries Arabs conquered the southern shores of the Mediterranean and its most easterly and westerly coasts. In the face of these enormous losses, a steadily shrinking remnant of the Empire continued to exist, based on Constantinople. In the course of these developments, the relatively unitary civilisation of antiquity was replaced by ones from which the histories of the different regions would emerge. These came to find that they had little in common. When our story begins, the constituent parts of the Empire looked towards each other across the waters of the Mediterranean; at its end, they give the impression of having decided to turn their backs on the sea.

Our topic, then, is the changes that took place as the greater part of the Roman Empire passed beyond Roman control, and the roles of the Germanic peoples, Slavs, Arabs and others in this process. This approach means that many important aspects of the period will not be covered as fully as they deserve. Developments in nearby areas, such as Ireland, much of Scotland and Armenia, will receive short shrift, while those in parts of the Empire that remained under imperial control will not be fully explored. Such important events as the preaching of Islam and the consolidation of Christianity and Judaism; the emergence of powerful institutions such as the papacy and caliphate; the definitive statement of Roman law and the beginnings of legislation among such disparate peoples as the Arabs and the English; and the coming of literacy to fill new functions among those significantly described by the Qur'an as 'People of the Book' will all be treated, but only as ancillary to the main theme, that of the impact of the newly arrived peoples.

Their impact is more difficult to understand than may be thought. One way of looking at it is to see it in terms of waves of newcomers, rolling in one after another. But what looks like the forward movement of a wave can also be seen as the upwards and downwards motion of water that does not really move forward, and as we shall see, each perception has some validity for the period with which we shall be concerned. Moreover, the Empire into which new groups came was already undergoing great change. Power was passing to great landowners, many cities were mutating, while the recent rise of the Christian church was already decisively changing the weight of religion in society. Such internal developments meant that the Empire was taking on what may be thought of as a medieval appearance, even down to its different parts becoming less like each other, independently of new arrivals.

In any case, the categories of Romans who were there in the first place and non-Romans who arrived later are not as clear-cut as the literary sources produced by Romans tend to suggest. Overwhelmingly the products of males who had found their way to metropolitan centres, these are a poor guide to the realities of life in the provinces, and their perspectives often conceal regional diversity. A member of the proletariat of Rome, an intellectual in Alexandria, an olive farmer in Syria or Africa, and a peasant in Britain had little in common, even at the level of language. For their part, the newcomers to the Empire were more difficult to categorise than many of our sources suggest. They were disparaged as 'barbarians'; some would now say that they were 'constructed' in a way that entailed their being seen as the 'Other'. Yet these people, who often had little in common with each other and whose very ethnic identities could be slippery, had long been drawn into the gravitational sphere of the Empire, by raiding or the more benign mechanisms of settlement, trade and military service. Generals of non-Roman background were prominent in late antiquity, and someone who loyally served Rome, adopted the Roman religion, married a Roman and gave his son a Roman name could be thought of as having left his origins behind. Such people supported rather than weakened the Empire. Indeed, the settlement of newcomers on Roman soil could be seen as the speeding-up of a process of becoming more like the Romans, to which they had long been subject. And as we shall see, in province after province, local grandees sought to bend the newcomers to their own purposes, so that their settlement often reflected the agendas of local elites as well as their own.

Such considerations suggest that the categories of Roman and non-Roman, which loom so large in our sources, were not always sharply defined, and that the coming to power of the latter may have been an event of less moment than some thought. Another tendency points in the same direction. During the fifth and later centuries, similar events often occurred at much the same times right across the lands of the old Empire, no matter who controlled them, which suggests the working out of tendencies independent of who controlled various blocks of territory. More generally, there are countless signs of the survival of Roman ways in the post-Roman west. It could be argued that this was more apparent than real. Viewed from the moon, what inhabitants of Earth experience as great distances doubtless seem small, and it is certainly true that some of those who experienced changes in this time wrote of them with great feeling. Perhaps, it may be thought, it was words and forms rather than realities that survived. But against this can be set real changes that were under way in some areas towards the end of our period. As this book goes on, and its focus shifts towards the east, we shall come to an emergent society that quickly came to differ from both what had preceded it and its contemporaries in radical ways. Indeed, not only did it undergo great change internally, but it almost immediately found itself part of a much larger unit, so that very quickly it came to look away from the other parts of the old Empire, to an extent which proved fatal to the degree of unity that remained.

There is a vast array of sources for the period. Many are literary, some of them overtly historical and remarkably detailed. But few people wrote without *parti pris*. Occasionally, authors deal with some things in more detail than we would wish, so that historians seeking to make the best use of their materials write about things they happen to know about at a length that may exaggerate their importance. Some texts seem to yield information almost in spite of themselves. The genre of hagiography has much to say of the miraculous and extraordinary, yet paradoxically the lives of saints are often rich sources for the realities of daily life. Against the vagaries of written sources, the apparent objectivity of material data may appear attractive, but their interpretation is also fraught with problems. Nothing, it may seem, is less problematic than a piece of pottery, and datable items that were imported into the regions where they were found allow us to trace networks of exchange. But it is very difficult to correlate their use with that of technologically less sophisticated pieces that cannot be dated, and attempts to connect developments in trading networks with political happenings all too easily segue into circular arguments. Again, an assemblage of goods found in a burial offers insight into the goods available at that time and place. But can the ethnicity of people be determined from the goods with which they were buried? It would be foolish to draw deductions as to the origins of the inhabitants of contemporary western countries from the provenance of the high-tech goods with which they surround themselves. Moreover, the connections of a deceased person may have sought to make a fine show by assembling for a burial goods that appealed to them precisely because they were atypical of their society. Again, our period was prolific in laws, although the extent to which they reflected real conditions rather than the aspirations of lawgivers can be elusive. Similar difficulties confront anyone wishing to use the evidence of coins. We can plot their minting without being clear as to why they were minted; we can sometimes establish their distribution without being sure how they came to be distributed. Perhaps most usefully, coins give contemporary evidence for the views, perhaps propagandistic, of those who were responsible for them, just as laws do.

Not merely are the sources difficult and diverse, but the chapters of this book are based on very dissimilar bodies of evidence. For some, a narrative of important events can be erected on the basis of written sources; for others, this is lacking. While discussion of the sources in their own right has been avoided, I hope that something of the differing textures of evidence comes through. Yet such differences dictate different ways of proceeding, and it is a worthwhile exercise to imagine how the better-documented areas would appear to us were they only known through the kinds of evidence we have for others. All historians are at the mercy of their sources, but the problematic nature of many of those drawn upon here, and their uneven distribution, make unusually high demands on whoever tries to use them.

Beyond this, some of the practices I have followed require comment. This is a book about significant developments. Peoples and areas that may have seemed important at various stages, but whose roles turned out to be secondary, are sometimes given summary treatment. I have more to say about Franks than Alamanni, Visigoths than Suevi, Sunni than Shi'ite Muslims, and more about the north than the south of Gaul.

In a book that ranges over such a wide area, it has proven difficult to know what references to supply. With reluctance, I decided not to supply references to modern works in the notes. This places me in the uncomfortable position of not being able to acknowledge scholars from whose works I have benefited greatly, but there are hundreds of them, and any attempt to cite their works systematically would have weighed down a book of this nature, while an unsystematic approach would have created invidious problems of selection. This principle has been deviated from in the case of one monograph cited in the last chapter, and on rare occasions when modern works provide easy access to primary sources, but the key modern works are cited in the Bibliography. This also supplies relatively full, but by no means complete, references to primary sources, including both editions and translations of texts and the chief publications of other data; sometimes it has seemed simplest to give in a note an abbreviated reference to an edition in one of the great collections of sources listed in the table of abbreviations. Occasionally, it has been difficult to know what to include, but I have been guided by the principle of including references that readers may wish to have. In general, narrative parts of the book have received less annotation than others.

The rendering into English of names in strange languages is a difficult enterprise. I have given the name of Persia's greatest shah as Chosroes, a word to be pronounced with three syllables, rather than the more correct Khusro. The last Sasanid shah, often represented in English as Yazdgard, is referred to in an important Armenian source as Yazkert and appears in the *Prosopography of the Later Roman Empire* as Isdigerdes, while Kairouan, as the chief early Arab settlement in Africa is generally known, is spelt Qayrawan in the *Encyclopaedia of Islam*. In the face of such diversity, I have not applied consistent principles, but used forms that seem natural. Readers for whom some appear strange should know that it would have been possible to have moved further away from what is customary in English. I have followed general practice in retaining the classical name 'Persia' for the state called by its inhabitants, then as now, 'Iran'.

Another question of nomenclature concerns the name by which the continuing Empire should be called. In its medieval form, modern scholars generally call it the Byzantine Empire, but it is a tricky question just when the name becomes appropriate. I have used it from the reign of Heraclius, early in the seventh century, although there are other possibilities.

The Pacific coast of Australia may seem an odd place to write a book such as this, but it has its advantages. One cannot avoid being aware that scholars working within the area it covers sometimes tend to centre their approach on their own region, and interpret developments elsewhere in the light of its fortunes. From the eastern coast of the South Pacific, distances that loom large when encountered from within tend to diminish, the distance between Arabia and where I am writing being twice that which separates Arabia from Spain, and it is sometimes the case that outsiders have different perspectives to those within a situation.

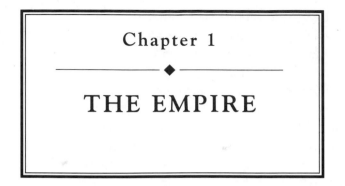

Chapter 1

◆

THE EMPIRE

It was the achievement of the Romans to create the largest political unit ever to have existed in that part of the world where Europe, Asia and Africa approach each other around the Mediterranean. As early as the fourth century BC, Alexander the Great had knitted together areas around the eastern shores of what the Greeks tended to refer to simply as 'the sea', so that a cosmopolitan poet who died a few centuries later could greet the readers of his epitaph in the languages of three places where he had lived: 'If you are Syrian, salaam! if Phoenician, naidus! if Greek, chaire!' Over some centuries the Romans were able to unify the lands around much of its western portion, particularly after they defeated Carthage in a series of wars in the third and second centuries BC, and during the first century BC they succeeded in bringing the eastern Mediterranean under their sway as well. They called it 'our sea', a term that acknowledged its status as the sea specifically connected with humans and distinguished it from the Atlantic and the great circumambulating Ocean. When a historian of the sixth century tried to conceptualise the extent of Roman power, it was natural for him to think of the Empire in terms of a block of territory lying around the sea. Its largest cities were all perched by its shores, and the advantages of speed and cost that transport by water had over that by land meant that, despite the excellence of the roads built by the Romans, through which they projected their power far inland, different coastal regions came to have a good deal in common.[1]

The true measure of the distances between the cities dotted around the Mediterranean was the time it took to sail between them. Communications could be remarkably quick, particularly between the northern and southern shores. On one dramatic occasion, Cato produced before the senate in Rome a ripe fig that he claimed had been picked at Carthage two days previously.[2]

Under favourable conditions, ships could travel between Narbonne on the coast of Gaul and Africa in five days, and between Constantinople and Alexandria in six. Communications across the length rather than the breadth of the sea were necessarily slower, but a letter written in Constantinople on 17 April 418 reached Arles in Gaul on 23 May, and, all going well, letters that popes wrote to emperors in Constantinople would take about a month to reach their destination. Sometimes communications were slower, as can be seen by the spread of news concerning the lynching of a bishop of Alexandria on 28 March 457, during Holy Week. Rumours reached Rome by 1 June, when pope Leo knew of it, but only on 11 July did he write to the emperor in Constantinople, having in the meantime received information from the bishop of that city.[3]

Exchanges of letters were hit and miss during winter, for the level of ancient naval technology allowed few sailings then. A letter written by the emperor Anastasius on 28 December 514 only reached pope Hormisdas on 14 May 515, by which time the pope had already received a letter written subsequently, while a letter that the emperor Justin wrote to the same pope on 17 December 519 was only received in Rome on 22 May 520, a full six months later. Only in May 603 did pope Gregory the Great write a letter of congratulations to an emperor who had acceded in November 602. Indeed, of the several hundred letters that Gregory wrote to destinations beyond Italy, most were written in the three months of summer, while none is dated to December and January. Nevertheless, while dealings between the cities around the shores of the sea could be played out in what now looks like slow motion, the speed with which they were conducted during much of the year meant that major cities on different shores were in some ways more tightly bound to each other than they were to their own hinterlands. The people of Rome and then those of Constantinople came to eat bread baked from grain imported from regions hundreds of kilometres to their south, and those who governed them were sometimes the victims of blackmail when threats were made to cut off the supply. A codex produced in Egypt during the late fifth century contains a cycle of illustrations of the book of Genesis, a part of the Bible that fascinated people of the period; pictures that are similar in ways too close to be accidental occur in the frescos of two churches of the fifth century in Rome, the throne of a bishop of Ravenna in the sixth century and, less surprisingly, Egyptian textiles of the seventh century. Behind these similarities stand chains of transmission that we cannot now identify.[4]

Yet although the civilisations of the ancient world continued to be based on the inland sea, the Roman Empire came to have a vast hinterland. Some of this was inherited from Alexander the Great, whose successors had established the Hellenistic kingdoms in Syria and Egypt, which diffused Mediterranean influences far inland from their capitals at Antioch and Alexandria, while the military prowess of the Romans, especially from the time of Julius Caesar and Pompey in the first century BC, allowed them to gain control over a broad swathe of territory far from the sea. Within a few generations all of Gaul and Spain, and much of Britain, became subject to Rome, together with portions of what is now German-speaking Europe. South of the Danube, all of the Balkans were subject to Rome, as for a while was Dacia on its northern bank. Doubtless the Empire could have expanded still further. Towards the end of his life the emperor Trajan (98–117), himself from Spain, one of the Empire's westernmost extremities, journeyed down the Tigris and gazed upon the Indian Ocean, where he lamented that he was no longer young enough to cross the sea to India, as Alexander had once done.[5] But the inland acquisitions of the Empire were immense and, as the Romans were dimly aware, would have great consequences.

In varying degrees, the conquered peoples underwent cultural assimilation and economic exploitation. In the period that followed the occupation of Britain, for example, a policy of building temples, fora and large houses was followed, and young men of important families were trained in the liberal arts, it being said that those who had disdained Latin came to long for rhetoric. But Tacitus, the Roman author who described the adoption by the Britons of the toga, colonnades, baths and elegant banquets, saw these things as a form of slavery which, he claimed, they were foolish enough to call 'civilisation'. Elsewhere, he represents the emperor Claudius as telling the senate that the people of Gaul, having been blended with the Romans by customs, culture and marriage, should bring their gold and wealth forward rather than keep them to themselves. Not surprisingly, the Romans encountered resistance. Tacitus credits a British leader trying to rally his people to fight for their freedom: 'Making off with wealth, butchering, snatching away, they falsely call these things "empire", and where they make a desert, they call it peace!'[6] Doubtless Tacitus was writing for effect, but if the physical remains of the Roman period in Britain still indicate the great impact that the Empire made there, the immense ruins of its capital show how successful the Romans were in making the wealth of others their own.

Yet the inhabitants of the inland areas of the Empire were also beneficiaries of Roman rule, for its thrusting away from the sea allowed Mediterranean ways to be widely diffused. The army in particular facilitated this process. Vines were planted by the river Moselle in the north of Gaul, in an area where legions were stationed; as early as the late first century an emperor had to act to preserve Italian production from competition. The founding of cities was one of the chief means by which the Romans imposed their rule. Identikit towns sprang up, each with its layout of streets based on two main roads intersecting at right angles, and buildings such as a forum, circus, amphitheatre and baths. Some of the works were paid for by the state, but largesse publicly displayed by the members of local elites eager to present themselves in a Roman light was responsible for the building of many, while right across the Empire, from a wealthy suburb of Antioch to the villas of Britain, the upper class installed mosaics displaying similar themes. More and more, indigenes came to be like Romans; from the early third century, virtually all the inhabitants of the Empire were Roman citizens. A poet of the early fifth century was able to pun: Rome had made a city (*urbs*) of what had formerly been a world (*orbis*).[7]

Another sign of increasing cultural homogenisation was the spread of the two imperial languages, Latin and Greek. As early as the time of Christ, the inscription on his cross had been written in these languages as well as Hebrew. Latin in particular benefited from its status, so that even in the east it gained currency as the language of imperial power and the army. But a multiplicity of tongues survived in the east, it being said that 72 languages were spoken in the streets of Constantinople. Some Armenians who came to a monastery near Jerusalem were told by the abbot to perform the liturgy in their own language, and only when some of them tried to add an heretical interpolation were they ordered to chant the Thrice-Holy hymn in Greek. In about 570 an Italian visitor found in an eastern monastery three abbots who knew Latin and Greek, Syriac and Coptic, and Bessic, which was spoken in Thrace. In the west, on the other hand, the spread of Latin led to the extinction of Celtic speech over almost all the continental parts of the Empire. This process took a longer period than our sources, none of them written in Celtic, would suggest. The bishop of a town in the south of Gaul in the late second century found it necessary to use Celtic, which he thought of as 'barbarous speech', and the father of the first great writer of Latin in Gaul, Ausonius, a native of Bordeaux who flourished in the late fourth century, may have been a Celtic speaker.[8] Yet outside Britain the fate of pre-Latin speech was sealed. In community after community, a stage of diglossia replaced Celtic monolingualism, and yielded in turn to Latin monolinguism. People who spoke only the indigenous language were succeeded by those who could speak both the indigenous language and the imperial one, who were themselves followed by people who spoke Latin alone.

Thus did the ways of the Mediterranean extend inland. But it was also true that the centre itself lay open to being influenced by people from the provinces. No less than Trajan, his successor Hadrian (117–38) was from Spain, while the emperor Septimius Severus (193–211), who was born in the African port city of Lepcis Magna, was said to have been moderately instructed in Latin, learned in Greek, but best at the Punic language that was indigenous to Africa. He married a woman from the inland Syrian town of Emesa (the modern Homs). In the middle of the third century, celebrations were held to mark the thousandth birthday of the city of Rome. They took a standard form, wild animals being killed in the Circus Maximus and games being held in the Campus Martius, but despite his Greek name, Philip, the emperor who presided over them, had been born near the inland Syrian town of Bostra, and he also bore the Arab name Sergius.[9] Pelagius, a Christian heretic of the early fifth century, was a native of Britain who made his way to Italy and ran afoul of Augustine, who had been born in an inland town in what is now Algeria. The gravitation of talented people from inland provinces to the centre is one of the most striking features of the Empire. And, as time passed, influences from beyond the Empire increasingly began to play.

FRONTIERS

Centred as it was on the sea, the Empire was ringed by its frontiers. Some of these, like the borders between most modern states, were clearly defined. In the West, they followed the Rhine upstream approximately as far as its junction with the Moselle, where the modern town of Coblenz takes its name from the 'confluence' of these rivers; the Roman side of the Rhine was lined by the military settlements from which such cities as Cologne and Bonn originated. From Coblenz the frontier proceeded overland to Regensburg, whence it followed the Danube to the Black Sea. In Britain, the frontier came to be marked by Hadrian's Wall, which ran across the island from the Solway Firth to the lower reaches of the Tyne. By contrast, the frontiers in the East and to the south were less sharply defined, and capable of being challenged. From the eastern edge of the Black Sea they ran southwards through the ancient Mesopotamia, an area of lasting tension with Persia, a powerful state fully capable of looking the Empire in the eye, and thence south-west from the Euphrates to Aqaba. On the African continent they incorporated Egypt as far south as the first cataract on the Nile, and the northern coast as far as the Atlantic. While at no point in Africa did the frontier extend as far from the sea as it did in Europe, in the modern Algeria and Tunisia in particular it ran some hundreds of kilometres inland.

The frontiers were an important part of the way in which the Romans thought of their Empire. They were accustomed to thinking of precisely defined zones. Caesar looked on the Rhine as constituting a border between the Gauls, a branch of the Celts, and the Germans, although this was at best a gross simplification. In a similar fashion, later Romans invested their borders with great significance. They could see themselves as being surrounded by howling nations which, in their tricky barbarism, were wont to attack the frontiers. One writer believed that the emperor Augustus had made the Empire strong 'by hedging it about with major obstacles, rivers and trenches and mountains and deserted regions which were difficult to traverse', while the author of a panegyric envisaged the Rhine as having been provided by nature as a dividing line that would protect the Roman provinces from barbarian savagery. Late in the fourth century, bishop Ambrose of Milan thought of this river as a 'noteworthy wall' that stood between the Roman Empire and fierce peoples, while his near contemporary, the historian Festus, whose life was memorably consummated as he died on the steps of a temple dedicated to Nemesis, considered that the Danube downstream from Augsburg formed a boundary between peoples whom he was happy to describe as Romans and barbarians.[10]

Those closer to the margins experienced a different reality. While Ovid, a Latin poet and man of the world at the time of Christ, was none too pleased at being exiled to a town on the Black Sea, in the midst of his sorrows he set himself to composing poetry in the language of the local people. Ill-defined borders running through semi-desert regions could not keep those on either side apart from each other, and even rivers can function as means of communication that bring zones together just as much as lines of demarcation. Trade across borders was expedited by the markets that flourished in frontier zones. By the 360s people living to the north of the Danube were so dependent on trade with the Empire that they lacked the necessities of life when the Romans forbade it, and in the late fifth century Rugians and Romans were attending each other's markets on either side of the river. In one area where the border with Persia was poorly delineated, the people on either side not only shared markets but happily intermarried, and elsewhere there were three towns specified in Roman law as places where trade could take place on the Persian frontier. A peace treaty that the Empire and Persia concluded in the sixth century treated the conduct of trade between the two states at length: the locations at which trade could take place between Roman and

Persian merchants were indicated, while trade undertaken by Saracens and other merchants was precisely regulated.[11]

Such trade was only one way in which ties extended across borders. The Franks and others who dwelt to the east of the Rhine and the Goths who lived to the north of the Danube in late antiquity were for the most part farmers; when some of the latter were allowed into imperial territory during the late fourth century, the authorities gave them food and land to cultivate.[12] In some areas their economies were becoming intertwined with that of the Empire. Downstream from Bonn the Rhine broadens, rich agricultural land lying on either side. The economy of the region was dominated by the need to provide for the legions stationed on its left bank, and farming patterns on the non-Roman side of the river seem to have been changing to cater for the welcome market opened up by their arrival. On the Roman side were stationed the *limitanei*, the frontier troops whom a law issued in 443 reveals cultivating lands for their own profit in border regions, but also 'barbarians' who had been given land in return for seeing to the border and its fortifications. Some of them were *laeti*, groups of soldiers who had been settled with their families on imperial territory: a law issued at the end of the fourth century explained that 'laetic land' had to be provided for those people from many nations who had sought the felicity of the Romans and come to the Empire. Some Germanic people, as we may call them for convenience, were peacefully entering the Empire as migrants and settling as farmers in the north of Gaul, while others settled further to the south, with the permission of the authorities. In 370 the emperor Theodosius I sent some Alamanni captives to Italy, where they farmed land around the Po.[13] One way of looking at the occupation of the western part of the Empire by Germanic peoples in the fifth century is to see it as the speeding-up of the processes of Romanisation and peaceful settlement that had been going on for a considerable time.

In such ways, the image of their borders that presented itself to the Romans was false, turning as it did what can be seen as zones of inclusion and integration into lines of exclusion and division. It would be impossible to deduce where the northern border ran in Britain on the basis of finds of Roman pottery, and in some ways the area in which such pottery was used, which extended northwards of Hadrian's Wall, is as valid a marker of the extent of Roman presence as the formal border. Across the frontier were people who enjoyed what the Empire offered and attempted to use it for their own ends. A treasure laid down in about 400 at Traprain Law, to the north of the wall in the Scottish lowlands, consisted of broken silver from the Empire which members of a local elite had prepared for use as bullion.[14]

Such treasures are a reminder that, while our sources are necessarily opaque as to the attitudes of people across the frontier towards Rome, there were people there who used what the Empire produced in ways that made sense within their own societies, just as the Empire sometimes sought to manipulate such people for its own ends. It will be worth our while turning to such people, concentrating on the West, for it was there that they became increasingly important in late antiquity.

BARBARIANS

Beyond the borders of the Empire dwelled people whom the Greeks and Romans termed 'barbarians'. These were people whom the inhabitants of the Empire found it difficult to like. Reproducing categories that had been used centuries earlier, Prudentius, a Latin author who wrote in about 400, was strikingly forceful: Romans differed from barbarians as animals with four legs from those with two, or the dumb from those who speak. About a hundred and fifty years later, Cassiodorus, whose fanciful etymologies are a constant reminder that the people of the period attributed to words a significance different from that which they have today, commented: 'The word "barbarian" [*barbarus*] comes from "beard" [*barba*] and "country" [*rus*], because it is known that he never lives in the city but dwells among the fields, like a wild beast.' For Victor of Vita, an African of the fifth century who had first-hand experience of the Vandals, the word 'barbarian' signified savagery, cruelty and terror. Such people were often looked on by the Romans in a heartless fashion. When 29 Saxon captives whom a senator had obtained to use as gladiators in games held to celebrate the appointment of his son to high office committed suicide, he shed no tears for the loss of human lives. Rather, he thought the misfortune was all his, and was driven to console himself through the teaching of Socrates.[15]

But such sentiments, the vehemence of which invites speculation as to the extent to which they involved the projection on to others of the anxieties of those who gave them utterance, as well as some scepticism in accepting what Greek and Roman authors say of such people, do not tell the whole story. Other perspectives were possible. Even Victor found it necessary to define his position against that of people 'who love barbarians and sometimes praise them', while an author of Gaul extolled the barbarians for the love they had for each other and their chastity, something which he believed the Vandals valued more highly than Socrates had. Julian the Apostate, the most intellectual emperor of late antiquity, was taught by someone of Scythian birth whom he described as a barbarian. A historian of Gothic background has Goths hoping to live with the Roman people so that they would be believed to be of one race. On one occasion in the fifth century, the eastern emperor Zeno, in a gesture of humility, professed that he was a barbarian and a person who bore arms.

It is sometimes hard to be certain of the tone of passages that appear critical of barbarians. A description of Burgundians that mentions their spreading sour butter on their hair and smelling of garlic and onions is alarming, but it occurs in a poem written in what its author called a jocose style, which is addressed to someone known to have enjoyed a good laugh, and perhaps the passage was meant to be funny rather than to be taken literally.[16] Indeed, the very word 'barbarian' is problematic. Whenever we use this word, we identify ourselves with a Roman perspective that was pejorative and credited the peoples of whom it was used with a unity that it would never have crossed their minds to claim for themselves. In a sense, therefore, we may think of the barbarians as having been invented by the Greeks and Romans. Just as the Latin word 'pagan' and its Greek counterpart 'Hellene' could be applied indiscriminately to highbrow senators who worshipped the ancient gods, Germanic peoples who worshipped such deities as Woden, and Persians who worshipped fire, the only unity they possessed being that attributed to them by Christians, who used these terms of them in hostile ways, and just as the word 'Arian' could be used by Catholic authors as a handy term of abuse to describe people who subscribed to a wide range of theological positions, so the word 'barbarian' was never used of themselves by those to whom it was applied, and betrays a perspective both hostile and falsely generalising. For that reason we shall use it only when quoting from or paraphrasing contemporary authors who employed it, relying elsewhere on the neutral term 'newcomers' to describe those who entered imperial territory.[17]

When the Greeks and Romans thought of 'barbarians', they conceived of them as belonging to different groups, the members of which were biologically related to each other. This understanding was reflected in the terms they applied to these groups, for such words in the classical languages as *genos*, *gens* and *natio* were derived from roots referring to birth. For their part, such people had similar notions of themselves. The reality, however, was more complicated.

Some scholars, taking literally a report by the historian Jordanes, believe that the Goths originated in Scandinavia, and that a movement of this people in a south-easterly direction across what is now Poland to an area between the Danube and Dnieper rivers can be traced by archaeological evidence.

Such theories fall far short of proof. Jordanes wrote in the middle of the sixth century, and it would be extraordinary if he were a reliable source for a migration that his own dating suggests occurred just over two millennia before he wrote.[18] Moreover, while Gothic, of which we have a reasonable quantity from the fourth century, was a Germanic language, by about the third century, when inscriptions give some sense of speech in Scandinavia, the people there were speaking a language quite different to Gothic. And while some have held that material artefacts point to migration from Scandinavia, even if it were agreed that the archaeological record unambiguously shows a diffusion of goods that can be connected with Scandinavia, it is not clear what would be proven, for the spread of a material culture need not be associated with the spread of a people. Indeed, the very notion of an ethnically distinct people retaining its purity across the millennia, which Jordanes' model entails, is implausible, for marriage with people outside the group and the adhesion of various people who threw in their lot with it would in time have lessened its ethnic specificity.

In any case, modern scholarship has developed a different approach to the origins of peoples, called 'ethnogenesis', which emphasises their ability to come into being and mutate. A military band, it is held, could develop stories of its origin, a kernel of tradition, and if it were successful it would, in the manner of an avalanche, draw other people to identify themselves with it. Such traditions would have been associated with royal families to which they attributed an endurance over long periods of time rarely to be found in families whose lineage can be securely documented. That the history of the Goths written by Jordanes could be held to represent this tendency outstandingly may be thought to strengthen the theory, or lead to speculation as to why other sources do not point more clearly in the same direction. In any case, it is easy to see that new members who threw in their lot with a group of warriors that was doing well for itself could identify themselves with it, precisely as we know happened with the Vandals, Franks and Alans. At another level of society, a group of farmers who settled densely in a region could assimilate people who were already there, as we shall see occurred in parts of both western and eastern Europe in the post-Roman period. Rather than being something entirely given, ethnicity may also have sometimes been a matter of choice, and those who chose to throw in their lot with a group could express this choice by the adoption of practices common amongst its members, some of which involved aspects of material culture that can be recovered by archaeologists, while others, for example language, are more difficult to trace.

This is not to say that different groups were not clearly distinct. An author of the eighth century was able to distinguish between groups of Gepids, Bulgars, Sarmatians, Pannonians, Saxons and Noricans.[19] We may further assume that marriage generally occurred within such groups; after all, most people marry those with whom they have things in common. But the period we shall examine in this book witnessed an extraordinarily rapid growth in the size of some groups, and the no less dramatic diminution of others, which can be more easily explained by people choosing to be members of a group on the one hand and opting out of membership on the other, than it can by invoking high birth rates and death rates respectively. It is worthwhile remembering the changing meanings attached to the word 'Roman': from referring to the inhabitant of a city, and then an empire, by late antiquity it had modulated so that it could refer to a Catholic Christian, who could have been a Frank, as opposed to a believer of the Arian persuasion, while the Greek-speaking inhabitants of the Byzantine Empire based on Constantinople called themselves Romans! Given such flexibility, it would not be surprising were the reality attached to the word 'Goth' to have been unstable across time. The people, assuming it was one people, referred to in classical texts as Gotones, Gothones or Gutones bore names that may have been variants of that of the Goths who, by 500, seemed of commanding importance in much of western Europe, but it may have been names rather than an ethnically distinct people that lasted across the centuries.[20]

NON-ROMANS

It could not be doubted that the peoples looked on as barbarians differed from the Romans in important ways. Those known in the west were in the main Germanic peoples whose political structures were, by the standards of the Mediterranean, underdeveloped. This characteristic was particularly evident in their system of law, which was customary rather than the product of legislation, transmitted orally rather than in writing, and emphasised the rights of the extended family. They spoke non-classical languages, of which only Gothic is known in any detail, but it was certainly a Germanic language, and what can be deduced from personal names indicates that others as well spoke tongues which, like Gothic, had diverged from a common Germanic ancestor. They could also be distinguished from the inhabitants of the Empire by their religious beliefs, for some were polytheists and others adherents of what had come to be considered a heretical form of Christianity, whereas by the end of the fourth century Catholic Christianity had become the official religion of the Empire. They responded to a different visual aesthetic, which found expression in the use of geometrical and stylised animal images rather than the representational, so that when Germanic artists appropriated themes from Roman art, the human figures became dematerialised and tended to turn into shapeless masses.[21] Their taste was shown in the beautification of utilitarian objects, rather than the practice, characteristic of the high art of the ancient world, of creating things of beauty for their own sake. In such ways they were very different to the peoples of the ancient world. Yet as we shall see, some of the qualities that have sometimes been thought of as proper to them must be set aside. Indeed, as time passed, it was remarkable how similar to the Romans some of the people they thought of as barbarians were becoming.

This was evident in material culture, for a wide variety of goods manufactured in the Empire came to circulate beyond its frontiers. It may be that hostile military action during the third century contributed to this, for raids then took place on a great scale. In the 260s people described as Goths ravaged towns in Asia Minor, while Athens was sacked by Heruls. Such was the scale of raids in Gaul that hundreds of people buried coins in hoards that have been excavated by modern archaeologists. Franks also raided Spain and advanced as far as Africa, while at the very heart of the Empire the ancient walls of Rome were strengthened in the 270s. Such developments were alarming, but transient. For most of the fourth century, the Empire enjoyed good relations with its neighbours in Europe, and in no way can the raids of the third century be seen as part of a continuum that culminated in the far more important events of the fifth century. Nevertheless, people who were taken prisoner or enslaved during the raids may have contributed to the diffusion of Roman speech, ideas and goods, the last of which would also have been carried away as booty by the raiders. Germanic troops in imperial service were another agency for the spread of Roman ways. The markets we have already mentioned, and more generally commerce, was another area of interaction. One of the oldest Latin words to enter the Germanic languages was *caupo*, which means shopkeeper and, more particularly, innkeeper. While the word failed to generate derivatives in the Romance languages that grew out of Latin, *caupo* lives on in the modern German word for a purchase, *Kauf*, the English word 'cheap' and the first part of the Danish placename 'København', while even beyond the Germanic languages it formed the basis of the Russian word for buying, *kupit*. The word had passed into Gothic as early as the fourth century, for it was then that a translator of the Bible into that language used the verb *kaupon*, meaning 'to trade', at Luke 19:13.

One of the commodities that it is easy to imagine Germanic people buying, especially from innkeepers, is wine, and indeed the word for this drink in the modern Germanic languages is derived from the Latin *vinum*. The partiality of 'barbarians' for this drink had long been noted by the Romans. One classical author suggested that, if they were given the amounts they wanted, their vices would allow them to be overcome as easily as they would have been by arms. Wine was certainly one of the commodities they expected the Empire to offer. A king of the sixth century was furious that enemies of his had been allowed to settle in the Empire, and a letter he wrote to the emperor shows him imagining what they would be doing there: trading in grain, enjoying wine cellars, leading a high life, bathing and wearing fine clothes with gold.[22] As the king was aware, the Empire offered goods at the luxury end of the market, and these were exported far beyond the frontiers of the Empire, to places such as Scandinavia, where imitations of them were sometimes produced. More bulky commodities enjoyed more local distribution.

In such ways were the European neighbours of the Empire coming under its influence. Words of Latin or Greek origin, like *caupo*, came to permeate their speech. By the time the English began to settle in Britain in large numbers during the fifth century, they had borrowed some 170 Latin words, using them for such domestic things as radishes, pepper, butter and cheese. But the interchange between Romans and non-Romans worked in both directions. The Latin word for soap, *sapo*, was borrowed from a Germanic word. We first hear of it being used to colour hair, rather than wash it, in the second century, when it is mentioned as being used by Germans in Gaul. Nevertheless, no lesser person than the emperor Constantine (306–37) was remembered in the following century as having had hair which was so difficult to manage that he had to use soap and a diadem to control it. Sometimes it is difficult to tell in which direction linguistic influence operated. The bishop who translated the Bible into Gothic in the fourth century rendered the Greek word for city, *polis*, by the Gothic *baugs*. But for some time the word *burgus* had been used in Latin inscriptions to denote forts, and it was used in a law issued in 400. In the early fifth century, the word was in common use in Latin, although one writer looked on it as a colloquialism. Whatever the origin of the word, which may be Greek rather than Latin or Gothic, the linguistic exchange suggests a coming together, which presumably occurred by way of the army rather than the wine shop.[23]

Indeed, when the Romans thought of 'barbarians', it was often in military terms, and in this capacity they sought to use them. The Empire could enrol military units as *foederati*, a word which referred to the treaties (*foedera*) that bound them to it, or as imperial allies (*symmachoi*). Some groups were thought of as being bound to the Empire by ties of 'friendship'. An army that the emperor Theodosius I led from the east to Italy towards the end of the fourth century was said to have included many 'untamed nations' that God had caused to have the one faith, so that it seemed to be made up of one race, although the suggestion of unity was belied by a detachment of Goths within it being led by its own commander, Alaric. And non-Romans did not only serve as auxiliaries, for the composition of the regular army became steadily more Germanic. By the sixth century, the Greek words for 'banner' and 'military band' had been driven out by the Germanic word *bandion*; so thorough was its adoption that by the early seventh century it was thought of as being a word of the ancestral tongue of the Romans.[24] But the Germanisation of the army was particularly strong in the west. There is no reason to interpret this development in a sinister light, for military service was immensely unpopular amongst the Romans. Officials, confronted with the likelihood of soldiers running away, had taken to branding them, which suggests that citizens of the Empire may have viewed the widespread enlistment of non-Romans with pleasure.[25]

Not everyone approved of these developments. A proposal was offered in the east that the army be manned not by 'Scythians', as Goths were sometimes called, but by philosophers, craftspeople, traders and the people who wasted their time laughing and groaning in the circus. However, having become a remarkably civilian people, to whom a law of 364 forbade the use of weapons, the Romans were pleased to have irksome military duties placed in the hands of competent people who were known to be good at that kind of thing.[26] The troops who were responsible for Julian becoming emperor at Paris in 361 were Germanic, and they elevated him in accordance with ancestral custom, raising him on a shield and acclaiming him just as they would a new chief. An inscription at Trier, a town in the north of Gaul where emperors came to live frequently in the fourth century, recorded the death of a Burgundian, Hariulf, whom it described as 'protector domestigus'. His name was Germanic and must mean 'army wolf', but his office was that of a bodyguard of the emperor. A panegyric delivered in honour of Theodosius I describes barbarian peoples wishing to fight for him. It has all the nations of Scythia, enticed by his kindness, as flowing together in such a way that they gave the impression of obeying an order. The Goth, the Hun and the Alan, former enemies of Rome, conducted themselves without the tumult, confusion and pillage that barbarians would have caused. Some Germanic troops were being used by the emperor in his capital. In 386 the histrionic bishop of

Milan, Ambrose, then involved in a controversy with the state over the use of churches in the city, claimed that against the emperor's weapons, soldiers and Goths, he could only use tears as arms.[27]

Not only the lower ranks were open to non-Romans. By the late fourth century, most of the commanders-in-chief of the Roman forces in the west had non-Roman names, a yardstick that may well underestimate their preponderance, and the weight they carried in the political life of the Empire was evident. In 383 a usurper, Maximus, was proclaimed emperor in the north of Gaul. Bishop Ambrose was sent from Milan on an embassy to his headquarters at Trier, and during their negotiations Maximus claimed that Bauto, a Frank from across the Rhine, had sent barbarians against him. This, he felt, was unjust, for he could have sent as many barbarians against Bauto. But Ambrose responded by claiming that Maximus had himself threatened to march on Rome with barbarians from across the frontier. Maximus was finally defeated by Theodosius, whose army was largely made up of barbarians. The affair made clear the extent to which armies made up of non-Romans had become important, the role of Germanic generals such as Bauto, and the use to which both troops and generals were put by Roman contenders for office. Such were the services that Bauto rendered the state that he was appointed consul for the year 385, on which occasion Augustine, then coming towards the end of his years as a non-Christian, delivered a speech in his honour.[28] Before long, Roman and Germanic elites were marrying each other. Arcadius, the elder son of Theodosius, married a daughter of Bauto, while Honorius, his brother, married one after the other two daughters of another great general, Stilicho, himself the son of a Vandal father and a Roman mother. But another family makes the integration of powerful Roman and Germanic more clear.

In 422 a Goth named Areobindus distinguished himself in the east when participating in a successful expedition against the Persians. Some years later he was made a consul, the highest, although by then purely honorary, office of the state, and he became a wealthy landowner, in which capacity he received correspondence from a nearby bishop. His son, Dagalaif, went on to become consul himself, and married the daughter of another non-Roman general. Their son, another Areobindus, became a military commander in the east during the early sixth century, held a consulship, and married an extremely wealthy Roman woman whose father had briefly been an emperor in the west, after whom they named their son. Another Areobindus, who may have been the grandson of this couple, married the niece of the emperor Justinian and served the Empire in Africa during the 540s. The fortunes of this family across several generations illustrate the remarkable coalescence that had come about at the highest levels of society between Germans and Romans.[29]

Despite the marriage of the younger Areobindus, these tendencies came to operate far more strongly in the West than in the East where, following a massacre of Gothic troops in Constantinople in 400, less use was made of such people. But in the West it became difficult to distinguish between the activities of the increasingly Germanised regular units and those of Germanic auxiliaries. The divergent histories of the two parts of the Empire were both natural developments of the situation that had come to obtain during the preceding century. As we shall see, the final collapse of Roman power in the West occurred in a world still recognisably Roman, for the co-option of Germans in the interest of the Romans meant that the destinies of the two in the West were necessarily linked. Ambrose of Milan, displeased at the behaviour of Gothic troops in his city, confronted them with a hard question: 'Where will you go, if these things are destroyed?' Such people had every interest in the preservation of the status quo.[30]

NAMES AND CLOTHING

Two of the ways in which people make statements about their identity are the names they give their children and the clothes they choose to wear. Developments in both these areas point to a coming together of Roman and alien traditions during late antiquity.

For centuries, the attractiveness of Rome to the Germans had been shown by their enthusiasm for adopting Roman names. As early as the first century, two took the names Iulius Civilis and Claudius Paulus, and the tendency accelerated in late antiquity. According to a writer of the late fourth century, Constantine was the first emperor to advance 'barbarians' to the office of consul. It happens that not one of the names known to us of the consuls appointed by Constantine is non-Roman, but this does not mean that what we are told of Constantine's appointment is wrong, for non-Romans could well be concealed behind Roman names. We know of an Alamannic general of the fourth century, Mederich. Knowledge he had gained of the Greek mysteries while he was a hostage in Gaul led him to change his son's Germanic name, Agenarich, to the exotic Serapion, after a deity of Egyptian origin in whose honour a temple had been built in Rome during the third century. The mother of the great Ostrogothic king Theoderic, Erelieva, adopted at her baptism the Greek name Eusebia, and her daughter was known by two names. One of them, Ostrogotho, preserved the name of her people, while the other, Ariagne, recalled a name from Greek mythology, Ariadne, which was borne by the empress of the time. We may see the giving of such names as astonishing examples of chutzpah, but it is more probable that it should be seen as revealing a kind of cultural symbiosis that developed as non-Romans were attracted to Roman ways and joined the elite of the Empire.

The reverse procedure, that of Romans adopting non-Roman names, is much harder to document in this period, although it became more common in later centuries. But we know of a native of Gaul whose name was the Latin word for 'wolf', Lupus. He had a brother named Magnulf and a son named Romulf, who became a bishop of Reims in the late sixth century. Such easy passage between the Latin for 'wolf' and names ending in 'ulf' suggests that the family moved in a world where identity, if important at all, was not reflected in personal names. Early in that century a woman in Italy who was recommended to students as 'the flower of Roman eloquence' bore what might have been thought of as the inappropriate name Barbara, and a few decades later a man erroneously named in a text as Gothigus is described as urging the emperor to commit resources to a war against the Goths. Such names suggest that distinctions between 'barbarian' and Roman, and Goth and Roman, were of little import to those who used them.[31]

Clothing was another area in which differences between Romans and non-Romans were dissolving. In the fifth century, many Catholics who worked for the Vandal king in Africa went to church dressed like Vandals, which both implies a difference in style of dress and suggests that it was ceasing to apply. Vandals who attacked Catholic churches are said to have turned altar cloths into shirts (*camisae*) and trousers (*femoralia*), yet there was nothing distinctively Vandal about such clothes, for Romans wore them as well. But we may suspect that some Romans would not have been seen dead in them, for shirts were considered vulgar, the kind of things that soldiers found it convenient to wear while fighting, which suggests that they had military and populist connotations. They were susceptible to various uses, for a shirt was among the clothes that a young man of Corinth was wearing when he entered a brothel and which he gave to a virgin so that she could escape dressed as a man. The same could be said of trousers. While official ideology continued to associate the wearing of these with barbarians, as on the Barberini ivory, an early sixth-century ivory of imperial victory, a good deal of evidence points to Romans wearing trousers or breeches (*brachae*). Perhaps such behaviour was only to be expected of a person who became an Arian bishop, who also wore a chain around his neck, and it was perhaps predictable that after the raids of the third century some country people in Gaul would imitate the enemy. But mosaics of the fourth century at the villa of Piazza Armerina in Sicily show Romans wearing trousers, while during the late fourth and early fifth centuries a series of emperors enacted laws forbidding the wearing of boots, trousers, clothes made of skins, and even long hair, in the city of Rome. Alas, such practices were deeply established, for no less a person than the eastern consul for 392 was accused of wearing skins and having assumed the customs and clothing of the Goths. Perhaps this legislation was directed against clothing that was perceived as being military as much as barbarian, but as we have seen, by then it was becoming difficult to prise the two categories apart, and a recently discovered letter of Augustine shows him conflating military and barbarian dress. We may postulate a craze among Roman civilians who wished to dress in the style of 'barbarian' soldiers. When, late in the eighth century, a historian considered the propensity of the Lombards to wear trousers, he hazarded the bizarre conjecture that they had adopted the practice from the Romans; by this time their true origins had been forgotten.[32]

Such tendencies did not prevent non-Romans who were trying to look smart from putting on Roman clothes. When the Visigoth Athaulf married Galla Placidia, the daughter of Theodosius I, in 414, at a ceremony that took place at the home of a leading citizen of Narbonne, the bride and groom were both dressed in Roman style, while the gifts that Athaulf made to Galla included precious stones that the Goths had carried off from Rome four years previously. Yet, as with non-Romans known to have adopted Roman names, the practices of Athaulf were those of a member of an elite group. At other levels of society, influences flowed in the opposite direction, as in the practice of cranial deformation. Artificially deformed skulls are known among the Huns, but they were also to be found among a wide range of peoples, among them Sarmatians, Avars, Goths, Gepids and Burgundians. One may be inclined to write these folk off as a motley crew of barbarians who shared a savage practice, but it was one they shared with the indigenous inhabitants of Roman Gaul, whose adoption of it made a statement of non-Roman leanings.[33]

Perhaps the world of late antiquity was full of poseurs striving to be seen as what they were not; perhaps a situation of cultural fluidity within which statements of identity could easily be made had developed. Whatever the mechanics that generated such developments, we may suspect that they were to be met in particular among high-status people of Germanic background, some of whom doubtless found reasons of prestige for adopting some of the trimmings of a Roman life. But someone who held high office in the Roman army (which entailed command of Latin and may have involved campaigning against 'barbarians'), took a Roman name and married a Roman woman had made a series of statements that, cumulatively, amounted to something very like a declaration of being Roman. Even if this were questioned, surely the offspring of a marriage between such a person and a member of a distinguished Roman family would have been seen as Roman. Yet, at the same time there were Romans who, in various ways, were making statements that implied identification with non-Roman ways. Indeed, as time passed, it became clear that the future lay in a mixture of elements that had begun to come together at a time when no one would have doubted that the Roman Empire, in the West as much as the East, had a brilliant future.

ROMAN SOCIETY

Our discussion may have given the impression that the Roman world was a constant, interacting with non-Romans in various ways. In fact, the Empire into which the newcomers were finding their way was undergoing rapid change, and it will be worth our while examining some aspects of this.

When the emperor Diocletian, in a move unusual among those of his rank, renounced office in 305, he moved to Split, an out-of-the-way place on the Adriatic coast where he had built a large villa. It contained a temple, baths, and his own mausoleum, virtually everything a retired emperor could be expected to need. His move to the country was one frequently made in the European and African parts of the Empire during late antiquity. The author of a poem on the river Moselle describes villas dotting its banks, the inhabitants of which could enjoy the life of the city while in the country. Like the villa built by Diocletian, theirs were largely self-contained and often fortified; Spanish towns of the middle ages whose names begin with 'Torre' may have been named for a tower (Latin *turris*) built to fortify a villa. Among the great villas of Gaul was Montaubin in its south-west, where a villa of the first century was largely rebuilt in the mid-fourth. Its impressive entrance, size and decorative mosaic and paintings breathed style and confidence. Bathing, hunting and fishing were available, while its kitchen, conveniently located between the garden and dining areas, prepared sumptuous meals at which oysters and snails were consumed in equal proportions. Another great villa was that at Piazza Armerina in Sicily. Whereas the layout of Montaubin is pleasingly symmetrical, that of the latter, probably erected in the early fourth century, seems chaotic, but it was cleverly designed so that lines of vision were blocked once it had been entered. Its amenities included a smart bathing complex, and it was decorated with the largest area of mosaics known in the ancient world, showing not only people wearing trousers but also a chariot race being held in the Circus Maximus in Rome.[34]

Such a gesture towards the presence of the city in the country was stylish, but it was directed towards something increasingly of the past. Urban life had not merely been a way for the Romans to impose their authority on conquered lands; it had also been, since the time of Socrates, conceived of as providing the space in which one could lead a life that was, literally, 'civilised'. The English words 'civil', 'urbane' and 'polite' are ultimately derived from Latin and Greek words for 'town' and 'city', while the words 'rustic' and, perhaps, 'pagan' come from classical words for the country. But in late antiquity, powerful currents were flowing against urban life. Constantine had to legislate against people who were removing marbles and columns from cities to the country. Long traditions of local autonomy, exercised through the town councils that had selected magistrates and overseen the collection of taxes, were being eroded by provincial governors answerable to the emperor. To be sure, the bishops who were becoming prominent were well placed to act as advocates for their fellow townspeople, but the ideology of the Christian religion was anti-urban. When the biographer of the monk Antony stated that his hero 'made the desert a city', the dictum represented a contradiction of the values of a thousand years of Greek civilisation, as did the very term 'monk' (alone); according to Aristotle, humans were by nature animals who lived in towns. The church fathers set themselves firmly against this understanding. John Chrysostom, writing in the great city of Constantinople, attacked those who built fora and baths, standard urban amenities, rather than churches, maintaining that a church built in the country is like God's paradise. For John, 'philosophy', which the Athenians had practised in their city, was really the product of quiet. One of his contemporaries, Augustine, held that the deserts of the wilderness were fertile. And if it were true, as pope Gregory believed, that Christ engaged in prayer on the mountain and worked miracles in the towns, his followers found his example easier to follow in the first respect.[35]

Yet while such teachings were diffused throughout the Empire, it was in the West that towns atrophied. Whereas cities in the East comfortably looked back to their history before the Romans came and remained integrated with the society and economy of their agricultural hinterlands, many of those in the West had been founded relatively recently by the Romans, and remained somewhat artificial. At some point they became less desirable as places of residence, and people able to move elsewhere began to do so. A law issued by the western emperor in 400 deals with members of guilds deserting cities to follow a rustic life in what are described as secret and out-of-the-way places. Later in the century, a scion of a distinguished family in Gaul accused one correspondent of neglecting his residence in a town for a rural life of 'suburbanity', and another of disdaining city affairs while busying himself with country activities. In this respect, the practices of the owners of the great estates conformed to the ideology of Christianity. In the following century, a servant of the Ostrogothic government in Italy wrote to the landowners and town councillors of the south of Italy, urging them to live in cities, for the fields and woods were suitable for wild animals. He lovingly described the lifestyle one could enjoy in a town of the ancient world:

> To stroll through the Forum, to look at some skilful craftsman at his work, to push one's own cause through the law courts, then between whiles to play with the counters of Palamedes, to go to the baths with one's acquaintances, to indulge in the friendly emulation of the banquet – these are the proper employments of a Roman noble; yet not one of them is tasted by the man who chooses to live always in the country with his farm-servants.

But such lives were those of a minority, supported by the surrounding countryside, and all over the West the tide was flowing away from the city towards the country.[36]

The villas to which the wealthy retreated were more than holiday homes. They were supported by broad estates (*latifundia*), which were growing at the expense of smallholdings. A story told in the Bible of how king Ahab improperly took over the vineyard of Naboth was of contemporary relevance in the West during the late Roman period. An author of the period described people losing their small properties to others who occupied them, or abandoning them as they fled from tax collectors. Such people sought the estates of great men and became the tenants (*coloni*) of the wealthy. Much of the working of the land came to be done by *coloni*, who were often tied to the soil and were obliged to render the estate owners varying proportions of money, rent in kind and, apparently to a lesser extent, labour services. They were starting to resemble the serfs of the middle ages, and they tended to replace slaves as a source of labour. Slaves, into whose situation St Paul's injunction that they obey their masters 'with fear and trembling' (Eph. 6:5) casts an eery light, may not have been maintaining their numbers, and the practice of groups of thugs who captured people in Africa and sold them as slaves overseas indicates that there was a market for them. Nevertheless, by late antiquity they were yielding to *coloni*, whose situation was not happy. It is possible that obscure rebellions, the work of people known as 'bacaudae', were a form of resistance on the part of peasants to an increasingly difficult life, and it was known that there could be found among the 'barbarians' Romans who preferred impoverished freedom to being anxious taxpayers. The outlook of the owners of large estates, by contrast, was bright.[37]

More and more of the wealth of the West was being concentrated in few hands. The villas that were rebuilt in Spain after the raids of the third century were the larger ones. While the great landowners were sometimes well connected politically and rarely averse to holding high public office, they were steadily turning their backs on the rest of the world, and the ties between them and the state were becoming loose. Increasingly, they stood between the state and the production of wealth. The Empire drew little benefit from people who were reluctant to pay tax and well placed to gain from the remissions that were periodically issued. Moreover, a law of 366 made them responsible for the taxes paid by the *coloni*.[38] The implications of this enactment were serious. It had long been a truism among the Romans that taxes were the sinews of the state, and the ability of the Empire to maintain its army depended upon its ability to draw wealth from the land by way of taxation. The taxes levied in late antiquity were overwhelmingly on the land, often in kind, and high in incidence. While we cannot estimate the proportion of wealth that was consumed by taxation, it is certain that much of the wealth created on the land found its way to the state. From there, it passed to the army. One way of looking at the role of the state in late antiquity is to see it as a gigantic apparatus that took wealth from the land with one hand and gave it to the military with the other. The failure of the state to enjoy direct access to the wealth was ominous.

For their part, the grandees found the state of diminishing importance, as they set to work privatising some of its functions. In 399 a Gothic general ravaging Pamphylia was defeated by a local leader who had organised farmers and slaves to resist, while shortly afterwards landowners in Spain supplied the slaves and farmers on their estates with arms. Military goods have been associated with cemeteries near a number of Spanish villas of late antiquity. In 440 the emperor told people living in parts of Italy threatened by Vandals to take their defence into their own hands. If the job of defence could be organised locally, what had the state to offer those who were coming to wield power in the regions where they lived? The authorities who, in the sixth century, instructed a senior person in the south of Italy to gather a group who would be able to deal with the country people who disrupted a market were of the post-Roman period, but the way in which they acted had become familiar. There were other signs of the retreat of the state. A water mill complex installed at Barbegal, near Arles in the south of Gaul, which was capable of producing enough flour to support 80,000 people, may have been privately constructed and operated by the proprietors of the villas that had been built nearby. Significantly, the water needed for its operation was drawn from a publicly owned aqueduct, and, although the owners may have paid for the right to use it, it is hard not to see the complex as the intrusion of private enterprise on to the domain of the state. Water mills were becoming more common. Palladius, the author of a tract on the management of estates, advocated their use, as St Benedict did in his Rule for monks. The self-sufficiency that Benedict intended for his monastic community precisely reflected the trend towards self-sufficient latifundia in the secular world. Turned in on themselves as they were, these units reflected the priorities of people for whom the state was becoming an irrelevance.[39]

In such ways did the powerful turn their backs on both the Empire and the life of the cities through which it had largely been expressed, as they put down deep roots in their own regions. Such tendencies would outlast the villas, for as late antiquity progressed they were falling out of use. Some were abandoned, while the buildings of others were put to new uses. There is no need to see this process as having been caused by the arrival of 'barbarians', nor did it spell disaster for the families that had resided in them, for over most of the west they remained a force with which the newcomers had to reckon. But whatever prompted the decline of the villas, wealthy families, rather than competing for prestige in the public places of towns and the military or civilian service of the state, continued to base more of their activities in their own localities, and their horizons became steadily more narrow.

The tendency for local grandees to become absorbed into regional life was connected with another development in late antiquity. As time passed, the different parts of the Empire were becoming less like each other. This could be seen at a macro-level in the divergence of the eastern and western parts of the Empire. Since the days of Augustus, it had been governed from Rome, but in the third century a system was devised whereby emperors were made responsible for various regions. In accordance with the logic of this system, Constantine established a new capital for the eastern part of the Empire. Named after himself, the city of Constantinople was established early in the fourth century on the site of the ancient Greek colony of Byzantium on the Bosporus. It grew rapidly, and by the end of the fourth century came to exercise more effective power than Rome. During the fourth century, one emperor would sometimes be responsible for the whole empire, but after the death of Theodosius I in 395 its two parts became in practical terms autonomous units, their interests sometimes coinciding and sometimes conflicting. They drifted apart in such areas as language. During the administration of a praetorian prefect who came from Egypt, Cyrus (439–41), Latin was replaced by Greek in the administration of the East, and although an antiquarian civil servant was still regretting the change a hundred years later, it was never turned back; while the corpus of Roman law was in Latin, the 'new laws' (*novels*) that the emperor Justinian issued were in Greek.[40]

In such ways did an autonomous East liberate itself from the linguistic inheritance of Rome. But it was not merely the case that the two halves of what had been a unified Empire were drifting apart; each part was also becoming more diverse. Inscriptions suggest that, from about the fifth century, the inhabitants of Spain, Gaul, Dalmatia and different regions within Italy were coming to speak diverging forms of Latin. Elsewhere, languages other than the classical pair gained in strength, especially in the East, where Syriac became the vehicle of Christian and Manichean theology, while an alphabet based on that of Greek came into use for Coptic, the language of Egypt, which enjoyed an extraordinary vogue. In a novel development, some of the Greek classics were translated into other languages and received commentaries in them. Towards the middle of the fifth century, Probha produced commentaries, and perhaps translations, of logical works by Aristotle into or in Syriac; a few decades later, an Italian scholar, Boethius, would begin his enormous project of translating into Latin and commentating upon the works of Plato and Aristotle, of which only a small proportion was completed. Boethius found himself hindered by the inability of Latin to express some of the concepts of Greek thought, but in the following centuries few would be worried about this issue.[41] In some respects, these endeavours constituted a recognition of the importance of a central body of teaching that was the common property of all learned people, but they also represented a retreat from a world in which Greek was a shared language of high culture to one in which people would appropriate the learning of the Greeks in their own languages. In some areas, the place-names imposed by Empire were in retreat. The names of towns founded by the Romans in Gaul were yielding to names based on the names of local Celtic tribes; by the beginning of the fourth century, some people were calling the town later to become the capital of France the 'town of the Parisii', rather than 'Lutetia', the name that the Romans had given it.

In different ways, these tendencies complemented the devolution of power away from the centre to regional potentates in the West. This is not to say that the arrival of newcomers and the dismemberment of the West into smaller political units did not speed matters up. When Melania, a wealthy Roman woman attracted to an ascetic life, liquidated her estates early in the fifth century, she had to deal with properties in Italy, Sicily, Africa and Britain;[42] by the end of the century, the falling apart of the Empire in the West would have made such scattered holdings difficult to sustain. But it is clear that a process of regionalisation was already well under way. Much of the history of the west in the following period would be the product of accommodations between the newcomers and the local landed aristocracies.

RELIGION

The period of these changes was also that of the definitive triumph of Christianity, another product of the ancient Mediterranean that spread far inland. When Constantine was converted early in the fourth century, Christians were a small minority of the population of the Empire, largely made up of socially undistinguished people, but towards the end of that century a series of laws was issued which prohibited public pagan practice. Doubtless more pagan belief survived than our sources, overwhelmingly Christian in the fifth century and virtually entirely so from the beginning of the sixth, would wish us to think; in religion, as in other areas, the material we have for the period is often one-sided to an extent that can screen realities. But it is clear that the greatest religious revolution in the history of the West was securely accomplished with great speed, comfortably within two lifespans. Moreover, it was not simply the case that one system of belief was replaced by another, for the triumph of Christianity opened a period during which religion came to bear a far heavier weight than it had previously or would subsequently.

The conversion of Constantine allowed Christianity to become the religion of the Empire. Before long it was part of the establishment, a situation that many clerics found all too congenial, and predisposed to accept the realities of the world around it. Yet such acquiescence would be in conflict with the radical instincts implicit in the teaching of the religion. In the fourth century, these came to the fore in the explosive growth of monasticism. The most important pioneer of the movement was a Coptic-speaking Egyptian hermit, Antony (c.251–356), whose longevity may suggest something of the rewards of holiness. The example of his life as a monk was widely followed. Within a few decades it was being imitated in Syria and Anatolia, and by the end of the century 'monasteries' had been established in Italy and Gaul. One of the means by which Antony's fame spread was a biography thought to have been written by Athanasius, a bishop of Alexandria. Some of the greatest scholars of recent centuries have regarded this work as having had a disastrous impact on later Christian thinking, and its emphasis on demons and ascetic practices makes it problematic for many readers. But Athanasius wrote works on other topics, the readers of which quickly find themselves in awe of his precise intelligence, and among those powerfully moved by the example of Antony was Augustine, one of the most intellectually rigorous people ever to have written in Latin. On hearing of the holy man, one of Augustine's friends cried out:

> Tell me, where is all the work we are doing leading? What is the point of it all? Why are we still serving the state? Can we hope for anything greater in the palace than being friends of the emperor? . . . If I want to be, I can become a friend of God right now.[43]

For such people, the friendship of God could easily trump anything the state could offer.

Figures such as Athanasius and Augustine confront us with extremely acute minds engaged in a radical project, that of overthrowing the traditional values of their world. This is not to say that they would not seek and welcome the support of earthly authority, but it was secondary. At a lower intellectual level, St Benedict, the most authoritative monastic author in the west, was praised for having been 'knowingly ignorant, and wise in his lack of education'. People like Benedict were part of a democratisation of culture associated with Christianity, another sign of which was the emergence of female writers. They were virtually unknown among the authors of antiquity, especially among those who wrote in Latin, and while their future in the Christian tradition was contested, it often being the case that areas of discourse to which women contributed were new ones which, as they became established, turned into the preserves of male authors, there can be no doubt that writing on explicitly Christian themes offered possibilities to women.

Such counter-cultural inclinations, uneasily coupled with the power it came to hold in society, made the new religion more of a force to be reckoned with than its predecessors in the ancient world had been. Moreover, it was doctrinally sharp-edged, and its tendency to operate in an intellectual world within which questions were approached in an 'either/or' rather than a 'both/and' manner made it little inclined towards compromise with enemies without or, for that matter, dissidents within.

Society was confronted by not only the Christian religion, but also the Christian church, with its power structure and ability to accumulate wealth. In each town there came to be a bishop. Men holding this office were often able, aggressive and adept at striking a demotic tone that enabled them to build support within the communities they led. An author of the ninth century told a funny story about Attila the Hun. It was said that, when he approached the city of Ravenna in the fifth century, its bishop went out to seek his mercy. Attila was told that the bishop was prepared to lay down his life for his children, whereupon the Hun was furious, demanding his advisers to tell him how one man could have so many children. Terrified, they replied that the inhabitants of the city, they being the children in question, were his spiritual children. At this it was Attila's turn to be alarmed, and he left the city unharmed. The story is completely untrue, although as we shall see, Attila did receive an embassy that included a pope. But apart from its being an example of the sometimes unexpected humour encountered in texts of the period, it shows the relationships that could be thought to exist between a bishop and the people of a town whose church he presided over. Bishops also enjoyed an authority that came from presiding over the cult of the dead, particularly the martyrs who had been put to death by Roman power. Ambrose of Milan described himself drawing on the patronage of two obscure martyrs, Gervasius and Protasius, whom he saw as defenders when he was threatened by the troops of an emperor who was then resident in the city.[44]

Yet bishops were not only the leaders of their congregations. They also looked to their episcopal counterparts elsewhere, so that, in a world of narrowing horizons, the church was an organism which, at least in theory, was universal. Despite the ever-present reality that local churches would come to be vehicles for furthering the interests of those who already held power, a reality often displayed in controversies over the appointment of bishops, the reach of the bishops of Rome, or popes as they were coming to be called, tended to lengthen. In these ways, the structures of the church were opposed to the growing regionalism. Even the cults that grew up around holy men had an integrative power which pulled disparate regions together. Symeon the Stylite, who lived for years on top of a pillar in Syria, is described as having been revered by Arabs, Persians, Armenians, Spaniards, Britons and Gauls, while his cult was so strong in Rome that many icons of him were placed there. The cult was widespread, and the origins of the saint's devotees indicate that there was no reason for its being confined to the territory of the

Empire. But the timing of the rise of Christianity meant that it came on line, so to speak, just as the arrival of newcomers into imperial territory was becoming more significant: the rise of the faith in the fourth century enabled it to operate during the fifth century as a mechanism that allowed newcomers to be integrated into Roman ways. For it was open to all. A theologian of the seventh century drew attention to the ability of the church to assimilate: within it could be found men, women and children beyond counting who were different in birth, looks, race, language and many other respects. Yet in Christ there was 'neither male nor female, neither Jew nor Greek, neither circumcision nor uncircumcision, neither barbarian nor Scythian, neither slave nor freeman'.[45]

Such was the growing power of the church that, while it profited from the support of the Empire, it came not to need it. This was clear in its great success in beginning to accumulate wealth, mainly in the form of land. From the time of Constantine, the Roman church was given estates over a wide part of the Empire, while the churches of Constantinople and Alexandria had come to possess villages a century later. Emperors and other patrons were endowing churches with splendid vessels for use in the liturgy, such as those to be seen in mosaics of the sixth century in the church of San Vitale in Ravenna, and cities were being reconfigured around places of worship. The author of a letter written in 400 mentions the squalor of the Capitol in Rome and all the temples of the city being covered with soot and spiders' webs, its people running quickly from the half-ruined temples to the tombs of the martyrs. The skylines of the towns and cities of late antiquity came increasingly to be dominated by churches. In the early centuries of the Empire, the provision of public buildings had given rise to competitive display by wealthy citizens, both within and between towns. But local patronage of secular buildings dried up, as those which continued to be built were financed by the state or bishops, while the proliferation of buildings erected for the cult of the church reflects not only the growing standing of the church, but also its access to wealth.[46]

The wealth and power that the leaders of the church accumulated in late antiquity meant that the institution had been transformed into a stakeholder in the status quo which stood to gain from the continuation of the existing order. Yet its degree of detachment from worldly structures, and the circumstance that its authority was in the main independent of the state, meant that its long-term interests did not necessarily lie with the Empire. Like the great landowners, it would be possible for the church to go it alone. Such considerations governed its relations with the newcomers on imperial territory.

The scale of the changes that we have been considering, and others which we shall consider later, was not fully understood by those who lived through them. The extraordinary situation that, by 400, there had come into being within the Roman Empire powerful elements that no longer needed the state, and which indeed may have found its interests antagonistic to their own, passed unremarked, as did the awkward reality that many of those looked down on as being barbarians tended to profit from their association with the Empire and had an interest in its continuance. Contemporary authors, and modern scholars who share their perspectives, often credit such people with malign intentions. But for most of them, the Empire was the goose that laid the golden eggs, and they did not stand to gain from its demise. In any case the Empire was widely believed to be in an excellent position. About three-quarters of the way through the fourth century one of the greatest biblical commentators in the history of the church, John Chrysostom, was in Antioch, preaching on the prophecy of Isaiah, 'nation shall not lift up sword against nation, neither shall they learn war any more' (Is. 4:2). He observed: 'Today, wherever the sun shines, from the Tigris to the British Isles, and Africa, Egypt and Palestine as well, indeed whatever is subject to the Romans, is fully at peace, and war is known only by hearsay.'[47] Our concern in this book will be to explore the ways in which this ceased to be true, while remaining alert to other processes of change that were under way, and to the complex ways in which newcomers to the Empire and these processes interacted.

Chapter 2

THE WESTERN MEDITERRANEAN TILL THE MID-SIXTH CENTURY

ITALY

The Goths Enter the Empire

Theodosius the Great was the last ruler of the whole Empire. Following his death in 395, it was divided between his two sons, the elder, Arcadius, succeeding to his power in Constantinople, while the younger, Honorius, reigned in Rome. There was nothing to wonder at here, for the Empire had been divided previously, and in any case it was becoming more regionalised. But within a hundred years unforeseen circumstances that developed quite quickly caused the territory under Honorius to pass beyond the control of the Empire.

As we have seen, relations between the Empire and those across its borders tended to be good in the fourth century, and it was in the context of such relations that a number of Germanic people, known as Goths, crossed the Danube into Roman territory in 376. There is no reason to envisage Goths leaving a Scandinavian homeland on a trajectory that would inevitably lead them to Rome, and certainly no reason to think of them as having laid deep plans to arrive there. In fact, we cannot take the Goths further back than late antiquity, when a people of this name lived to the north of the Danube, and Roman emperors were awarding themselves the title 'Gothicus' to commemorate victories won over them.[1] The oldest surviving text in a Germanic language, a portion of a translation of the Bible into Gothic undertaken by bishop Ulphilas, is apparently a product of this milieu. It came from a society familiar with Roman ways; in St Mark's gospel, the word 'tribute' (Mark 12:14) is translated *kaisaragild*, literally 'emperor-money'.

The Goths were a people with whom the Romans found it worth their while keeping on good terms. Many Roman coins, presumably paid as subsidies, have been found in the region, while items of largesse found in the town of Kerč (Bosporus) may have been imperial presents to local aristocrats. The presence of the Goths may have been associated with the artefacts of a material culture, dating from about 200 to 400, found between the rivers Danube and Don, which has been called, after a site near Kiev, Černjachov. The farming tools used by the people of this culture were more advanced than those of other peoples in the area, a reflection of their close relations with Rome, and while a factory devoted to the production of combs indicates fondness for this characteristic Germanic product, the scale of its production suggests that strong networks of exchange had developed. The society was by no means warlike, for weapons are found in only a few of its burials; rather, it was a settled population that supported itself by agriculture, not by pastoralism and still less by fighting. The entry of many of its members into Roman territory, and the sudden end of the Černjachov culture, was the result of contingent circumstances that no one could have foreseen.[2]

The onslaught of the Huns was devastating. This people had been unknown to the ancient world, the very word 'Hun' being first used by Roman authors at the time of their appearance. Answering to impulses unknown to us, they had come from central Asia. In the sixth century, Jordanes told a lurid story of their origins, according to which the Huns were the product of unions between Gothic women and unclean spirits, testimony to the dread with which they were remembered and, perhaps, the apologetic need of a Gothic author to explain the devastating impact they had on the Goths. Such was the fear their coming inspired among the Goths living to the north of the Danube that their leader, Ermaneric, took his life. In their hour of need the Goths sent spokespersons, who may have included bishop Ulphilas, to the emperor Valens, who asked humbly to be allowed into the Empire and promised they would live quietly and provide it with military assistance if required. Long experience of the Goths as neighbours indicated that the Empire stood to gain from this proposal. Some of the emperor's advisers drew attention to the usefulness of the new soldiers they would gain, and Valens allowed Goths, referred to from the sixth century as 'Visigoths', to cross the Danube into Roman territory. So it was that many Goths, described in one source as variously making the crossing in boats or on rafts and hollow tree trunks, with others attempting to swim, made their way across the Danube and into Roman territory, in numbers that cannot be estimated. They were refugees, peasants rather than soldiers. Valens ordered that they were to be given food and land to cultivate, and the Empire could congratulate itself on having gained productive and useful new inhabitants.[3]

It is also likely that this was the time when most of the Goths agreed to accept Christianity. Their decision would later be a cause of tension between the Romans and themselves, for the Goths received the religion in a form associated with a priest of Alexandria, Arius, which came to be regarded as deviate. Christianity, in common with Judaism and Islam, holds that all that exists is either God, the Creator, or belongs to the realm of created beings. To which category, then, would Jesus Christ, the Son of God, belong? For Arius, and those who thought like him, he fell into the latter category, but their view was rejected by the Council of Nicaea, summoned by the emperor Constantine in 325, which used the language of Greek philosophy to teach that Christ was 'of one substance with the Father'. This view was to prevail, but as it happened Ulphilas was of anti-Nicene conviction, and Valens inclined towards a theology that subordinated the Son, so that Christianity came to the Goths in this form. The form of Christianity accepted by the Goths enjoyed all the prestige of being the emperor's belief, and was part of a package that eased their assimilation into the Empire. Alas, Valens was the last anti-Nicene emperor, and it could not have been foreseen that the loyal adherence of the Goths to what was seen as Arianism would come to distinguish them from the Catholic Romans.

Such developments lay in the future. Very quickly, however, it became clear that the benefits that each side had hoped would accrue from the entry of the Goths into the Empire would be short-lived. The coming of so many hungry mouths into a part of the Empire not known for its wealth strained local resources, and Roman officials exploited the Goths, causing them to take to arms. Much later, a Gothic historian was to represent the change in status that this implied in the language of the Bible, which came so readily to authors dealing with the arrival and settlement of newcomers: after an incident in which Roman soldiers murdered the companions of a Gothic leader at a feast, the Goths were no longer 'strangers and pilgrims', but citizens and lords. Within a few years, some of the refugee farmers had become threatening warriors. Valens made his way to Thrace to deal with them, and gave battle without waiting for reinforcements to arrive. On 9 August 378 a Gothic army in which cavalry played an important role inflicted an exceptionally heavy defeat on the Romans at Adrianople. Valens was killed; not until the ninth century would another emperor die in battle. Gothic troops, joined by groups of Huns and Alans, moved quickly towards Constantinople itself, but before they reached it they were themselves attacked by a group of Arabs, one of whom alarmed them by sucking the blood of a man he had killed. Disconcerted by this and the immensity of the city, the Goths withdrew. But the existence of hostile forces within the Empire was a new situation that called for a response.[4]

In 382 the emperor Theodosius, who succeeded Valens as emperor in the East, came to a settlement with the Goths which gave them the use of land in the Danube area. They were to keep their own laws, which meant that the legislation of Theodosius against heresy, now including the Arian style of Christianity, did not apply to them. They were also obliged to render military service to Theodosius. In accordance with this obligation, a force of Goths commanded by Alaric fought within the emperor's army at the battle of the Frigidus in 394, helping defeat an army supporting the emperor Eugenius, which was commanded by a Frankish general, Arbogast. The role they played showed that Goths could be loyal allies of legitimate Roman authority. But their losses had been severe, and following the death of Theodosius in the following year Alaric, disappointed at not having been given a Roman command, rebelled. Years of devastating raids in the Balkans followed, during which Alaric sometimes received support from Romans. On one occasion, when advancing southwards through Greece, he sent a message to the general Gerontius, who controlled the crucial pass at Thermopylae, whereupon the general kindly withdrew his forces to allow him through.[5] In 401, perhaps in annoyance at a withdrawal of subsidies that he had been receiving, Alaric took an important decision. He determined to invade Italy.

Italy from Alaric to Odovacer

The West was not well governed when Alaric arrived. Perhaps in recognition that it was less important than the East, Theodosius had assigned it to the younger of his sons, and Honorius achieved little in his long reign (395–423). Not only did he disdain to leave Italy, but in response to fears that Alaric would attack Rome, he retreated from the city, so that by the end of 402 he was issuing laws from a town on the Adriatic coast, Ravenna. Surrounded as it then was by marshes and some of the arms of the river Po, its inaccessibility made it a retreat in troubled times, and it remained the favoured residence for emperors for most of the time left to the Empire in the West. In 405, when Alaric had left Italy, it was invaded by a Goth named Radagaisus, who was defeated and put to death near Florence in the following year. It had fallen to another general of non-Roman background, Stilicho, whose career had benefited alike from his military skill and adroit management, to lead the Roman resistance to Alaric and Radagaisus, but he was executed for treason in August 408. In that year Alaric returned to Italy and, receiving support from many of the troops who had served Stilicho, he besieged Rome. He only withdrew when he received 5,000 lb of gold, 30,000 lb of silver, 4,000 silk robes, 3,000 skins died in purple and 3,000 lb of pepper. The sums of gold and silver were substantial, for a prosperous family drew 4,000 lb of gold annually from its estates, but the other items that Alaric received reflect a surprisingly sophisticated taste for imported items. Silk was produced in China, and pepper, the word for which in Greek and Latin is derived from an Indian word, came from the subcontinent. Similarly, a few decades later, a leading woman among the Huns was given three silver bowls, red skins, Indian pepper, dates and other dried fruits. Not surprisingly, slaves were keen to join Alaric's army; we are told that nearly all the slaves in Rome left the city and mingled with his men.[6] In the summer of 410 Alaric returned to Rome, and on 24 August the city that for centuries people had been calling 'eternal' was captured, and then sacked for three days.

So there took place what has been seen as one of the most important happenings of late antiquity. But care is needed is assessing its importance. Much of what we know of the sack comes from a series of letters written by the biblical scholar Jerome, then living near Bethlehem, in which he suggested that something immense had happened: 'In one city the whole world has perished.' Jerome made his point by punning on the Latin words for 'city' (*urbs*) and 'world' (*orbis*). It was a clever turn of phrase, but scarcely original; Jerome's near contemporary, Rutilius Namatianus, had made the same pun, and Ovid had said much the same thing four centuries earlier.[7] Moreover, the descriptions that Jerome provides of what transpired in Rome are verbally similar to the account of the sack of Troy by the victorious Greeks found in the second book of Vergil's *Aeneid*, and reflect literary borrowing rather than contemporary reality. That he saw the events of 410 in the light of the fall of Troy certainly indicates that he considered them important, but it also suggests that we are dealing with a literary topos. Our second source for the events of 410 originated in a response to the polemic of non-Christians, who, pointing to the sack having occurred shortly after Christian emperors suppressed the traditional cults, blamed the new official religion. To these charges Augustine responded in his massive *City of God*, in which he sought to diminish the sack by contextualising it. He argued that Rome had known many difficulties, a line that was taken further in the *History* written by his follower Orosius. Augustine felt able to take a more sunny view than some modern commentators: 'The

Roman Empire has been shaken rather than transformed . . . there is no need to despair of its recovery at this present time.'[8] To judge from the copying of a manuscript containing a large part of his work in Verona early in the fifth century, very shortly after it was written, his message was quick to find readers in Italy.

The apologetic concern of Augustine led him to diminish the impact of the Goths. Yet the significance of the sack lay more in the imaginations of the fathers of the church who wrote about it than in its impact on the functioning of the city. The authorities at Ravenna seem to have addressed a law to the prefect of the city just a month after the sack,[9] by which time Alaric had withdrawn southwards in search of further profit. But before he could cross to Sicily and Africa, as he had planned, he died in the far south of Italy. From there his followers moved into Gaul, whence they were driven into Spain, where it was hoped they would be unable to receive effective provisioning. In 416 a plan to go to Africa was ruined by a storm that destroyed many ships, and thereafter the Goths came to an accommodation with the Romans. By about 420 they were established around Toulouse with the status of *foederati*, according to which they were allies of Rome settled on imperial soil and obliged to provide military service. Now a settled people, provision had to be made for them, and it may well be that they received a share in the revenues of the state rather than land. The territory that they were allocated was scarcely prime real estate, for it had no access to the Mediterranean, and its only coastline was on the Bay of Biscay. The Goths give the impression of having been sidelined and settled satisfactorily within the land and structures of the Empire.

Meanwhile, life in Italy continued. For some time it was shielded from further attacks. But as the fifth century progressed, the power of Rome steadily contracted, so that, with provinces being lost one by one and emperors reluctant to move beyond Italy, it moved from being the centre of the Empire in the West to what was virtually a free-standing political unit. We shall later consider the impact of these developments beyond Italy, but they did not pass unnoticed there, where their serious impact on the functioning of the state was observed. Unlike modern states, the Roman Empire had no concept of deficit financing, and therefore relied on regular income from taxation to cover military expenses. But the emperor Valentinian (425–55) found it increasingly hard to bring in the taxes; even in territory still part of the Empire, the 'exhausted circumstances and the afflicted condition of the State' made it difficult to maintain the army. The outcome was the imposition in 444 of a new sales tax, the siliquaticum, levied at the rate of 1/24, of which the seller and buyer were each to contribute half. It is hard to envisage how it was collected, although post-Roman governments in Italy found it worth retaining. But people within Italy whose fortunes were not closely bound to those of the state could take a more optimistic view of affairs. Preaching to the people of Rome on the feast of SS Peter and Paul in 441, pope Leo punned on the same words as Jerome had, but to very different effect; while the birth of the Apostles demanded reverence from the whole world, it received special veneration from this city. Rome had been founded by the twin brothers Romulus and Remus, who later quarrelled, one of them killing the other, but now, through the sacred see of blessed Peter, Rome had become the head of the whole world, so that religion allowed the city to enjoy a wider dominion than it had exercised through earthly domination![10] There was a marked contrast between the buoyant view of Leo and the despair of Valentinian, his exact contemporary.

A round of invasions that lay just ahead affected Italy more directly. In 452 Attila the Hun led an army that sacked Aquileia and went on to take the largest city in northern Italy, Milan. But near the river Mincio, north of the Po, he met an embassy from Rome. The versatile Leo, together with two distinguished members of the laity, sought peace, and Attila retreated, although it may have been famine and the threat of disease rather than respect for his visitors that prompted him to move out of Italy. He died in the following year; rumour had it that this was the result of a haemorrhage that struck him when he was drunk on the night of what turned out to be his last wedding.[11]

Greater danger loomed from the south, where the Vandals had established a kingdom in Africa. In 455 king Geiseric subjected Rome to its second sack. The reasons that impelled him to make the short sailing from Africa are obscure. But, in a match typical of the period, Valentinian's daughter had been betrothed to Geiseric's son Huneric, and according to one tradition, which shows Romans and 'barbarians' using each other, after Valentinian was assassinated in 455 by dissident Romans his widow asked Geiseric to intervene. The intervention, if such it was, was a blow to Rome, perhaps more serious than Alaric's better-known sack; a book decribing the deeds of popes compiled early in the following century described the sack of 410 as 'the Gothic conflagration', but that of 455 as 'the Vandal disaster'.[12] Valentinian was the last emperor in Rome with any claim to strength. His successors, nine of whom reigned in the next 21 years, were ineffectual. In the face of such nonentities, it is not surprising that power passed to a series of military strongmen; nor, given the role that Germanic generals had come to play in the army, is it a cause for wonder that these people were 'barbarians'. And while one of them, Ricimer, married the daughter of an emperor, no one seems to have thought that such a person could himself become emperor. In these circumstances, the office of emperor was becoming increasingly superfluous.

Its end came in August 476 when Odovacer, a successful general and a member of the imperial bodyguard, was made king by rebellious soldiers. His office was a new one, and Odovacer's accession to it was followed by the deposition of the emperor Romulus, generally referred to as 'augustulus' because of his youth, who was allocated a handsome annual income of 6,000 solidi and sent to live in a villa near Naples. With him out of the way, an embassy was sent to Constantinople, which informed Zeno, the eastern emperor, that there was no further need for a separate emperor in the West, for one emperor was enough for both parts. As a sign of this, its members offered Zeno the imperial regalia that they had brought with them. Moreover, as Odovacer was a suitable person, they asked that the government of Italy be entrusted to him. It was believed that the embassy took place at the behest of Romulus himself.[13] Zeno, who doubtless felt that he had no choice in the matter, agreed, and appointed Odovacer to the lofty office of patrician, although he tempered his acceptance of the *fait accompli* by advising the new ruler of Italy to respect the authority of a claimant to the imperial title, who, prior to an early death, was living in Dalmatia.

So did Italy move into the post-imperial period. At the beginning of the century, power in the West had lain with the general Stilicho rather than the emperor Honorius, and little had happened since then to indicate that the imperial office was not redundant. Odovacer did no more than bring a process that had been going on for generations to a sensible conclusion. He was a military man who had never held a formal Roman office prior to being appointed patrician, and the thought that he was leading Italy into a post-Roman period would have been beyond his imagination. Doubtless the state he ruled as king was independent of the Empire, a reality coyly suggested by his minting a small number of coins bearing his own portrait. Yet his regime was noteworthy for its adherence to established norms. A consul for the west was appointed annually, and the senate continued to function in Rome. According to one report, the deposition of Romulus occurred after he had forced the senate to send an embassy to Constantinople alleging that it had selected Odovacer, and that his relations with this body were good is indicated by his restoration of the seats of the senators in the Flavian amphitheatre.[14] Moreover, under his rule the steady weakening of the position of Italy was reversed. Although the last part of Gaul to remain under Roman power was ceded to the Visigoths, Vandal attacks ceased, and in return for an annual payment they relinquished control over Sicily. One of the best rulers Italy knew in late antiquity, it was Odovacer's misfortune to be overthrown by a better one.

Italy under the Ostrogoths

In 489 king Theoderic came into Italy at the head of many Ostrogoths. The recent history of this people had not been glorious, for they had been among an assemblage of peoples who had fallen under the sway of the Huns in the time of Attila, and the attempts they made to extort subsidies from the Empire following his death in 453 suggest that, far from turning their backs on his nefarious ways, they attempted to emulate his successes. They rampaged around the Balkans, and in an inspired stroke Zeno, the very emperor who had accepted Odovacer's *fait accompli* in Italy, proposed to Theoderic that he take Italy on his behalf. At the very least, the destructive energies of the Goths would be turned away from the east. So it was that Theoderic arrived in the north-east of Italy, at the head not merely of an army but of a people, accompanied by their household goods and livestock. Odovacer, having been defeated in early fighting, retired to Ravenna, just as Honorius had. But the consequent siege took its toll, and in 493, in a reflection of where authority was coming to reside in cities, the bishop of Ravenna came forth to treat with Theoderic. An agreement that Theoderic and Odovacer would share the rule of Italy came to an abrupt end a few weeks later, when Theoderic murdered his colleague at a banquet. One might interpret this treacherous act as a sign of primitive barbarism. Yet Romans had killed Gothic troops at a feast shortly after their crossing of the Danube, and new emperors frequently found murder a worthwhile tool; in 520 Justinian saw to the murder of a leading general. Theoderic's wielding of his sword against Odovacer was simply an act of statecraft at the beginning of a long and successful reign (493–526), which was to comprise the greater part of the lifespan of Ostrogothic Italy.

His first task as ruler of Italy was to make provision for his followers. A precedent for this was to hand in the Roman practice of billeting soldiers, although it was liable to abuses, as when Gothic soldiers who were billeted with the townspeople of Edessa in Mesopotamia early in the sixth century plundered their hosts and tried to kill the general who attempted to restrain their drunken and outrageous behaviour.[15] But Theoderic followed the example of Odovacer, who, on coming to power, had allotted to his soldiers what our sources describe as 'thirds'.[16] It is unclear exactly what these 'thirds' were. Taken literally, the terminology would indicate that they were units of land, although it may be that they were the tax revenues produced by land, perhaps passed on to the Goths by local rather than central authorities. The precise language of our texts supports an interpretation of the thirds as units of land; the surprising lack of an outcry from dispossessed landowners, an understanding of them as payments from state revenues. Our sources do not register any sudden vast accretion of wealth at the disposal of the Goths, and perhaps they received much less than a 'third', however it be understood. In any case, whether directly by land or indirectly via taxation chiefly drawn from the land, the agricultural surplus that had formerly supported the 'Roman' army, which had become overwhelmingly 'barbarian' in its composition, was now diverted towards a 'Gothic' army, which doubtless included men who a short time before would not have been thought of as Goths. Moreover, the allocation of resources to the military still took place under the auspices of the state, and was the responsibility of Roman officials. Structurally, little had changed.

The most striking characteristic of Ostrogothic Italy is its continuity with the regime of Odovacer, and beyond it with the Empire. Historical atlases frequently show maps that refer to 'Ostrogothic Italy'. Yet, while it was possible for the Goths to be thought of in biblical language as comparable in number to grains of sand or stars,[17] the newcomers constituted a tiny proportion of the population, and many of the indigenous people could go about their business rarely encountering one of them, for most of them lived in a small part of Italy, to the north of the Po and, within this area, in the east. This was the very area where the Roman army had been concentrated, with a view to blocking the invasion route that the Goths themselves, among others, had followed into Italy. The newcomers were simply discharging the responsibility of the Roman army.

At the time of their coming into Italy, many if not most of the Goths spoke Gothic, while the inhabitants of Italy were speakers of Latin. A situation had come to exist that, in one form or another, was common in late antiquity and the early middle ages, that of two languages being spoken in one area. But it was clear where the linguistic future of Italy lay. The correspondence of Cassiodorus, a civil servant in Theoderic's employ, includes some 60 letters to people with Gothic names written in Latin, and while they tend to be short and devoid of the rhetoric that Cassiodorus loved to lavish on letters to members of the Roman intelligentsia, he gives no indication that he expected their readers to have trouble understanding his messages. Indeed, Goths had long been exposed to Latin, for they had been exchanging letters with Romans as early as the late fourth century.[18] While many Goths knew Latin, and Theoderic's daughter Amalasuintha was proficient in Greek as well as Latin and Gothic, few Romans found it necessary to master Gothic.

Similarly, there was a drift away from the ancestral Arianism of the Goths towards Catholicism, far stronger than the reverse movement among the Romans. To be sure, the religious communities remained distinct. In Rome the Arians had their own church in Subura, an area known for its colourful nightlife, while Goths in Ravenna worshipped in churches decorated with lavish mosaics executed in the style of the mosaics in nearby Catholic churches. Their theologies were different, and the survival of seven manuscripts, copied in Italy or Gaul in the fifth and sixth centuries, of the *De Trinitate* written in the fourth century by Hilary of Poitiers indicates the continued relevance of an anti-Arian case. Yet in 530 a deacon of the Roman church, Boniface the son of Sigibuld, became pope. To judge by the name of his father he was of Germanic ancestry, although he may have been from a Roman family with a penchant for Germanic names. Perhaps the distinction between German and Roman was breaking down. Viliarit, a copyist of books who was attached to a Gothic church at Ravenna, produced works that include the oldest surviving manuscript of the *History* of Orosius, now kept at Florence. It is extraordinary to think that our oldest text of a work that minimises the impact of the Goths on Rome in 410 was written in the workshop of a man with a Gothic name associated with an Arian church.

There was not always a great difference between a Roman and a Goth. The state recommended the virtue of *civilitas*, living in accordance with the laws, and the two peoples were to be judged by the same law code, issued by Theoderic and based on Roman law. It is true that they were to be tried before different courts, but the distinction between them was seen as primarily between civilian and military, rather than specifically Roman and Gothic courts. What was there for the Romans to do but live in peace, while the army of the Goths made war? Most of the indigenous inhabitants of Italy could go about their daily lives just as they had before the coming of the Goths, while the newcomers became steadily more like them. Not all of them, however, assimilated at the same rate. On one occasion, Theoderic observed that the poor Roman imitated the Goth, whereas the well-to-do Goth imitated the Roman, and the second part of his dictum seems to be confirmed by the prevalence of Roman items in the burials of wealthy people whom we may deduce to have been Goths.[19]

In about 497 a senatorial embassy sent to Constantinople succeeded in obtaining recognition for Theoderic's regime from the emperor Anastasius, who had succeeded Zeno. Theoderic, like Odovacer, referred to himself as king. But his embassy brought back to Italy the ornaments of the palace that his predecessor had sent to Constantinople, and to all intents and purposes Theoderic acted as an emperor. A mosaic in the church of Sant' Apollinare Nuovo at Ravenna, his capital, shows the palace he built there, in imitation of that of the emperor in Constantinople; as late as the ninth century its entrance was known as the Chalke, just as the entrance to the imperial palace was.[20] When two popes were elected on the one day in 498, the matter was referred to Theoderic for arbitration, just as it could have been to an emperor. An imperial feeling was definitely in the air in 500, when Theoderic paid his only recorded visit to Rome.[21] He made the trip at the time of his tricennalia, to commemorate the thirtieth anniversary of an important event in his early life. Such occasions had been deemed appropriate for emperors to visit Rome, and Theoderic's was a formal visit, modelled on the ceremonial arrival of an emperor in his city. Approaching Rome, he prayed devoutly at St Peter's and was met outside the walls of the city by the pope, senate and people of Rome, precisely in accordance with the practice of emperors who visited the tomb of the Apostle and were met outside the walls by the dignitaries of the city. Entering it, he visited the senate and addressed the people, assuring them that he would maintain what emperors had previously established. He then made his way to the palace, presented circus games, gave rations to the people, and made funds available for the restoration of public buildings, these being among the palaces, baths, aqueducts and one amphitheatre that our sources credit him with erecting in various places. Only after spending six months in the city did he leave.

These events could be taken as a text-book account of a formal visit paid by an emperor to the old capital of the Empire. A few decades after Theoderic died, an eastern author commented that he had invested himself with all the qualities appropriate to an emperor; although he was in name a usurper, in reality he was as truly an emperor as any who had held that title. One of the significant figures of his reign was Ennodius, a rhetorician whose pupils, trained in the expectation that the old ways would continue, went on to occupy offices of state; they included all but one of the quaestors known to have held office from 500 to 530. When Cassiodorus wrote to one of them formally advising him of his appointment, he recommended that he be to Theoderic as Pliny had been to Trajan. Indeed, there were many who compared Theoderic to the great emperor, then four centuries in the past, and it may have been in imitation of Pliny that Cassiodorus published letters that he wrote on behalf of Theoderic and his successors. Authors of the period took delight in a rhetoric of renewal, renovation and restoration; they displayed a chronological self-consciousness that found expression in the widespread use, for the first time, of the Latin adjective for 'very recent', *modernus*. Cassiodorus observed, in a letter written in Theoderic's name to the people of the northern Italian town of Este, that old columns and stones should not lie about unused giving rise to sad thoughts, but be reused. Whereas the city of Rome was traditionally thought of as being an aged woman, the author of a panegyric on Theoderic represented her as having regained her youth during his reign.[22]

Such emphases comported well with the sentiments of the senate. It issued coins depicting the Roman eagle, Romulus and Remus being suckled by the she-wolf and the fig-tree beneath which this was said to have taken place – themes that reflect an understanding of Roman history very different to that of pope Leo. Senators devoted themselves to emending texts of classical authors. Whereas the fifth century, as far as we can judge, had been a quiet period for the copying of non-Christian texts, under the Ostrogoths elite groups cultivated nostalgia; the three oldest nearly complete manuscripts of Vergil's *Aeneid* seem to have been copied in Italy during Theoderic's reign. The senator Symmachus, whose great-grandfather had unsuccessfully defended a classical altar against Ambrose, wrote a history of Rome in seven books, and undertook repairs to one of Rome's great public buildings, the theatre of Pompey in the Campus Martius. His son-in-law, the philosopher Boethius, possessed of an excellent education and a formidable intellect, wrote works that made Greek thought available in Latin; while he came to a sad end, it was one for which, as he recognised in his last work, the *Consolation of Philosophy*, there were numerous classical precedents. Doubtless the loss of the various provinces led to a narrowing of the horizons of the senators, who may have been turning into an aristocracy based in regions of Italy, although we know of a Symmachus who still kept a house in Constantinople.[23] But whatever losses lay behind the more locally based lives that the senators were now living, at least some of them inhabited a world of lofty ideals.

The Gothic state in Italy was very much a going concern, yet in some ways its position was precarious. Its new status as a free-standing unit made Italy vulnerable. In Gaul, the Franks were coming to exercise greatly increased power, while the Vandals in Africa were difficult neighbours. The last years of Theoderic's life were sad. Albinus, a senator who may have been in an inner circle of his Roman advisers, was accused of treachery. The philosopher Boethius was imprisoned and killed, his father-in-law Symmachus was executed, and one of his friends, pope John, was imprisoned on his return from an embassy to Constantinople and died shortly afterwards. Such events were a reminder that the surviving Empire hovered like a gigantic cloud to the east of the first post-Roman states around the western shores of the Mediterranean, and there were voices encouraging any imperial ambitions to recover lost ground. At the beginning of the sixth century, Priscian, an African intellectual who lived in Constantinople, wrote a panegyric of the emperor Anastasius in which he expressed the hope that Rome as well as Constantinople would come to obey the emperor alone. Nevertheless, it is hard to see a powerful Gothic king being greatly disquieted at whatever dealings such people as Boethius and John had with Constantinople, and the difficulties that beset his government in the 520s were chiefly caused by the lack of a secure succession, for it became clear that the ageing Theoderic would not leave a son, and jockeying for power broke out among the officers of his administration. Such problems were largely of a contingent kind.

Yet there were others that made manifest tendencies at work throughout the west of the old empire. A threatening concentration of land in the hands of powerful individuals was taking place. Theoderic rewarded one of his most successful generals, Tuluin, by making him the lord of lands that he had conquered in Provence; on the margin of the kingdom, these could have formed a semi-independent block of territory. Another general who was sent into Spain married a wealthy land-owning woman and thereafter declined invitations to visit Theoderic. Within Italy itself, the king's nephew Theodahad built up enormous landholdings centred in Tuscany, often by seizing the lands of other people, and played the role of a Roman noble, building baths, composing poetry and reading philosophical texts. In the 530s, after he had become king, an ambassador of the emperor Justinian bluntly told him that his philosophical interests made him unfit to conduct war. This extraordinary figure provided an example of a Goth ceasing to be a Goth. That people such as he and the military men were doing so well, even under the strong government of Theoderic, was a gloomy portent.

Moreover, despite its bright façade, the economy of Ostrogothic Italy was not buoyant. To be sure, there were still large fortunes in private hands. A banker, Julianus, was responsible during this period for beginning the construction of a number of churches in Ravenna and its port, Classe, which were dedicated in the latter half of the 540s. The greatest of them, that dedicated to San Vitale in Ravenna, cost 26,000 solidi, a sign of the wealth available in the first half of the century. But at about this time Italy was moving into recession, as archaeological evidence from a number of sites makes clear. The most significant of these is an agricultural complex at San Vincenzo al Volturno, located in an upland area of Molise, to the north-east of Monte

Cassino, where St Benedict founded his famous monastery.[24] Founded or thoroughly rebuilt early in the fifth century, and extended in about 475, San Vincenzo had fallen into a state of decay by the second quarter of the sixth century. It is not clear why this occurred. Perhaps, at a time when trade around the Mediterranean was tending to diminish, inland areas were ceasing to participate in networks of exchange, although a precise correlation between the difficulties of San Vincenzo and global patterns of trade is difficult to establish; perhaps its economy was geared to the supply of pork to Rome, and its atrophy was caused by a lessening of the requirements of the city. In any case, less wealth was being produced over the career of the Ostrogothic state; the economy which emerged after the tragic events that terminated it would be on a much diminished basis.

AFRICA

While Italy had been the political centre of the Western empire, Africa was by far its most economically developed region.[25] It supplied much of the grain that fed the inhabitants of Rome, a trade so significant that early in the fifth century the count of Africa was able to place pressure on the authorities in Rome by threatening to withhold supplies from the city; 200 years later, the governor of Africa saw fit to withhold grain from Constantinople. It was also thought to have supplied all peoples with oil, virtually alone. More significant was an enormous pottery export business that it had built up.[26] By about AD 100, factories in what is now Tunisia were beginning to export what is called African red slip-ware, pottery of an orange-red colour made especially for use at table. It enjoyed tremendous success as, first in the west and then in the east, it drove locally produced wares out of production. By the end of the fourth century it was being used in the west of Spain and far up the Nile. Africa was also a source of ivory for the Empire, which was brought across the Sahara Desert to the port of Lepcis Magna, whence it was shipped to Rome. It was also vibrant with intellectual energies, for early Christian thinking in the west would have been in a sad state without Africa, and was respected for its style, it being felt in Constantinople that Africans conversed more elegantly than Italians. Africa was vibrant as it entered the fifth century of the Christian era.

A major upheaval was soon to follow. Unlike the Goths, who had enjoyed a long-term exposure to Roman ways north of the Danube, the Vandals seemed to come from nowhere. The troubled events in Italy at the beginning of the fifth century had caused troops to be withdrawn from the frontier along the Rhine, and it seems to have been on New Year's Eve 406, when the great river was frozen, that Vandals crossed it on foot, probably between Mainz and Worms. There have not been many times in recorded history when such a crossing could have been made, but a period of cold weather, which would last until the era of Charlemagne, was setting in; not long before, the emperor Julian had seen blocks of ice in the Seine at Paris. The Vandals are said to have been accompanied by Alans and Suevi. The way lay open before them, especially when Gaul fell under the control of a usurper, although the speed with which they advanced cannot be established. They are represented as ravaging much of Gaul in 409, but this may have reflected a recent expansion of their activities made possible by a conflict between rival Romans. In the spring of that year, they entered Spain with the connivance of local authorities; as so often happened, newcomers advanced into Roman territory with Roman co-operation. After some two decades of wild living in Gaul and Spain, in about 429 they crossed to Africa under their king Geiseric, succeeding where the Goths had recently failed. Here again, it was widely said that Boniface, the Roman commander in Africa, who had recently married a woman who was probably a Visigoth, had asked them to come to his aid when he was in difficulty with the imperial authorities.[27]

The coming of the Vandals and their associates was marked by behaviour reminiscent of events that disfigured much of the history of the twentieth century. The bishop of Carthage wrote to those present at an important church council held at Ephesus in 431 that he was unable to join them because of a multitude of enemies and widespread devastation, and sent a deacon to represent him.[28] In 435 Geiseric concluded a peace with Valentinian, but before long he went on to attack the rich proconsular province, capturing its capital, Carthage, in 439. This was a great success, for Carthage, perhaps the second city in the western part of the empire, had long been a rival to Rome. Vergil told how queen Dido of Carthage, when she was stood up by Aeneas, whose descendants were to found Rome, uttered a dreadful curse: there would be no love or treaties between the peoples, but their shores, waves and arms would ever be opposed to each other.[29] The ancient antagonism between the cities did not end with Rome's victory in the Punic Wars, and may later have been transposed to rivalry between their bishops. After an invasion launched from Constantinople against the Vandals failed to reach Africa in 441, a second peace was concluded, which ceded to them control of most of Roman Africa. From there they sacked Rome in 455, perhaps with the support of elements in the city, captured the major islands of the western Mediterranean, including Corsica, Sardinia and Sicily, and raided the more distant Crete. Later expeditions against the Vandal state having failed, the eastern Empire concluded a final peace in 474. Geiseric was succeeded as king by his son Huneric (477–84), a fervent Arian who set under way a savage persecution of Catholics, during which Victor of Vita wrote an emotive account of Vandal persecution that emphasised their wickedness (*impietas*). As time passed, the newcomers appear to have become quieter, especially in the reign of king Thrasamund (496–523), who married the sister of Theoderic and enjoyed debates with Catholic bishops. Their kingdom lasted for just over a century, until another army sent from Constantinople defeated it in the 530s.

The Vandals left a vivid impression. There is no mistaking their self-confidence. Whereas the Ostrogoths could claim to have gone to Italy at the behest of the emperor, the Vandals appealed to a higher authority, claiming that a command from God had moved them to go to Africa, and when the pilot of Geiseric's ship asked the king against whom his fleet was proceeding, he replied, 'Plainly, against those with whom God is angry.'[30] The Vandals dated years from their capture of Carthage or according to the regnal year of the current king, rather than according to the consuls of the year, as was the practice in Italy under the Ostrogoths. They were long remembered; centuries later, texts written far away in Old English and an old form of German still referred to the Mediterranean as the 'Vandal Sea', and we can only speculate what lay between the Vandals and these northern writings of the ninth century.[31] But their contemporaries found the Vandals noteworthy for two reasons: it was held that they were impelled by greed to act badly towards the Africans, in particular by confiscating land, and that they were ferocious persecutors of Catholics. In both respects their behaviour seems very different from that of the Ostrogoths in Italy, and as they touch on deep issues it will be worth our while considering them in turn.

Land and the economy

When the Vandals arrived in Africa, they helped themselves to the wealth of many of the indigenous people, committing what one author referred to as 'wild and frenzied acts of wickedness', and after the capture of Carthage they deliberately set about confiscating land. Different sources report that virtually all the senators lost their property and sailed to Italy, and that Geiseric made all the Africans who were conspicuous for their wealth the slaves of his sons, to whom he delivered their estates and money; others who lost their lands, which were given to the other Vandals, nevertheless retained their freedom.[32]

Such evidence, while somewhat inconsistent, cannot be easily laid aside. Yet wealth remained in the hands of the indigenes. Half way through the Vandal period, one of Huneric's officers was deprived of his house and wealth when he refused to become an Arian, while someone described as the most wealthy man in the regions of Africa similarly spurned the royal blandishments. Moreover, estates remained in the hands of old families. When Geiseric confiscated the property of the grandfather of Fulgentius, later bishop of Ruspe (c.507–33), he sailed to Italy. But his sons later returned to Africa and received back part of the property, which Fulgentius himself was later expected to manage. A set of documents registering land transfers made in the late fifth century around Tebessa, the Tablettes Albertini, show a non-Vandal family, the Geminii, actively buying land; the names of the sovereigns in the dates of the documents are the only indications of Vandal presence. To judge by the frequent references to olive trees in these texts, oil was the principal product of the family's estates; fig trees are mentioned a third as often, while there is a scattering of references to other trees, including almonds and pistachios. The cultivation of trees of such kinds points to stability during the preceding decades.[33]

Another indication of continuity is provided by a large farm building, some 50 m by 30 m in extent, at the site of Nador. Its location, facing the road between two coastal towns, suggests that it produced oil and wine in commercial quantities, perhaps for export. Erected with fortified towers in the second quarter of the fourth century on the site of an earlier building, the building provides a good example of the fortified farms that were becoming common in Africa, although the ostentatious display of power may have been more important than any defensive function. In the early fifth century its interior space was remodelled, and its rooms were subdivided. But this need not indicate economic decline, and the red slip-ware pottery found on the site is preponderantly from the fourth and fifth centuries. The complex was abandoned and the site fell into decay in about the first quarter of the sixth century, perhaps a little too early to be associated with the imperial conquest of the 530s. It provides clear evidence for continuity over the greater part of the Vandal period, and it is impossible to correlate such changes as took place with any impact that the Vandals may have had. The evidence from the site points in a very different direction to the chief narrative account for Vandal Africa, which has almost the entire population of Tipasa, less than 10 km away, sailing to Spain to escape the Vandals in the 480s.[34]

The occupation of estates by Vandals was therefore probably partial, and not necessarily permanent. It is also possible that such confiscations, rather than reflecting greed, were a sign of the newcomers' need, for our sources are silent as to any peaceable settling of the Vandals in accordance with any system such as that of the thirds which applied in Italy. One might be inclined to think that provisioning for the Vandals along these lines could not have been expected, given that Geiseric, unlike Theoderic, came to hold his territory by right of conquest rather than with the approval of the Empire, and the confiscation of estates may have been a way of providing for a ruling class of newcomers who intended to be long-term stayers. But the maintenance of a functioning civil service indicates that the Vandal kingdom, like every strong state of the period, continued to raise taxes. As we have seen, taxes were chiefly expended on the army, and this is precisely how the Vandals presented themselves to the people of Africa, for when Victor of Vita mentions them, he sometimes speaks of them as an army where we would expect 'people'.[35] Given that they entered Africa in the guise of an army, much of the revenue must have been directed towards them, giving them a share in the wealth of Africa quite apart from the estates they took.

The state of the economy of Africa during the century of the Vandals' power is not easy to assess. They did not mint gold coins, but paradoxically this may be a sign that wealth, whether the fruit of trade or raiding, was readily available in their kingdom. Exports certainly continued. Although the fate of the grain shipments to Rome is difficult to trace, pottery continued to be exported, although at a lower level, as we shall see later (pp. 250–51). The diminution is hard to account for. While it is possible that the coming of the Vandals was bad for trade, the competitiveness of rival products may have contributed to it, and it occurred against the background of declining trans-Mediterranean trade in the fifth century. The archaeological record at Carthage reveals that the city did not prosper. Indeed, there is no evidence for the construction of houses in Africa in the Vandal period, or the following one when it was reintegrated into the Empire, and while finds of coins and pottery suggest an optimistic picture, the public buildings of Carthage were decaying. Some of them, such as the great Antonine baths, apparently fell into disuse, as did some private ones, as rubbish was tipped into houses. There is very little evidence for new building at all. Developments at Cherchel, a large town with a good harbour in the modern Algeria, are similar to those at Nador in that, while they point to overall decline, it is difficult to connect this with the activities of the Vandals. Cherchel seems to have flourished into the Vandal period, but change came early in the sixth century, when a church was set on fire and its walls were demolished down to floor level, soil began to accumulate on the paving of the forum, and a basilica was pulled down.[36]

Such developments were gloomy, but similar things occurred in Italy during the late-Roman and Ostrogothic periods for reasons unconnected with the arrival of newcomers (see below, pp. 144–48), and general social and economic trends operating throughout the west were probably more important than the establishment of new states and their activities. And the picture in Africa was not universally depressing. When the young Fulgentius adopted an ascetic life towards the end of the fifth century, he is said to have stopped visiting the baths, which suggests the survival of urban pleasures. Moreover, as was the case in Ostrogothic Italy, wealth may have been displayed in ways that one may not have thought likely, for lovely mosaics were installed during the period of Vandal power. When forces from Constantinople arrived at Carthage in 533, a crowd of merchants was among those who complained about the conduct of the soldiers, and we know that many merchants from the east had been imprisoned not long before on suspicion of having encouraged Justinian to make war. Their presence suggests that trade remained brisk.[37]

Religion

A second charge was made against the Vandals, that of engaging in religious persecution. The Vandals were Arians, unlike the Catholic Romans among whom they settled; the author of a pilgrim account of the sixth century could refer to two monasteries at Memphis in Egypt as being of the religion of the Vandals and the religion of the Romans respectively. But tensions between the adherents of the two faiths were far stronger in Africa than they were in Italy, where the Ostrogoths were also Arians. When the Vandals arrived, the elderly Augustine found himself writing a long letter to a bishop on whether it was right for clergy to withdraw from threatened cities, and Catholic churches were confiscated. Doubtless this was partly a consequence of the church having become an established arm of society, and hence vulnerable in times of upheaval. But persecution motivated solely by religion took place. As bishops died, Geiseric forbade the ordination of replacements in some parts of the territory under his control; when a bishop was ordained for Carthage in 481, the see had been vacant for over 20 years.

But whatever animosity the Vandals displayed to Catholics in the reign of Geiseric was insignificant compared to that which developed in the reign of Huneric. He sent thousands of the clergy and laypeople of Carthage into exile, and in 484 ordered that the Catholic churches were to be closed. Accounts of tortures inflicted upon Catholics make much of the physical agonies they endured, although it is hard to detect many who were killed. Not surprisingly, some Catholics converted to Arianism. After the death of

Huneric, persecution occurred at a lower level. When king Thrasamund did not allow bishops to be ordained to replace those who died, the remaining bishops decided to proceed with ordinations anyway, among them that of the theologian Fulgentius to the see of Ruspe in Byzacena. It was in this climate that the story was told of the Arian bishop Barbas, whose attempt to baptise someone using an heretical formula was foiled when the water disappeared and the vessel that had contained it shattered. The candidate for baptism prudently sought it from Catholics. But before long Fulgentius, with some 60 other bishops, was exiled to Sardinia. Thrasamund, who had intellectual interests, recalled him for discussions and then sent him back.[38]

The persecution of Catholics by the Vandal state is a grim story, without parallel in our period. Nevertheless, as with the dispossession of some of the landowning class, it may not have been as bad as it may appear, for the author of our chief source, Victor of Vita, may have heightened its nefarious qualities with an eye to mobilising readers outside Africa against the Vandals. Their persecution may have had a political as well as a religious basis. On one occasion, a group of Catholic African monks were arrested and accused of wishing to overthrow 'Christian' – that is, Arian – kings, and the tempo of persecution may have been linked with fluctuations in relations between the Vandals and the Empire. The development of separate states in the post-Roman west had brought about an edgy situation in which governments could use the treatment of religious groups as a way of putting pressure on other states, in particular the Empire, for the status that emperors enjoyed within orthodox Christianity made them feel obliged to see to the welfare of Catholics wherever they were. Moreover, the rage of Huneric was not only directed against Catholics, for under him Manichaeans and even an Arian bishop were burned.[39] But there was another, more important reason for the sad experience of African Catholics under the Vandals.

For centuries, African Christians had been at loggerheads with the governments under which they lived. The language that Victor of Vita used to describe the tortures inflicted by the Vandals is remarkably similar to that which had earlier been used of tortures applied to Africans in the time of the pre-Christian Empire, and centuries-old language of martyrdom came easily to him. Thumbing its nose at the state, the African church had abounded in martyrs during its early centuries, and the conversion of Constantine coincided with the emergence in Africa of a combative and schismatic church, that of the Donatists, which in some ways preserved the old anti-establishment traditions of African Christianity. What could the Vandals throw at the feisty Africans which they were not all too familiar with from their own past?

Events at the coastal town of Tipasa during the reign of Huneric were striking: when the king had the tongues of the people of the region pulled out and their right hands cut off, they kept on speaking. Yet the town had a history of religious turbulence. It was one of the places where Catholics were persecuted during the reign of Julian the Apostate, when men were torn to pieces, married women roughed up, infants killed and foetuses aborted. In those days, Donatist bishops ordered that the Catholic eucharist be thrown to the dogs, while they cast a container of chrism from a window; fortunately, this was caught by angels and did not break.[40] Some of the responsibility for the bad relations between Arians and Catholics in Vandal Africa lay with the latter, irascible and battle-hardened as they were. Later, when Justinian's troops came to Africa thinking that they were liberating the Africans from the tyranny of the Vandals, the combative African church quickly found fault with the emperor's faith.

Moreover, the religious policy of the Vandal regime was in some ways typical of a late-Roman government. While it is true, for example, that under it Carthage lacked a Catholic bishop for many years, after taking the city Geiseric had exiled its Catholic bishop and delivered the cathedral to Arian clergy, who at some stage included a bishop; in these circumstances, the existence within a town of a second bishop who lacked a cathedral would have been anomalous. When Huneric issued a comprehensive law, 'flowing from the fount of justice', against Catholics, he could locate it within the context of imperial legislation. As he proudly pointed out, his law was largely based on laws that various Catholic emperors had enacted against Arians, and simply represented a 'twisting round' of their legislation by another ruler, whose claim that his convictions had been validated by a thousand and more bishops from the whole world constitutes a reminder that Arian belief had been an alternative to Nicene belief, and sometimes a powerful one, in late antiquity.[41] Similarly, when Huneric sought out Manichaeans, burning some and making slaves of others, he was simply punishing a deviate belief that emperors and popes of the period also acted against. The Vandals governed according to the model provided by the Empire. Until about 490, they issued silver coins bearing the name of the emperor Honorius, and when the old provincial capital Hadrumentum was renamed 'Hunericopolis', the gesture was an imperial one; before long it was to become 'Justinianopolis'.

The Moors

More important in the long run was an erosion of the power of the Vandals in their hinterland, where the indigenous Moors, or 'Berbers', were becoming stronger. Associated as they were with camels and herds of sheep, they had been looked down upon by the Romans, for whom their speech resembled the barking of dogs, and the Vandals were in the habit of exiling troublesome Catholics to their territory. But their economy was complementary to that of settled peoples, and symbiotic with that of the coastal areas devoted to farming. Ancient writers did not see things in these terms, but as so often their rhetoric implied a greater degree of exclusion than really existed. Some Moors independent of Roman power had concluded, just as others in their position did in Europe, that they had more to gain by co-operating with Rome than by attacking it. In particular, Rome could be emulated and its patronage sought for reasons of lifestyle or prestige, which could be used to enhance a leader's position among his own people. Others felt honour bound to resist. So it was that the Moors were not of one mind when it came to dealing with Rome. In about 372 a Moor with the Roman name Firmus was illegally proclaimed emperor. He enjoyed the support of his sister, who used her wealth to gain support among various peoples, but was opposed by one of his brothers, the owner of a fortified estate who secured the loyalty to Rome of nearby tribes. The revolt was defeated, but another brother, Gildo, who served Rome as a general, later revolted and cut off the grain supply to Rome, only to be defeated by yet another brother.

The Moors remained a problem for the Vandals. One Iugmena, credited in an inscription with the very Roman title 'prefect', was responsible for the beginning of work on a church built in the name of the Holy Spirit near Berrouaghia, in modern Algeria, which others finished in 474. An inscription placed at Arris in the Aurès mountains by one Masties begins with an abbreviation of the pre-Christian Latin formula *dis manibus sacrum*, 'sacred to the spirits of the dead'. Masties is described as having been a duke for 57 years and an emperor for 40, and a man who kept faith with both Romans and Moors, obedient in both war and peace and well treated by God, in accordance with his deeds. It is a confusing description, especially in its use of the title 'emperor' (*imperator*), but it certainly implies good relations between Romans and Moors, apparently to the exclusion of Vandals. Similarly, it was during the reign of one Masuna, described in an inscription as 'king of Moors and Romans', that a fort was constructed at Altava in 508. In about 500 a Moorish leader, Guenfan, consulted a woman capable of telling the future, who gave him encouraging news: the fates had decreed ruin for the Vandals and Africans alike, while the yoke and reins were going to pass to the Moors. Indeed, she could see mountain streams running with Vandal blood, and African cities burning.[42]

The story about Guenfan occurs in a work written in the middle of the sixth century after the demise of the Vandal kingdom, and is doubtless a case of prophecy after the event. But the rise of the Moors could not be ignored. They cleverly played on the sentiments of Catholics mistreated by Vandals: stories were told of Moors cleaning up churches desecrated by the Vandals.[43] One group of Catholics, sent to Moors who were not Christians, began to convert them. Developments among the Vandals played into their hands. Following the death of king Thrasamund in 523, the throne passed to Hilderic. Now elderly, he was the son of Huneric and his wife, a daughter of the emperor Valentinian III, and so a perfect example of the coming together of Roman and Germanic elites. An old friend of Justinian, soon to become emperor, he quickly moved to overthrow the traditional policies of the Vandal state. He appointed a bishop of Carthage, and the first council of Catholic bishops to meet during the Vandal period convened at Carthage in 525. Exiled bishops were recalled, and new ordinations allowed. But Hilderic could not deal with the Moors. In 530 they won an impressive victory over the Vandals, so serious that the king was thrown into prison and replaced by Gelimer, a proven general who was a descendant of Geiseric. As it turned out, the elevation of Gelimer was to do the Vandals no good. But as their kingdom moved towards its end, the rise in the power of the Moors was plain. They even ravaged the area around Ruspe, a coastal town south of Sousse.[44] The development boded ill, not only for the Vandals but also for the Empire when it took Africa from them.

Vandal identity

While the Moors retained their identity, the Vandal kingdom witnessed a coming together of different peoples. Our source closest to its beginning describes those who invaded Africa in 429 as 'a mixed group of savage Vandals and Alans, together with a Gothic tribe and people of different races'. Although the monarchs continued to be styled 'King of the Vandals and Alans', our texts tend to fall silent concerning all groups but the Vandals, and as we have no reason to believe that elements of Geiseric's forces were foolish enough to leave Africa following their success, we may conclude that people who were not originally thought of as Vandals came to be identified with them. What we know of the early history of the Alans suggests that they themselves had emerged from a similar process. As a Roman historian of the fourth century understood it, they caused peoples whom they defeated to be called by their name, so that various peoples came to be called Alans because of their common customs, wild manner of living, and arms; doubtless in a similar way, the names of the Alans and others who arrived in Africa 'were united in the name of Vandals'.[45]

There is nothing to wonder at here, given our understanding of Germanic peoples as often being in states of flux. More significant are indications of fluidity between Catholics and Arians in Africa. We have assumed in the foregoing discussion that Vandals were Arians and the local people Catholics, but this was not necessarily true. We know the names of two Arian bishops of Carthage: Jucundus bore a Roman name and Cyrila a Germanic one, while Antony, the most ferocious of the Arian bishops, shared his name with the great Egyptian monk. The 403 inscriptions in a basilica in Carthage that the Vandals occupied, St Monica, contain only six names of Germanic origin. On the other hand, some of the Catholics tortured by the Vandal state had Germanic names. Sometimes the Vandals made adherence to Arianism a requirement for employment in the royal service, which suggests that some Catholics were prepared to move in that direction. To what extent did choice of religion involve wider issues of identity? Even many of the Catholics who worked for the state dressed like Vandals in 'barbarian clothes', to the annoyance of the Arian bishops, which suggests that it was sometimes hard to tell the Vandals and indigenous Africans apart.[46]

In such ways, Vandal Africa saw a level of *rapprochement* for which the tales of expropriated estates and religious persecution do not prepare us. And intellectual life flourished. Martianus Capella, the author of the immensely learned *The Marriage of Philology and Mercury*, in which the seven liberal arts introduce their subjects at what some readers have found inordinate length, was almost certainly a non-Christian writing in Africa towards the end of the fifth century, and seems to have had a good knowledge of Greek. Fulgentius of Ruspe, a theologian who continued the Augustinian tradition of African Christianity, was said to have spoken Greek excellently, although his works show little sign of his having read material in that language. A collection of poems called by modern scholars 'the Latin anthology' seems to be based on a collection first put together in Africa towards the end of the Vandal period, perhaps for educational use, at the very time that scholars in Italy were producing copies of Vergil. The Vandals themselves were not immune from such scholarly enthusiasms. Felicianus, a teacher of grammar in Carthage, numbered Vandals among his pupils, and Fulgentius wrote a refutation of a work, doubtless written in Latin, by an Arian bishop.

This is not the kind of thing that the negative impression which the Vandals have acquired would lead one to expect. Yet by the end of their time in Africa they are reported to have taken to daily bathing, the banquet, the wearing of silk, and enjoying themselves in theatres, hippodromes and hunting, while living in villas. The last king of the Vandals had a palace not far outside Carthage with a beautiful park where there were springs, woods and fruit trees.[47] This could be a description of the villa of a Roman aristocrat; within a hundred years it could be said that the Vandal ruling class had gone native.

SPAIN

Today we think of Spain, as we may conveniently call the Iberian peninsula, as forming part of Europe, separated from Africa by the Strait of Gibraltar. Yet the Pyrenees, which cut Spain off from the rest of Europe, constitute at least as important a boundary, and across the millennia Spain has often looked towards Africa rather than Europe. Much of the peninsula was long subject to the African city of Carthage, which founded such cities as Carthagena, often simply known as 'New Carthage', on its south-eastern coast. The city remained orientated towards Africa. A fleet that the Romans assembled in the fifth century to attack the Vandals came together not far from it, and when, following the defeat of the Vandals, a force from Constantinople occupied the parts of Spain nearest Africa, Carthegena became a major stronghold; a surviving inscription records the strengthening of its gates. Not surprisingly, when the Visigoths recaptured the town, which was much closer to Africa than to Toledo, their capital city, they overthrew it. While Rome's victory in the Punic Wars opened Spain decisively to its influence, in some ways it continued to turn its face towards Africa. Early Spanish Christianity is tied up with that of Africa, and it was to a bishop of Carthage that Spaniards who were uncertain as to the relationship of the divine and human elements in Christ turned for advice.[48] The tension between the two orientations that its position made possible is a constant theme in the history of Spain.

Despite its location on an edge of the Empire, Spain played its part in the affairs of the wider Roman Empire. As early as the first century of the Christian era, three Spanish authors, Seneca, Martial and Lucan, were flourishing in Rome itself, and shortly afterwards two Spanish emperors, Trajan and Hadrian, successfully ruled for 40 years between them. After the conversion of Constantine, a bishop of Cordova named Hosius was for over four decades central to the religious affairs of the Empire, while the birth of Theodosius I in Galicia, the north-west corner of Spain, allowed Spain to be referred to as 'mother of governors and emperors', and at the beginning of the fifth century another Spaniard, Prudentius, found himself in Rome, where he wrote a long poem on a controversy that had exercised the people of Italy some two decades previously.

Spain was still an area of large villas, its ruling class possessed of broad horizons: a praetorian prefect in Italy towards the end of the fourth century was the son of Pacianus, a bishop of Barcelona who wrote on theological subjects. It was also involved in the exchange of goods. In the days of the early empire, Spain had exported olive oil, wine and the fish sauce for which it was famous; Horace wrote of a dinner party in Rome at which 'garum', made from the juices of Spanish mackerel, had been used in the cooking.[49] But as time passed, the circulation of goods within the Empire came increasingly to reflect the needs of the state. Spanish pottery found in the military zone of the Rhineland will have reached there in response to the requirements of the army. As late as the 520s, the Ostrogothic government in Italy arranged for Spanish grain to be shipped to Rome in time of need, and even after the demise of state purchases in the western Mediterranean Spain continued to produce exports, for Spanish goods continued to arrive in Marseilles, where they were bought by private individuals.[50] Yet, despite its ties with the wider world, Spain occupied a marginal position. It lacked the political centrality that Italy had traditionally enjoyed and the religious centrality that succeeded it, while it could not compete with the economic and intellectual power of Africa. Indeed, as events unrolled it may have seemed the destiny of Spain to be the territory of those losers among the newcomers to the Empire who failed to acquire more glittering prizes elsewhere. Yet by the end of the seventh century the state that emerged in Spain was the strongest in Europe.

In 409 the Vandals and other peoples who had crossed the Rhine a few years earlier made their way into the peninsula. It was a propitious time for them, Gaul and Spain having fallen under the control of the usurper Constantine, and they were able to enter Spain when it was not under central control, perhaps with the acquiescence of local authorities (see above, p. 50). After some tumultuous years, the Vandals and Alans found their way to Africa, leaving the Suevi in the remote region of Galicia. From there they extended their power towards the southern and eastern parts of the peninsula. Our primary source for these events, a chronicle written by Hydatius, a bishop in Galicia, paints a grim picture, which it is tempting to link with the emergence of hill forts and the virtual end of the occupation of large villas at this period, although the Suevi may only have administered the *coup de grâce* to entities that were already struggling. As a child, Hydatius had been to Jerusalem, where he had seen the great scholar Jerome, but when he wrote, he thought of himself as living at the very edge of the world, and found the edge was bleak. His chronicle finishes with reports of signs and wonders, obscure but threatening.[51] Under king Rechila (438–48) the Suevi advanced to take Mérida, which became their capital, and Seville. His son Rechiarius (448–55) made further progress, and co-operated with rebels in Roman territory, the bacaudi. The kingdom of the Suevi had grown to encompass the greater part of Spain. Its kings minted gold coins modelled on those of the Empire, and were able to maintain a gold coinage for more than a century. But the state they established was not destined to last.

The coming of the Goths

Just over the Pyrenees lay the territory that the Visigoths had acquired in the south of Gaul shortly after the Suevi came to Spain. They had briefly intervened there in the Roman interest early in the century, and it continued to tempt them. The emperor Avitus (455–6) was a native of Gaul who enjoyed good relations with the Visigoths, and it was probably with his support that they advanced into Spain against the Suevi, defeating and killing Rechiarius. As the Suevi fell back to Galicia, the Goths exploited the free hand that the weakening of Roman power had left them. By the 470s their king Euric had incorporated most of the peninsula into his kingdom based in Toulouse.

The Visigoths were strong enough to dominate the history of Gaul for some decades. But after the battle of Voulon, sometimes thought to have been fought at Vouillé (507), and the consequent loss of most of their possessions in Gaul to the Franks, a migration into Spain that had begun some time earlier seems to have picked up speed. The presence of apparently Visigothic goods in early cemeteries suggests that the new arrivals were then concentrated in the central areas of the northern part of Spain, most them settling in Old Castile and some finding homes in New Castile, about as far south as Toledo. No more than the Ostrogoths, they do not seem to have scattered widely. The adoption of Toledo as the capital of the kingdom later in the sixth century may have been connected with wider dispersion of Goths, for tombs of the late sixth and seventh centuries indicative of Gothic presence were scattered over the whole of the peninsula, although their contents became steadily less Germanic. In any case, after 507 Spain was no longer an appendage to the main territory of the Visigoths; thereafter the centre of gravity of their kingdom was firmly to the south of the Pyrenees, and the progressive shifts in the location of their capital, from Narbonne to Barcelona and finally to Toledo, in the very centre of the peninsula, anchored it ever more firmly within its land-mass. The shifts also marked a move away from the Roman past. Toulouse had been a major classical city where work on a lavish cathedral had been completed less than two decades before the Goths decisively took it in 462. Toledo, on the other hand, had been looked down on by the Romans as no more than a small town on a well-protected site.[52] The Visigothic state would be less beholden to the past than those of the Ostrogoths and Vandals, who retained Roman capitals.

While the Goths would bring major changes to Spain, they entered it at a time when important developments were already under way, more so than in Africa. In particular, two interacting processes were changing the bases of its economy and society. Under the Empire, large estates geared to producing goods for the market had developed. Yet their markets, both domestic and external, ultimately dried up. The towns that drew on their products were declining in population and, apparently, wealth. They were losing ground to villas, which sought self-sufficiency – an impulse that was sometimes taken to extremes, as when olives were planted in northerly areas where the climate was unsuitable. Similarly, goods that had been produced to supply the needs of the Roman state were no longer needed as it ceased to exist in the West. A lower production for the market meant that economic life was increasingly regionalised. Moreover, Spain was becoming more self-sufficient. While African pottery and some wares of eastern origin were still imported along the Mediterranean coast during the sixth century, the demand for pottery in inland regions was satisfied by locally produced wares. Even the coastal regions were moving towards self-sufficiency, as hand-moulded pottery, of a kind also found in inland areas, came to be used. The reason for this development is unclear, for while it involved a decline in technological sophistication, it may primarily reflect a new kind of demand. In either case, more of what people consumed was being produced locally.

Such tendencies in economic life were reflected in the political life of the kingdom. Whatever its aspirations, political authority was decentralised in the Visigothic state. Theudis, a commander whom Theoderic sent to govern Spain in 511, married a wealthy Spanish woman whose landed wealth was sufficient to support a force of about 2,000 soldiers; such a family must have enjoyed a large measure of *de facto* independence. In 575 king Leovigild captured one Aspidius, the leading man of a region in Galicia, and brought under his power the wealth and places he had held. There may have been other local grandees of whom we know nothing.[53] The regional diversity of Visigothic Spain was also shown in its coinage. The Suevi, and then the Visigoths, minted coins; the failure of the Romans to do so is testimony to the relatively small number of soldiers who had been stationed there. The activity of the post-Roman states was another consequence of the emergence of independent political units in western Europe, but the number of mints was high, over 80 mints being known to have produced gold coins. The existence of many small mints in Galicia, which one would have thought of as an economically backward area, is particularly striking. Such a multiplication of mints points not merely to Iberian independence from foreign authority, but also to regionalism within Spain.

The peninsula was also divided in an important non-geographic way, for two law codes operated simultaneously in Visigothic territory. One, which Euric had originally issued in Gaul, applied to the Goths, although its content was not specifically Germanic. For example, at one point the code provided that a person who took someone else's ox for his own use without the knowledge of its owner was to give its owner another of the same value when he returned it. This law is closely paralleled by a provision in a law code that the Burgundians issued shortly afterwards in Gaul, according to which two oxen were to be handed over in such a case. But it is also similar to a provision in a Byzantine law code, the Farmer's Law, which most scholars believe to have originated in a rural part of the empire in the seventh or eighth century, according to which a person who took someone else's ox, ass or beast of any kind without permission was to pay for its hire twice over, and if it died was to give two for it.[54] The similarities between the Farmer's Law and the western law codes may be no more than sensible solutions to what was doubtless a common problem, arrived at independently. But it may well be that they all grew out of a common source, termed by scholars 'vulgar law', which was not the classical law of Rome but a form of it that had developed in the late Empire, perhaps during the fourth century, to cater for people who lacked the legal knowledge that major reforms had made necessary. That the compilers of law codes issued by early Germanic states, no less than the compilers of a legal text in the Empire, may have drawn on this source is another sign of the influence on post-Roman society of non-classical forms that developed in the Empire during late antiquity. The other early law code of the Visigothic state, the Breviarium issued by Euric's son Alaric in 506, was still more Roman. Prepared by the bishops and noble men of his kingdom, it was based on the Theodosian code promulgated in 438 and other legal sources of the period, and applied to Romans. The situation was therefore different to that in Ostrogothic Italy, where the one code applied to both Goths and Romans; in Spain, each people had its own law, although both were substantially Roman in origin.

If this were not enough to suggest a kingdom divided within itself, the survival rate of the earliest Visigothic kings in Spain was appalling. Amalric, who was made king by Theoderic the Ostrogoth in 511, was a wife-beater who was killed when trying to escape from his wrathful Frankish brother-in-law; Theudis was assassinated; Theudegisel was murdered when drunk at a banquet; and Agila was in his turn murdered. An author across the Pyrenees wrote of the Goths' nasty habit of murdering kings they did not care for.[55] Later kings erected a powerful state, but the circumstances to which it owed its strength had not become apparent by the middle of the sixth century.

The immediate post-Roman destinies of Italy, Africa and Spain may seem to have been very different. But in all three cases, what is sometimes thought of as 'the fall of the Roman Empire' emerges as having been a gentle process. The newcomers, who were usually well on the way to being like the Romans, were invited or sent into the territories they occupied, and the states they established were entirely within the frontiers of the former Empire. Few battles were fought. Indeed, after the battle of Adrianople, which was itself the product of contingent circumstances, it is hard to point to a single significant engagement that allowed the Goths or Vandals to occupy Roman territory. In some ways, the impact of the newcomers was bad. The depredations of wandering armies, such as the Vandals and their allies prior to their settlement in Africa, raiding, such as the Suevi practised in Spain, the sacking of cities, such as Rome itself, and the ability of various groups to operate what amounted to protection rackets brought about widespread insecurity, of which the atrophy of villas may be a sign, and were all felt keenly. Yet as the dust settled, the new rulers tended to maintain or imitate systems already in operation, although because these were often the products of late antiquity rather than the classical period they can look less Roman than they really were. Wherever they went, they found local elites keen to co-operate with them. By and large, the post-Roman states that had emerged around the western Mediterranean by the early sixth century maintained the status quo.

Chapter 3

◆

FROM GAUL TO FRANCE

As the Romans had been uneasily aware, Gaul stretched a long way inland. Its south had long been subject to Greek and Roman influences. Greeks from Asia Minor founded Marseilles in about 600 BC, and some 500 years later the Romans founded their 'province', after which Provence is now named, with its capital at Narbonne. What place could be more pleasant than Marseilles, happily combining Greek elegance with appropriate provincial restraint? Romans interested in rhetoric and philosophy could find such a place more attractive than Athens. When people in the north thought of the lands around the Rhône and Saône, vineyards, olive trees and a kind of intellectual snobbery came to mind. In the sixth century, the abbot of a monastery in Paris declined to become bishop of Avignon, professing that in his 'simplicity' he had no desire to be placed among sophistic senators and counts who were philosophers. Subsequently, he was appointed to the more suitable see of Le Mans. Influences from the Mediterranean were weaker in the north. Christianisation had occurred more slowly there: while the bishops who attended the council of Arles in 314 came from as far away as Cologne, most of them were from south of Lyons. On the other hand, most of the nine weapons factories in Roman Gaul were to the north-east of the Seine. When the Romans distinguished between that part of Gaul south of the Alps, where people wore the toga in the manner of Roman citizens, and the northerly part where people had long hair, it was not to the advantage of the latter. And, as time passed, the distinction took on political overtones.[1]

From the late third century, the north became a hotbed of military unrest. In about 260 one Postumus, confusingly described in our sources as both the leader of the barbarians in Gaul and the duke of the frontier across the Rhine, was proclaimed emperor to deal with the attacks of Franks and others. He received recognition in Britain and Spain and unexpectedly enjoyed the support of some Franks, inaugurating a line of emperors in the north of Gaul which lasted for some years after he died in 268. Soon afterwards a general in Britain of Celtic origin, Carausius, proclaimed himself emperor. He was thought to be in league with the Franks and Saxons who were raiding the coasts, and held territory in the north of Gaul as well as Britain. Another usurper was Magnentius, thought to have been the son of a British father and a Frankish mother, who was raised to the purple at Autun in 350 and defeated three years later. Thereafter Julian was raised to imperial office at Paris by troops from across the Rhine, and in 383 the general Magnus Maximus was proclaimed emperor by troops in Britain. Crossing to Gaul, he established himself at Trier, and enjoyed some success. In the early fifth century, the armies in Britain proclaimed another soldier, Constantine, emperor, inaugurating a line of short-lived usurpers, while a native of Gaul, Jovinus, was proclaimed emperor in the modern Belgium, with the support of various groups of Germans. These events, the scale of which cannot be paralleled elsewhere, repeatedly saw the less Romanised north of Gaul, together with Britain, generate military rebellions in which both Romans and non-Romans participated.

If this were not enough, the north was also subject to pressures from beyond the Rhine. After the great raids of the third century, the Romans adopted a new strategy of developing defensive works away from the frontier and concentrating on the defence of roads. Resources were poured into Trier, the northerly headquarters of the praetorian prefect of the Gauls, which acquired an amphitheatre capable of seating 50,000 people and other monumental buildings, many of which still survive. Yet the north was experiencing depopulation, towns becoming smaller and many rural sites being deserted. It is hard to account for this. Declines in the markets for which rural producers had catered, the impact of the mysterious bacaudae, who are known to have been active towards the end of the third century and, during the fifth, specifically in the north, and the fear of aggressors from across the Rhine are likely to have been more important than whatever damage such aggressors may have done. Some of the abandoned land became forest, but by the late third century Germanic people were abandoning their settlements to the east of the Rhine and occupying vacant land within imperial territory. By the early fourth century, groups of Franks were being officially settled. The author of a panegyric on the emperor Constantine was not certain what to say of the nations within Francia, whom he saw as no longer based in places formerly invaded by the Romans but now placed in regions of Gaul that had been uninhabited, aiding the peace of Rome with their way of life and its arms with their recruits.[2] The settlement of such Franks in what is now Belgium may have caused bishops to move from Tournai to Noyon and Tongeren to Maastricht. Various cemeteries in northern Gaul, in which men were often buried with weapons and women with Germanic jewellery, were presumably their burial places.

These developments pointed in a very different direction to the events that we considered in the preceding chapter. Whereas peoples who had travelled long distances brought an end to Roman rule around the western Mediterranean, in the north of Gaul developments arising from internal disruption and the peaceable settlement of outsiders would bring this about. It was into this unstable environment, which saw the headquarters of the praetorian prefect transferred from Trier to the southern town of Arles at about the turn of the century, that invaders came.

NEWCOMERS AND THE OLD ESTABLISHMENT

While the breaching of the Rhine by the Vandals and others ushered in a period of turbulence, its impact on Gaul is unclear. In 409 Jerome lamented that 'most ferocious nations' had occupied all the Gauls, that Mainz had been destroyed and Worms ruined, and that various other cities had suffered sad fates.[3] But Jerome, who lived far away in Bethlehem and was never averse to rhetoric, may not be a sound guide. A Gallic author of the period may seem to provide more substance:

> Neither dense and savage forests nor high mountains, nor rivers rushing down through swift rapids, nor citadels on remote heights nor cities protected by their walls, not the barrier of the sea nor the sad solitude of the desert, not holes in the ground nor caves under forbidding cliffs could escape from the barbarians' raids.

But such passages can easily be paralleled. We read of contemporaries in Africa hiding from the Vandals in the caves of mountains, steep places and remote areas, while Britons are said to have hid in mountains, caves and forests.[4] Such similarities suggest a high level of rhetoric, rather than independent accounts of remarkably similar occurrences. Times were doubtless difficult in some areas. At Sisteron, on the middle reaches of the Durance, a successful civil servant, Dardanus, founded an establishment named Theopolis, where an inscription emphasised its strong defences, although they need not have been erected against non-Romans. The great villa at Montaubin was abandoned in about 400, and attacks are a possible reason for this, although there may well have been deeper, structural causes, as there were for similar events in Spain. But the raids of the third century are better reflected archaeologically than the activities of the Vandals and their allies. There is some evidence for human habitation in caves during this period in Gaul, but this could merely reflect the sleeping habits of shepherds at a time of increased pastoralism. In any case, the new arrivals quickly left Gaul, and soon afterwards the Visigoths were officially settled in the south (see above p. 40). An autobiographical poem provides a fascinating picture of events in the south-west of Gaul as the Visigoths moved in.

Influenced by the *Confessions* of St Augustine, Paulinus, a landowner near Bordeaux, published in 459 his *Eucharisticos*, a work, as its name implies, of thanksgiving for his long life.[5] He was a grandson of the poet and civil servant Ausonius, a daughter of whom had married a man whose career took him to Greece and Africa, and their son, born in the Greek town of Pella, was Paulinus, for whom Greek remained his first language. He aspired to a traditional life of leisure and moderation, and his early labours in his property near Bordeaux, no less than his marriage to an heiress, were designed to assure its attainment. Yet such ambitions, testimony to the spread into a remote corner of the Empire of a Roman ideal of a life of retirement in which elevated pursuits could be followed, could not easily be fulfilled in the fifth century. Paulinus suffered losses from enemies who poured into the Empire at the time of the Vandal irruption, but more important was the arrival of the Goths in 414, because his estate, not having a Gothic 'guest', lacked protection. He describes Bordeaux being burned by the Goths, but this occurred before the newcomers were settled in about 418, after which it was in their interest to maintain existing structures. He also laments that he lost all his goods and outlived his fatherland, although he knew that others who enjoyed the favour of the Goths flourished, and we may suspect that Paulinus, who complained that even members of his own family wrongfully gained control of some of his property, had not been astute in accommodating himself to changing realities. In any case, his losses were not total. Having moved to Marseilles, towards the end of his life he looked forward to being able to pass on his property, and he sold a parcel of land to a Goth, although he claimed that the sum he received was less than its worth. Doubtless Paulinus was one of the losers in a changing world, but reading between the lines of his account we may deduce that there were winners.

Members of another Germanic people, the Burgundians, seem to have crossed into Gaul with the Vandals. As were the Goths, they were later thought of as having originated in Scandinavia,[6] but this was simply the recycling of a familiar topos. After a disastrous defeat at Roman hands in 436 they settled around Lake Geneva as Roman allies. A garbled later tradition has Romans inviting the Burgundians so that they would not have to pay taxes, where-upon they settled with their wives and children, while a source nearer the period represents them occupying part of Gaul and dividing the land with Roman senators. The stories suggest that they settled in a peaceable fashion, and people described as senators remained a force in the political life of the Burgundian kingdom.[7] From there they expanded, establishing a capital where the waters of the Saône join those of the Rhône at Lyons, and came to share a border with the Visigoths to the west. At the end of the fifth century, a church dedicated to a Gallic saint, St Martin, was erected on top of the sunken dwellings often associated with Germanic peoples at St Julien-en-Genevois, near Geneva. By the early sixth century their territory was called 'Burgundia', a name that persists in the modern 'Bourgogne'. King Gundobad (474?–516), a Christian of the Arian persuasion, and his successor Sigismund (516–23), who made a gesture of identification with the local people by adopting Catholicism, enjoyed the services of the local elite, among them bishop Avitus of Vienne. A well-connected man related to the emperor Avitus, the bishop was a member of the old Gallic aristocracy who had succeeded his father in office; among the letters he wrote were three in the name of Sigismund to the emperor in Constantinople, seeking to maintain good relations. As did the Visigoths, the Burgundians issued one code of law for themselves, influenced by Roman law, and one for the Romans living in their kingdom, and it must have seemed that their state was destined for a long future.

Other groups were also establishing themselves in Gaul. The Alamanni, whose name, originating from roots that lie behind the modern English 'all men', witnesses to their diverse origins, and which lingers in the modern French word for Germany, 'Allemagne', moved across the Rhine early in the fifth century, and occupied territory to the north of the Burgundians.[8] Another Germanic group, the Saxons, important in the history of Britain, made inroads. Skilled seafarers, they were feared as far away as the Bay of Biscay, and communities of them settled in the maritime regions of northern and western Gaul. Groups of Alans made themselves at home in various areas, while parts of north-eastern Gaul were being settled by Bretons, inhab-itants of Britain who, for reasons that are unclear, were making their way to the Continent.

The complicated inroads made by these peoples may seem to have taken us a long way from the principles stated at the beginning of this chapter. But in most cases their important settlements were confined to the parts of Gaul south of the Loire. It would be with a group to the north, the people after whom France takes its name, that the future lay.

The Franks were not a unified people; rather, like the Alamanni, they were a coalition of small tribes. They had long been entering Roman territory, unambiguously as friends of the Empire. Some, such as Arbogast, had served as generals at the highest levels, and when the Vandals crossed the Rhine, Frankish forces attempted to block them on behalf of the Romans. Military dealings between the Empire and the Franks were better than those between the Empire and the Goths; there would never be an Adrianople in Frankish history. Meanwhile, many Franks were settling quietly as farmers on the left bank of the Rhine, where modern Germanic placenames suggest their settlements. In this respect as well the Franks, whose journey into imperial territory only involved short distances, can be contrasted with the Goths, whose settlement in Gaul and Spain, as well as that in Italy, came after long treks. Trier was taken on a number of occasions early in the fifth century, but the original population seems to have continued to inhabit the inner area, where the grid formed by Roman streets is still recognisable in the street-plan of the modern city, while Franks settled round about it; in the 470s the city had a count with a Frankish name.

Other Franks took over Cologne, but their presence there was not new. Some graves from the Roman period at Cologne contain Germanic goods, such as the one containing a goblet on which was written, in Latin, the encouraging message 'Let's drink happily!' Perhaps the Franks of Cologne saw themselves as continuing rather than overthrowing the life of the town, although this took new forms. A young woman and a boy of six were buried in separate graves beneath what is now the cathedral, contrary to Roman law which prohibited burials within the walls of a town; the timber from which goods in the latter grave were made was from trees felled in about 537. Outside the town are a number of cemeteries in which the graves are laid out in rows, a custom associated with Roman frontier society. When Gall, a cleric from Clermont, arrived there in the early sixth century, he found a temple with wooden idols, to which he set fire. Our source describes those who worshipped there as 'barbarians', and they may have been Franks. But they may have been descendants of people living on a fringe of the empire who had abandoned Christianity when Roman laws against the public practice of polytheism ceased to apply; perhaps by then the distinction between such people and Franks was unclear.[9]

By the middle of the century, a balance of political forces had developed in Gaul, as Attila the Hun discovered. In 451 he led his army of Huns and other peoples into Gaul, where he was opposed by a coalition of a Roman army under the general Aetius, Visigoths, Burgundians, Franks, Alans and others, all stakeholders in the existing situation. When the town of Orléans was besieged, it was saved by the arrival of forces under Aetius and a Visigothic leader, and at the battle of the Catalaunian Plains, in Champagne, Attila failed to defeat his combined enemies. It was the beginning of the end, and he was dead two years later. Perhaps the most startling aspect of the invasion of 451 was the role played by an inhabitant of Paris, the virgin Genevieve, who is said to have performed miracles on a scale for which the deeds of earlier holy women provided no precedent. She led a campaign of prayer that deflected the Huns from the town. Her name, which is given in our Latin sources as 'Genovefa', is Germanic, yet her parents, Severus and Gerontia, bore classical names. Presumably her father was a Frank who had adopted a Roman name. Despite the dichotomy that had existed between Romans and 'barbarians', we may doubt whether the question as to which group she belonged to would have occurred to her contemporaries. Not merely were Romans and non-Romans co-operating; in the north of Gaul it was already becoming difficult to tell them apart.

The decades that followed the battle of the Catalaunian Plains belonged to the Visigoths. This was largely due to the ability of king Euric (466–84) who took the Auvergne, Arles and Marseilles. Sidonius Apollinaris, the bishop of Clermont, deplored the fact that between the ocean, the Loire and the Rhône, his town alone resisted the Goths, and many powers found it worthwhile to send representatives to his court.[10] Euric was a rough diamond. He had murdered his way to the throne, and Visigothic kingship during this period was more attractive to the ambitious than the prudent: of the eight kings who ruled in Gaul, four were murdered and another two died in battle. Moreover, he was an Arian noted for anti-Catholic policies, in particular a refusal to allow deceased bishops to be replaced. In such circumstances, local elites walked carefully. Among them was Sidonius, whose father-in-law Avitus had briefly been emperor in 455–6, having been elevated with Gothic support, although in a sign of regional affiliation a panegyric that Sidonius wrote in his honour portrays him as from the Auvergne more than Gaul. Some years later, Sidonius expressed the hope that his sons would be consuls, but the only one known to us acted in the two capacities with the greatest futures in the post-Roman west. He served the Goths in a military capacity and ended his days as a bishop.[11]

So it was that the aristocrats of Gaul, far from displaying the apathy that has sometimes been thought to mark their posture before the newcomers, frequently tried to turn developments to their advantage. Often, this led them to turn their backs on the diminishing Empire. In about 460 the general Agrippinus, a native of Gaul, was accused of supporting barbarians and wishing to remove provinces from the Roman state, which seems to have led to a trial in Rome, while in the 470s one Seronatus, who had held office in the Auvergne, was executed for treason with the Goths. Leo, an adviser and speech writer of Euric, looked with such complaisance on recent history that he suggested to Sidonius that he write history; his correspondent tactfully relied that Leo would be the better author. Leo was the kind of Catholic who was quite prepared to lower the height of a church that interfered with the view from the palace of an Arian king. Such people had little to fear as Gaul moved into the post-Roman period.[12]

CLOVIS

Towards the end of the fifth century, the complex political situation in Gaul underwent a remarkable simplification. Following a series of victories in the north, the Frankish king Childeric (c.456–c.481) was buried, on the edge of a Roman cemetery at Tournai. The contents of his grave, which was discovered in 1653, reveal him as a Romanized figure who, judging from a signet ring inscribed CHILDERICI REGIS ('of king Childeric'), dispatched documents under his seal. He fastened his clothes with a gold cruciform fibula, as did the high officials depicted in the mosaic of Justinian's court at San Vitale. Intriguingly, he was buried with a large number of gold solidi from the east, most of them recently minted. Such largesse, which implies that Childeric was being backed from Constantinople, recalls a story that on a trip to that city Childeric had asked an emperor to send him to Gaul as his servant. In ways that we cannot trace, the continuing Empire in the east remained interested in Gaul. The emperor Leo (457–74) was so impressed with what he heard of one valiant inhabitant of Gaul, Titus, that he summoned him with his following to Constantinople, but to the annoyance of the emperor he fell under the influence of the holy man Daniel and became a monk. Perhaps the indigenous populations of Gaul saw the Franks as their allies against other newcomers.[13]

Under Childeric's son Clovis (king c.481–511), the Franks moved against the other major powers in Gaul. Shortly after succeeding his father, having being lifted up on a shield just as the emperor Julian had been, Clovis received a letter from bishop Remigius of Reims. The bishop informed him that he had heard of his having assumed the administration of the province of Secunda Belgica, and encouraged him to govern in a moral way and listen to the advice of his bishops, so that his province would stand firm.[14] Remigius belonged to the local elite. His brother was bishop of Soissons, where he would in turn be succeeded by a nephew, and he wrote as the head of the church in a province to its new political head. Writing of Clovis's 'administration', he used the technical word for the government of a Roman province,[15] and by mentioning 'your bishops', 'your province' and 'your citizens', and advising him to 'let your praetorium be open to all', he acknowledged him as its legitimate governor. In this capacity, Clovis turned against the other regimes in Gaul. The first was that of Syagrius, a shadowy figure later known as king or patrician of the Romans, who had inherited a claim to what was left of Roman power in the north. Defeated in 486 or 487, he fled to Toulouse, whence king Alaric handed him over to Clovis, who later saw to his murder. Franks later seized Bordeaux from the Visigoths, and in 507, at a battle probably fought at Voulon, south of Poitiers and comfortably within Visigothic territory, Clovis decisively defeated the Visigoths. Alaric was killed, and his people abandoned most of their territories in Gaul, some of which were occupied by the Franks and others by the Ostrogoths. Victories were also won against the Alamanni, and Clovis intervened in Burgundian affairs. It was a staggering expansion. Towards the end of his life, in a decisive move towards strong monarchy, Clovis turned against rival members of his family. A later tradition has the royal family, by then known as Merovingians, as being descended from one Merovech, conceived by a princess in an encounter with a sea-monster. But Merovech was the grandfather of Clovis, so speedily had the family risen. Moreover, its members were distinguished for their long hair, and who could have been surprised at its emergence in that part of Gaul known for the long hair of its people?[16]

Clovis set about doing the things that high imperial officials, and indeed emperors, did. Towards the end of his reign he issued a code of laws by which one Frankish group, the Salians, was to be judged, and he presided over the army in a Campus Martius, just as emperors did. Following his defeat of the Visigoths, the emperor in Constantinople made him an honorary consul and granted him the title 'gloriosissimus', as did bishops meeting at a synod in Orléans three years later; the word was often used of high imperial officials. In Paris, a town with imperial traditions since the time of Julian, Clovis built over the tomb of St Genevieve a basilica dedicated to the Holy Apostles, in which he was buried. The dedication was resonant, for Constantine had built a church with the same dedication in Constantinople in which emperors were buried, and later, when Milan briefly had imperial pretensions, its bishop Ambrose founded a church with the same dedication. Indeed, a historian of the late sixth century depicted the baptism of Clovis as that of a 'new Constantine', using language that anticipates later legends of the first Christian emperor being cleansed of leprosy when baptised by pope Silvester. He also claimed that Clovis was called 'consul or augustus'. The reality was less grandiose: after the emperor appointed him consul, Clovis had entered Tours, crowned himself with a diadem, and processed across the city distributing largesse. This solemn entry into Tours resembled that of Theoderic into Rome eight years previously. But whereas Theoderic teetered on the brink of being an illegitimate emperor, Clovis was recognised as being the ally of the emperor.[17]

At about the turn of the century, Clovis took another important step. His father had died a non-Christian. Excavations near his tomb have uncovered the skeletons of horses that had been ritually killed and buried, presumably in connection with his burial; its flamboyance may have been a defiant response to a Christianity that increasingly seemed inescapable. Clovis, on the other hand, married a Catholic, and may have decided to adopt her faith having won a victory after invoking Christ. But the most attractive feature of Catholicism was its being the religion of the people of Gaul. This is not to say that adhesion to it gained him their support. At the battle of Voulon a contingent from Clermont led by Apollinaris, the son of Sidonius who later became its bishop himself, had been happy to support the Arian Visigoths, and the career of Caesarius, bishop of the southern town of Arles (502–42), indicates that political and religious loyalties were independent. A member of an old noble family, he had been trained at the monastery of Lérins, which had been founded early in the fifth century offshore from the modern Cannes and become famous as a nursery of bishops. Like many members of his class, Caesarius was a man of the world who dealt with Arian and Catholic rulers as circumstances required. Alaric the Goth had approved his becoming bishop, but following an accusation that he wished to bring Arles and its territory under the Burgundians, whose king was another Arian, he was exiled to the distant town of Bordeaux, whence 'the abominable prince' later ordered his return to Arles. Subsequently, while the Ostrogoths were resisting a Frankish siege of Arles, he was imprisoned, but later, when summoned to Ravenna, he made a great impression on Theoderic.[18] There was an element of nervous edginess in the career of Caesarius, for the emergence of new political structures encouraged tensions, but allegiance did not follow religion. When Clovis converted, he was not bidding for the support of the people among whom the Franks were coming to live, but indicating his identification with them.

In some respects the Franks remained visibly non-Roman. The Salic law provides for trial by ordeal. When Theoderic sought a harp player to be sent to Clovis, he envisaged someone like Orpheus, who would tame the savage hearts of barbarians with his sweet sound, and the picture of him which emerges from texts written in the sixth century is overwhelmingly that of a man of war. Not all the Franks followed him into Catholicism; a group who fought in Italy in the 530s terrified the Goths when they offered human sacrifices, and the progress of the new faith among Franks in the Rhineland and to its east was slow. Nevertheless, in the middle of the sixth century, people in Constantinople thought of the Franks as sharing the orthodox faith with themselves, unlike the Goths, and as having a system of government, administration and laws modelled on those of the Romans.[19] The new force that had emerged in the north of Gaul by the death of Clovis was recognisably antique in its ways.

THE SIXTH CENTURY

Clovis was succeeded by four sons, perhaps in accordance with a Frankish practice of dividing a man's assets among his male offspring. Under them, the Franks enjoyed further success. In 531 Narbonne, the headquarters of what remained of the Visigoths' power in Gaul, was attacked, whereupon their king withdrew to Barcelona. In 541 a force even entered Spain and besieged Zaragosa, but withdrew, unnerved when the townspeople marched around the walls singing psalms and bearing the tunic of their patron saint, St Vincent. Burgundy was incorporated into the Frankish kingdom in 534, as was the territory of the Thuringians across the Rhine, after their king mysteriously died falling from a wall. Moreover, a way into Italy appeared. After the battle of Voulon, the Ostrogoths had occupied Provence. Among those who administered it on behalf of Ravenna was Parthenius, a well-connected man who had the distinction, which may have made the Franks uneasy, of being a scholar of Caesar's *Gallic War*. But before long the boot was on the other foot, for the beginning of a war between the Ostrogoths and the Empire in the 530s seemed to offer the Franks an entrée into Italy. The war began just after the accession of the most ambitious Merovingian sovereign, Theudebert (533–47), a staunch warrior who had already shown what he was made of by defeating a force of Danish raiders. Hard pressed by the Empire, the Goths ceded Provence, including the great port of Marseilles, to him. But this did not deter him from leading a large army into northern Italy in 539, and the Franks maintained a presence there for decades.

Theudebert was ambitious. He minted gold coins bearing his name, a prerogative some thought reserved to the emperor, and wrote to Justinian boasting that he controlled lands extending from the Danube and the borders of Pannonia as far as the Ocean; the scale of his claim, and its including 'parts of Italy', where the army of Justinian was fighting at that very time, was breathtaking. The people of Constantinople feared that he planned to lead an army as far as the city itself. The kingdom of the Franks certainly had wide horizons; a duke was thought worthy of being applauded by the Roman on the lyre, the barbarian on the harp, the Greek as if he were Achilles, and the Breton on an indigenous instrument. The empress Sophia sent a portion of the True Cross from Constantinople to Radegund, a Thuringian captive who had married a Frankish king and gone on to found a convent at Poitiers. Radegund's coup, which made the local bishop envious, led the poet Venantius Fortunatus to write a series of hymns, and one of these, the rhythm of which has been said to be that of Roman military marches, is still widely sung. Another king, Chilperic (561–84), acted the part of an emperor, debating theology with bishops, seeking to add new letters to the alphabet and, apparently, erecting circuses where he put on shows at Soissons and Paris. When kings issued acts referring to themselves as 'most clement', they were laying claim to an imperial title.[20]

Yet such accomplishments occurred in the midst of civil wars. Bishop Gregory of Tours (bishop 573–94) was alarmed at the wars being fought among the Franks, which partly arose from their inheritance practice, although military unrest was not a new problem in Gaul. Just as worrying was a halt in their expansion. The coming of the Lombards into Italy complicated affairs there, and by the end of the sixth century military interaction between Gaul and Italy had ceased, only to be resumed well into the eighth century. A series of attacks on the Visigoths across the Pyrenees came to nothing, the Bretons proved difficult to tame, and across the Rhine the Saxons showed signs of insubordination. In 631 they were excused from a tribute of 500 cows that they had given the Franks annually since the middle of the sixth century, in return for a promise that they would resist another people, the Slavic Wends. In 639 a duke of Thuringia established by king Dagobert to strengthen the position of the Franks in central Europe successfully rebelled, whereupon he deemed himself the king in Thuringia.[21] While the Franks had done stunningly well, the powerful image that their kings projected of themselves was showing signs of becoming remote from reality.

FRANKS AND INDIGENES

Our chief narrative source for the history of Gaul in the sixth century is a long work written towards its end by bishop Gregory of Tours. It is often called the *History of the Franks*, but the name is misleading, for Gregory's own title for his work was simply 'Books of Histories', and he wrote less about the Franks than might have been thought likely. His uses of the word 'Franks' are significant. He first mentions them as fighting Attila (2.7) and then gives a long account, based on earlier writers, of their prior history, in which they spend all their time fighting. After a description of the Franks in the time of Childeric (2.12), Gregory describes them fighting the Goths (2.18) and Saxons (2.19). On almost every occasion, the word 'Franks' has a military connotation, and as their history progressed, Gregory continued to think of them in this way. When a meeting of the Franks was told of the evil deeds of the Thuringians in 531, they all agreed to invade Thuringia (3.7); 'the Franks' are represented as bodies of soldiers more inclined towards warfare than their kings (3.11, 4.14), and in the closing stages of Gregory's narrative they are still seen as members of armies (9.25, 10.3). It is a small step from this to Isidore of Seville's suggestion that they may have been called Franks from their 'ferocity', their manners being rude and their spirits naturally ferocious.

They may have cultivated such an image. A text of the seventh century tells how Clovis, being told at the time of his baptism of the passion of Christ, exclaimed, 'If I had been there with my Franks I would have avenged his injury!' Yet this emphasis comports ill with other things we know of the Franks. The Salic law issued by Clovis deals with issues likely to arise in small agricultural communities. After treating summonses to court, its opening titles are concerned with thefts of pigs, cattle, sheep, goats, dogs, birds and bees, and subsequently it prescribes punishments for thefts from gardens, in particular turnip, bean, pea and lentil patches. The people whose affairs it regulated were settled enough to have water mills. While the name 'Franks' was associated with a warrior aristocracy, there were clearly many Franks who did not belong to it.[22]

Moreover, they proved capable of accommodating other people. They were concentrated in the north. The sons of Clovis, although they had most of Gaul at their disposal, established their capitals in Orléans, Soissons, Paris and Reims, in the region traditionally least susceptible to classical influences. Here, where the Franks were seen as a prestigious group in society who could be distinguished from 'weaker people',[23] others wished to identify with them. The indigenous population began to give their children Frankish names, as did the family of one Lupus in the second half of the sixth century. Said to have been a native of Gaul, he served Frankish kings in the north-eastern area later known as Austrasia. His brother, Magnulf, served as an administrator in the Rhineland, while his son, Romulf, became bishop of the northerly see of Reims. Oddly enough, the Latin word *lupus* means 'wolf', which suggests continuity across a period when the family was drawing names from both Roman and Germanic traditions. The great-uncle of Gregory of Tours was named Gundulf, and he played a role in the education of Arnulph, later bishop of Metz. As late as the early ninth century, a bishop of the same see bore the name Gondulf, and it is tempting to see him as a member of Gregory's family; if he were, the family had been able to retain its interests in the region for centuries.[24]

Most of the bishops who attended church councils in the north of Gaul in the seventh century had Germanic names, which reflect the spread of such names among the indigenous population more than the entry of newcomers into the episcopate. Indeed, the personal names used in Frankish territories were ultimately overwhelmingly Germanic; of the characters in the *Song of Roland*, an epic poem written down in about 1100 but which is based on material centuries older, only one, Roland's wise friend Oliver, bears a name that is in any way classical. People came to be buried in accordance with frontier custom, as can be seen from a cemetery that was in continuous use from the fourth to the seventh centuries at Frénouville, 10 km south-west of Caen. In the early fifth century, graves began to be orientated so that people were buried facing the east, according to the practice known to scholars as Reihengräber; from the middle of that century, goods associated with Franks occur; and towards the end of the sixth century, men began to be buried with weapons. Yet these changes occurred within a homogeneous population, which became culturally Germanic with minimal genetic change.

Such developments show how hard it became to distinguish Frank from indigene. From the second half of the fourth century, people in the north of Gaul lived increasingly often in wooden cabins; the evidence for such structures in the south is slight. Such dwellings may have revived pre-Roman practice, in line with developments that occurred elsewhere in the Empire, but the practice was also known on the far side of the Rhine and may have been specifically Frankish, for the Salic law deals with setting houses on fire, and we hear of Romans burning Frankish houses. Perhaps, then, its reintroduction into Gaul and subsequent spread was associated with the arrival of newcomers. However, wood was also used as the main or sole building material on sites in Gaul where there is nothing else of a Germanic character, and here it was presumably linked with a renunciation of old Roman ways by indigenous people.[25] The evidence of burial customs is also problematic. Cemeteries in which graves were arranged by rows, as they came to be at Frénouville, have frequently been associated with the Franks. Yet the practice originated in the frontier zone of northern Gaul. From there it spread both east of the Rhine, where no antecedents to it can be found, and into the lands of the old Empire.[26] But during the seventh century, the style of burial practised at sites such as Frénouville became outmoded. People ceased to be buried with arms, and by 700 old cemeteries were being abandoned as people came to prefer burial near churches. This development, a clear reversal of the preference of the Romans, was an important step towards the villages of the middle ages.

The indigenous people of northern Gaul having chosen to identify with the Franks, it became plausible to see the area as being inhabited entirely by this people. Nomenclature reflected this understanding. By the late sixth century, the north, but not the south of Gaul could be thought of as 'Francia',[27] and ultimately everyone living north of the Loire was considered a Frank, distinct from the Romans and Aquitainians, thought of as absolutely different in race, who resided in the south. Bishop Eligius of Noyon (641–60) was a southerner who came to Paris, located in what his biographer of the eighth century described as 'the land of the Franks'. Having become a bishop, he preached against 'the abominable games of demons and unspeakable dances and all other inane superstitions'. Not surprisingly, he encountered opposition. Those involved in these practices made their feelings clear:

> Never, Roman, . . . will you be able put an end to our customs, but we shall carry out our solemnities just as we have until now, and celebrate them for ever and always, and no one will ever be able to prohibit the pleasant games we enjoy so much.

Such were the difficulties that a 'Roman' who came to the north could find himself in. The south retained a distinctive Mediterranean flavour. In 529 the council of Vaison decreed that the Kyrie eleison was to be sung in the liturgy with fervour, as was done in the apostolic see and throughout the East and the provinces of Italy, and a council at Narbonne, which decreed in 589 that no one was to work on the Lord's Day, specified that the provision applied to Goths, Romans, Syrians, Greeks and Jews, without mentioning Franks. Writing in the ninth century, Einhard knew of a 'Francia' in the north, where Charles Martel tamed tyrants, and a 'Gaul' in the south, which the Saracens tried to occupy. Such an understanding made it plausible to believe that conquering Franks had exterminated or expelled Romans, but the indigenous people had disappeared not because they had been exterminated, but because they had become Franks.[28]

For their part, the Franks shortened the distance between themselves and the Romans by thinking of themselves as descendants of the Trojans. These were the people from whom the Romans traced their foundation, and it was possible to see in Rome the very ship aboard which the Trojan refugee Aeneas arrived there. The story first occurs in the seventh century, but oddly enough a writer of the fourth century reports a tradition that after Troy had been destroyed some of the fugitives occupied Gaul, and it is possible that the Franks applied to themselves a story already current in lands they occupied.[29] But whether derived from existing tradition or invented by themselves, the fiction brought the Franks close to the Romans.

Unlike kings of the Visigoths and Burgundians, Clovis did not issue a code of law for the indigenous people within the land that came under his control. Such people would be judged in accordance with laws that also applied to the Franks, although in some fields, especially church affairs, Roman law continued to be observed. Its longevity in Gaul was remarkable. A church council of 511 decreed that the canons of the church and Roman law were to determine what happened to those guilty of various crimes who fled to churches, while in 567 the council of Tours quoted a portion of Roman law. In the following century, one Bonitus was 'instructed in the decrees of Theodosius', and in 664 the bishop of Clermont, Praejectus, argued that he did not have to answer charges on Easter Saturday, 'according to the statutes of the canons and the law called Roman'.[30] But despite the continuing operation of two systems of law, the peoples coalesced. The phenomenon can most easily be seen in the elites. We have already encountered the Frankish general Arbogast, active in Roman service towards the end of the fourth century. In about 470 a bishop of Toul addressed a poem to another Argobast, the count of Trier, in which he mentioned the count's wish to become a bishop. Sidonius Apollinaris also wrote to him, praising him, among others things,

> for your urbanity which leads you to make a most amusing profession of clumsiness when, as a matter of fact, you have drunk deep from the spring of Roman eloquence and, dwelling by the Moselle, you speak the true Latin of the Tiber: you are an intimate of the barbarians but are innocent of barbarisms . . . Thus the splendour of Roman speech, if it still exists anywhere, has survived in you.

As it turned out, an Arbogast was bishop of Chartres in the 490s, and there is every reason to identify him with Sidonius's correspondent and to see him as the grandson of the general with the same name. The grandson of a

Frankish war lord had joined the civilian and, indeed, religious ruling class of the north; so quickly did assimilation occur.[31]

In the south, by contrast, the church was a means by which the old great families maintained their position. Men could be intruded into sees where their families had an interest, and bishops who had fathered a family prior to taking orders could be succeeded in office by their own sons. Advantageous marriages were arranged. Leontius, bishop of Bordeaux in the mid-sixth century, had married the daughter of a king's close ally who was a great-granddaughter of Sidonius Apollinaris. Leontius even counted as an ancestor a patrician of the fourth century, Philagrius, who was remembered for his excellent library. He displayed his style by not merely building a basilica in honour of St Martin, but also restoring villas near Bordeaux. One has the feeling of an age-old aristocracy comfortably accommodating itself to changes in the political climate that were doubtless viewed with more equanimity from pleasant retreats in the country. The habits of such people were all too predictable: the people of Rion expected a priest to celebrate Christmas mass while drunk, for he was a noble from a senatorial family. Gregory of Tours, who claimed to be able to trace his ancestry back to a noble who died as a martyr at Lyons in AD 177, was certainly from a distinguished family, and he claimed 13 of the 18 preceding bishops of the see as his relations. Church affairs were a means by which such families maintained their power. Whereas the bishops of Africa were distinguished for their theological acumen, those of Gaul, while they drew some prestige from their cultivation of letters, chiefly brought administrative competence and social standing to their office.[32]

CENTRE AND PERIPHERIES

A chronicler writing in the middle of the seventh century told a story about the wedding night of Clovis's parents. Three times, the new wife sent her husband outside the palace to report on what he saw. The first time, he returned with the news that he had seen lions, unicorns and leopards passing by, on the second, wolves and bears, and on the third, dogs and lesser beasts which pulled each other down and rolled about. She believed that this referred to the generations of their descendants; ultimately, they would be like dogs.[33] Alas, in broad terms the vision was correct.

One of the greatest Merovingian kings was Lothar (584–629; sole king 613–29). The early part of his reign was marked by discord, which contemporaries attributed to trouble stirred up by Brunhild, a Visigoth who had come to exercise great power after marrying into the Merovingian family. In 613 she was brought before Lothar, who, aided by a group of nobles, had enjoyed military success within her territory. Accused of having murdered ten kings of the Franks, she was tortured for three days and led through the army on a camel. Then, bound to the tail of an unbroken horse by her hair, an arm and a leg, she was dashed to pieces as it ran. Such behaviour was not gracious, but the punishment can be placed beside that of a Byzantine official accused of plotting against the emperor just a few years earlier: 'Elpidius had his tongue cut out and his 4 extremities removed; he was paraded on a stretcher and carried down to the sea; when his eyes had been gouged out, he was thrown into a skiff and burnt.'[34]

As so often in this period, behaviour we might think typical of one part of the Christian world was in fact widespread. The same was true of the 'edict of Paris', which Lothar issued in 614. Providing as it did that judges were to be drawn from the regions in which they officiated, so that they could make reparations from their own property for any wrong they committed, it suggests a world of powerful local elites. But the Pragmatic Sanction that Justinian issued for Italy in 554 was the product of the same world, providing as it did that provincial judges were to be selected by the bishops and leading men of their provinces. The charters issued by some of the Merovingians survive; they were modelled on Roman chancery practice, and in an unRoman way signed by kings, although emperors in Constantinople had begun to sign such documents. In such ways, the post-Roman world remained a unit. An illegitimate son of the emperor Heraclius bore two names, John and Athalarich, the latter being the name of Theoderic's grandson.[35]

Frankish monarchy was part of a wide world. Yet tendencies were operating that would tell against it. The edict of 614 is the eighth decree of a Merovingian king to have come down to us, and the last. In the north, two Merovingian kingdoms developed, their names based on geography. Austrasia, or Austria, was the area in the 'east', near the rivers Meuse, Moselle and Rhine, while 'Neustria' was the name given to lands further west, which, in terms of the expansion of the Franks, were 'new'. Each kingdom had its own administration, which remained the case even after 679, when there was only one king. These administrations were headed by officials known as mayors of the palace, and a family with deep roots in the Rhineland that came to dominate the office in Austrasia was destined for great things. It originated in a marriage alliance between two of Dagobert's advisers, Pippin of Landen and Gundulf's old pupil, bishop Arnulf of Metz. At a battle fought at Tertry in 687, their grandson, Pippin, defeated the Neustrian mayor, opening the way to his family's later taking power in Neustria as well as Austrasia. His son Charles 'Martel', who succeeded him as mayor, defeated a Saracen force at the battle of Poitiers in 732 and brought under his authority the region of Aquitaine, hitherto largely left to its own devices. His leadership in battle, which the Germanic peoples considered a basic function of kingship, and the expansion of his authority into the south, made Charles king in all but name.

The dominance that the mayors came to hold was the subject of the opening portion of the *Life of Charlemagne*, written in the ninth century by Einhard. An enthusiastic supporter of the Carolingian dynasty that had by then come to power, he depicted the later Merovingians as impotent figures of fun who travelled about in a rustic manner, in a cart (*carpentum*) drawn by oxen. This seems a very undignified way for kings to travel, but when the emperor Constantius entered Rome in 357, it was in a *carpentum* drawn by horses; Cassiodorus describes the rumbling wheels of a *carpentum* as indicating the presence of a prefect; and an eastern text of the sixth century mentions patricians processing in carriages. The Merovingian practice therefore continued that of the Romans. Perhaps Einhard failed to understand a practice that may only have been dimly remembered when he wrote; perhaps he did understand, but chose to misrepresent it in a sly way.[36] But towards its end the Merovingian dynasty was beset with problems. One of them was the growth of rival sources of authority.

From the fifth century, when the prospect of careers in imperial service disappeared, the church beckoned.[37] Hitherto, the able and ambitious had lived in a world of broad horizons. The father of the poet Ausonius had been praetorian prefect in Illyricum; he was praetorian prefect over much of western Europe, as was one of his sons, while a son-in-law held office in Greece and Africa. But such options were not available to his grandson, the beleaguered Paulinus, whose own two sons became a priest and an associate of a Gothic king. Their career choices reflect precisely the possibilities that were then available.

Bishops enjoyed great authority in late antiquity, as the towns over whose churches they presided became overwhelmingly Christian. Even in such a strongly governed state as Ostrogothic Italy, a bishop could be asked to distribute grain on behalf of the government.[38] The bishops of Gaul, both northern and southern, could turn their hands to many tasks. A correspondent of Justinian, the enterprising Nicetius of Trier, turned a villa into a fortress equipped with a ballista, near which he planted vines, while Desiderius of Cahors asked another bishop for technical assistance in conveying water into his town through underground pipes.[39] Inevitably, kings took an interest in the appointment of such important figures. As early as the time of Clovis, bishop Remigius of Reims had to defend his having ordained a priest on the king's recommendation, and it was said that the poor man who took the exiled Brunhild to one of her grandsons in 599 was rewarded with the see of Auxerre. The edict of Paris provided that when a bishop died, a man elected by the metropolitan with the bishops of the province, the clergy and the people was to be ordained; if suitable, he would be ordained through an ordinance of the prince; if someone from the palace were elected, he should certainly be ordained because of the merit of his person and doctrine. Such legislative clumsiness betokens a murky reality, and the following provision, which forbade bishops from nominating their successors, doubtless sought to curb succession within families. Prior to becoming bishop of Cahors, Desiderius had spent many years in the service of Lothar and Dagobert. Yet one of his brothers governed Marseilles, while another had been his predecessor as bishop of Cahors. One has the impression of experienced hands at the wheel.[40]

The *History* of Gregory of Tours reveals the power that bishops enjoyed in their towns and, even more clearly, their determination to withstand competition. For their authority was not unchallenged. Each *civitas*, technically a town with the adjacent land, had its own *comes*, or count. Counts were familiar figures in the post-Roman west, known in the kingdoms of the Ostrogoths, Visigoths and Burgundians and, apparently, in Italy after its conquest by Justinian, although the use of a Germanic term for them in the Salic law (*grafio*) indicates that their background was not purely Roman. They exercised military responsibility for the town to which the king appointed them, and seem also to have been concerned with the maintenance of law and order and the collection of taxes. Some counts, such as Leudast in Tours, could be looked down on. The son of a slave and a former kitchen hand, he had appalling relations with bishop Gregory and engaged in various acts of skulduggery before being tortured to death.[41] Numerous stories tell of their decisions being miraculously brought to nothing by the power of saints, while the practice of clearing oneself of an accusation by swearing on the relics of saints also challenged their authority. Yet the very animosity that counts aroused among the clergy points to the threat they posed to episcopal power. Many of them, no less than bishops, were natives of the towns where they held office, such as all of the five known to us from Clermont in the sixth century. They could be scholars, like the philosophical counts who terrified the northern abbot offered the see of Avignon. Only in the seventh century did counts come overwhelmingly to have Germanic names, and the change presumably reflects the growing popularity of Frankish names among the population at large.

Bishops and counts, drawn from and responsive to the communities in which they operated, threatened the hold of the centre. Their world was one in which the rural sphere was becoming more important. When Gregory of Tours represented himself as a 'rustic' speaker, he associated himself with the manners of country people, although doubtless there was a large degree of metaphor in the way he used the word. Such people were well placed to withstand the atrophy of the towns, from which political power had been exercised in the ancient world. To be sure, bishops found themselves threatened by it, and had to legislate against chapels built on the villas of the powerful, which threatened to escape their control. But what hope was there for kings who came to live in villas in the country? Dagobert I spent a lot of time at the villa of Clichy, where councils of bishops were held. In 680 a secular authority summoned bishops to meet 'in a certain villa'.[42] The contrast with Spain is revealing. While Gaul was losing the notion of the city from which government was conducted, Spain was increasingly centred on Toledo, a capital city where kings reigned and bishops met in council. The contrasting developments were reflected in the strength of the Visigothic and Merovingian monarchies.

CONTROL OF RESOURCES

The Merovingian state was therefore one in which political power was dispersed. There was a centre, made up of the kings and their immediate following, and there were bishops and counts scattered throughout the kingdom. We may ask who controlled its wealth.

Much lay in ecclesiastical hands. By 700 the great estates of the medieval church had been largely built up. One has sympathy for the position of king Chilperic:

> My treasury is always empty. All our wealth has fallen into the hands of the churches. There is no one with any power left except the bishops. Nobody respects me as king; all respect has passed to the bishops in their cities.

He therefore tore up wills in which property had been left to bishops. The making of wills was a Roman rather than Germanic custom, but the edict of Theoderic the Ostrogoth gave 'barbarians' the power to do so, and Gregory of Tours, in a passage it is possible to interpret in a sinister light, describes a Frankish queen making a will leaving legacies to churches while he looked on. A practice that allowed wealth to be diverted away from one's family towards churches would not have been universally popular, and wills leaving property to churches were contested even in Roman lands. The growing wealth of the church in the period attracted widespread hostile comment, and it was widely felt that the military arm of society suffered in consequence of it. The Byzantine administration in Italy cast covetous eyes on it, wondering why so much wealth had been accumulated in the Lateran, the papal head-quarters, which was of no use to the army, while an English bishop of the eighth century was advised to tear up the deeds and documents by which land had been conveyed to 'pseudo-monasteries', leaving no land for kings to give to military men who would protect the kingdom. Churchmen also promoted the payment of tithes, a payment of a tenth part of what the land produced, which a council held in Gaul in 585 ruled had to be paid on pain of excommunication.[43]

By comparison with the resources passing to churches, those available to the state were weak. When bishop Remigius wrote to Clovis on his coming to power, he treated him as the head of a Roman province, except in one respect: he remarked that the new ruler should free captives, possessing as he did the wealth of his father. The tomb of Childeric indicates that such wealth was considerable, but the Roman Empire had relied on taxation rather than access to treasure, and the emphasis that narrative sources persistently place on the Merovingians' control of treasure reflects their lack of the steady income that a strong tax base would have provided. The early Franks, who had lived in a tax-free world prior to entering Roman territory, hated the very idea of paying tax.[44] Others were scarcely more enthusiastic. When two assessors came to Tours with tax-lists in their hands in 589, the bishop proved awkward, telling them that earlier kings had not taxed the city, and on being apprised of the situation the king ordered that the city's freedom from tax was to be maintained. Church lands in particular benefited from royal grants of 'immunity'. The concept was known to Roman law by the fourth century, and precedents were long remembered, for towards the end of the sixth century the town of Lyons claimed immunity from taxation on the basis of events that occurred in the reign of the emperor Leo, presumably to be identified with the eastern emperor of that name (457–74). But Frankish kings were generous in granting it, and pope Gregory was astonished to hear that church estates in Gaul were not liable to taxation.[45] One has the impression that the payment of taxes was increasingly voluntary.

Fortunately, the state had other sources of income, particularly tolls. These had been levied in Roman times, the senator Symmachus having held late in the fourth century that senators who transported wild animals for gladiatorial shows should not have to pay such taxes, for these things were suitable for those who sold bears, but not quaestors. The useful income that tolls provided made control of Marseilles, a Mediterranean port, important to kings during the sixth century. It was then that a new extra-mural suburb developed, and the supply of pottery from Africa held up, contrary to what was occurring in Italy and Spain. The port had close connections with Italy, for the first leg of the journey made by missionaries whom pope Gregory sent from Rome to England was thither, and Jewish merchants are known to have travelled frequently between Italy and the port. It handled goods from the east, such as the cargoes of papyrus from Alexandria which a demon once mockingly suggested be loaded on a girl he possessed.[46] A ship wrecked near Marseilles late in the century went down with a cargo of African amphorae filled with olive oil and garum; another was carrying African pitch and grain when it sank at the beginning of the seventh century. But in a society where wealth was based on the land, a regime that taxed effectively would have regarded income from tolls as icing on the cake.

Nevertheless, the reduced income of the Merovingians answered to the diminished outlays of their state. The chief expense of the Empire had been its standing army, and much of the imperial apparatus was directed towards maintaining it. The location of mints suggests that coins were minted to pay soldiers, and perhaps subsidies, at least as much as to facilitate trade. At the beginning of the fourth century there were mints in the West at London, Trier, Lyons, Carthage, Rome, Aquileia and Pavia. For an empire based on the sea, their distribution was remarkably inland, and it fits the placement of legions better than centres of trade. Moreover, the Romans had no concept of deficit financing, which made it important to bring in the taxes each year. But whereas the standing army of the Romans was supported by taxation, the armies of the Franks were organised on a very different basis, for the troops depended on what they produced from their own lands or what their commander gave them. Perhaps of less economic importance, but of great ideological significance, was income that the warriors derived from booty. Soldiers were also bound to their leaders by ties of personal loyalty. So it was that the state, freed from the expense of running an army whose members came to look to commanders as well as kings, had less need for income.

It is possible that the freeing of coinage from the need to pay troops brought its function in the Frankish kingdom closer to that which it plays in a modern economy. In the 660s, gold coins ceased to be minted in Gaul. This was not necessarily a backwards move, for Persia maintained a purely silver currency, and the change may merely have reflected the exhaustion of massive payments in gold that the Franks had received from the Empire in return for undertakings to make war on the Lombards late in the sixth century. In any case, prior to the introduction of an all-silver coinage, the gold coinage had been steadily debased. That coinage was economically useful is shown by the passing of its minting away from central hands. The names of over 1,600 moneyers are known from the Merovingian period; whereas the Lombard kings of Italy asserted that coins could be minted only by royal command, Frankish sovereigns seem to have been acquiescent in this right passing out of their hands. There was also significant production for the market. For centuries, pottery had been manufactured in the region of Argonne, to the west of the Moselle. The industry had been well placed to supply the needs of the Roman frontier zone, but easily outlasted its demise, and during the sixth century pottery produced there was used 100–200 km away from the place of manufacture, an extraordinary range considering the difficulty of overland trade.[47] Before long, other northern centres of production were diffusing their goods over wide areas. By the standards of the post-Roman west, distribution across land on this scale is remarkable, and it cannot be paralleled in the south. With this in mind, it will be worth our while turning again towards the dichotomy with which this chapter began, that between the north and the south of Gaul.

THE NORTH

In some ways, Gaul was open to the south. During the sixth and seventh centuries, many Frankish women took to wearing items of pearl jewellery similar to those worn by the members of Theodora's court in a mosaic in the church of San Vitale at Ravenna.[48] But this was a symptom of Romanisation, and the external contacts that Gaul continued to enjoy tended to be with the north. In about 590 an Irishman, St Columban, arrived from County Down, allegedly with the suspiciously apostolic number of 12 companions, and before long he founded several monasteries, the most famous of them Luxeuil in the Haut Saône. Irish monks were much given to the practice of *peregrinatio*, a kind of pilgrimage without a definite goal. Their exploits in this regard are astonishing; when the Vikings arrived in Iceland in about 870, they found that Irish monks had beaten them there. By the standards of earlier monasticism, theirs was an eccentric if not deviate impulse. The fathers of the Egyptian desert had regarded sitting in one's cell as a virtue, while St Benedict's Rule has more to say about stability than about chastity. The Irish may have been very like the wondering monks, the *gyrovagi*, whom Benedict accused of being always wandering and never stable, although his accusation that such people served their own will[49] could not be made against the Irish, whose wanderings involved renunciation of self-will. A series of quarrels took Columban, an awkward person incapable of anything other than plain speaking, from Luxeuil to Bobbio, in the north of Italy, where he died in 615. But he left behind a new kind of religion. Hitherto, Christianity in Gaul had emphasised corporate adherence to cultic practices, such as solemn acts of worship in brilliantly illuminated churches, communal prayer and fasting in the form of rogations, and the observance of the Lord's Day, and while it is hard to warm to the rigorous penances that Columban imposed upon his monks, which easily dispel the notion sometimes entertained that Celts practised a gentle style of Christianity, the prospect of a religion offering a strong interior life was too good to pass by. By 700 there were some 550 monasteries in Gaul, well over half of them founded within the preceding century and most of them in the north. They quickly came to set the pace in the Frankish church. By about 669 Luxeuil was producing manuscripts with a distinctive form of handwriting, and such developments lay behind the minuscule script that was to characterise the Carolingian renaissance.

The participants in the new movement included people such as Fara, also known as Burgundofara. Her family, who lived not far from Luxeuil, had been close to Columban, and her father endowed a monastery for both men and women not far to the west of Paris, at the place still called Faremoutiers after her. Fara became abbess of this community, and testament shows her giving away her share of various villas, mills, slaves and other property; a good deal of wealth lay behind the new monastic movement. Before long, its members were involved in evangelistic activities across the Rhine, and an ecclesiastical elite developed for which the English Channel was the slightest of inconveniences. Agilbert, a Frank who had gone to Ireland to study the Scriptures, was made bishop of Winchester in about 650. But he did not speak English well and, finding this more of a hardship than did some bishops after the Norman conquest, he became bishop of Paris in about 668. There he was among those who consecrated the Englishman Wilfrid bishop and played host to an archbishop-elect of Canterbury on his journey towards his see.[50]

Ties across the English Channel became stronger. Some time earlier, pope Gregory had instructed his agent in Gaul to have English slaves placed in monasteries, doubtless with a view to the subsequent evangelisation of the English. It was later believed that his desire to convert them had been inspired by his seeing English slaves for sale in the forum of Rome. The English church looked to Gaul for high-status products. When Benedict Biscop founded the monastery of Wearmouth in the north of England, he obtained the services of builders from Gaul who could erect a church made of stone, in the style of the Romans, and when their work was nearly done, he sent to Gaul for glass makers, whose craft was at that time unknown in Britain. Having been captured and taken to Gaul, the English woman Balthild was sold as a slave and entered the household of Erchinoald, a mayor of the palace. Attracted by her Saxon looks, he wanted to marry her, but she was unwilling, and later became the wife of a king. After his death she governed with her son until, the political wind having changed direction, she entered a convent at Chelles, which had been among the religious communities to benefit from her largesse in earlier years. There she died in about 680. Oddly enough, she was not thought well of in England. One author levelled against her a charge that would have made Brunhild blush – that of having put to death nine bishops, among them the bishop of Lyons.[51] Bertila, an abbess of Chelles, sent people to teach and found monasteries at the request of kings 'from parts of Saxony beyond the seas', which can only refer to England. Another beneficiary of her largesse was Burgundofara's house, her generosity towards which may have been connected with the two women who suc-ceeded her as abbess both being English princesses. Bishop Amandus of Maastricht bought captives and slaves from 'across the sea', presumably Britain, whom he baptised, educated and passed on to churches, where many became bishops, priests or respected abbots.[52]

Such stories reflect growing economic ties between England and Gaul, in particular the Rhineland. From about 600, coins were being minted at Quentovic, a site on the river Canche near the modern Étaples, and the tex-tiles and glass which have been excavated suggest that goods were manu-factured there. The port, much closer to the Thames than to the Seine, was superbly placed for trade with much of southern England, and it may not be coincidental that the English port of Ipswich was being occupied from early in the seventh century. The earliest evidence for the name Quentovic is the inscription on a coin included in a hoard, probably put together in about 620, which was buried at Sutton Hoo, not far from Ipswich in England, and the names of the moneyers found on the coins, one of them intriguingly given as 'Anglus', are often English. The port became a familiar stopping-off place for those crossing the English Channel.[53]

Another growing commercial centre was Dorestad, on an old arm of the Rhine south of Utrecht, where coins were being minted in the period

630–50. The site was then under Merovingian control; later in the century, while Frisians held it, it grew into an enormous complex with large jetties, and the scale of the goods it produced indicates that several thousand people may have been involved in its activities. These may have included the sale of slaves. Archaeology does not allow us to detect trade in humans, but we know of a captive who was sold to a Frisian in London and who may well have been consigned to Dorestad had it not been for supernatural aid.[54] The itineraries of travellers changed. Whereas, at the end of the sixth century, the missionary Augustine seems to have proceeded towards England northward through Paris, in the late seventh century, archbishop Theodore finished his journey from Rome to Canterbury by way of Quentovic, and nearly a century later Alcuin, an English scholar on his way to Rome, proceeded via Dorestad and the lower Rhine. That Franks and Frisians disputed for control of the city in the seventh century was a sign of the wealth to be gained from the northern port; in the preceding century, Marseilles in the south had been a bone of contention between Frankish kings for the same reason.

Such developments were important in more than one way. They were connected with a tendency for Frankish rulers to claim an ill-defined authority over the some of the English.[55] Of more practical importance was the growing prosperity of north-western Gaul and eastern England, which would soon make them tempting targets for Vikings. But Scandinavia had been reorientating itself towards western Europe for some time. Traditionally, it had imported high-status items from the Mediterranean, often conveyed across central and eastern Europe. But the coming of Avars and Slavs into that region disturbed the trade routes, and by the seventh century the land of the Franks was supplying it with such goods, which were similar to the goods it was exporting to Britain. The liveliness of the northern economy was reflected in the establishment of new mints. For much of the post-Roman period, coinage was a commodity in search of a function. But whereas the Romans had minted currency to pay troops, the coins were minted in the north to facilitate exchange. So it was that the north of Gaul became an economic centre. This was seen in the rise of a great monastery near Paris. King Dagobert, who in something like a decade as sole king of the Franks never found himself closer to the Mediterranean than he was to the English Channel, had provided the monastery of St Denis with an annual income from his share of the tolls of Marseilles. He chose to be buried there, where his tomb, rebuilt in the thirteenth century, can still be seen, together with those of later kings. Dagobert also renounced royal rights over a fair held there annually, although the generosity of the gift did not stop the monks of

St Denis from forging greater privileges on a well-nigh industrial scale for centuries. The foundations of the monastery's great wealth had been laid; in economic, as in political terms, Gaul had come to look to the north.

CHANGES IN LATIN

Other changes were under way in the period. No one would imagine that the writings of Ausonius and Paulinus, who sought to write formal and correct Latin, and the accounts that were written of the lives of Merovingian saints, the style of which can induce extreme distaste in those brought up to read classical Latin, were the products of the same society. But there is more than one way of looking at this development, and examination of it will highlight some aspects of the broad changes that occurred in Gaul and elsewhere in late antiquity.

It is true that Latin was changing. Gregory of Tours professed that he made mistakes in genders and cases when he wrote.[56] Doubtless this was partly a conventional deployment of a topos of humility, but Gregory lived in a world in which written Latin was being increasingly influenced by spoken language, which was steadily diverging from it. Pronunciation was changing; when the learned Isidore of Seville tried to correct the pronunciation of those who read in church, they laughed at him. But there is no need to blame 'barbarians' for changes away from classical norms. Isidore himself believed that Latin had taken four successive forms. The third of these, which he called 'Roman', began when Rome became a republic, and his list of authors who wrote in it concludes with Vergil. The last form, 'mixed', began after the empire was widely extended; this, he felt, came to influence the city, corrupting the integrity of the language by solecisms and barbarisms.[57] For Isidore, the most recent form of Latin was that of the Empire, and when he thought of 'barbarisms' it was in connection with the Empire's expansion rather than any fall it may have suffered. And while people often wrote in ways that are aberrant by the standards of classical written Latin during late antiquity, they usually had nothing to do with non-Romans. Words hitherto found in graffiti leaped into formal writing. Translations of the Bible into Latin, including the famous Vulgate, were pitched at a populist level, going so far as to use the extraordinary form *abante*, which later yielded the words for 'before' in Italian (*avanti*) and French (*avant*); the first-known use of the latter was in an oath sworn at Strasbourg in 842.[58] The stirring injunction that opens Benedict's Rule for monks, 'Listen, son, to the precepts of the master', is wildly aberrant by the standards of classical Latin, for the first word appears as *obsculta*, rather than the correct *ausculta*. Our oldest surviving manuscript of the Rule, written in England in the first half of the eighth century, tried to clean up Benedict's Latin by substituting the correct form, but a manuscript of the early ninth century, not far removed from Benedict's autograph copy, makes it clear that he used an unclassical form.[59]

The changes occurring in the writing of Latin, in Gaul and elsewhere, took place independently of the coming of the Germanic peoples. They occur in the Latin of native speakers, and that people were writing words which had hitherto only occurred in speech and adopting more phonetic forms of spelling indicates that written Latin was now open to the language of the streets and expressing wider registers of usage. Except in the frontier regions, which experienced considerable Germanic settlement during the imperial period, the Franks made no great difference to the language spoken in Gaul. Remigius of Reims wrote to Clovis in that language, the Salic law was in Latin, and Gregory of Tours took it for granted that Franks could understand passages of the Bible that they heard in church.[60] The voluminous works of Gregory of Tours contain only six words of Germanic origin, just as they do six Celtic words, and although any impact that the Franks had would have been stronger on spoken than written Latin, we may conclude that over most of Gaul the Franks made little difference to the language.

It was along such routes that Gaul entered its post-Roman period. As in other areas, the newcomers arrived in a world already changing, but the Franks were unlike the Goths and Vandals in having been a part of the changes. Some stayed to the west of the Rhine, while those who made the short trip into what had been imperial territory could be seen both as continuing imperially sanctioned settlement there and as playing the role of imperial allies in a continuation of the military turbulence of the northern area. It became clear in the sixth century that the ambitions of their ruling class were rather grander, but by this time the indigenous people were already starting to identify with them. The most important new development occurred at the end of our period, with the establishment of a new political centre in the north of Gaul, particularly in the Rhineland, an area that was becoming an economic centre at just the same time. In a world in which political and economic units had steadily become smaller, this marked a modest turning of the tide. Moreover, these developments unexpectedly transformed what had been a periphery of the old Empire into a centre. At this point, it will be worth our while crossing the English Channel.

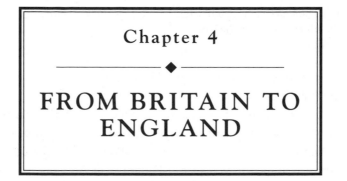

Chapter 4

◆

FROM BRITAIN TO ENGLAND

Of all the areas that made up the Roman Empire in the west, Britain experienced the greatest change as it moved into the post-imperial period. The Romans evacuated it early in the fifth century, leaving a society already undergoing rapid change, and Britain became subject to unwelcome interest from its neighbours. Some of its leaders summoned military help from the Continent, but the Germanic newcomers, who had already been settling in Britain and whom we may call the English, began to migrate there in what seem to have been large numbers, and by a mixture of conquest and settlement came to dominate the indigenous population over much of the island. Indeed, unlike the Franks they give the impression of having created, over a few centuries, a new country that owed scarcely anything to its original inhabitants. The replacement of Celtic speech by English, a Germanic language, over most of Britain and the failure of the polytheistic newcomers to accept from the Britons the Christian faith that many of them had adopted, suggest that Britain underwent immense change in the post-Roman centuries.

Such a view is supported by some of the texts of the period. Much of the infrastructure built by the Romans was still to be seen, and the early English can give the appearance of having come into a land that had once been far more advanced and blundered about it uncomprehendingly. The sentiment could be poetically expressed: 'Cities can be seen from far away, the skilful work of giants, which remain in this world, the splendid stone-walled forts.' A few hundred years after the Romans left Britain, the author of another poem contemplated with astonishment the remains of stone buildings, halls and bath houses that they had erected, perhaps in Bath:

Splendid this rampart is, though fate destroyed it
The city buildings fell apart, the works
Of giants crumble . . .

Such language may be thought to reveal a high degree of misapprehension, and to imply the utter remoteness of Roman Britain from the centuries that followed it. Yet Old English poetry is rarely cheerful, and the taking of pleasure in mournful thoughts prompted by ruins has been a trait of the English across their history. Moreover, even in Italy it was possible to write sad poetry about the destruction of towns, as did Paulinus on Aquileia (below p. 145). And sometimes the English looked on Roman remains with pride: when, in the seventh century, a missionary came to what had been the most north-western city of the Empire, Carlisle, the townspeople showed him the city's walls and a wonderfully constructed fountain built by the Romans.[1] Perhaps the poets were attempting to create a mood rather than give realistic expression to the way the English felt.

ROMAN BRITAIN

Despite its distance from the centre, Britain had been a flourishing part of the Empire until well into the fourth century. During the Roman period, it developed in a way similar to Gaul. Towns, linked by good roads, sprang up, and the prosperity that Britain enjoyed is indicated by a hoard of Christian plate laid down at Water Newton, near Peterborough, probably in the third century. The region was one where pottery was produced, and it is tempting to see the hoard as evidence for prosperity created by a successful local industry. But, as was general in the west, towns were becoming less important in late antiquity. Wealthy people were moving into villas, often built at a convenient distance from towns and decorated with expensive mosaics. Again in conformity to a general trend, by 400 some of these were falling into disuse, earth having sometimes come to lie on top of the mosaics. To deal with attacks from the Continent, the Romans had erected a series of coastal fortresses from the Wash to the Isle of Wight, under the command of the Count of the Saxon Shore. Somewhat later, we hear of Saxon trouble-makers furrowing the British waters with hides and cleaving the blue seas in stitched boats. They may have been the foes against whom a military writer of the early fifth century encouraged the Romans to take measures that might be deemed eccentric. His work contained a passage devoted to the use of fast vessels, in which he wrote:

In case ships sent out to reconnoitre are given away by their bright appearance, the sails and ropes are dyed a blue colour, similar to the waves of the sea, and even the wax with which they usually smear the ships is made like this. The sailors and soldiers wear blue clothes so that those on reconnaissance may more easily be concealed, not only by night but also by day.

It is hard to imagine such measures as being successful.[2]

Against this background, the Romans pulled out. This may have occurred in stages, for the propensity of generals in Britain to rebel against central authority – as Magnus Maximus, perhaps significantly later thought of as having been born in Britain, did in 383 – may have led them to withdraw troops that were never made up. But however the rundown occurred, when the western emperor Honorius wrote to the Britons in about 410, telling them to see to their own defence, it was to cities, presumably seen as independent centres of authority, rather than officials of the Empire, that he addressed his advice.[3] Power devolved locally, to units that a writer of the sixth century, Gildas, thought of as kingdoms, and Britain entered a period of which we know far less than we would like to. Nevertheless, some trends are apparent.

Economic dislocation quickly became evident. Late in the fourth century, the minting of coins, which had been going on in Britain since pre-Roman times, ceased, and a new issue of coins that was introduced on the Continent at the beginning of the fifth century was not used there. Given the close connection in Roman times between minting and the payment of troops, the move away from the use of coins must have been a product of the departure of the legions. Although coins can remain in use for some time after they are issued, early in the fifth century many were buried in hoards for safety, which suggests that the passing of coins out of circulation, and hence the coming of an economy where coinage was not used, was a speedy process. A hoard of coins discovered in 1997 at Littlehampton in West Sussex contained items minted as late as 461, but they do not seem to have been used for exchange; by then, the economy had come to function without money.[4]

Less easy to assess are developments in the manufacture of pottery. At the time when African wares were carrying all before them in the Mediterranean, a strong industry had developed in Britain, but, as far as we can tell from evidence that it is hard to date with confidence, mass production ceased at about the same time as the minting of coins did. The transition may not have been as dramatic as it may seem. There is good evidence for more of the pottery used in Spain at this time having been hand-thrown; such pottery is known to have been produced in Campania during the sixth and seventh centuries; and even in Carthage hand-made pottery represents a fifth of that produced after the Byzantine conquest. Furthermore, difficulties in dating hand-thrown pottery, which is often found in archaeological contexts with few indications of date, may lead us to underestimate its prevalence in all areas. But in Gaul, pottery continued to be mass-produced and coins to be minted across the fifth century.

This is not to say that British society relapsed into primitivism after the Romans left. The biography of Germanus, a bishop of the Gallic town of Auxerre, written late in the fifth century, suggests that the people were in fine shape when he twice visited the island of Britain, 'the first and greatest of them all', early in the century: he encountered wealthy people with bright clothes surrounded by followers and a man described as exercising the power of a tribune, and even helped the Britons in a defeat of Saxons and Picts who were attacking 'the most wealthy island'.[5] But the destiny of Britain had been diverging from that of Gaul even before the coming of the English. The newcomers to Britain made their way into a remarkably unstable society.

In Britain, as elsewhere, the civilians of the Empire had relied on the legions to defend them. Indeed, Tacitus represented Roman policy in Britain as seeking to accustom to idleness a people who were easily moved to war. The departure of the army therefore left Britain open to attacks. These came from various directions. From the west the Irish launched raids, one of which was presumably the origin of a hoard of Roman silver items and coins found at Coleraine in Northern Ireland. On another occasion a British teenager with a reasonable command of Latin and a remarkably Roman name, St Patrick, was captured; subsequently, he evangelised many of the Irish.[6] More important were attacks from the north, mounted by enemies who had already caused the Romans trouble, the Picts. They were indigenous inhabitants of the north of Scotland, unlike the Scots, the name confusingly given to Irish who had begun to settle in Scotland. Centuries later, an English author poured scorn on the Britons for their indolence when these peoples attacked,[7] but the charge was unreasonable, for the provincials had effectively been demilitarised by the Romans.

In the face of these difficulties and denied assistance from the Empire, the British ruling class sought the help of professionals. Probably about the middle of the fifth century, a British leader later named, it seems wrongly, as Vortigern asked people living across the sea for military help. Our source closest to the event describes the invitation in the precise terminology appropriate to the employment by the Romans of *foederati*,[8] and Germanic troops were by no means a novelty in Britain, where the Roman legions, like those on the continent, included many such people. Indeed, the Saxon Shore that the Romans had established may have been named for those who manned its defences rather than those whom it sought to deter. The invitation was accepted. We are told that the newcomers came in three boats under the command of two brothers, Hengist and Horsa, and that they subsequently rebelled against the Britons. But this may well be legendary. Stories of the Goths had them depart from Scandinavia in three ships, while the names of the commanders are suspicious, for although a man named Hengist is known from elsewhere to have been a Dane living in Frisia, his name means 'stallion', and that his brother's means 'horse' or 'mare' suggests that we are dealing with nicknames, if not fictitious persons.[9] We may suspect that legendary material occurs in our earliest written sources for the coming of the English to Britain, and that caution is needed in evaluating whatever they tell us.

NEWCOMERS

In a famous passage written early in the eighth century, Bede, the greatest historian of the early middle ages, wrote of the newcomers who arrived in Britain in response to the alleged invitation of Vortigern. He identified them as three of the most powerful peoples of Germany, the Saxons, Angles and Jutes, and named the area on the Continent from which each group had come and the part of Britain in which it had settled.[10] Alas, there are problems with this account. A few sentences before he so carefully distinguished between the three peoples, Bede wrote of 'Angles or Saxons' coming to Britain, but the word he used for 'or' (*sive*) means 'or' in an inclusive sense, so that it could also be translated 'and'. Here, 'Angles' and 'Saxons' seem to be two words for the one people. Perhaps the passage that so precisely differentiates between them is an interpolation inserted by Bede at a late stage in his writing when he was unable to revise other passages to make them conform to it. A more helpful guide to the origins of the newcomers occurs later in Bede's work, where he describes the desire of a missionary to preach on the Continent. The evangelist knew that there were many nations in Germany from which the 'Angles or [*vel*, another weak conjunction] Saxons' who had come to live in Britain took their origin, and Bede names them as Frisians, Rugians, Danes, Huns, Old Saxons and Boructuarians.[11] Perhaps Bede, writing long after the first arrivals, was the victim of an origin myth such as we have encountered for newcomers on the Continent. But evidence from the coastal area between the Elbe and Weser indicates that many people left that region during the fifth century, perhaps for Britain. We can only speculate as to why they moved: an invitation to provide military help might have encouraged them, but overpopulation, a deteriorating ecological situation and the pressure of other groups, perhaps Franks, are all possible. We do not know to what extent the English jumped and to what extent they were pushed to Britain.

According to the Anglo-Saxon Chronicles, which seem to have originated late in the ninth century, the earliest English landed at Ebbesfleet, on the southernmost tip of what was then the Isle of Thanet. The evidence is not beyond reproach, but plausible, and prompts thought as to what aspect would have presented itself to the new arrivals. Ebbesfleet was a very convenient place for people arriving in Britain to make land. In the time of Caesar, Kent was the landing place for nearly all ships from Gaul, and the Romans had erected an impressive fort, part of the Saxon Shore, at Richborough, just a few kilometres away from the Isle, on a site that had been a familiar point of disembarkation for visitors from the continent. It was probably there that the emperor Claudius disembarked in AD 43 when he began the definitive Roman conquest of Britain, and later emperors certainly made landing there; in the early fifth century, the crossing between Boulogne and Richborough was known to be the shortest between Belgic Gaul and Britain. The spot was some 20 km distant by a Roman road from Canterbury, the town in Britain closest to the continent. It was a provincial town of a kind found throughout the Empire, among its public buildings a theatre capable of accommodating perhaps 7,000 people. From the middle of the fifth century, the time when our sources state the newcomers were arriving, sunken huts of Germanic style were being built in a part of Canterbury where a goldsmith's hoard was located, which suggests that English people, or conceivably Britons who had adopted English ways, were living there. While the town cannot be shown to have been inhabited throughout the sixth century, it was certainly a going concern at its end, for when missionaries arrived from Rome in 597 it was the capital (*metropolis*) of a Germanic ruler. His title, 'king of the Cantuarii', preserved the classical Latin word for the indigenous people of Kent, the Cantii, and invites speculation as to whether he ruled a population group largely stable since pre-Roman times. His Frankish wife was a Christian who used to pray in a church built in the town in honour of a saint who had been a bishop in Gaul in the fourth century. English life in Britain did not begin on a *tabula rasa*. And while the Anglo-Saxon Chronicles have the Britons abandoning Kent and fleeing in terror after losing four men in a battle seven years after the English arrived, the early English tended to settle near sites used in the Roman period, while conversely most of the known Roman sites are near early English burials. The early English penetration of Kent may have been a process of gradual infiltration, perhaps involving intermarriage, rather than a catastrophic invasion.[12]

A good deal of archaeological evidence from other parts of Britain supports such an interpretation. For example, the people who lived from about 400 to 600 in a settlement at West Stow, by the river Lark near Bury St Edmunds, had settled on the edge of an area of Romano-British settlement. They occupied six rectangular 'halls', one larger than the others, around each of which were a number of smaller sunken buildings, all made from organic materials. The village would have resembled another, mentioned by Bede, when he wrote of a king who, wishing to set fire to a town, carried away from a nearby village 'beams, rafters, wattled walls and thatched roofs'. The inhabitants of West Stow cultivated a number of grains, kept cattle, sheep and pigs, and engaged in craft pursuits. Some of the sunken buildings were used for weaving, and combs, always important for Germanic peoples, were made on the site. Although weapons were placed in burials at West Stow, fighting did not play an important part in the lives of its inhabitants, whose village had no defences. In the west midlands, a cemetery at Wasperton was used during both the late-Roman and early-English periods. On the basis of artefacts associated with the burials and their orientation, it has been suggested that 124 of those buried were English, and 47 Romano-British indigenes, while of 21 cremations, 20 were English. Although difficult to interpret, this evidence seems to indicate that the English continued to use an established cemetery, and coexisted peacefully with the indigenous community. At Stretton-in-Fosse, cemeteries containing Romano-British goods overlapped in time with those containing English goods, and some of the earlier female graves in the latter contained studded boots and items woven in a Romano-British style, suggesting that, at a time when two groups were living near each other, females who identified with one tradition were marrying males who identified with the other.[13]

Such findings point in a different direction from the perspective of our narrative sources. These describe the English turning against the Britons who had invited them and setting about what turned out to be the conquest of the greater part of Britain. Their accounts are couched in strong language. Gildas describes the Britons experiencing military disasters of a kind that can scarcely be paralleled in the history of the Continent at the time, although it seems that when he wrote, some way into the sixth century, Britain knew peace. Bede describes a few Britons surviving in desperate circumstances.[14] A verse passage in one version of the Anglo-Saxon Chronicles has war-loving Angles and Saxons coming to Britain from the east, overcoming the 'Welsh' and seizing the country.[15] Such emphases may be reflected in burials, for English males were often laid to rest with swords, spears and shields, as occurred in the great burial at Sutton Hoo, while other weapons were passed on; a prince who died in the early eleventh century left to his brother a sword that had been the property of king Offa, over 200 years earlier. Warfare seems to have been staple of the early English imagination, although it is not clear that they devoted more of their resources to it than the Romans had. The arrival of the English led some of the indigenous population to take serious precautions. An extraordinarily large hoard, comprising over 14,000 coins and some 200 objects of gold and silver, was buried in a chest at Hoxne in Suffolk.[16] A disconcerting absence of British placenames in Sussex may be a consequence of heavy fighting mentioned in the Chronicles.

Our evidence therefore seems to point in different directions. But it must be said that the narrative accounts are problematic. The major discussion of the Britons in Bede's narrative concludes with their fighting each other, not the English, and thereafter he describes English sovereigns imposing their power on the Britons without implying that the latter were in any danger.[17] Elsewhere Bede, a distinguished scholar of the Bible who thought of the English as a chosen people foreknown by God, using the precise term that St Paul had used of the Jewish people, extrapolated from the settlement of the Jews in the promised land to that of the English in Britain. But these biblical concepts need not have been applicable.[18] Similarly, the authors of the Anglo-Saxon Chronicles may have been misled by the hostile activities of the contemporary Vikings, which they may in any case have misunderstood, into interpreting the coming of the English in similar terms. Rather than adopting a model of military conquest on the basis of Bede and the Chronicles, it may be better to think of the coming of the English as occurring in a similar way to that of the Franks. Any reader of Gregory of Tours would conclude that the Franks were no more than a military group who forced their way into territory occupied by others, yet many of them were settled farming people. In the same way, while the perspective of our narrative sources for the early English doubtless reflects some of the truth, complementary sources of evidence suggest that they included many farmers, and that a degree of symbiosis with the indigenous population occurred, just as took place across the Channel. The coming of the English was later construed as having been far more violent than it was; indeed, as we shall see, some of their expansion was more apparent than real.

INDIGENES

While the English occupied most of Britain over a few centuries, some of the Britons in the west retained their independence, in the course of time becoming the peoples now called Welsh and Cornish. They minted no coins and, lacking strong government, erected hill forts at places such as South Cadbury (Somerset), the site of a pre-Roman fortified place, presumably under the command of local war-lords. Latin survived well enough to be used in a large number of post-Roman funerary inscriptions, particularly in Wales, and in donations made to churches. It has even been suggested that an illuminated manuscript of Vergil, the *Vergilius Romanus*, was produced in post-Roman Britain. But the Britons did not merely preserve what had gone before. By the seventh century, charters were being written in western Britain, Brittany and Ireland in a form that seems to have originated in late- or post-Roman Britain. The Britons took to monasticism, which was apparently unknown in Roman Britain, with great enthusiasm; the monk Samson can be placed against his Italian contemporary Benedict, even down to their both being victims of attempted poisoning by people who were envious of them.[19]

It was probably in this period that Britons migrated in large numbers to the part of France whose name today, Brittany (French 'Bretagne'), preserves an echo of their settlement, just as a region in its far west, Cornouaille, took its name from the Celtic tribe after which Cornwall is named. Links between the Britons and the Continent were strong, despite the English seizure of eastern Britain. In the fifth century, unworthy British candidates for the priesthood were reputed to sail overseas for ordination, while from the fifth to the early seventh centuries Tintagel, a site on the north coast of Cornwall which was later to figure prominently in legends of king Arthur, imported goods of Mediterranean manufacture, although it is not clear whether they were shipped direct or entered Britain via Gaul. Such goods were also arriving at Dinas Powys, in the south of Wales, in the seventh century.[20] While the volume of surviving evidence does not imply regular long-distance trade, it certainly reflects the wealth and cultural aspirations of an elite British group. Paradoxically, a recognisably late-antique way of life was sustained in what had been the least Romanised part of Roman Britain.

Yet the future lay elsewhere. Located as it is beyond the westernmost end of a great plain which, interrupted only by the North Sea, runs across northern Europe as far as the Urals, Wales is precisely the point at which the settlement of newcomers to Britain was likely to have ceased. Dominant in the lowlands, the English may not have thought it worth their while moving into the difficult and less productive territory beyond. To judge from the earliest surviving Welsh poetry, the Britons who remained independent reconciled themselves to their reduced circumstances, and over the greater part of the land where they retained their independence the British became 'Welsh', as the English called foreigners. Bede reckoned that in his day, five languages were current in Britain: English, British, Irish, Pictish and Latin. But a version of the Anglo-Saxon Chronicles based on this passage listed six languages: 'English and British and Welsh and Scottish and Pictish and Book-language'.[21] The second of Bede's terms has been expanded, perhaps to differentiate between British speakers under English authority and those inhabiting Wales. It will be worth our while going on to examine interactions between the English and the Britons in the lands that came under the sway of the former.

NEWCOMERS AND INDIGENES

When the Roman missionary Augustine arrived in Britain at the end of the sixth century to convert the English, he was aware that there were already Christians in the island, and a story was transmitted of a discussion he had with a group of British bishops. It was said that, when the Britons refused to abandon their own practices and join him in preaching to the English, Augustine proposed that a sick person be brought, so that God's will would be shown as both sides tried to heal him. The Britons were thereupon unable to heal a blind Englishman, but when Augustine prayed his sight was restored.[22] Any medieval reader of this narrative would have deduced that the English needed illumination, and that this was to be provided not by the Britons but by the Roman missionaries. But such an interpretation may have involved a misreading of the situation. To be sure, in Roman Britain Christianity had been strongest in the towns and the villas, the breakdown of which severely limited its power to reach out to newcomers; there is no sign of British bishops of the stature of Remigius in Gaul. Moreover, the inhabitants of the old Empire had taken little interest in converting 'barbarians'; the example of Patrick, who actively sought to convert the Irish, was rarely followed. Yet Bede mentions that when an Englishman, Chad, was consecrated a bishop in Wessex in about 665, it was at the hands of one English and two British bishops.[23] His narrative flows on around these unnamed Britons, who are never mentioned again. But given that he was writing a history of the English, rather than the British church, there was no need for him to have done so, and behind their apparently inconsequential appearance in his narrative may lie a strong British church in the west whose clergy were more interested in the spiritual welfare of the English than those who failed to heal the blind man. An English monastery founded at Sherborne in Wessex at about the same time counted among its early benefactors Geraint, a British king, and there could have been a good deal of peaceable interaction between Britons and English. The lament of an English poet over what may have been the ruins of Roman Bath (above p. 96) suggests total rupture with the past. Yet Bede was aware of springs being used for hot baths, which suggests continuity or at least resumption of the bathing practices of Rome, and as we shall see, a complex of buildings that the English erected at Yeavering in Northumbria was on a site that had been used by the British.[24]

Only friendly relations between the Britons and the English can explain some developments, such as many people in English society having British names. Among them was Cædmon, an animal keeper who lived in Northumbria late in the seventh century, and who has the distinction of being the earliest poet in English whose work has survived. A shy man who left parties when he saw the harp making its rounds, he was visited in his sleep by someone who ordered him to sing and, despite his protestations of inability, he began to sing, having received a miraculous gift of composing poetry in 'his own tongue, that is that of the English'. Yet the name Cædmon is British, and he may plausibly be seen as a Briton who had adopted the English language. Over a century earlier, even the vehemently anti-English author Gildas knew the proper English word for the ships in which the newcomers made their earliest crossings, whereas late in the seventh century Guthlac, an Englishman who later became a famous hermit, had taken refuge among Britons and come to understand their speech. Many people living in Northumbria during Cædmon's period are unambiguously named as Britons by our sources, and those who sheltered an English boy when his parents left the neighbourhood, like the Briton who gathered soil from the place where Oswald was buried and went on to a feast and drinking party that villagers were holding in a house, apparently enjoyed good relations with the English.[25] On the other hand, every English king of Wessex prior to Cynewulf, in the eighth century, bore a British name; one of them, Cædwalla, shared his name with the British king of Gwynedd. The occurrence of such names among the leaders of the English suggests that they were marrying indigenes, just as the leaders among the Germanic newcomers were doing in other parts of the old Empire.

In some areas that came under English control, the Britons were largely left to their own devices. It is striking how English power in Northumbria, a kingdom that extended from the North Sea to the Irish Sea, was concentrated within the east of its territory. It was there that the royal centres such as Bamburgh and Yeavering, the four known episcopal sees and the great monasteries were all located. There is a striking absence of such centres in the west of the kingdom, and the names by which the area is still known, Cumbria and Cumberland, preserve the word that the Britons used of themselves, 'Cymry'. Speaking at the inland centre of Ripon, an English bishop observed that holy places in different regions had been abandoned by British clergy fleeing from the swords of the English, but it does not follow from this that the Britons in general had fled. A text of the early eighth century explains that, after the martyrdom of St Alban in Roman times, a shrine was built where the healing of sick people and the working of miracles 'continues to occur often, to this day', and the words suggest that the cult of the British saint had continued across the coming of the English.[26] Similarly, king Ine of Wessex (688–726) extended a church at Glastonbury which the Britons had founded and which may have enjoyed a seamless history as British political supremacy yielded to that of the English. Under the year 913 the Anglo-Saxon Chronicles refer to a river in Hertfordshire as 'Bene ficcan', the second element of which corresponds to a British adjective for 'little'. But adjectives only came to follow nouns in British speech from the late sixth century, so behind the name of the river lies British speech that remained in use after the coming of the English, in which form it was transmitted to them.

It may be thought that an interpretation of the coming of the English along these lines is contradicted by other, more basic linguistic evidence. As we have seen, the ending of Roman power in Italy, Spain and even Gaul had little linguistic impact: in all cases, the newcomers learned Latin within a few generations. The reverse occurred in Britain. There, the Germanic language of the newcomers, which we may call Old English, came to a position of dominance in most of the island. The comparison with the Continent is not entirely fair, for at the end of the Roman period in Britain, Celtic speech was used more widely than Latin there. But the Britons' success in resisting the imperial language of Latin makes their linguistic capitulation in the face of English the more noteworthy. Indeed, not only did the English go on speaking their own language and impose it on the Britons, but Old English shows few signs of having been influenced by British speech, for there are few British loan-words in its lexicon. Indeed, Old English contains far more words derived from Latin, many of which must have joined the word hoard before its speakers moved to Britain.

Nevertheless, it does not follow from the catastrophic fate of British speech that its speakers suffered a similar fate. To be sure, the evidence seems strong: the contribution of British to the vocabulary of modern English runs to a mere 15 or 16 words, many of which, such as 'coomb' and 'dun', now have a quaint air about them. But the spread of Latin in Gaul and Spain in Roman times was not due to a change in the population group; for the greater part, it occurred as population groups, in an unforced way over some generations, abandoned their own Celtic language for that of the Romans. Indeed, it has been argued that the spread of Indo-European in prehistoric times may have resulted from changes of speech within stable populations as well as population movements. Such could well have been the case in Britain. Some British place-names survived, particularly in Cornwall, although only a small minority of current English place-names can be traced to pre-English roots; for what the comparison is worth, the proportion of place-names of Aboriginal origin that have remained in use across a period of massive dis-location for the indigenous inhabitants of Australia is far higher. But this need not be very significant. Most of the British names known from before the arrival of the English survive today. Again, of the names that can be docu-mented in the period of early English settlement, the proportion of Celtic names is far higher than it is for later periods, and the low overall proportion may partially reflect the very high proportion among the towns of modern England that were founded in later centuries, when Celtic names could not be looked for. The proportion of rivers, which are obviously much the same now as they were millennia ago, still called by Celtic names is far higher than the proportion of places.

As with the triumph of Latin in Gaul and Spain, that of English in Britain was due not so much to the numerical preponderance of its speakers as to its being a high-status language. Speakers of the local language would have found it worth their while to acquire the language spoken by a group with political and military dominance. Some Latin speakers did the same in Italy and Gaul when Goths and Burgundians arrived. But English was more important than its Germanic counterparts on the Continent, for it quickly came to fill some of the functions that Latin filled there. The churchmen who debated at the synod of Whitby did so in English, and the long tradition of translations of the Bible into English goes at least as far back as Bede, who was working on a translation of St John's Gospel as he died. Moreover, whereas Germanic monarchs on the Continent legislated in Latin, from the turn of the seventh century English sovereigns were publishing laws in their own language, which Britons who went to law would have been well advised to know. So it was that English established itself in a way that no other Germanic language did in the territory of the former Empire. Moreover, if the case of Cædmon is anything to go by, its literary expression was attractive to the Britons. Hence, whereas in the north of Gaul the indigenous population came to see themselves as Franks but retained their own language, many of the people of Britain went a step further and adopted English.

Seen in this light, the volume of Germanic artefacts that archaeologists have uncovered in post-Roman Britain, particularly in the lowlands, and which could be thought to suggest a massive change in ethnicity may partly reflect cultural choice among an indigenous population, for the coming of Germanic artefacts need not have been associated with the coming of Germanic people. As we have seen, during the late fourth century and early fifth century, the indigenous people of Italy, and indeed Rome itself, were taking to wearing Germanic fashions, and it would be difficult, on the basis of material culture, to tell the difference between an English person and a Briton who had adopted the accoutrements of a Germanic life. The laws issued by king Ine of Wessex refer to Britons, whom it calls 'Welsh', while those issued by Alfred of Wessex 200 years later do not. Perhaps the descendants of Ine's Welsh had come to think of themselves, and to be thought of, as 'English' by Alfred's time. Theoderic the Ostrogoth had remarked that 'the poor Roman imitates the Goth, and the well-to-do Goth the Roman'.[27] But the crisis-stricken civilisation that the English encountered in Britain may not have seemed worth imitating, whereas the success of the English, together with whatever process of assimilation that the enslavement of some of the Britons entailed, may have been enough for them to begin to identify themselves with the English, adopting such characteristics as their language, laws and material culture.

One other consideration suggests that we need not despair of British survival. Scholars have drawn attention to the invisibility of the Britons in the archaeological record. Yet invisibility does not entail non-existence, and the Britons may have been entering a period of invisibility quite independently of the coming of the English. Throughout Britain, new villas ceased to be constructed in the last quarter of the fourth century, just as thrown pottery ceased to be manufactured and coinage ceased to be used for exchange shortly afterwards. These changes created a situation in which the kinds of goods that would have enabled us to identify British life were no longer produced, just as the chronological markers they would have provided ceased to exist. As we shall see, there is little archaeological evidence for the indigenous population of Italy in parts of the Lombard period, yet it is certain that this population continued to exist, and we may take it that the same was true in Britain.

But such accommodation as the Britons reached with the newcomers would not be influential in the history of England. Increasingly, the influences that played upon the developing civilisation of the English arose from their contacts with other parts of Europe. The bodies of water that surround Britain to its east, south and west allow it easy contact with the peoples living on their farther sides. The relative ease of communication by water allowed such contacts to be close, for the North Sea is no broader than the greater part of the Mediterranean, across which contacts were so close in antiquity, while large parts of Britain were closer to Ireland and Gaul than they were to other parts of the island. And, as has usually been the case in England, it was those areas nearest the Continent where such influences were most intensely felt.

FRANKISH INFLUENCE

During the later Empire, Britain had been part of the praetorian prefecture of the Gauls, and in similar fashion some of the Franks claimed hegemony over the English (see above, p. 92). Moreover, during the various rebellions that broke out in the later Roman Empire, forces on both sides of the Channel tended to find themselves marching together. Relations across the Channel in the post-Roman period were not always friendly, as an extraordinary story found in an eastern author indicates. He tells us that when, in the sixth century, king Radigis of the Warni, a minor people on the right bank of the Rhine, broke his betrothal to the sister of an English king in Britain with a view to marrying the sister of the powerful Merovingian king Theudebert, the rejected woman led an enormous force against the Warni. It was successful, whereupon she had Radigis brought to her and they married.[28] Yet it would be reasonable to suppose that there were close and potentially friendly ties between the English and the Franks from an early time.

That there were can be seen clearly in the case of their political elites. King Æthelberht of Kent, four generations removed from an early immigrant to Britain, married a Frankish princess, Bertha. She was a Christian, who arrived in her new home with a chaplain. Æthelberht may have been expected to adopt the religion of his wife, but he frustrated any such hopes, only accepting the faith from missionaries led by the monk Augustine, who arrived at the head of a team of 40 monks in 597, having been sent from Rome by pope Gregory. They landed on the Isle of Thanet, where the earliest English were said to have landed some 150 years earlier. The king's decision to accept the new religion when it was transmitted from a distant city, rather than through his wife and the nearby Franks, may have been an assertion of independence from his powerful neighbours, but the church that sprang up in England was closely linked to that of Gaul. Augustine had been consecrated a bishop there, his mission was supported by Frankish monarchs, particularly Brunhild, and Frankish interpreters accompanied him to England. Close ties were maintained. Two churchmen from England attended the council of Paris which Lothar summoned in 614. Æthelberht's son Eadbald, while reluctant to follow his father into Christianity, imitated his example in marrying a Frankish woman, who has been identified as the daughter of a mayor of the palace. His sister married king Edwin of Northumbria, and after the death of Edwin in battle, two of his children and one grandchild were sent to the Merovingian king Dagobert, the 'friend' of his widow. Not long before, an East Anglian king, Sigeberht, had been an exile in Gaul, where he became a Christian. Eadbald's granddaughter Eorcengota later entered a convent just to the west of Paris, and we have already seen the role that the Englishwoman Balthilde played in the political and religious life of the Franks (see above, p. 91). Ties between the English and the Frankish churches were close and sustained.

The two peoples were also bound together by their material culture. So many Frankish artefacts were imported into Kent that some scholars have unwisely concluded that substantial Frankish settlement occurred. Some two-thirds of the glass vessels of the early English period that have been excavated have turned up in Kent, and it is likely that a great many of these were imported, for the north-west of Gaul had become an important centre of glass-making in Roman times and there is good reason to believe that the industry continued into the Frankish period.[29] Many of these items were bottles, which may have contained expensive products. Such was the volume of trade that the early kings of Kent employed toll collectors. Visitors from other parts of England must have been struck by a visibly higher standard of living in Kent. By the middle of the sixth century, coins from the Continent, especially those minted in Gaul, were finding their way into Britain, although they need not have been used for exchange. A number of Kentish men were buried in the seventh century with sets of balances and weights, just as people in the least monetarised parts of Frankland were at that time, which may indicate trade being conducted with coins used as bullion.

Before long this situation was tidied up. During the reign of Æthelberht, the first English coins were minted, although it may be safer to describe them as coin-like objects, it not being clear for what purpose they were produced. They were certainly used in necklaces, and the burials within which they have been found tend to be those of females. Many of the Roman coins used by the inhabitants of West Stow were pierced or modified to allow their use as ornaments, as were the Roman, Byzantine and Frankish coins deposited in St Martin's church at Canterbury. The use of coins for adornment may seem bizarre, but there were precedents for it at the edges of the Roman Empire, as in a treasure hoard hidden during the early fourth century in what is now Belgium.[30] Decades passed before English coins supplanted those minted in Gaul. A ship burial at Sutton Hoo in East Anglia included 37 Merovingian coins, which may have been brought together in the 620s, but a hoard buried in about the middle of the century at Crondall, a town now in Hampshire near its border with Surrey, is mainly composed of coins minted in England. Only 24 of the 100 coins it contains are clearly Frankish or Frisian, and over a quarter of these were from the mint that had recently been established at Quentovic, where many English moneyers seem to have worked. But the English kept a close eye on the coinage of the Franks. When the latter moved away from the minting of gold coins in the 660s, the English followed their lead. By the end of the century they had abandoned the practice, and the silver coins on which they came to rely, the famous sceattas, had the same weight as the silver deniers minted under the Merovingians.

SCANDINAVIAN INFLUENCE

To the north of Kent lay East Anglia, which, when it looked overseas, often did so across the North Sea, towards lands far less influenced by the Mediterranean than those which Kent faced. Such an orientation is revealed by the greatest archaeological find from Anglo-Saxon England, that at Sutton Hoo, where an unknown person, perhaps king Redwald of the East Angles (died c.624), was laid to rest overlooking the river Deben in a boat, some 27 m long and over 4 m wide. Whereas Æthelberht of Kent had been buried as a Christian in a church, the burial at Sutton Hoo made an explicitly anti-Christian statement, as did another burial of about the same time beneath a high mound at Taplow, overlooking the upper Thames. Burials in large barrows or mounds that could be seen from far out to sea, and specifically burials within ships, are known from Sweden. They are also described in *Beowulf*, the great Old English epic poem, significantly set in Scandinavia, which seems to have been written between the seventh and ninth centuries, although it contains material from earlier times. Indeed, a sceptre, perhaps of British manufacture, with a carved stag or hart on top, found in the burial at Sutton Hoo[31] recalls the name of king Hrothgar's great hall in *Beowulf*, Heorot or 'hart'.

The contents of the burial at Sutton Hoo are extraordinarily rich. Some were of Mediterranean origin, such as a pair of silver spoons that bear the names Saul and Paul in Greek, and a large silver dish with control stamps which show that it was made in the Empire during the reign of Anastasius (481–518). Other items, such as a belt buckle and a pair of shoulder clasps, while of exceptional beauty, are products of an aesthetic which, in the fascination it took in interlacing design and its disinterest in the depiction of the human body, was remote from the taste of the ancient Mediterranean. The treasure contains items remarkably similar to those found in Swedish boat-graves of the sixth and seventh centuries. While its ancestry was probably Roman, the fine helmet with wonderful figural designs buried at Sutton Hoo, as well as a sword and shield, were probably made in Sweden, or failing this almost certainly made by Swedish craftspeople elsewhere. Despite the presence of some explicitly Christian artefacts, the burial at Sutton Hoo is that of a staunchly non-Christian world, perhaps one that chose to display defiance in the face of Christian encroachment, for nearby burials indicate that human sacrifices were offered. In both its lavishness and its location at the edge of Christendom, the Sutton Hoo burial recalls that of Childeric the Frank at Tournai. It was a world of heroic drinking, for the treasure contained a pair of drinking vessels made of the horns of an aurochs, a kind of ox now extinct. Thin, curved vessels some 90 cm long, they would have been impossible to put down once a drink was poured. The use of aurochs' horns was traditional among Germans, for Caesar records their being used at banquets,[32] and perhaps widespread, for similar vessels were included in the burial at Taplow.

Scandinavian influence was present in other areas of English life. Artefacts of Scandinavian type, such as clasps and brooches, were common in Kent as well as East Anglia, pointing at the least to sustained economic exchange, of which the export of English glassware to Scandinavia, especially Sweden, in the seventh century was also a part. Links across the North Sea are also implied by 'bracteates', thin discs of gold or silver on which designs based on those of Roman coins were stamped in the middle, and which were worn on necklaces.[33] Something like a thousand of these have been discovered, the great majority of them in Scandinavia, but there is a scattering in England, especially in Kent and East Anglia. The pieces found in Britain date from the fifth and sixth centuries, some apparently of Scandinavian manufacture and others English. While based on Roman models, the designs make no attempt to render the human body in a naturalistic way, and are sometimes virtually abstract, but we may attribute this to a different aesthetic rather than to any lack of competence on the part of the northern artists.

Scandinavian, or at any rate Germanic, influence was also displayed in the use of the runic alphabet. Of obscure origin, it was widely employed in Scandinavia, although its coming to England may have been by way of Frisia. The earliest example of its use in England, which may date from as early as the late fourth century, occurs on an ankle-bone at Caistor-by-Norwich, and other early examples also come from East Anglia, although it was later employed much more widely in Northumbria. While they were widely deployed in non-Christian media, runic letters were also used in prestigious and definitely Christian contexts. The runic and Roman alphabets were both used in inscriptions on the coffin of Cuthbert, bishop of Lindisfarne, and they were also employed on a cross erected at Ruthwell in the modern Dumfriesshire, which contains in runic characters verses very similar to some that make up part of one of the best-known Old English poems, *The Dream of the Rood*. The two alphabets also occur in inscriptions on the Franks Casket, a box carved from whalebone in about 700, on which juxtaposed carvings of scenes from the Germanic, biblical and Roman traditions bear witness to learned eclecticism.[34] England's possession of an alphabet widely used in Scandinavia, which formed an alternative to the Roman alphabet, suggests the varying influences to which it was subject in the early English period.

IRISH INFLUENCE

Beyond East Anglia lay Northumbria, named for its being to the north of the wide river Humber. Bede, the author of our chief narrative source for early English history, was a Northumbrian, so we are better informed about its early history than about those of Kent and East Anglia. Extending both southwards and northwards of Hadrian's Wall, Northumbria, like the state of the Franks, was a sign of tendencies that diminished the significance of the Roman borders. It was made up of two kingdoms with Celtic names, Bernicia and Deira. One of the greatest Northumbrian monarchs was King Edwin (616–33). Banished by the king of Bernicia, he took refuge among Britons, by whom, according to a later tradition, he was baptised. But he was also involved with the other English kingdoms. He married a daughter of king Æthelberht of Kent, Æthelburgh, who was followed to Northumbria by missionaries. It was only in 627, according to the generally accepted story, that the king was baptised by one of them, Paulinus, who, himself from Italy, set about building a stone church at York, the old Roman headquarters in northern Britain.[35] But in 633 Edwin was killed in battle, when fighting a coalition of Britons from Wales and English from Mercia. It fell to his son, king Oswald (634–42), to restore unity to Northumbria and revive the church. But, Paulinus having fled to Kent following the death of Edwin, Oswald decided to look elsewhere for the leadership of the church in Northumbria.

Ireland, never part of the Roman Empire, was one of the unexpected success stories of early Christianity. The religion arrived there early, its cause being strengthened by St Patrick in the fifth century, and the Irish cultivated learning. The oldest surviving Irish manuscript dates from about the beginning of the sixth century, and Irish scholars of the following century produced a handy summary of pope Gregory's exposition of Job, a learned contribution to debate concerning the date of Easter, and in the *Hisperica Famina* a Latin text so dazzling in its difficulty that few modern scholars would care to be asked to translate it unseen. The Irish were also enthusiastic missionaries. We have already considered the activity of Columban in Gaul, and a few decades before he arrived there the similarly named Columba, a feisty monk much given to quarrels, had sailed from Ireland to establish a monastery on the Isle of Iona, off the west coast of Scotland, from which he was later believed to have set about converting the Picts and to have cursed, to no apparent effect, a monster dwelling in Loch Ness. It was to the monks of Iona that Oswald, who had lived for some time among the Irish as an exile, turned when Northumbria needed a bishop, and it was Christianity of this tradition that rose to prominence in his kingdom. This was well suited to the English, for whereas Christianity within the Roman Empire had been structured around bishops in their towns, in Ireland, where urbanisation had remained at the level characteristic of other parts of Celtic Europe prior to the coming of the Romans, bishops resided in monasteries. This system answered well to the society of post-Roman Britain.

In 635 the monks of Iona dispatched one of their number, Aidan, to be bishop in Northumbria. He straightaway founded a monastery on the island of Lindisfarne. As islands went, it was quite an accessible one, being only separated from the mainland at high tide, but the degree of separation it enjoyed meant that Aidan would have failed to live up to the standards of the bishops in Gaul, who were even forbidden to keep dogs which might deter people from seeking their hospitality. And although Lindisfarne was within sight of the royal stronghold of Bamburgh, and Aidan died at one of the king's villas near it, he made a point of dining with the king only rarely. The Irish clergy and those influenced by them, such as Chad and Cuthbert, went on preaching tours around the countryside of Northumbria. The Irish were men of modest tastes; Aidan's successor as bishop of Lindisfarne, Finan, built a church explicitly described in our source as 'not of stone', a phrase that distinguished it from structures such as that erected by Paulinus at York, but of oaken wood, thatched with reeds. The methods of the Irish, whose contribution to English Christianity lives on in such words as 'cross' and its numerous derivatives, offered a remarkable contrast to those of the missionaries from Rome and those influenced by them, who were much more comfortable with political establishments.[36]

MEDITERRANEAN INFLUENCE

Yet despite the influences playing upon it from the immediate south, the east and the west, warm breezes blowing from the Mediterranean were increasingly felt in England. Christianity came to Kent directly from Rome, in a very up-to-date form. Augustine brought with him a Gospel book, which may be identical with a manuscript now in Cambridge, written and richly illuminated in Italy during the sixth century. He also came with an 'image' of Christ painted on a board, probably an example of the icons just coming to prominence. The English never forgot the source of their religion. More churches were dedicated in early England to the very Roman figure of St Peter than to any other saint. A cult of pope Gregory, who had dispatched the first missionaries and whom the English regarded as their own apostle, sprang up, which produced the earliest significant biography of that pope, written in England early in the eighth century. Popes sought the goodwill of English royalty by sending what they deemed suitable presents. Edwin of Northumbria received a tunic with a golden ornament and a cloak from the distant town of Ancyra, the modern Ankara, as far away from Rome as Northumbria, which had been destroyed by Persians a few years earlier. With due regard for gender difference, Edwin's wife was given a silver mirror and a comb of gold and ivory, presumably made from the tusk of an elephant. In such ways, the early English church was more closely linked with the papacy than churches in other parts of Europe that were closer to Rome.[37]

This was clearly shown in the life of the Northumbrian noble Biscop, who adopted the name of the great Italian monk Benedict. Having already made three trips to Rome, in the course of one of which he became a monk at Lérins, in 674 he founded a monastery at Wearmouth, some 100 km south of Lindisfarne. Many nobles in Gaul were doing the same, but Benedict's monastery was dedicated to St Peter. Only the best would do for Benedict. From Gaul he obtained the services of masons who could build in stone. To the English, who thought of buildings as things made of wood, their scholars translating the Latin word for 'build' as *getimbran*, works such as those of Benedict were executed in 'the Roman manner'. After the church was finished, he sent again to Gaul for glass makers, whose craft was then unknown in England. Work having advanced sufficiently, Benedict set off on his fourth trip to Rome, from which he returned with countless books, relics of saints, an expert at singing and the conduct of church services, and images of the saints and biblical stories. Later, having founded another monastery nearby at Jarrow dedicated to St Paul, generally thought of as Peter's colleague in the foundation of the church of Rome, he made a fifth trip there, whence he returned with more books and images. Rome had become important to the English. Churchmen and even kings ended their days there, and in an unexpected example of tourist graffiti, several people from the north of Europe carved their names in runes to mark their visits to the sites of Rome at about the middle of the seventh century.[38]

The English were remarkably good pupils, who took to learning with gusto. Doubtless there were losers in the rush towards book-learning: the bearers of traditional, pre-Christian knowledge and traditions, many of them women, may have found themselves disempowered and their lore marginalised, if not demonised. But the books collected by Benedict Biscop in Rome were the basis of a library rich enough to nourish the intellectual life of Bede, the most learned scholar in western Europe during the period. So difficult was the Latin written by Aldhelm, a scholar in the west of England, that people who copied his works added explanatory glosses in English and Latin. Aldhelm was aware of being the first person of Germanic race to write on the metres of classical poetry. Before long, the English were able to offer gifts to their benefactors. In 716, almost a hundred years after Edwin and his wife received their presents, an abbot of Jarrow set off for Rome with a gift for the pope, the oldest surviving complete manuscript of the Vulgate Bible, the Codex Amiatinus. So big was it that the skins of some 1,550 calves were needed to produce it. The great monasteries of Northumbria produced books that can be placed next to the greatest items of world art. At about the end of the eighth century, Lindisfarne produced several sets of gospel books, of which the most famous, the Lindisfarne Gospels now kept in the British Library, is noteworthy for the simple elegance of its script and the beauty of its artwork.[39] An English scribe who made a copy of the Rule of Benedict early in the eighth century cleaned up Benedict's Latin, to make it more correct. By then the intellectual leadership of western Europe, held by Spain a century earlier (below p. 152), had passed to England. And as it turned out, the horizons that Christianity opened up for the English extended even beyond Rome.

The coming of the Irish monks into Northumbria had introduced tensions into the church there. In particular, the Irish calculated the date of Easter, the greatest feast of the church, in a way that led them often to celebrate it on a day other than that observed by the missionaries from Rome and their followers. A council that Oswald's successor, king Oswiu, summoned to deal with this problem at Whitby in 664 is often taken as the moment when English Christianity turned decisively away from the Irish tradition towards that of Rome. But, as Bede chose to tell the story, there was more to it than that. When he wrote his account of the council, he had before him an earlier version of its proceedings, which occurs in the biography of bishop Wilfrid written by Stephanus, sometimes called 'Eddius', the emphasis of which he subverted.

Stephanus had represented the controversy at Whitby as having been between 'the custom of the Britons and the Irish and all the northern region' and 'the practice of the apostolic see'. Bede took a more general view, seeing it as a clash between the traditions of the Irish and the custom of the universal church. He played off the practice of 'the Picts and Scots, who live in the most remote islands of the ocean, and not the whole of these', against what Wilfrid, an English adherent of Roman ways, had discovered:

> The Easter which we keep we saw celebrated by everyone at Rome, where the blessed apostles Peter and Paul lived, suffered and were buried; we noticed that it was followed by everyone in Italy and Gaul, which we traversed in order to study and pray. We have learned that it is observed in Africa, Asia, Egypt, Greece and the whole world, wherever the church of Christ had spread, at the very same time . . . [The Irish] and their obstinate allies, the Picts and Britons . . . foolishly struggle against the whole world.

Bede concluded his account by quoting words that Christ spoke to Peter: 'Thou art Peter, and upon this rock I will build my church; and the gates of hell shall not prevail against it. And I will give unto thee the keys of the kingdom of heaven' (Matt. 16:18f). There is nothing papal in Bede's use of these words, for in his narrative Peter plays the role of a disciple who correctly calculated the date of Easter, and whose method it would be prudent to follow, given his possession of the keys of the kingdom of heaven. Stephanus, on the other hand, does not discuss the method that Peter followed to calculate the date of Easter, and when he provides a quotation of Christ's words to him, it is in a fuller form, which goes on to speak of his having been given the power of binding and loosing, a meaning that can only be juridical. For Bede, Christianity inducted the English into a wide community. When he recommended the frequent reception of holy communion, it was with reference to 'the practice of Italy, Gaul, Africa, Greece and the whole East'.[40] It was a spacious world that the English had joined. Bede showed the breadth of his horizons in time as well as space by being the first major historian to express dates in accordance with what he understood as the number of years that had passed since the birth of Christ. The forms in which dates came to Bede were expressed according to a variety of confusing systems, but he processed them in a way that allowed them to be expressed in an absolute chronology since Christ's birth.

The warm breezes of the south even influenced the clothes that the English chose to wear. During the seventh century, the brooches traditionally worn by Germanic women yielded to pins. At the same time, women were abandoning beads in favour of necklaces, similar to those worn by Theodora and members of her court depicted in a mosaic at San Vitale in Ravenna. And some of the fashions castigated by an English poet of the late seventh century were by no means Germanic: clothes embroidered with silk were a fashion of the Mediterranean, while the veils that yielded to headdresses extending to the ankles which he describes recall veils worn by virgins in a mosaic installed in the church of Sant'Apollinare Nuovo in Ravenna. Whereas some Romans in the late fourth and fifth centuries had adopted Germanic garb, the English, in a way that would have staggered their ancestors when they settled in Britain, came to ape the fashions of the Mediterranean. English churchmen visiting Charlemagne, who prided himself on plain dressing, had to be warned to dress down.[41]

Links between England and the south were strengthened in 669, when an archbishop of Canterbury with a Greek name arrived. Theodore had been born in Tarsus, a strategically significant town that controlled communications between Syria and Anatolia. He seems to have studied at Edessa, for centuries an intellectual centre of Christianity in Syria, and expounded the Bible in a way that had developed in Antioch, which emphasised the literal rather than the allegorical meaning of the text. When the Arabs invaded Syria, he moved to Constantinople, from which he journeyed to Rome, where he would have learned Latin. He and the African abbot who accompanied him thence to England, Hadrian, were native speakers of Greek, capable of widening the horizons of the English immensely. They brought first-hand information on all kinds of puzzling things, such as a phrase in the book of Numbers (11:5):

> Cucumbers . . . and melons: are the same thing, but cucumbers are called *pepones* when they grow large, and often one *pepon* will weigh thirty pounds. In the city of Edessa they grow so large that a camel can scarcely carry two of them.

Such information, the strangeness of which clearly lost nothing in the telling, must have astonished the English, unfamiliar with such foods. But beyond it, Theodore was a genuine scholar and intellectual. In 680 a pope wrote to the emperor expressing regret that the 'archbishop of the great island of Britain and philosopher' had not been able to help express papal views.[42] The world inhabited by Cuthbert, a bishop of Lindisfarne, was more narrow. But even he was laid to rest towards the end of the seventh century with a comb made of elephant ivory and a pectoral cross at the centre of which was a shell that may have come from the Indian Ocean. By then, England had taken its place within a very wide world.

This was also true of its economic life. As early as 604, London was a market to which many peoples came by land and sea. In the following century, a trading area developed to the west of the former Roman town, in the area of the Strand, with perhaps a particular concentration around the modern Trafalgar Square. No less than Marseilles had been, the wealth that passed through London made it worth controlling, and it may explain its confused political history in the seventh century. By the end of the century, kings of Kent were legislating concerning men of Kent who bought property in the city. People were also settling at Ipswich, a site whose location, directly opposite the mouths of the Rhine, made it handy for Frankish and Frisian traders. During the second half of the century, wheel-turned pottery, the production of which seems to have ceased in Britain at about the time the Romans left, was being manufactured there. From about 700 another centre of production and trade was emerging at Hamwic, near Southampton on the south coast, the population of which grew to several thousand people. Such towns were not just centres of administration and consumption by elite groups, as many Roman towns had been, but also, as foreign and locally produced coins found at Hamwic show, of production and exchange as well. Kings responded to the boom in trade by minting large numbers of silver coins; whatever role earlier coins may have been designed to fill, the volume of coins that survive from the eighth century indicates that they were meant to facilitate exchange. Later, king Offa of Mercia (757–96) promised to send to the pope every year 365 'mancuses' for the feeding of the poor and the upkeep of lights. The mancuses, coins minted for almsgiving rather than for commercial purposes, were imitations of dinars minted by the Abbasid caliphs of Baghdad, and one of Offa's productions survives, its inscription in the Kufic script of the Arabs except for the words 'OFFA REX', which are upside down in relation to the Arabic text. The mancus is dated in the 157th year after the prophet Muhammad's hijra to Madina.[43] The possession by Offa's moneyers of a coin minted so far away, and his ability to act so generously to the pope, indicate the distance that the English economy had travelled.

MONARCHY

Our discussion of England has largely been couched in terms of its relations with other parts of the world. Yet these centuries saw important internal developments. In particular, kings came to play an enhanced role.

People in this period who thought about the entry of newcomers often interpreted events in the light of the historical books of Old Testament, and no reader of these could be unaware that the entry of the chosen people into the promised land was shortly followed by the institution of monarchy:

> When thou art come into the land which the Lord thy God giveth thee, and shalt possess it, and shalt dwell therein, and shalt say, I will set a king over me, as all the nations that are about me . . . (Deut. 17:14)

It would have come as no surprise to Bede, who looked on the English as a new chosen people, that kingship developed rapidly after their settlement in Britain. Æthelberht of Kent, whose family had been in Britain a mere four generations, already discharged many of the functions of an established medieval king. He promulgated laws, so becoming the first of a distinguished series of English legislators, and minted coins, reviving a practice that had lapsed before the departure of the Romans. Before long, the kings of Kent and Wessex were making grants of land to churches. King Edwin, who had a royal standard carried before him wherever he went, maintained an impressive wooden hall at Yeavering in the Cheviot Hills, inland from Bamburgh. On the site, previously occupied by Britons, a series of wooden halls was erected from the late-sixth to the mid-seventh centuries, the largest of which could accommodate perhaps 300 people. Nearby stood a structure which resembles part of a wooden amphitheatre; perhaps the evangelist Paulinus preached there. No more than the humble settlement at West Stow, Yeavering had no defences. The architectural antecedents of these buildings are unclear. The earliest of them may have been erected by Britons, although some of the ground plans and the sunken floors reflect Germanic tradition. This may be a case where it would be unhelpful to draw a distinction between British and English practice. The styles favoured by the English in Britain may have differed from forms current in the parts of the Continent from which they had come, and may have owed something to what they found in Britain; timber halls with doors on their long sides may have imitated stone buildings that have been found on late villa sites. In any case, the wooden structures at Yeavering were not permanent, and by the early eighth century the 'palace' had been deserted, and another built elsewhere.[44]

Kings of the period can also be dimly perceived displaying an interest in taxation. That the streets of Hamwic form a grid indicates that it did not develop in an unplanned way, but was created for a reason. The mastermind may have been Ine, king of Wessex, and his purpose profiting from tolls on trade, such as those which charters reveal were being levied on ships at London some way into the eighth century. The Tribal Hidage, a mysterious document that may have been drawn up for a king of Mercia towards the end of the seventh century, lists over 30 territories south of the Humber and the number of 'hides' in each. Notionally, a hide was a unit of land large enough to support a free family, and Bede had at his disposal figures that allowed him to indicate the size of various areas with reference to the number of hides they contained, from five in the Isle of Iona to 7,000 in the case of the land of the West Saxons. Such figures suggest an ability to measure areas, not merely naturally occurring ones such as islands, but also politically defined ones, and in at least some cases the hide may have been used as a unit of taxation. Perhaps the Tribal Hidage was compiled with a view to gathering tribute; however this may be, the person in whose interest it was produced was some-one able to gather precise information that could have been used to raise taxes over a large part of England, in a way that would have challenged the autonomy of various areas.

Christianisation was another way in which the power of kings was streng-thened. Oswiu's conduct at the council of Whitby would not have been amiss in a Byzantine emperor, used as such rulers were to taking a prominent part in ecclesiastical deliberations, and not long afterwards his son was present at an important synod at which archbishop Theodore sought to unify the church in England. Churches gained from the support of kings. When king Æthelberht's code prescribed that losses suffered by God's property and the church were to be compensated twelve-fold, it significantly modified in the interests of the church a position attributed to pope Gregory, according to which the church was not to benefit from any losses it underwent. But kings in turn benefited from what the clergy had to offer, insistently placing as they did earthly kingdoms beside the kingdom of heaven.[45] It was not accidental that many of the activities we associate with monarchs were first undertaken in England by Æthelberht, just as they first were among the Franks by Clovis. And while pre-Christian notions could be used to strengthen kingship, as when Hengist and Horsa were said (in a genealogy probably only constructed after the coming of the English to Britain, which invites comparison with others concocted on the Continent) to have been four generations removed from Woden, the northern god of war, the ideological support that Christianity had offered monarchs was stronger. Kings also laid claim to classical ancestry. A text that seems to reflect an understanding current in the eighth century offers a novel descent for the kings of East Anglia: while it began with Woden and proceeded by way of one Wuffa, after whom the dynasty was named, Caesar was now placed next to Woden. Roman origins were also suggested in a coin issued towards the end of the century in East Anglia, which shows the twins Romulus and Remus, the legendary co-founders of Rome, being suckled by the she-wolf, a story well known to the English.[46] Just as Lupus and Magnulf were brothers in Gaul, so the Roman wolf could co-exist with Wuffa among the East Anglians, and whereas the Franks staked a place for themselves in the classical past by claiming descent from the Trojans, so did the East Anglians, audaciously claiming Caesar as a forebear of their ruling dynasty.

OLD AND NEW

In these various ways, the English came to take their place on a stage far wider than their ancestors of the fifth century could have imagined. Yet it would be wrong to see England as becoming a cosmopolitan place, for its inhabitants remained resolutely attached to many of their old ways, quite capable of filling new forms with old content. The narrative of Bede, from which much of our knowledge of English history in this period is derived, can hide this reality. This is partly because the author's life in a monastery distanced him from many of the concerns of people in the world, but it also arose from the intensely Christian nature of his thought and the metaphorical cast of his mind. But even Bede tells of a newly converted king being murdered by two of his relatives, who hated him because he would spare his enemies and forgive those who asked for pardon, which Bede glossed as observing the precepts of the Gospel.[47] And against Bede may be set the poem *Beowulf*, which, despite being the work of someone familiar with the Bible, haunts its readers by the emotional loyalty its author displays towards the pre-Christian and heroic values of Germanic society. Indeed, the very speed with which the English adopted Christianity may have allowed them to bring a good deal of baggage with them. Thoughtful churchmen were concerned at the worldliness of monasteries that had been founded for unworthy purposes, and at the danger that abbots could be appointed by hereditary succession.[48] The biography of the greatest native-born church-man of the period, Wilfrid (intermittently bishop of York, from *c*.665), by Stephanus shows how close the values of even a bishop could be to those of the secular Germanic world.[49]

Modern readers of this text can find Wilfrid a hard man to like, but they may be looking for the wrong virtues. His biographer expects us to be impressed by the pertinacity with which Wilfrid defended the rights of his church and pursued quarrels with other bishops, the assets that he accumulated, and the style with which he travelled. A gospel book that he bought is described in terms that could have been applied to treasure: written in the most pure gold on purple parchment, it was kept in a container made of the purest gold and precious gems. Even when he left home at the age of 14, Wilfrid had arms, horses, clothing and slaves such as would not have been out of place in the presence of kings, and the 'honourable' way in which he later presented himself and the size of his following is stressed. For such a person, the line between secular and sacred was a fine one. When he became abbot of Whitby, 'the wide door of this world was opened', a phrase with most unfortunate biblical echoes, and money was never an object. It was therefore nothing more than common sense that, as he came towards his end, Wilfrid gave treasure to abbots, so that they in turn would be able to maintain the friendship of the powerful with gifts. To an extent that one may not have expected in a monk, he was concerned with family. While he left his father and stepmother when young, better fathers proved to be available: the archbishop of Lyons wanted to adopt him as a son and give him his niece in marriage, and when archbishop Theodore was reconciled to Wilfrid, he sought to place their relationship on the level of father and son, and adopted the younger man as his heir. When Wilfrid had 'children', they were of the highest standing: a king of the West Saxons is described as becoming his obedient son, and towards the end of his life Wilfrid adopted the young king of the Northumbrians as his son. No less distinguished were his friends: a well-placed deacon in Rome and king Dagobert were 'faithful friends', and Theodore became a friend as well. That Wilfrid's values were those of a man of the world made it fitting that nobles sent him their sons for training. Some of these entered the service of God, while others were recommended to the king as armed men. One suspects that no sense of failure was attached to the latter group.[50]

Such currents were widespread in English Christianity. The success of monasteries and convents in obtaining grants of land in perpetuity, a practice that overthrew the traditional way in which families transmitted their wealth, and in recruiting members from the highest levels of society, ensured their success. A convent where nuns passed their time weaving fine clothes, planning to adorn themselves like brides or gain the friendship of strange men was destroyed by fire from heaven; they had been living such evil lives when no less a woman than a sister of king Oswiu was their abbess.[51] Even those parts of the church that had developed under Irish influence were affected. Bishop Cuthbert was a man of the greatest simplicity of life, who undertook long preaching tours in remote areas and became a hermit, growing his own food. But just a decade after his death, the Lindisfarne Gospels were produced in connection with his cult. The community that generated them was one prepared to pour its resources into a project that not only produced something of great beauty, but also allowed its wealth to be displayed. The Gospels have no superior in works produced in the Christian world at the time, but the community that produced them valued treasure far more than Cuthbert had. Doubtless such tendencies partly answered to the rapid progress of Christianity, and while it is true that the scholarly maturity of Bede, almost certainly the grandson of non-Christians, indicates that the English could make the new religion their own with extraordinary speed, it is also true that the faith had to make its way among the newcomers to Britain without the infrastructure already in place elsewhere in the post-Roman west. In this situation, pre-Christian mind-sets could easily linger.

The history of Britain as it moved into the early medieval period was different from that of the other parts of the Roman Empire in the West. To an extent unparalleled elsewhere, the indigenous people failed to transmit the ways of the ancient world to the people who came to settle on their soil. This was in part bound up with developments which, quite independent of any newcomers, were already taking Britain on a distinctive path, and in part the consequence of settlement by newcomers who had been less exposed to Roman ways than many of the groups who settled elsewhere. But it was also the consequence of the kind of interaction that took place between the old residents of Britain and those who joined them. As we shall see, interactions of a similar nature were occurring in other parts of the former Empire.

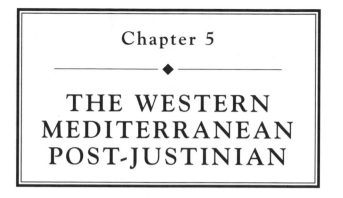

Chapter 5

◆

THE WESTERN MEDITERRANEAN POST-JUSTINIAN

BYZANTIUM AND THE WEST

Seeing as it did the loss of two-thirds of its territory, the fifth century was a disaster for the Empire. Yet it could have been thought that, if losses were going to happen, they occurred where they should have. The borders in the East stood unchanged, excepting only the Balkans, still enclosing the most desirable parts of the old Empire. The East was far more urbanised than the West, containing three of the old Empire's four largest cities; it boasted many free, property-owning farmers; and its intellectual sophistication was evident from both a continuing tradition of philosophical thought and a far greater incidence of Christian heresy than occurred in the West. This area emerged largely unscathed from the turbulence of the fifth century.

This is not to say that it was free of dislocations. As in the West, people from the provinces and non-Romans gained in power. Even in the church, one Fravitta, who shared his name with a famous Gothic general, became patriarch of Constantinople in 489, and the army was full of such people. The emperor Leo I (457–74) was a Bessian from Thrace, while Zeno (474–91), like many of the soldiers of his day, was one of the wild Isaurian people from the south of Asia Minor. When circumstances called for it, Zeno was prepared to describe himself as a barbarian, but a better guide to his aspirations was furnished by his adopting a classical name in place of his rebarbative original one, which was something like 'Tarasiccodissa'. Another prominent general, Aspar, was an Alan who was said to have been asked by the senate to become emperor, an honour that he declined. When disturbances threatened to break out over the possession of the relics of Symeon the Stylite in 459,

Aspar's son sent a detachment of Gothic soldiers to bring the body back to Antioch. Some years later, a patrician with a Germanic name, Dagalaif, took into his home another stylite, Daniel, when a crowd in Constantinople threatened to crush him, and his son married the daughter of an emperor. Basiliscus, who on one occasion made an unsuccessful attempt to take the throne from Zeno, was thought of as a barbarian.[1] But whereas Odovacer's usurpation in Italy, which took place at almost the same time, meant the end of a western emperor till Charlemagne, Basiliscus took the continuation of the imperial office for granted.

So it was that the structures of the East accommodated newcomers. In any case, the influx of such people to high office did not last. In 518 a new emperor, Justin, came to the throne. He too was something of an outsider, having been born near Niš; stories were told that he had walked all the way to Constantinople to join the army. But before long the last great general of Germanic origins had died in suspicious circumstances,[2] and radical developments occurred when Justin was succeeded by his nephew, Justinian (527–65). Within a few years, he and his resourceful wife Theodora were engaged in an unprecedented blitz of activity. A new legal code and ancillary texts were issued, and a vast number of buildings, among them the great cathedral of Constantinople, Hagia Sophia, and innumerable military constructions, were erected. And although Justinian was no more than an armchair general, he presided over some of the greatest military successes in the history of the Empire, which saw the recapture of much of the territory lost during the fifth century.

For people at the time, no less than modern scholars, the loss of the West was a problem needing to be explained. To Justinian and those around him, one reason seemed foremost: the incompetence and laziness of earlier emperors. They thought of the emperor Honorius as having been startled while living at Ravenna by news that Rome had perished, believing it referred to a pet cock by that name, and having been relieved to be told that only the city had been lost.[3] Such idleness and frivolity were displayed in lands about which the easterners were remarkably uninformed. They had no idea of the role that Ravenna had come to play in the governance of the west. Ivory diptychs issued by consuls in both the east and the west depicted the figure of Rome standing on the superior, right of the consul and that of Constantinople to his left, and the elder city remained central to the way people thought. What they thought of as its loss in 476 was something that the easterners took seriously. The chronicler Marcellinus stated the position solemnly:

With this Augustulus perished the Western empire of the Roman people, which the first Augustus, Octavian, began to rule in the seven hundredth and ninth year from the foundation of the city. This occurred in the five hundredth and twenty-second year of the kingdom of the departed emperors, with Gothic kings thereafter holding Rome.[4]

Paradoxically, the deposition of Romulus was seen as a momentous turning-point not by contemporaries in the West, but by people in the East two generations later.

The elites of the west did not only accommodate themselves to the new order. They looked down on easterners, whom they disparagingly termed 'Greeks'. Churchmen often made hostile use of the word. A pope complained to a bishop in Gaul of 'Greeks' expressing a desire for peace with the Roman church with their mouths rather than with sincerity; they spoke of just things rather than doing them, and boasted of wanting to do things which their conduct indicated that they really did not want to do. A collection of papal biographies produced in Rome twice uses the formula 'a report came from Greece' to introduce bad news. The pejorative western usage was picked up by the Greek historian Procopius, who used it to good effect in speeches that he attributed to Goths. He has a Gothic king rebuking the people of Rome for exchanging the rule of the Goths for that of 'Greeks', although the only Greeks they had seen in Italy were actors in tragedies, mimes and thieving sailors, and encouraging his troops before battle with the thought that they only had few enemies, and these Greeks; Gothic commanders represented their opponents as '[Greeks] and unmanly by nature'. Significantly, the word was used of an emperor dispatched from Constantinople to the west in 467, when the eastern emperor appointed a military man, Anthemius, to the office there. The reaction was not positive. A Roman official in Gaul advised the Gothic king Euric against making peace with the 'Greek emperor' and to divide Gaul with the Burgundians, while the general representing Roman power in Italy is said to have styled Anthemius 'the little Greek'. He was murdered in 472. What would occur if the East again sought to intervene in the west?[5]

AFRICA

King Gelimer's deposition of Justinian's friend Hilderic in 530 and his subsequent description of himself as the emperor's equal were not the actions of a wise man.[6] In 532 the emperor concluded a 'perpetual peace' with his most potent enemy, Persia, and while we may mock at the period for which it was expected to run, contemporaries believed it would last.[7] A year later Justinian, against the advice of some of his counsellors, dispatched to Africa an army led by Belisarius, a general of hitherto modest achievements. The campaign was an astonishing success. Having landed unopposed, the force made rapid headway overland towards Carthage. Gelimer fled from a battle fought not far from the city, which Belisarius entered, to dine on food already prepared for the Vandal king. After being put to flight at a second battle, Gelimer took up residence among some Moors; later, he was taken as a captive to Constantinople.

The collapse of the Vandals had been stunning. The booty that Belisarius took back to Constantinople included treasures of the Jews which the emperor Titus had removed from Jerusalem to Rome in the first century and the Vandals had taken to Carthage in 455. The city was speedily renamed Carthago Justiniana, after its new sovereign. A passage in a law published in 534 that Justinian himself may have written provided an impressive context for the victory:

> Through us Africa received its freedom very quickly. It had been held in captivity for 105 years by the Vandals, enemies both of souls and bodies . . . By what work or deeds can I thank God, who through me, the least of his servants, has seen fit to avenge the wrongs done to his church and to pluck the population of such great provinces from the yoke of servitude? My predecessors were not worthy of this: not only were they not allowed to free Africa, but they saw Rome itself captured by the same Vandals.

The wreck off the east coast of Sicily of a ship, apparently on its way to Africa, containing a pre-fabricated church, suggests that necessary goods were dispatched thither. New laws dealt with the return of property occupied by the Vandals, and Justinian's apologists portrayed the opening of a new era. At Caput Vada (Ras Kaboudia), for example:

> The rustics have thrown aside the plough and lead the existence of a community, no longer going the round of country tasks but living a city life. They pass their days in the market-place and hold assemblies to deliberate on questions which concern them; and they traffic with one another, and conduct all the other affairs which pertain to the dignity of a city.

A move of rustics (ἄγρικοι) to the market-place (ἀγορά) is nicely described, but, like the holding of public assemblies at such a late date, it is probably a fantasy. To be sure, such rhetoric occurs elsewhere, but such descriptions probably reflect a lack of first-hand information in the East and resort being made to topoi.[8]

In some ways, the conquest changed little. People with Germanic names remained in Africa; an epitaph of the late sixth or early seventh century records someone who seems to have had both Germanic and Roman names. And expectations of a sunny relationship between Constantinople and the newly conquered Africa would have been misplaced. While Justinian's rhetoric represented Africa as having regained its freedom through his war, and the senate of Rome informed him that Africa had deserved to regain her freedom, the author of a poem honouring Justinian's successor could describe Africa as having become his slave.[9] There was more than one way of looking at the position of Africa, and the resultant tensions were expressed in theology.

In 451, a few months after Attila the Hun encountered forces under Roman and non-Roman command at the battle of the Catalaunian Plains, a council of the church held at Chalcedon, near Constantinople, declared that there were in the one person of Christ two natures, divine and human, 'without confusion, without change, without division, without separation'. Alas, many held that Christ had just one nature, and these people, the Monophysites, were particularly strong in Egypt, the Empire's wealthiest province. Not only were the two positions incompatible, but it is hard to see how they could possibly be reconciled. Attempting to do so, Justinian hit upon the notion of condemning writings of three long-dead theologians which could be held to have overemphasised the distance between Christ's divine and human components, and he extorted assent from most of the patriarchs of the church. Pope Vigilius, who was believed to have owed his office to a deal with Theodora, was unceremoniously arrested and conveyed from Rome to the royal city. There, in 553 a council dutifully condemned the Three Chapters, as they were called, and the prevaricating Vigilius was coerced into accepting its verdict; he was later punningly remembered as not having been very vigilant. The three condemned theologians had never made big waves in the west, and indeed were virtually unknown there until the 560s, when a deacon of Carthage produced a dossier of key documents. But by then a council of African bishops had excommunicated Vigilius, while Justinian deposed the bishop of Carthage who had been consecrated after the defeat of the Vandals and arrested various African bishops. One of them recommended to Justinian that he imitate the humility of an earlier Christian emperor. The military successes of Theodosius I could not be compared to those of Trajan, a son of hell; he had been worthy of true glory by humbly performing penance when castigated by Ambrose. Justinian could not have been expected to concur with this view. A bishop from the north of Gaul told him that all Italy, the whole of Africa, Spain and Gaul wept over him:

'O sweet Justinian of ours, who has so deceived you, who has persuaded you to act in such a way?'[10]

Controversies such as that concerning the Three Chapters can easily take on a disembodied air, and they cannot have been as important to most people as the mass of material that they generated might suggest. Doubtless the impassioned quality of African resistance to Justinian's policies owed something to the long established combative traditions of African Christianity. But, coming as it did so soon after the conquest, it also reflects the uneasy feelings that Africans had about the new regime.

Some of these were due to military problems. Many of Belisarius's troops married Vandal women. Justinian's legislation for the return of property confiscated by the Vandals threatened their interests, and they were easily persuaded to rebel. A more important problem was posed by the Moors, in response to which fortifications were erected that would provide defence in depth rather than straight-line defence. Some of the ruins can still be seen. The town of Thamugadi (the modern Timgad), which Moors had sacked in the late fifth century, was safeguarded by walls over 15 m high. The general who built them, Solomon, was an easterner who had been born near the Persian frontier, typical of the men Justinian appointed to high office in the conquered West. John Troglita, another important general, seems to have been born in Thrace. The Africans cannot have enjoyed being under such foreigners, particularly as they proved unable to deal with the Moors. Other means of dealing with them were tried: in an amazing compromise, coins were minted at Carthage displaying the portrait of Justinian and the monogram of a Moorish leader, Mastinas. Yet in 545 a Moorish advance caused alarm in Carthage itself, and a steady stream of refugees left Africa.[11] Desperate remedies were called for, and by the end of the sixth century the administration of Africa had been placed on a new footing. For centuries the civil and military arms of the Roman state had been independent of each other, but a new office was created, that of exarch, which combined civil and military functions. It was a powerful office; in 610 the son of an exarch of Carthage, Heraclius, sailed to Constantinople and became emperor. In practice, the amalgamation of offices meant that civilian authority was absorbed by that of the army. This foreshadowed both the atrophy of independent civil authority in the early medieval west and a tendency in the Empire where, within a century, generals would command blocks of territory.

More theological controversy arose in the seventh century. Influenced by the patriarch of Constantinople, Heraclius, now emperor (610–41), sought a formula that would satisfy both the adherents of the council of Chalcedon and the Monophysites. He finally settled on the doctrine that Christ had only one will (Monothelitism), which was expressed in the Ekthesis issued in 638. His position may be incompatible with the teaching of Chalcedon: if a will is part of a nature, and Christ has two natures, he must have two wills. Initial responses to the proposal, including that of the pope, were encouraging. But, just as happened with the Three Chapters, the imperial position was strongly opposed in Africa, and this time opposition took on a political colouring. This was connected with the arrival in Africa of one of the greatest theologians in the Orthodox tradition, Maximus the Confessor, who took to campaigning against the Ekthesis and a later edict that forbade discussion of the issues. It is a misfortune of Christian history that during his decades in the west Maximus seems never to have read anything by Augustine of Hippo; the future of Christian thought might have been very different had he done so. In a public debate with Pyrrhus, a former patriarch of Constantinople and a strong advocate of the one-will position, presided over by the governor of Africa, Gregory, Maximus triumphed. That the position of the emperor had been refuted in a meeting he chaired placed Gregory in a difficult position, and in 645 or 646 he proclaimed himself emperor. But while Heraclius had been able to use his position as the son of an exarch as the launching pad for his bid for the purple, Gregory was soon killed by invading Arabs.

Despite the end of Gregory's rebellion, discontent rumbled on. In 649 a council of bishops, mainly Italian and African, was held at the Lateran basilica in Rome, which roundly condemned the doctrinal line taken by the emperor. Much of the work in preparing the texts used by the council was done by Theodore of Tarsus, the later archbishop of Canterbury, who was then living in Rome. The emperor was not pleased, and his anger worsened when troops were unable to arrest pope Martin and their commander rebelled. Only in 653 was Martin successfully arrested and sent to Constantinople, where, accused of treason, he was flogged and exiled; later, people thought of him as a martyr. A similar fate awaited Maximus. In 653 he was taken from Carthage to Constantinople, to be accused of treason. But this time the accusation was not merely on theological grounds, for Maximus was accused of having encouraged a Roman commander not to undertake an expedition against the Saracens, thereby being responsible for the loss of Egypt and Africa to them, and of having had a vision of two groups of angels, one to the east and one to the west. The former cried out 'Constantine augustus, may you conquer!', while the latter uttered the words 'Gregory augustus, may you conquer!', and the voices of those on the west were louder than the voices of those on the east.[12] This was a sinister charge, associating Maximus with the rebellion of a few years earlier. Maximus was sent into exile; in 662, after a second trial, his tongue was pulled out and his right hand amputated, and he was banished to an unutterably remote location in what is now Georgia, where he died in the same year.

Such controversies suggest that the imperial authorities had failed to win the adherence of the Africans. There were good reasons for this. The impact of the Moors on the towns and taxpayers of Africa steadily grew. Moreover, Africa did not know prosperity as part of the Empire. Our evidence here is sketchy and hard to interpret, and special circumstances may lie behind what look like clear-cut patterns in the data. But it is apparent that whatever ground the economy lost in the Vandal period was not regained. While pottery exports were strong for a while after the reintegration of Africa into the Empire, there was little building in the towns. Burials took place within the walls of Carthage, where the apparently random nature of their distribution suggests that they were not confined to special areas. By the end of the sixth century, people were living in the old theatre and circus of what had once been a great city. Indeed, the range of public buildings had been radically reduced in African towns, so that it came to consist of those devoted to the needs of religion or the needs of the state, particularly its military needs. In these respects, despite its incorporation into the Empire, Africa was following a similar pattern to the Germanic states to its north, and becoming steadily less like other parts of the Empire. Indirect evidence is suggestive in this regard. Later, after the Arabs had taken Syria and Egypt, town life there flourished, whereas in Africa even Carthage failed to make a good showing. Indeed, when the Arabs took Carthage, they were surprised at how few people they found in the city.[13] We may deduce that the Arabs may have done no more than administer the *coup de grâce* to African towns that were already in dire straits.

In some ways, Africa remained of solidly Roman inheritance. An epitaph that cannot be dated more closely than the period from the sixth century to the early Arab centuries, which described a girl who died at the age of 12 as 'ripe for a husband, whose full years made her ready for marriage', did no more than quote Vergil.[14] Yet Africa's life in the seventh century was impaired. The great flow of African theological writers, who had dominated the intellectual life of western Christianity since the second century, ended with the generation who opposed Justinian. The great Maximus was a Greek-speaking outsider, and only a few scraps of African Christian writing in Latin can be dated to the seventh century. In intellectual as in economic life, whatever losses Africa sustained under the Vandals were not recouped under the Empire. It would not be well placed to respond to the threat of the Arabs.

ITALY

The misfortune suffered by the Ostrogoths when king Theoderic died without leaving a strong successor in 526 was compounded in the following year, when Justinian ascended to the imperial throne. From the early 530s he issued laws that he expected to apply in Italy, and in 533 he ordered that copies of his legal works were to be placed in the royal cities, presumably Rome and Constantinople.[15] After the lightning swift collapse of the Vandal kingdom, his eyes turned northwards. An agent was installed at Ceuta, on the far west of the African coastline, to keep an eye on developments in 'the parts of Spain, Gaul and the Franks'. But Italy, so close to Africa, was of more immediate concern, and the murder of a Gothic queen in 535 yielded a plausible excuse for intervention there. By the end of the year Sicily was in the hands of Belisarius, who invaded the Italian mainland in 536. Justinian's ambitions swelled. In April 535 he issued a law within which, in a passage so awkwardly worded as to suggest excitement, he envisaged the regaining of territory on a grand scale:

> God has allowed us to make peace with the Persians and to bind fast the Vandals, Alans and Moors and the whole of Africa, and to possess Sicily as well, and to have good hopes that God will grant us possession of the other lands which the Romans of old held as far as the edge of the Ocean on either side, lost through the carelessness of their successors. We, trusting in divine help, hasten to change things for the better.[16]

Early in 537 Rome fell, and a complaisant pope was installed. The Goths asked the Franks for help, although once involved in Italian affairs they proved hard to dislodge, for at the very end of the century they still controlled parts of the diocese of Turin, and an author in Gaul distinguished 'lesser Italy' under the sway of king Theudebert from 'greater Italy' that lay beyond. The Goths were said to have razed the great city of Milan to the ground in 539, but following the capture of their capital, Ravenna, in 540, Belisarius returned to Constantinople, taking with him members of the Gothic elite, who did obeisance to Justinian.[17]

Had the war ended then, the history of Italy would have been very different. But some Goths continued to resist, while the new administration showed itself corrupt and quickly became unpopular. In 541 one Totila became king, and quickly made himself master of most of Italy. Deprived of necessary resources, Justinian's troops found themselves on the defensive, and in the midst of this Italy was struck by the plague. Totila vacillated between acting the emperor, praying at St Peter's church in Rome and presiding over horse races, presumably the last ones held in Rome, and actions of great ruthless-ness.[18] As the situation deteriorated, Justinian appointed as commander a cousin who had married a granddaughter of Theoderic. It was an intelligent choice, but the general died before leaving for Italy, and the task of finishing the war was entrusted to Narses, an Armenian with considerable military experience. He entered Italy at the head of a vast force, which included many non-Roman soldiers, to which it was beyond Totila's power to respond ade-quately. Narses entered Ravenna unopposed, and in the summer of 552 the Gothic army was decisively defeated, Totila being killed while fleeing. It took another decade for the resistance of the Goths to be suppressed, but many of them continued to live peacefully in Italy.

Seen from the east, all had gone well. As early as 540, Justinian was thought of as having recovered for the Roman Empire half of the land and sea, and liberated all the west from being the slaves of the usurpers. At the church of San Vitale in Ravenna, mosaics were installed showing Justinian, in the company of Maximianus, a local man whom he had appointed bishop of Ravenna, and Theodora in solemn processions. The royal couple were shown carrying respectively a paten and chalice for use in the Eucharist, per-haps acting out an offering of liturgical vessels such as Justinian is known to have presented to St Peter's in Rome. Italy, the mosaics suggested, had been reintegrated into the emperor's domain.[19]

Such grandeur could not conceal the massive change that Italy had under-gone. The Pragmatic Sanction issued by Justinian in 554 prescribed that provincial judges who judged wrongly were to make satisfaction from their own resources, anticipating the edict of Paris issued by Lothar in 614, and made popes and the senate responsible for weights and measures, legislation scarcely in accordance with traditional Roman law.[20] Burials within the city of Rome became common, in open defiance of it. The estates that had become so large in late antiquity suffered a savage blow, from which the aristocracy would never recover. The secular literary traditions that found expression under the Goths in a panegyric on Theoderic delivered by Ennodius, who felt that 'rhetoric rules the world', and the immense intellectual achieve-ment of Boethius, effectively ended with the demise of the society that had sustained them. Many of the Italian landowning class had fled to Con-stantinople during the war, and were reluctant to return. The travails of Rome affected the regions whose economies had been orientated towards supplying it with food, such as the Po valley had with grain and the south with pork and lard, and Campania, described as the pantry of Rome in a text of the fourth century.

Moreover, Italy had lost its independence. Formerly the head of the Empire, and after 476 an autonomous unit, it was now controlled by Constantinople. Ravenna became the branch-office of a corporation whose headquarters were a month's journey away, from where its senior officials were appointed. Following his defeat of Totila, Narses enjoyed supreme power in Italy until his death, perhaps in 574, and by the end of the century military men with the office of exarch held sway in Italy, just as they did in Africa. Civil offices that had offered generations the means of advancement and the assertion of status disappeared; as it turned out, the aristocrats of Italy would have done better to seek the control of churches, as had their counterparts in Gaul. Even the appointment of popes was subject to imperial approval. During the period of the Goths, the interregna between popes rarely lasted more than a few weeks. But of the 12 popes who succeeded Vigilius, only two came to office within three months of the death of their predecessors, while four had to wait for over 10 months as imperial consent was obtained. Far from restoring Italy to the position it had enjoyed prior to 476, the imperial conquest imposed a new situation of dependence.

Not surprisingly, the new regime was vastly unpopular. A contemporary account describes the people of Rome informing Justinian and Theodora that, having been subjected to slavery by Narses, they would rather serve the Goths than the Greeks. Just as in Africa, resentment crystallised around opposition to Justinian's attempt to bring peace to the churches by condemning the Three Chapters. When Pelagius, appointed by Justinian to succeed pope Vigilius, arrived in Rome it proved difficult to find bishops prepared to ordain him, and many of the people of Rome withdrew from communion with him. Worse, Pelagius had the embarrassing experience of having to assure a king of the Franks that his theology was sound. Before long many bishops withdrew from communion with the pope, and a schism concerning the Three Chapters sprang up in Italy.[21]

Lombards

If this was not enough, Italy did not enjoy peace for long after the defeat of the Goths. For some time a largely non-Christian people known as Lombards (Latin 'Langobardi', a name thought to have been derived from their 'long beards') had been living along the middle Danube, in the old Roman province of Pannonia, and in 568 their king Alboin led his army and people from there into Italy. Their relocation is hard to explain. Prudence may have led them to move southwards, for, unable to get on with a neighbouring people, the Gepids, they had turned for assistance to a recently arrived nomadic group of mounted warriors, the Avars. The short work that their new allies made of the Gepids may have alarmed the Lombards in turn. But another explanation is possible. Thousands of Lombards had participated in the great expedition that Narses launched against the Goths in 552. Their behaviour on this occasion was not good, their practice of arson and rape being such as to make them roughnecks even by the standard of the troops whom Narses commanded, and they were sent home. But such taste as they acquired for the Italian *dolce vita* may have encouraged them to return, while a tradition of co-operating with the Empire and the difficulties that Narses had in pacifying northern Italy may even have led the authorities to summon them to Italy. In Gaul, their move to Italy was seen as a migration rather than an invasion, and our source closest to the events describes Narses, seeking revenge for complaints that the Romans had made against him to the imperial authorities, inviting the Lombards to come and possess Italy.[22] As so often with incomers to the Empire, it is hard to judge whether the Lombards jumped or were pushed, the extent to which local authorities were attempting to manipulate them for their own purposes, and whether there was a major non-military aspect to their move.

Whatever the reason for their coming, the loss of the Gothic army that had been stationed in the north had rendered Italy vulnerable, and the tardiness of imperial resistance suggests either a lack of resources or a degree of complicity. Milan fell in 569 and Pavia in 572. In the same year Alboin was murdered, whether because of tensions among his people or imperial intrigue. His successor reigned for two years before being murdered by a slave, a common fate among the kings, emperors and caliphs of the period was the same. Thereafter there was no Lombard king for 10 years; perhaps the sad ends of its recent incumbents had made the post less attractive, although it is again possible that imperial agents had successfully plotted to weaken their enemy. While their settlement, like that of the Goths, was strongest in the north, before long the Lombards established strong duchies at Spoleto and the southern town of Benevento. In 582 Naples was besieged; a notary of the cathedral, Peter, took the opportunity to correct a text of extracts from the writings of St Augustine. St Benedict's monastery at Monte Cassino was destroyed, and Lombards were even able to interfere with communications between Rome and Ravenna, the capital of the exarchate. Traditionally, the cities had been linked by the Via Flaminia, which ran northwards from Rome to meet the Adriatic at Fano. But the duchy of Spoleto, and the situation that is indicated by a large early Lombard cemetery near the road at Nocera Umbra, full of men buried with weapons, demanded a change. Traffic came to pass along the more westerly Via Amerina, which proceeded by way of Perugia. The strategic importance of this town, perched on a hill on the right bank of the Tiber, had meant that it was fiercely contested during the Gothic war; Totila had besieged it for seven years. Its new prominence revealed the growing importance of fortified places, and the militarisation of the Italian landscape, some of which was the work of private persons and not the state. Writing of his home town, Squillace, in the sixth century, Cassiodorus had playfully observed that its not having walls meant that it was a town in the country, or a villa in the city; a manuscript of the eighth century, however, shows the monastery he founded there protected by walls with towers.[23]

The seventh century: broad horizons

Gregory I (590–604), one of history's most important popes, lived in a spacious world. We happen to know of the baptism, at Christmas 597, of more than 10,000 English, 'a people placed in a corner of the world', from a letter he wrote to a churchman in Egypt. He exchanged letters with the royal family in Constantinople, where he had lived for some years, the patriarchs of Constantinople, Alexandria, Antioch and Jerusalem, monarchs in Gaul, Spain and Britain, and various people in Africa. He was grateful when a bishop in Egypt sent him a particular kind of drink that he enjoyed, for the product sold by the merchants in Rome under its name was not the real thing, and he reciprocated by sending his colleague supplies of timber.[24] His books had an extraordinary reach. One of them, his *Pastoral Care*, was almost immediately translated into Greek by the patriarch of Antioch; another, a collection of miracle stories known as the *Dialogues*, was drawn on very soon by John Moschus, an easterner then resident in Rome, for his *Spiritual Meadow*; 150 years later it was translated into Greek and 300 years later into English. An Irish monk and a Spanish bishop produced excerpts of his works during the seventh century.

The popes lived in a world still centred on Constantinople. Gregory regarded himself as a loyal son of the Empire, which remained keenly interested in the west. While Gregory was pope, the emperor Maurice drew up a will appointing his elder son lord of Constantinople and the second emperor of Old Rome, although nothing came of the plan. At this time a spell in the royal city as papal ambassador was a desirable item in the curriculum vitae of aspirants for papal office. Yet the agendas of emperors seeking middle ground with the Monophysites of Egypt and Syria were different from those of popes, and the latter had to maintain constant vigilance to ensure that the emperors were not tempted to deviate from sound teaching. Pope Honorius (625–38) let down his guard when he accepted Heraclius's suggestion that Christ had only one will, but the sufferings that pope Martin endured while opposing monothelitism are impressive. By then, it was becoming clear that the seventh century would be the most oriental century in papal history, subsequent to its beginnings. From 642, when Theodore, who had been born in Jerusalem and was the son of an eastern bishop, became pope, there was a run of eastern popes, reflecting the arrival of refugees from the rapidly expanding power of the Arabs and the coming of many Greek speakers to the south of Italy. In 663 the emperor Constans II came to Rome, the first eastern emperor to do so since the fourth century. Contemporaries tried to make sense of this unexpected move by placing it in contexts with which they were familiar, but the successes of the Arabs may furnish the most plausible motive: the possibility of an alliance with the Lombards, securing a reliable grain supply from Sicily, or simply a wish to flee may have prompted his journey.[25] In any case, his entry into Rome recalled that of Theoderic. Six miles outside the city he was met by the pope and clergy, whence he made his way to St Peter's, to pray and make a gift. On Saturday he went to St Mary's, where he made a gift, and on Sunday to St Peter's, with his army. All had candles, and before mass was celebrated he offered on the altar a golden pallium. On the following Saturday he was entertained at the Lateran palace; the next day he returned to St Peter's, and after mass emperor and pope farewelled each other. Constans had stayed in Rome for 12 days. Alas, he helped himself to some of the wealth of the city on leaving. Proceeding to Sicily, he lived there for some years before being murdered by a slave while taking a bath.

The seventh century emerges as a puzzling one in papal history, and a discouraging one for those who believe that people who see more of each other will get on better: although numerous easterners became pope, more often than not relations between Rome and the empire were cool, and popes were increasingly happy to go their own way. A small incident that occurred at the end of the century allows us to see this happening. The emperor Justinian II, perhaps seeking to emulate his great namesake, caused a church council to be held in Constantinople in 692, the council in Trullo. Pope Sergius I (687–701) did not attend, although the archbishop of Ravenna did; the proceedings of the council included a place tactfully left blank for Sergius to sign, but although pressure was brought to bear on him, he refused to put his name to its decrees. Some of these, such as that which sought to mingle the different practices of the churches of Rome and Constantinople concerning marriage among the clergy, would have been unacceptable to him. Another of its decrees, which reflected the changing role of images in Byzantine religious life, forbade the depiction of Christ as a lamb in representations of the biblical scene in which John the Baptist pointed to him, declaring 'Behold the lamb of God, behold him who takes away the sins of the world', as he had been shown, for example, on the great ivory throne of bishop Maximianus of Ravenna. Henceforth, the council decreed, Christ was to be shown in human form. Pope Sergius disapproved, and offered a sly rejoinder, ordering that the words 'Lamb of God, that takest away the sins of the world, have mercy on us' were henceforth to be sung at mass. Doubtless his response was a subtle one, but popes were masters of subtle gestures, and in this way Sergius showed just what he thought of the emperor's council.[26]

The seventh century: reduced circumstances

Meanwhile, the Lombards were settling with some violence into what had been imperial territory in Italy. In Gaul, it was believed they needed an interpreter to communicate with Latin speakers, and some two centuries later it was recorded that they killed many Roman nobles and forced the survivors to pay one third of their 'produce'; indeed, the Lombards were said to have despoiled churches, killed priests, razed cities to the ground, and exterminated the population. Whatever the truth of this, pope Gregory wrote of the devastation they caused and the fear they produced.[27] By whatever mechanism, wealth was redirected towards the newcomers, and Gregory's contemporary king Agilulf (590/1–616) laid the foundations of a Lombard state. Although he did not become a Catholic, he conveyed a respectable late antique style. He had his son Adaloald 'lifted up' to be king in the circus at Milan in 604, a gesture of Germanic origin that had become thoroughly Roman; a few years earlier the Byzantine soldier Phocas seems to have been elevated to the office of emperor in the same way. Something of his ideology is revealed in a depiction of him on a helmet plate.[28] Looking for all the world like a Germanic leader, he is nevertheless seated on a throne, making the gesture of exhortation that emperors made to their troops. An inscription reads 'Victory to our lord king Agilulf'. On each side stands a bodyguard, with lance and shield, flanked by Victories, for centuries familiar figures in Roman art, holding standards bearing the word 'VICTURIA'. Beyond the Victories are two suppliant figures, a clean-shaven one on the king's right and a bearded one on his left, possibly intended to suggest a Roman and a German respectively; if so, the former occupied the position of honour.

Yet Agilulf devoted a good deal of energy to warfare, and, whatever the breadth of his horizons, Gregory had to deal with a grim reality. A tomb of the late sixth century excavated in the western part of Rome contains weapons used by Germanic warriors: was their bearer a Lombard, or an imperial soldier equipped as a German?[29] Gregory wrote of having seen Lombards leading Romans for sale in France as if they were dogs. 'Where is the senate, where is the people?' he once asked. 'There is no senate, the people has perished . . . and Rome burns, empty.' Considering the prophecy 'Where is the dwelling of the lions, and the feeding place of the lion cubs?' (Nahum 2:11), he observed, thinking of Rome's imperial past:

> Are not the lions these commanders and princes who, running across the different provinces of the world, used to snatch their prey with murderous raging? Here the lion cubs found their feeding place, because boys, youths, young men of the world and the sons of men of the world ran about hither and thither, wishing to gain worldly advantage. But now you see it desolate, you see it wasted, you see it oppressed by groans. No one goes to it now to gain worldly advantage; no strong and violent person is left, who might snatch his prey by oppressing others.

In accordance with another prophecy (Mich. 1:16), Gregory held that Rome had become bald, like an eagle that had shed its feathers. It was a neat image, for the eagle had been the standard of the Roman legions. But when Augustine had preached on the sack of Rome in 410, the biblical reference to eagles that came to mind was more positive: whatever happened in the world, people's strength would be renewed, like that of an eagle. Gregory lived in a less buoyant world. Providing for the people of Rome besieged by Lombards, he drew on the resources of the church in Sicily and Gaul, having come, just as emperors had centuries earlier, to preside over a transfer of resources from the country to the people of his city. As for the world beyond Rome:

> Lo, all things in the regions of Europe are given up into the power of barbarians, cities are destroyed, camps overthrown, provinces depopulated, no cultivator inhabits the land, worshippers of idols rage and dominate daily for the slaughter of the faithful.[30]

 But Gregory's words reflect a particular point of crisis, and as the Lombards settled in, they came to terms with the natives of Italy. While king Authari (584–90) had prohibited the baptism of Lombard children as Catholics,[31] Agilulf married a Catholic, and their son Adaloald was baptised into her faith. And although king Rothari (636–52) was an aggressive ruler, Arian by conviction and anti-Byzantine in policy, under whom the last Byzantine possessions in Liguria were conquered, he published the laws of the Lombards in written form. By the end of the century peace had been made with the

Byzantines, and Lombard kings were minting coins, on which the absence of the name of an emperor showed their legal as well as practical independence. These often bore representations of St Michael, to whom the cathedral in Pavia, their capital city, was dedicated. The leaders of the Lombards could have been excused for anticipating a bright future for their state. Yet, the Lombard monarchy did not see out the eighth century.

Regionalism

The coming of the Lombards made the long-foreshadowed political disunity of Italy inescapable. It created Lombard and imperial zones, and pope Gregory did not write to bishops in the former. The political division provided the context for the Three Chapters schism to linger until the end of the seventh century, and texts concerning the council of Chalcedon, the teachings of which Justinian and the papacy had allegedly overthrown in 553, were copied in such Lombard-held towns as Verona. The conquests that had caused Justinian so much trouble had, by the end of the seventh century, been reduced to some territory around Ravenna, the duchy of Rome, two pieces of Calabria in the south, Sicily and Sardinia.

Yet the two parts into which Italy had been divided were not hermetically sealed. The emergence of the powerful dukes of Spoleto and Benevento put a brake on the authority of Lombard kings; the son of a duke of Benevento who made his way to Pavia in 642 did so by way of Ravenna, the Byzantine capital. Neither were the Byzantine lands a tight unit, for within them the popes enjoyed *de facto* independence in Rome, and were beginning to feel their way towards an understanding that they controlled the territories which would later become the papal estates. The Roman church was fortunate in being able to draw on lands it held in regions untouched by war, as was the church of Ravenna, whose holdings in Sicily enabled it to forward foodstuffs, items of clothing, and gold and silver vessels each year to Constantinople as well as Ravenna.[32] But the secular landowning aristocracy was shattered. By the time of Odovacer, it had largely been reduced to living off its estates in Italy. That many of these were concentrated in particular regions made them vulnerable during the Gothic war, while the Pragmatic Sanction suggests that the landowners may have found it difficult to exercise control over their estates. The coming of the Lombards may simply have put an end to their possession of them. Far more than in Gaul, by the end of the sixth century the fate of the class that at its beginning had produced Boethius was utterly grim.

In such circumstances, trade between the regions declined further. To be sure, when pope Gregory sought an image for the sharing of gifts between the saints, he hit upon that of trade: one area has wine and another an abundance of oil, one has a multitude of flocks and another is rich in the fruits of the earth, but they are joined together in exchange.[33] But the image would have occurred far more readily to someone who controlled the far-flung properties of the Roman church than to a scion of a family that used to hold estates, and the scarcity of coins minted in Italy during the seventh century points to local self-sufficiency. Although some coastal areas may have imported more African goods following the imperial conquests of the sixth century, by then inland centres were ceasing to use imported pottery. Some areas sought to fill the gap by producing imitations of African wares, but many people must have found themselves eating from hand-thrown pottery or wooden vessels, and perhaps cooking in stone ware.[34] Such reduced circumstances in material culture are not entirely easy to account for, as the apparent disappearance of the Roman tax system under the Lombards and the weakening of the great estates that *coloni* had worked may have meant that more wealth remained with those who produced it. Nevertheless, inland regions, in particular, were becoming detached from trading networks and thrown back on their own resources.

The operation of such tendencies throughout Italy meant that the Byzantine and Lombard zones had more in common than one may have thought likely. The Lombards minted coins designed to resemble those that the Byzantines minted in Ravenna, and a provision in Rothari's edict that those who minted coins without the approval of the king were to have a hand cut off may have followed a provision in Byzantine law. A legal text produced in Byzantine Italy during the seventh century, the *Summa Perusina*, assumes the Germanic practice of feud; oddly enough Rothari was opposed to it. The Byzantines undertook little building in the parts of Italy they held. The inscriptions that allow us to document the military works undertaken in Africa are almost totally lacking in Italy, and the great churches of Ravenna were begun in the Ostrogothic period; the seventh century was a quiet time for church building in Italy. To judge by the very limited evidence at our disposal, the Lombards failed to collect taxation in any effective manner, and it is clear that their monarchs had less wealth at their disposal than Roman emperors and Ostrogothic kings had enjoyed in Italy.[35] Yet, although the Byzantine authorities in Italy did their best to retain the traditional taxation system, military landowners did their best to evade it, and by the late seventh century the Byzantine army in Italy had come largely to depend directly on the land for its sustenance, just like any other army in western Europe. The future lay not merely with the leaders of armies, but specifically with leaders who could draw wealth from land they owned, and were therefore less responsive to control from the centre.

Ethnicity

That different parts of Italy were moving in the same direction raises the question of the significance of race. As early as the beginning of the fifth century, when slaves mingled with Alaric's forces, such people were throwing in their lot with invading armies, and in the 540s the army of Totila was joined by slaves. Given that the Goths constituted the military arm of Italian society, this was a sign of identification with them, and comports well with Theoderic's observation that the poor Roman imitated the Goth. But identities need not have been clear cut. What are we to make of a woman buried at Ficarolo who, on the basis of the goods with which she was buried, has been identified as a Goth or Gepid who moved to an area around Basel and then, after events that occurred in either 496–7 or 505–6, migrated to Italy? Perhaps it would be simpler to see her as having been someone whose material culture, and possibly ethnic identity, were not firm. This was certainly true of the general Droctulf. Originally from among the Sueves, a people who could be taken as Alamanni, his epitaph punningly alludes to his being a Lombard with a 'long beard' who entered the service of the Empire, in which capacity he destroyed his own people, and was buried as a Catholic in the church of San Vitale near the famous mosaics of Justinian and Theodora.[36]

Two developments were at work. No less than 'Vandal' Africa, 'Lombard' Italy witnessed the folding into the dominant group of non-Romans people hitherto thought of as distinct from it; an impressive tally of peoples reported as arriving in Italy with the Lombards was slimmed down remarkably. But other changes were more important. The habit of people to identify themselves by their clothing makes changes in the dress of women buried at Castel Trosino, in the duchy of Spoleto, revealing. Graves of the late sixth century contain brooches in a style familiar from Pannonia, where the Lombards had lived prior to their coming to Italy. The women buried there had put Roman things to their own use, one being buried with a necklace in which five Byzantine gold solidi were interlaced. But brooches in Roman style occur from the beginning of the following century, and in the last phase of the cemetery, which ceased to be used at about the middle of the seventh century, brooch-pins are found. The disappearance of grave goods in that period may have been connected with a general conversion of the Lombards to Catholicism, another marker of identification with the indigenous population. But it was not merely the case that newcomers moved towards the cultural practices of the indigenes. By the end of the seventh century, people with Roman names were starting to give their children Lombard names. Roman names were best represented among the lowest strata of society, slaves and *coloni* remaining more likely to have Roman than Lombard names.[37] Perhaps Italy had now come to observe the reverse of Theoderic's dictum: whereas poor Romans had previously imitated Goths, wealthy Romans were now imitating Lombards.

Italy may seem to have been reeling under the impact of one disaster after another in the sixth and seventh centuries, and our sources often give the impression that it was full of things best not spoken of.[38] Doubtless many individuals, families and institutions sustained heavy losses. Yet the reasons for change were complex, and the period saw some fruitful beginnings. It will be worth our while to consider the evidence bearing on one of the pillars of life in the ancient world, for which Italy provides plentiful evidence.

Towns

Italy had been highly urbanised in antiquity. Yet before the empire came to an end, a widespread atrophy of towns was under way, the result of a process of general depopulation as well as the movement of their residents into the country. It was also connected with a shift in ideology, amply reflected in Italian evidence. Urban institutions were challenged, as when bishop Epiphanius of Pavia, said to have paradoxically regarded baths as 'friendly towards filthiness', decided against using them, to preserve his inner strength. Negative attitudes were made clear in a mosaic installed in the basilica of Sta Maria Maggiore in Rome during the fifth century, which illustrates the biblical story of the separation of Abraham and Lot. On the left stand Abraham, Sarah and their son Isaac, whose parents extend their hands protectively over his head. On their side of the scene are a house and tree, anticipating the tent and oak in the plains of Mamre, where Abraham and Sarah would later be met by God, mysteriously both three and one. To the right, at the head of a group of people, stand Lot and his wife. Lot gestures towards Sodom, later revealed as a place of debauchery and vice, but his daughters, who subsequently made their father drunk and enticed him to sexual intercourse, are already boldly making their way towards it. The representation of Sodom is the earliest known depiction of a city in Christian art; its connotations could hardly have been more plain.[39]

Urban life was thus precarious before the warfare that ravaged Italy in the sixth century. But fighting did no good. In 592 pope Gregory wrote to the bishop of Velletri, just out of Rome, telling him that his see was to be transferred to a higher place that would be more secure from dangers caused by barbarians. Other towns were in the midst of fields, to judge from the ability of a bishop of Cagliari in Sardinia to plough up someone's harvest before mass, and return to pull out his boundary markers afterwards. But towns remained more important in Italy than elsewhere in the west. Lombard kings, unlike their Frankish contemporaries, resided in a capital, and charters show that landowners often lived in towns, which they clearly did not in France. Moreover, the evidence for urban decay is sometimes ambiguous. Probably before the end of the sixth century, houses built of perishable material, presumably wood, were being erected in a corner of the forum at Luni. Yet wooden dwellings had been erected in the forum of Rome centuries earlier; the emperor Zeno, in prosperous Constantinople, had to deal with the problem of balconies being built of wood; and in any case, business activities were being relocated away from fora in the well-to-do eastern Mediterranean region at just that time. Luni was by no means an economic basket case: Jewish merchants who owned Christian slaves lived there, and a monastery established nearby was well endowed, having a silver paten weighing two pounds and a silver chalice of half a pound. Indeed, during this period, work was undertaken on a large church, decorated with a mosaic containing themes found in African art of the time. The ultimate decline of Luni may have resulted from the demise of nearby marble quarries, which were faced with old spolia being used in new buildings, the declining use of sarcophagi, and perhaps international competition. We have no reason to connect fluctuations in the economy of Luni with its capture by Lombards during the reign of Rothari.[40]

Another example is provided by Aquileia, at the north of the Adriatic Gulf, which was considered the fourth city in Italy in the late fourth century. Seeking to explain the utter obscurity into which it sank, authors later invoked catastrophic explanations: in the sixth century it was thought to have been 'captured, burned and destroyed', perhaps by Attila, while a poet of the ninth century believed that Attila's army of half a million men had destroyed it as punishment for the high living of its people and pride. Formerly a city of nobles, it had become a cave of rustics; formerly full of wonderful homes adorned with marble, it was now measured by the ropes of country people.[41] Such explanations can hardly be taken seriously, for towns could bounce back: sources close to the events describe a terrible fate befalling Milan and its people in 539, yet the heir to the Lombard throne was elevated there in 604; in the same way, the bishop of Aquileia was a figure of sufficient importance to warrant politicking far from the city when an incumbent died early in the sixth century.[42] Aquileia declined because circumstances that made it important ceased to apply. Located at the intersection of four major roads, it had become a crucial base for the defence of Italy at a time when invasions were funnelled through the coastal area between the Adriatic and the Alps. Other towns, which had discharged less impressive functions, declined as the functions they had discharged became irrelevant in a changed world. In any case, in 568 the see of Aquileia was transferred to the nearby town of Grado, where a church dedicated to St Euphemia, the saint to whom the church in which the council of Chalcedon met was dedicated, was handsomely refurbished. A large mosaic was installed, paid for by lay and clerical donors whose names can still be read on an inscription. And against Luni and Aquileia could be set post-Roman success stories, such as Amalfi, first mentioned in a letter of pope Gregory, and Venice itself. The trees used for the earliest wharves of what was to be Italy's greatest trading city were chopped down in the sixth century.

The former capital of the empire, Rome had grown fat on the wealth of the provinces. But by the third century its population was falling. Emperors of the fourth century knew of buildings falling into ruin and being pillaged. Dwellings of the poor were springing up in unexpected places; a law of 399 provided for the savage punishment of those who erected hovels and huts in the Campus Martius, along the old flood-plain of the Tiber:

> If any person should attempt to locate a hovel or a hut in the Campus Martius, we command that, by the decree of the illustrious prefect, he shall be stripped of all his resources and delivered into exile in perpetuity.

Writing in the 530s, Cassiodorus deduced from its infrastructure that Rome had once been far more populous than it was in his day:

> The vast numbers of the Roman people in old times are evidenced by the extensive Provinces from which their food supply was drawn, as well as by the wide circuit of their walls, the massive structure of their amphitheatre, the marvellous bigness of their public baths, and the enormous multitude of mills, which could only have been made for use, not for adornment.[43]

Late in the fifth century, probably during the reign of Odovacer, the Colosseum was repaired, but during the early part of the sixth century part of it was filled with embankments, cemeteries developed round about and it was pillaged for building materials. Worse times were at hand. In the winter of 546–7 Totila, infuriated by the conduct of Justinian, decided to raze the city to the ground. He had already begun to destroy the walls when he received a letter from Belisarius. As presented by Procopius, it offers another assessment of Rome:

> Now among all the cities under the sun Rome is agreed to be the greatest and most noteworthy. For it has not been created by the ability of one man, nor has it attained such greatness and beauty by a power of short duration, but a multitude of monarchs, many companies of the best men, a great lapse of time, and an extraordinary abundance of wealth have availed to bring together in that city all other things that are in the whole world, and skilled workers besides.

Totila, having read the letter several times, was foolish enough to abandon the city, whereupon Belisarius occupied it and began refortifying it. But in the meantime, for 40 days Rome had been inhabited only by wild animals. Some urban amenities continued to be available to its inhabitants, for in a sermon to the Roman people pope Gregory envisaged someone inviting another person to go to the forum or the baths. But the distinction between the city and its rural surrounds was becoming blurred. When it was besieged by Totila a few years after its resettlement, grain was sown in all parts of the city, and Gregory forbade the people to work in the fields at the time of the litanies. The changed circumstances of the city are revealed in a donation that pope Sergius I made to the church of Santa Susanna. He bestowed on it a number of properties, among them some in the city itself, containing gardens and vineyards. By then cultivation within the walls of the old city would have been taken for granted. Just as the distinction between towns where bodies were not allowed to rest and zones beyond the walls in which people could be buried had broken down, so the black earth that archaeologists have discovered within walls of many towns points to an invasion of urban space by the country, the very process described by the poem on Aquileia. By Sergius' time, the inhabitants of Rome would have numbered in the tens of thousands, although whether they were thinly dispersed over a wide area or concentrated in a few areas is unclear. Either way, its aspect would have been overwhelmingly rural.[44]

Rome's status as the home of the papacy made its position secure, but in the early middle ages it was much diminished, and the centrality it came to hold as the see of Peter was very different to that which it had formerly occupied. Yet despite its unique position, some of the changes it underwent were typical of towns in the post-Roman west. The atrophy of towns in the western European part of the Empire was well under way in the imperial period, and the broad changes that diminished their roles as mediators between distant centres, where political power was located and goods produced, and the regions in which they were located, had more impact than whatever the newcomers may have done to them. That contemporaries thought the newcomers were not necessarily implicated in the process is indicated by a prophecy concerning

Rome attributed to St Benedict: it would not be destroyed by barbarians (*gentibus*), but it would fall into ruins because of bad weather and earthquakes. Structural changes would be more important than the arrival of new peoples.[45]

SPAIN

The sixth century

Justinian's ambitions did not stop with Africa and Italy. The conquest of Africa opened the way for a move into Spain, with which it was so closely linked, and, just as he did in Italy and Africa, Justinian exploited tensions within the kingdom. When the leader of a rebellion asked for assistance in 551, troops were sent, and a slice of territory along the south-western coastline was added to the Empire, so isolating the Visigothic State from Africa. It was governed by military officials who, like the new rulers of Italy, tended to come from far away. Comentiolus, who strengthened the defences of Carthagena in about 589, was a Thracian who had already fought Avars and Slavs and was to go on to fight the Persians; for such an officer, a tour of duty in Spain was no more than one assignment among many. The limited conquest allowed people in Constantinople to see Spain as part of a world that the wise emperor had encircled:

> Go now thou Roman traveller, unescorted over the whole continent and leap in triumph . . . Yea, and walk fearless too over the dark lands of the West, and seek the pillars of Heracles; rest unalarmed on the sands of Spain where, above the threshold of the lovely sea, the twin horns of the continents meet and silence one's hope of progress by land.[46]

But most of Spain remained with the Visigoths, and before long they responded. King Leovigild (568–86), an aggressive and successful leader, began pushing back the imperial forces. He also imposed control over dissident Goths, defeated Basques, and overcame the last king of the Suevi, whose territory in Galicia was absorbed into his own. For such a king, a capital city was appropriate, and Leovigild established one at Toledo, a formerly undistinguished town which, as would the later Spanish capital of Madrid, may have owed its rise to its central location. The monarchy adopted a more imperial style. Leovigild was the first Visigothic king to sit on a throne and wear royal garments. He founded a new city near the river Tajo, about 60 km to the east of where Madrid is now located, which he named Recopolis, after his son, Reccared. While the town was small, only measuring 580 by 450 m, it was impressively fortified and boasted a mint, a palace and a basilica. The bestowing of its name was an imperial gesture. A few decades previously Justinian had founded a city in the Balkans named Justiniana Prima, and Huneric, the most imperially minded Vandal king, had renamed the ancient Hadrumentum 'Hunericopolis'. The confidence of the emerging Spain was reflected in a new coinage, which bore full-face portraits of Leovigild, hair falling down to his chin on both sides; the coins they replaced had depicted the emperor, in profile.[47]

Leovigild also sought a *rapprochement* between the Goths and Romans in his kingdom. In about 570 he issued a new law code; its provisions included one allowing Visigothic men to marry Roman women, and Gothic women Roman men. The hierarchy of gender implicit in the order of the terms was to endure, but that of ethnicity was weakening. An army of 400 Goths said to have defeated 40,000 Franks in 593 was led by a learned Roman general, Claudius, while the churchman and chronicler John of Biclaro was Gothic by birth. The legalisation of intermarriage doomed any distinction between Goths and Romans, for how would the offspring of such marriages be classified? Leovigild also made a pronouncement concerning the Trinity: the Son was equal to the Father, and henceforth only the Holy Spirit was to be seen as inferior. Arians sought to pass themselves off as Catholics, such as an envoy of Leovigild who spent Easter at Tours in 584. When the bishop raised the question of his religion, he asserted that he believed what Catholics believed, and went with the bishop to mass. Only when he failed to share in the kiss of peace and take communion did the bishop realise that he had lied when he said that he was a Catholic, and a long debate ensued. Goths and indigenes became more like each other. That nearly half the Catholic bishops of Spain had Germanic names towards the end of the seventh century tells us more about the spread of such names throughout society than the ethnic origins of the episcopate. A collection of slate tablets that date from the time of Reccared until well into the seventh century already contains almost as many names of Germanic as of Latin origin, and suggests a change in personal names similar to that which was occurring in Gaul at the time. By the late sixth century, women who would have passed as Visigoths were being buried with accoutrements of a Mediterranean style. The system of separate laws for Goths and Romans would have been becoming unworkable by the time the *Lex Visigothorum* was promulgated in 654. In Spain as elsewhere, symbiosis occurred.[48]

While the Visigothic monarchy was in theory elective, a strong king could be succeeded by a son, and so it was that in 586 Leovigild was followed on the throne by his younger son Reccared. The new king moved quickly on the religious front. In the following year he became a Catholic, making Arianism a lost cause among the Goths. But the change of religion turned out to be a matter of state as much as of religion.

In 589 Reccared ordered that a synod be held at Toledo, at which he presented a document in his own handwriting rejecting the teachings of Arius and accepting the Catholic faith. Henceforth, he stated, in the liturgy the creed was to be recited before the Lord's Prayer was said and the people took communion, just as happened in the eastern churches. As much of the Nicene creed is explicity anti-Arian, its liturgical use was timely. But its introduction had another aspect. While the practice of reciting the creed during the liturgy was known in Constantinople early in the sixth century, it took place after the reading of the Gospel. It was only transferred before the Lord's Prayer by the emperor Justin II in the first year of his reign (565–78). Oddly enough, our only source for Justin's innovation is a chronicle written by John of Biclaro, a Spaniard who had lived in Constantinople, and it may be that Reccared learned of Justin's innovation and determined to imitate in Spain the conduct of that emperor. John's description of Reccared's synod is interesting. He states that when the king, whom he describes as 'princeps', a title frequently used of emperors, was present at the council, he 'renewed' the old 'princeps' Constantine, who was present at the synod of Nicaea which condemned the Arian heresy, and 'the most christian emperor' Marcian, at whose behest the decrees of the synod of Chalcedon were strengthened. So now, at the insistence of the 'princeps' Reccared, the synod of Toledo had put an end to the long-lived Arian misbelief, cutting it off at the root. In words the bishops used to acclaim him:

> To whom has God conceded eternal merit unless to the truly Catholic king Reccared?
> To whom the eternal crown, unless to the truly orthodox king Reccared? To whom
> present and eternal glory, unless to the true lover of God Reccared? He is the con-
> queror of new peoples for the Catholic church! He truly deserves the reward of an
> apostle who has fulfilled the office of an apostle! [49]

Leadership among the Visigoths had come a long way since their passage across the Danube a little over two centuries previously.

Seventh-century strength

When Isidore of Seville (bishop c.600–36) contemplated the history of the Goths, the picture he painted of Spain's relationship with them was upbeat:

> Rightly did golden Rome, the head of peoples, already lust after you. And although
> that same Romulean strength, at first victorious, went on to wed you to itself, yet

Plate 1

The contrast between a Roman medallion of the fourth century (right), and a representation on a brooch found near the Rhine, illustrates two approaches to the portrayal of the human body. (p. 17)

After Klein-Pfeuffer, M. (1993) *Merowingerzeitliche Fibeln und Anhänger aus Pressblech* (Marburg: Hitzeroth), p. 181.

Plate 2

A villa of the fourth century in a rural setting, depicted in a mosaic at Carthage. Its fortified appearance may have been a matter of style rather than necessity. (p. 24)

Source: Ancient Art & Architecture Collection Ltd.

Plate 3

Theoderic's palace at Ravenna, as represented in a mosaic in the church of Sant'Apollinare Nuovo in the town; the word 'PALATIUM' can be made out. (p. 46)

Source: Ancient Art & Architecture Collection Ltd.

Plate 4
The gold seal ring of King Childeric; the back-to-front words 'CHILDERICI REGIS'
would spell 'of King Childeric' when pressed unto wax. (p. 73)
Source: © Ashmolean Museum Oxford. All rights reserved.

Plate 5
Part of a treasure laid down at Hoxne early in the fifth century. It contained 565 gold
solidi and over 14,000 silver coins, as well as pieces of gold and silver, a sign of the
wealth of Roman Britain and the suddenness of its end. (p. 102)
Source: © British Museum

Plate 6
A diptych showing Rome and Constantinople standing on either side of the last
western consul, Orestes, who held office in 530. At the bottom, slaves pour coins
out of bags in a gesture of *sparsio*, 'scattering'. (p. 126)
Source: © The Board and Trustees of the Victoria & Albert Museum

Plate 7

The emperor Justinian (527–565), shown offering a vessel for the liturgy, with clergy, officials and soldiers, in a mosaic in the church of San Vitale at Ravenna. (p. 134)

Source: Ancient Art & Architecture Collection Ltd.

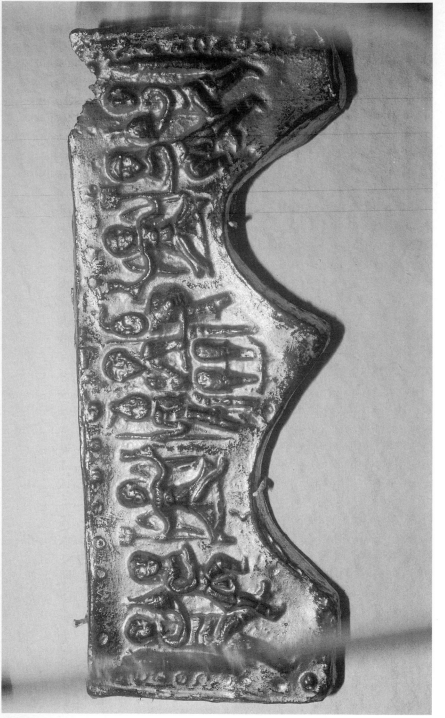

Plate 8
This mysterious artefact has been interpreted as the helmet plate of the Lombard king Agilulf, found near Lucca. (p. 139)
Source: Ancient Art & Architecture Collection Ltd.

Plate 9
A mosaic of the mid-sixth century at Poreč. On the left within the apse the martyr
Maurus, bishop Euphrasius and others are being presented by an angel to Mary and
Jesus. (p. 156)
Source: Scala

Plate 10
St Demetrius, the protector of Thessaloniki, in a mosaic of the
early seventh century. In a gesture of patronage in difficult times,
the saint shows his concern for vulnerable members of the
community. (p. 178)
Source: Sonia Halliday Photographs. Photo by André Held.

Plate 11
The wealth of Syria. This silver patten, diameter 35 cm, showing the communion of
the apostles, was discovered at Riha. It was produced during the reign of the emperor
Justin II (565–578), probably in Constantinople. (p. 188)
Source: © 2001 DUMBARTON OAKS, Trustees for Harvard University,
Washington, D.C.

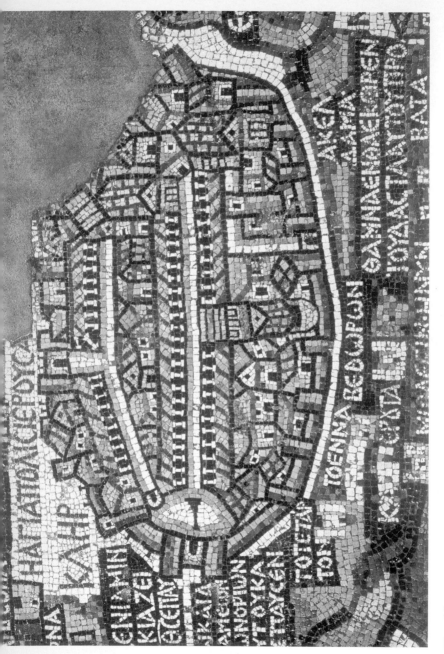

Plate 12

Jerusalem, as shown in a map of the second half of the sixth century in a mosaic on the floor of a church at Madaba in Jordan. The main street can be clearly seen, as can the church of the Holy Sepulchre, upside down halfway along the street. The city is named 'The holy city Jerusalem'. (p. 194)

Source: Ancient Art & Architecture Collection Ltd.

Plate 13
The great mosque of Damascus, early eighth century. That the façade of the exterior
recalls a representation of Theoderic's palace at Ravenna (see Plate 3) suggests a
common source for these post-Roman buildings in areas far apart. (p. 229f)
Source: Ancient Art & Architecture Collection Ltd.

Plate 14

While much restored, the unpeopled landscape on the mosaics of the mosque at Damascus suggests official artistic practice early in the eighth century, and anticipates the future of Islamic art. (p. 230)

Source: Ancient Art & Architecture Collection Ltd.

finally its rival, the most flourishing people of the Goths, after numerous victories in the world, took hold of you and loved you, and still enjoys you amid royal adornments and the abundant treasures of empire, secure in its happiness.

In this powerful passage, in which five verbs sustain a metaphor of sexual and marital relations, Isidore indicates the fittingness of Gothic rule in Spain. Later in the century, the author of a work of history wrote of 'Spaniards' and 'the army of Spain' – terms that point to the degree to which the Goths had become integrated into Spain.[50] Whereas much of Gaul became known as Francia in the post-Roman period, in Spain the Goths seem to have settled comfortably into what was already there. They maintained some Germanic traditions. Wonderful fibulae of eagles suggest their continuance, and cultural complexities are indicated by an extraordinary poem in Latin hexameters which a man wrote to his betrothed early in the seventh century. Having described some good marriages mentioned in the Bible, he lists the gifts he will make to his beautiful beloved, one of which, a generous one, is made in accordance with the old Gothic practice of the 'Morgingeba', the 'morning gift' that a groom paid to his wife after their marriage. Yet the Visigoths lived in a Mediterranean world. Their kings presented votive crowns to the church in accordance with a practice also followed in Constantinople, and in some ways the crowns recall that which Justinian is shown wearing in the mosaic at San Vitale. While the use of chunky stones and gems and the pendants spelling the name of the king in Visigothic crowns may seem to reflect a decadent taste, the patterning of such pieces recalls that found in Byzantine necklaces of the period. The provenance of such artefacts can therefore be obscure; a pair of earrings formerly thought of as Visigothic is now considered to have been made in Constantinople in about 600.[51]

After Justinian's establishment of an enclave in Spain, which endured until the early seventh century, the Spanish could hardly be blamed for displaying lasting hostility to Byzantium. While Gregory of Tours is an early witness to the legend that Constantine was baptised by pope Silvester, Isidore of Seville more accurately recounted his baptism by an Arian bishop, something that he professed caused him grief, and regarded Justinian as having accepted heresy. He pointedly excluded that emperor from a list of lawgivers, Constantinople from a list of churches with patriarchs, and the council of Constantinople convoked by Justinian in 553 from a list of chief synods. The Spanish church, no less than much of the church in Italy, proved extraordinarily reluctant to accept Justinian's council. A council of Spanish bishops meeting at Toledo in 681 gave its assent to five preceding universal synods, but the list excluded Justinian's council, unlike a council that Theodore, the archbishop of Canterbury, had presided over a few years earlier, which explicitly accepted it. In 682 pope Leo II wrote to the bishops of Spain describing a council of 680–1 as the sixth in the sequence of universal councils, and he wrote to a layman in the same vein. But in 684 another council at Toledo reasserted that the recent council was fifth in the sequence, and placed it immediately after the council of Chalcedon in 451. Such defiance of papal wishes indicates both independence from Rome and lingering animosity towards Justinian.[52]

It was in the context of having something to define itself against that Visigothic monarchy developed into a formidable institution. Increasingly, power was exercised from Toledo, which grew to become the headquarters of the most powerful government in Europe, where 18 church councils were held from 589 to 694. In this respect it emulated the role that Constantinople played in the Empire from the fifth century onwards. From 653 the councils were usually held in the royal church of SS Peter and Paul, a dedication that recalled the basilica Constantine had erected in honour of the Holy Apostles and its western imitations; their minutes were signed by royal officials. The stature of the capital city was evident in the role it came to occupy in intellectual life. Spain was the success story of western letters in the seventh century, comfortably filling the position that Africa vacated. At the beginning of the seventh century, the centre of gravity still lay in the old Roman towns, particularly Seville, where the remarkable Isidore wrote the great book of the century, the *Etymologies*, an encyclopedia that usually explains the meanings of words by providing them with etymologies. These are often false, but readers of this book are unfailingly impressed with the width of Isidore's knowledge. But king Sisebut (612–20) wrote Latin poetry in hexameters, and under a series of impressive bishops the church of Toledo came to a position of effortless superiority during the second half of the century. Bishop Eugenius was a poet, who edited and extended works of Dracontius, an African poet of the late fifth century; his successor, Ildefonsus, a keen devotee of the Blessed Virgin Mary, wrote defending her perpetual virginity; while the following bishop, Julian, who was capable of exchanging cool letters with the pope on doctrinal matters, wrote a variety of works, among them pieces for the liturgy. By the end of the century, Toledo was the intellectual leader of the Latin-speaking world. Ildephonsus wrote a book about 14 recent illustrious men: 12 were Spanish, and of these seven were bishops of Toledo.

Inevitably, such a concentration of power marginalised outsiders. The bad turn that relations between Jews and Christians were later to take can blind us to the strength and attractiveness of Judaism in late antiquity. Early in the seventh century, a bishop of Toledo found it necessary to excommunicate a count for his Jewish sympathies. But soon after becoming king, Sisebut sought to coerce the Jews of his kingdom into accepting baptism. Such fervour caused churchmen to raise their eyebrows. Isidore of Seville felt that the king had compelled them not according to knowledge but by power, but consoled himself with the thought that Christ had been announced, whether by convenience or in truth. Legislation by later kings prohibited the observance of the Passover and the Sabbath and the practice of circumcision. Finally, in 694, king Eciga ordered the enslavement of all the Jews in Spain. The need to reiterate laws frequently shows that the attempt to wipe out Judaism failed, while such success as the legislation enjoyed created a new problem, for no one could be certain that baptised Jews had sincerely accepted Christianity, and their behaviour could only be policed with difficulty; members of the clergy had to be forbidden to supervise converted women during Jewish festivals, because such supervision all too easily became an occasion for lust.

While the official attitude of the Christian church to Judaism was rarely friendly, the savagery of Visigothic legislation is unprecedented over the centuries that had passed since Christianity began to influence Roman law in the early fourth century. There is no reason to believe that economic considerations prompted it. Rather, the centrality of the Catholic religion to the high degree of unity that Visigothic Spain saw itself as possessing made the Jews an awkward anomaly. Theoderic the Ostrogoth had taken a benign attitude towards the Jews of Italy, holding that they could not be ordered to adhere to a new faith, since people could not be forced to believe against their will, and ordered the Roman population of Ravenna to pay for the rebuilding of synagogues burned down in the course of riots. But he had been a non-Catholic, the member of another religious minority, and may have thought it wise for minorities to hang together.[53] When the political and religious arms of society coalesced in Spain, the way was open for policies of a very different kind. Moreover, as we shall see, the policies of the Visigoths developed during a century decisive in relations between the adherents of monotheistic faiths.

Such developments were the product of the strength projected by the state. But in some ways this was a façade. As elsewhere in Europe, people were orientating themselves locally. Although the wealthy had access to a variety of costly imported items, regions were increasingly coming to depend on what they produced. The slate tablets mentioned above suggest an economy regionally self-sufficient, indicating as they do areas in which grains, especially wheat and barley, were grown, together with vines and olives, and cattle were raised. Much of the minting that occurred may have been the fruit of local initiative. The persistent repetition of laws against Jews indicates their ineffectiveness, and measures taken to prevent people from supporting them provides heartening evidence that they were sometimes disregarded. One of the last kings issued a law allowing judges to settle some cases by ordeal.[54] And while Catholicism was a powerful unifying tool, the last church council held in Visigothic Spain found it necessary to deal with bishops who celebrated requiem masses for people still alive, hoping thereby to cause their deaths. This suggests not so much the corruption of Christianity as its failure ever to take deep root.

Moreover, even the sources of royal strength could be double-edged. King Wamba (672–80) is the first king in European history known to have been anointed. Julian of Toledo described the background to his elevation: he was the person 'whom the Lord desired to be *princeps*, whom priestly anointing disclosed, whom the community of the whole people and the native land [*patria*] elected'. Wamba's array of supporters was certainly impressive, and the ceremony of anointing to which Julian alludes was doubtless solemn, but it made king-making less dependent on the will of the army and more on that of churchmen. Wamba was a monarch capable of powerful gestures. At the beginning of his reign he put down a rebellion that sprang up in the territory the Goths still held in the south of Gaul, testimony to the practical weakness of central authority. The ringleaders, their heads and beards shaven, shoeless and wearing filthy clothes, were placed in vehicles drawn by camels which conveyed them for the last four miles into Toledo, and the person who had fomented the trouble was mockingly crowned with a fish bone. Such treatment may seem extreme, although it was widespread in Christian states during the period. Yet Wamba's power was not secure. His anointing had been in accordance with biblical precedent, the prophet Samuel having anointed Saul to be the first king of the chosen people. But while Saul was still alive, Samuel anointed David to the same office, and precedent was followed in this regard as well. In 680 Wamba mysteriously fell unconscious, in which state he was tonsured and clothed in a monastic habit. Reviving to discover he had become a monk, all he could do was nominate his successor, Erwig, and spend his remaining years in a monastery; it may well be that the very clergy who had made him king were later responsible for his being deposed. The beginning and the end of Wamba's reign showed the gap that existed between the ideology of Visigothic monarchy and its practical reach. Such a state would find it difficult to deal with an invasion.[55]

The lands of the old empire around the western Mediterranean had turned into politically independent regions that were themselves unstable. The regime in Carthage controlled a diminishing portion of Africa, Italy splintered into Lombard and Byzantine zones, neither of them particularly cohesive, and while Spain remained a unit, the impression of strength that its monarchs gave was illusory. Not only were political units becoming smaller, but different regions were becoming more economically self-sufficient and generating their own cultural life more than had been the case in 400. But other routes away from the Roman Empire were possible, to which we shall now turn.

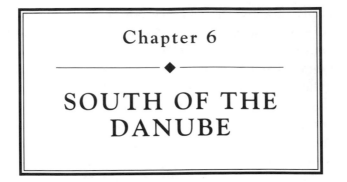

Chapter 6

SOUTH OF THE DANUBE

At about the middle of the sixth century, the church of Parentium, the modern Poreč on the Adriatic coast of Croatia, was governed by bishop Euphrasius. He was heartily disliked by the pope of the time, Pelagius, who knew of him as an adherent of the Three Chapters schism and as someone guilty of both homicide and incestuous adultery. But like many churchmen of his time, Euphrasius was a builder, and he undertook the rebuilding of a major ecclesiastical complex. In some ways, his undertaking was decidedly provincial. The episcopal throne in which he sat was far more modest than that of Maximianus in Ravenna, and the Latin used in a dedicatory inscription is that of the contemporary spoken language rather than the correct written language usually found in such contexts.[1] Yet Euphrasius' aspirations transcended the provincial. In the apse of the basilica he installed a mosaic that can still be seen. In its centre is the seated figure of Mary, with Jesus in her lap, to whose right (that is, to the left of someone viewing the scene) stands an angel who is presenting to them four people, standing in a line. The first is a figure about whom scarcely anything is known, Maurus, who holds a martyr's crown. He is followed by Euphrasius himself, bearing a model of the church for which he was responsible, and the archdeacon Claudius, who carries a gospel book, brings up the rear; between Euphrasius and Claudius is the tiny figure of a boy carrying candles. An angel presents them to Mary and her Son, just as another presents to them a group of unnamed people to their left.

At almost exactly the same time as work was proceeding at Parentium, less than 200 km away across the Adriatic, bishop Maximianus was involved in a mosaic placed in the apse of the church of San Vitale at Ravenna. It shows a seated figure of Christ, who presents a crown to the martyr Vitale, standing to his right, while bishop Ecclesius, who holds a model of the church, stands on the other side, each of them being presented to Christ by an angel in the guise of a court official.[2] While the mosaic at Ravenna is more delicate than that at Parentium, their similarities indicate that both towns remained part of a Christian, Mediterranean world well into the sixth century. In 700, both were still part of the Empire, but by then they were only parts of a series of isolated coastal settlements holding out against encroachments. We have seen how the Lombards gained a hold in northern Italy; by the end of the seventh century, Byzantine power in what we now call the Balkans had been even more reduced, till only a series of small enclaves along the coasts of the Adriatic, the Aegean and the extreme south-west of the Black Sea remained part of the Empire. This transformation, far more radical than that which took place in Italy, will be the subject of this chapter.

The lands that the Romans won in the Balkans were shaped like a triangle, the sides of which were the mighty river Danube in the north, the Adriatic Sea looking towards Italy in the west, and the Aegean Sea and part of the Black Sea in the east. The terrain tended to be hilly, heavily wooded and vulnerable, for the mountain chains other than the Balkan Mountains (Stara Planina) and Rhodopes, the rivers that flowed into the Danube or the Mediterranean and some of the most important roads ran north–south, giving easy access to invaders from across the Danube. In various ways the area was divided along east–west lines in Roman times. For administrative purposes, a western part came to be subject to the praetorian prefect of Italy and a more eastern part to the praetorian prefect of Illyricum, based in Sirmium, and so part of the eastern Empire; some of it was ruled from Constantinople. The Balkans were also linguistically divided. In the west, most people spoke Latin, as they did north of the Balkan Mountains, and during the second and third centuries the language may even have extended its sway across the Danube to include Dacia. Nevertheless, just as occurred in Britain, languages that had been spoken before the Romans came survived; it is possible that the modern Albanian language is the direct descendant of such a tongue. In the east, which included Greece itself, Greek retained the position it had long held, although here too other languages continued to be spoken. Another division between west and east in the Balkans was ecclesiastical, for the churches in the west looked for leadership to the bishop of Rome, while those in the east turned to Constantinople, although in this respect the dividing line was further to the east. But despite their importance, such fault-lines were not the most significant in the Balkans. There, no less than in Gaul, the most important distinction was between the territory near the Mediterranean and the less-Romanized lands that lay towards the northern edge of the Empire.

Home to the olive tree and the vine, the south and the coastal areas enjoyed a Mediterranean climate. Heavily urbanised and long integrated into the wider world of the Mediterranean, they came under Roman power early. Macedonia became a Roman province in the second century BC, and part of the region was allotted to Caesar in 59 BC. By the sea stood major cities, such as Thessaloniki and Athens. The former was a centre of administration, but in late antiquity the latter city, like so many in Europe, was much diminished from its glory days. Watermills were operating in the agora, and in about 530 the last great building to be constructed there, the so-called Palace of the Giants that had been erected at the beginning of the fourth century, was abandoned.[3] Nevertheless, in late antiquity Athens became a centre of lively philosophical thinking, as the 'Neoplatonists' who taught there developed a system of thought based on that of the great Plato. One of the most important Roman roads, the Via Egnatia, ran westwards from Constantinople through Thessaloniki to the port of Dyrrachium (the modern Durazzo), from which Italy was easily accessible. But it is significant that the main road running east–west was located in the south. Life in the north was different.

The Romans arrived later there, it being only during the reign of the emperor Augustus that they were able to consolidate their hold along the south bank of the Danube. From the early second century, when the emperor Trajan succeeded in building a bridge across the river, they held a block of territory on the other side, but in the 270s this was abandoned, and the river, along which fleets were maintained, thereafter served as the border. Some urbanisation occurred in the north, where the city of Nikopolis, its streets laid out in accordance with Roman principles of town planning, was founded, probably by Trajan in 110, but such developments were largely the result of the Roman military presence. The northern lands were marginal to the empire. Their economic contribution was modest, as was shown when Constantinople became a great city and the grain that fed its people had to be imported from Egypt rather than the Balkans, despite their being much closer to hand. Intellectuals treated the region with disinterest, and the inhabitants of Pannonia, to the south of the middle Danube, were looked down on as people who grew no olives and only a small amount of poor wine.[4] Ethnically distinct groups readily maintained their identities in the north. The medieval Vlachs, speakers of a Romance tongue whose transhumant ways were to cause trouble for the Byzantines in later centuries, were descended from autochthonous inhabitants of the Balkans. And the Danube frontier, no more than that along the Rhine, did not demarcate utterly dissimilar zones. As we have seen, the Černjachov culture which developed, possibly under Gothic auspices, to the north of the river was influenced by Roman ways, while in the early fourth century some Goths were settled near Nikopolis. Influences flowed across the river in both directions.

All these lands were destined to know turmoil during the post-Roman period. Some of this was of no lasting significance, but by 700 structures were emerging amid the turbulence which would have lasting importance.

THE FIFTH CENTURY

The late fourth and fifth centuries were a difficult period in the Balkans. The defeat of the Romans at the battle of Adrianople in 378 opened the way for the later activities of the Gothic general Alaric. In turn a servant of the Empire, as when he contributed to the victory of Theodosius I in Italy in 394, and its enemy, as when he ravaged lands in the Balkans immediately thereafter and sacked Rome in 410, his career remained chequered until he died, shortly after the sack of Rome. The Balkans were left in an uneasy situation. In 412 measures were taken to build walls, and when Paulinus of Pella went to Greece in the early fifth century, he found that the estates of his family had been wasted both by 'barbarians', who pillaged in accordance with the laws of war, and by Romans, who acted wrongly and against all laws, implying that the former posed the lesser threat to his property.[5]

More lasting damage was done by the Huns. Their sudden coming remains mysterious. Mounted horsemen who had caused dread among the Goths, they invaded imperial territory early in the fifth century, but their impact was felt most strongly when their great leader Attila, perhaps profiting from the weakening of Roman influence, made himself master of a block of territory that briefly extended from the Ukraine to the Rhine. Towards the middle of the century he occupied Pannonia, pocketed large sums of tribute and raided as far south as Thermopylae, the pass controlling access to southern Greece which a heroic Spartan force had failed to hold against invading Persians just under a millennium earlier. Among the cities he sacked was Sirmium on the river Sava, one of the empire's great frontier cities. It was of military significance, for emperors had resided there and it had possessed an arms factory and a woollen mill. But after Attila struck (440–1) it was only intermittently part of the empire. Nikopolis was destroyed. A few years later it was reoccupied, a bishop had taken up residence, and its walls were rebuilt, but the area within them was scarcely a quarter of that which the old walls had enclosed, and much of the diminished interior was not built on. It was a sign of the times that a settlement established 18 km away at Veliko Turnovo was on a hill, where defence would be easier. Singidunum, the modern Belgrade, was sacked, as was Serdica, the modern Sophia in Bulgaria, although in 469 an emperor was able to take refuge from a usurper in the latter. In 441 Attila attacked Niš with sophisticated siege engines, among them the battering rams that were responsible for the fall of the city; by 448 it lay in ruins.

Such events may give the impression of wanton and aimless destruction. But Attila had been exploiting a window of opportunity. Not only was Roman administration in the West increasingly feeble as the century progressed, but for a time the East was overextended. It mounted costly expeditions against the Vandals, which failed. Other endeavours, however, were successful, for during the middle years of the century imperial forces defeated Arabs, Isaurians and Nubians, and the last years of Attila were overshadowed by the reviving power of the Empire. In any case, Attila had never been bent on destroying the Empire; rather, the operation he mounted depended for its continuing success upon its ability to pay him subsidies, the force of arms being simply the means that allowed him to operate a very successful protection racket. During the 440s he obtained from Constantinople some 13,000 lb in gold. By the standards of the Huns, it was an extraordinarily large sum, and the sudden influx of wealth into their society is readily observable in the archaeological record of the region. But for the Empire, it was little more than small change. When the emperor Marcian died in 457, he was said to have left hundreds of thousands of pounds of gold in the treasury, of which 65,000 were spent on a single expedition against the Vandals.[6] The transfer of wealth to the Huns meant far more to them than it did to the Empire. Moreover, the Huns were not as bad as we might think. From the 420s a 'fashion of the Danube' was spread from the Atlantic to the Caucasus, answering not to the presence of Huns but to their prestige far and wide. A historian who participated in an embassy from Constantinople to the court of Attila was surprised when a man, wearing the clothes of a Hun and sporting a Hunnish haircut, addressed him with the Greek word *chaire*, the very word that the poet Meleager had employed to address those who read his epitaph in Greek. He thought the man was a Hun, but in conversation learned that he was a Greek who, having been captured by Huns, went on to fight for them, was freed and married a Hunnish woman, who became the mother of his children. The two men enjoyed a lengthy discussion on the respective merits of Roman and Hunnish society.[7] As so often in these centuries, one is struck by an apparently ambiguous case of identity.

Attila caused devastation in the Balkans on an unprecedented scale, with which it is plausible to associate the disappearance in the region of villas, which had outlasted most of those in what had been the western provinces of the Empire. Despite this impact, Attila's death in 453, which came shortly after he made unsuccessful attempts to extract wealth from the West, meant the end of Hunnish power. No longer able to extract wealth from the Empire, his sons could not maintain their father's authority, and in 469 the head of one of them was taken to Constantinople, to be paraded and fixed on a pole. By then, Germanic peoples who had been subordinate to the Huns had freed themselves from their sway. Two of them, the Gepids and the Ostrogoths, were played off against each other by the authorities in Constantinople; it is striking that, in the decades immediately prior to the establishment of his much-praised administration in Italy, Theoderic the Ostrogoth acted in much the same way as Alaric and Attila had. Sometimes he intervened to support various players in imperial politics, and sometimes he attacked important towns. In 487 he led an army to the walls of Constantinople itself, from which it had to be paid to depart. Indeed, so vulnerable were the outskirts of the royal city that a Long Wall had been built some 65 km to its west, to provide an outer defence. Less imposing than the original walls of the city, it was nevertheless a serious piece of defensive architecture, surviving portions of it being over 3 m thick and up to 5 m high.

Some troubles continued after Theoderic departed for Italy in the year after his foray against Constantinople. Early in the sixth century, another general who may have been of Gothic ancestry, Vitalian, launched several attacks against Constantinople at the head of imperial troops. He was supported by many farmers, so that when he marched on Constantinople in 513 he was said to have been accompanied by 50,000 soldiers and country men. But he was murdered, almost certainly on the orders of the already powerful Justinian, in 520. By the time Justinian came to power in his own right in 527, although Sirmium was in the hands of the Ostrogoths, Thrace had been troubled by Bulgars and another attacking force had reached as far as Thermopylae, the eastern parts of the Balkans were more peaceful than they had been since the fourth century.

THE LOSS OF NORICUM

Conditions were worse to the west. A vivid account of the last period of Roman rule in Noricum Ripense, an area to the south of the Danube which lay to the west of Pannonia, is given in the *Life* of a monk, Severin, which

Eugippius, the abbot of a monastery near Naples, wrote early in the sixth century, and it will be worth our while looking at it in some detail.[8]

Eugippius's text represents Noricum as distinctly a backwoods kind of place. Non-Christian religious practices were still followed there, and oil, so important in Mediterranean life, was hard to obtain. We hear of a church built of wood. The economy he describes was one in which some exchanges took place in kind, rather than being facilitated by money. This semi-civilised area was subject to attacks by 'barbarians', specifically Rugians, a Germanic people who, having become active in their own right after the death of Attila, were ravaging towns and enslaving the local people. Yet, as so often occurs in narrative texts written in this period, the work of Eugippius contains pointers to a more benign interpretation of these events. He describes his hero Severin as enjoying good relations with a number of rulers, among them Odovacer who, having received his blessing, remembered him kindly when he went on to become king in Italy. One of the members of Severin's monastic community was described as a barbarian. Such people and Romans frequented each other's markets, and in the latter one could pick up the most unexpected items. Who would have thought that relics of the Milanese martyrs Gervasius and Protasius were to be had at one of them?

Severin died in 482, and a few years later Odovacer, by then the ruler of Italy, decided that the region was not worth defending. According to Eugippius's report, Severin had used biblical imagery to predict what would take place:

> as the sons of Israel were rescued from the land of Egypt so all the people of this land will surely be freed from the unjust rule of the barbarians. They all, with their property, will leave these towns and go to the Roman province without falling into captivity.

Just as Bede would, Severin is represented as using the biblical image of the chosen people. But whereas the English author appropriated it as a remarkably positive way of describing newcomers, Eugippius describes an Exodus undertaken by a wretched group of refugees. Before he died, Severin predicted that 'all the peoples of the land would be freed, and that all would go forth from their towns', and a few years later the order came from Odovacer that all the 'Romans' were to migrate to Italy.[9] Such language is puzzling. Elsewhere, Eugippius uses the word 'Romans' of townspeople and defending troops, and his apparent assimilation of Romans and town dwellers is symptomatic of this attitude. His view of Roman society in Noricum is restricted to the people who lived in towns, and while towns had been the centres from which Roman influences were diffused, some Romanised inhabitants of Noricum must have stayed behind.

Indeed, other evidence points to continuity after the evacuation of the so-called Romans. People identified by the geographical term 'Noricans' rather than by the name of a people are said to have participated in the Lombard invasion of Italy. The name of the town Lauriacum, which the *Life* of Severin suggests received migrants from the surrounding countryside, was retained, to evolve into the modern Lorsch in Austria. There is also archaeological evidence for continuity of both settlement and Christian practice. Moreover, some philologists hold that the Bavarian tongue that came to be spoken in the region of Noricum after the arrival of another Germanic group is not a pure Germanic dialect but a creole, based on a fusion between the speech of the Alamanni and a form of Romance speech. If this were so, the Bavarian speech, and perhaps the Bavarian people, would almost certainly have been the result of intermarriage between speakers of Romance and Germanic languages. The offspring of such marriages would have learned, as their first language, the pidgin in which their parents, speakers of mutually incomprehensible languages, communicated. As the creole developed its own structures, quite possibly over a very short period, the new language of Bavarian, which later became a dialect of German, would have taken form. Seen in this light, the evacuation of the 'Romans' from Noricum would have involved the withdrawal of the army and the emigration of urban elites, who left behind a partially Romanised population to carry on without the structures of the Empire. Their position would have been similar to that of the Britons earlier in the century. A few decades after the withdrawal, Theoderic the Ostrogoth wrote a letter concerning an exchange of cattle between the people of the province of Noricum and the Alemanni. Unusually in his correspondence, the letter is not addressed to an official who would have seen to the business, but merely to 'the provincials of Noricum', just as the emperor Honorius had written to the cities of Britain a century earlier without naming officials.[10] In both cases, the Romans had pulled out, leaving the local populace to shift for itself as best it could.

JUSTINIAN

Such losses, occurring as they did in an inland area of what had formerly been the western part of the Empire, were not a matter of concern in Constantinople. When Justinian became emperor, the lands south of the Danube seemed in better shape than they had for a long time. The days of the great Germanic and Hunnish commanders of the fifth century had passed, and despite their ravages most of the lands remained under imperial control. When, in about 554, the historian Procopius came to write his *Buildings*, he seems to have thought of imperial territory as extending along the Danube as far west as its junction with the Sava, where Singidunum was located. The city was, he says, restored and fortified by Justinian.[11] Indeed, that emperor, never one to rest, quickly began to strengthen the Empire's position in the Balkans in a variety of ways.

One of his methods was a thorough overhaul of defences. Earlier emperors, especially Diocletian (284–305), had developed a strong system of defences, but Anastasius and more particularly Justinian strengthened the network considerably. Procopius was able to list some 600 fortresses that Justinian had erected or restored in the Balkans.[12] The data are suspect, for Procopius is generous in his attribution of works to this emperor, and credited him with some works for which preceding emperors were responsible. But it is clear that a strong system of fortresses was established. Some were located along the Danube downstream from Singidunum, while others were erected to the south of the river, some of them apparently intended as places of refuge. Natural defences were strengthened. In Greece, walls were erected at Thermopylae which would deny enemies easy access to land beyond. Any who were able to breach this defence would encounter, further to the south, a wall built across the isthmus of Corinth, which sealed off the Peloponnesos. Elsewhere, a high wall protected by a moat was erected which blocked access to the isthmus of Gallipoli, where stores were built to hold grain and wine. City after city, among them Serdica, had its walls strengthened. Another way of providing for defence was to transfer settlements to more secure places, just as was happening in parts of the west. Among these was the town of Diocletianopolis, later known as Kastoria. Lying as it did by a lake, it was exposed, but Justinian moved it to a high hill surrounded by the lake, except for one narrow approach.

Some of these works were undertaken a long way to the south of the frontier, but it does not follow that a tacit decision had been made to abandon the Danube region; rather, because it was impossible to police so long a river border, it was sensible to provide defences at points that could be expected to tempt enemies who crossed the river. Moreover, Justinian's strategy was based on a principle widely used by the Empire in the period, for at just the same time his commanders in the newly conquered Africa were seeking to provide defence in depth, and a similar policy was being followed in the east as well. In general terms, the wall across the isthmus of Corinth recalled the

strategy that informed the building of Hadrian's Wall, that of fortifying a narrow stretch of land so as to deny entry to a much broader area. But whereas
Hadrian had built his wall on the windswept, northernmost edge of the
Empire, the isthmus of Corinth was between two inlets of the Mediterranean. So it was that the policy of defence in depth overthrew earlier ways
of doing things. One of Justinian's architects, Victorinos, was responsible
for a series of fortifications in various parts of the Balkans. That three of
them were at Byllis, in the coastal area of the modern Albania, is clear evidence for the strategy of defending locations far from the frontier.[13]

The most significant of all the sites developed by Justinian was one named
after him, Justiniana Prima, which has been identified with Caričin Grad,
54 km south of Niš. Built in the mid-sixth century near the place where the
emperor had been born, it was called 'prima', 'the first', to distinguish it from
a nearby town that was also named in honour of the emperor. When Procopius
described the new city, it was in terms no less formulaic than those he used
to describe Caput Vada following the conquest of Africa, but archaeologists
have found few traces of the great stoas, fine market-places, fountains, streets
and baths with which he credits Justiniana Prima. Rather than calling to mind
an ancient city, Justinian's small foundation on its elevated position would have
resembled Recopolis, which the Visigoths were to found in Spain a few decades
later. And although Justiniana Prima had few of the appurtenances of a classical
city, its agora being little more than a space where roads intersected and devoid
of the monumental buildings that would have surrounded the agora of a
major classical town, it was richly endowed with churches. In 535 Justinian
made the bishop of the new city a metropolitan and archbishop, dignities he
soon lost in the face of papal complaints. In another confident gesture, the
headquarters of the praetorian prefect of Illyricum were relocated from the
coastal city of Thessaloniki, to which they had been moved in the fifth century, to the new inland town. Justinian intended his foundation to be a centre
of both civil and ecclesiastical authority. But the town was poorly located on
a hitherto unoccupied site that was distant from major rivers and roads.
Large, locally made ceramic vessels were commonly used by its inhabitants to
hold supplies of food, but few of the amphorae that were used to transport
goods over long distances were to be found in the town. Whatever administrative importance Justinian expected the town to have, Justiniana Prima was
an extreme example of a town that would have to rely on local resources, during a period when regions were increasingly turning in on themselves.[14]

Justinian adopted another strategy, a standard one in the repertoire of
Roman emperors, in persistently seeking to play one group of enemies off

against another. In 528 Grepes, king of the Heruls, a minor Germanic people, was baptised and promised to support the empire, for, just as it did in England, the reception of Christianity from a major power conveyed an expectation of alliance with that power. Previously, the Heruls had been allies of the Ostrogoths. One of their kings had become the 'son in arms' of Theoderic, just as Theoderic himself had become the son in arms of the emperor Zeno. But the baptism of Grepes signalled a move towards the Empire, at a time of clouded relations between the Empire and the Ostrogoths, and Herul troops fought for Justinian against the Persians, Vandals and ultimately Ostrogoths. Another sign of changing loyalties was given when Mundus, a Gepid who had spent time with the Ostrogoths in Italy, returned to the east and did useful work for the Empire. In 535 the Empire and its Gepid allies were able to take Sirmium from the Ostrogoths. But when the Gepids showed signs of becoming too strong, Justinian turned to another people, the Lombards, whom he encouraged to settle in imperial territory. In 552 the Gepids suffered a major defeat at the hands of imperial and Lombard forces; ironically, the former were led by an Ostrogothic general who had been taken to Constantinople after the apparent defeat of his people in 540. The year of the defeat of the Gepids was that in which thousands of Lombard troops joined the great host that Narses led into Italy to destroy the kingdom of the Goths. Meanwhile, a commander in Thrace, Chilbudius, who may have been a Slav, had been taking war to the enemies' territory north of the Danube, where he won a number of successes before being killed in 533. Justinian was like a chess grand master, choosing the best of a potentially infinite number of combinations and always thinking several moves ahead. However, such tactics were risky. Making payments to secure peace or loyalty from those who had the potential to harm the state was dangerous, for what one side saw as subsidies, the other could claim as tribute, and it was also expensive, particularly at a time when wars were being waged virtually without intermission in the west, and sometimes against the Persians. Moreover, the settlement of newcomers on imperial soil could backfire, as happened with the Goths late in the fourth century.

Nevertheless, there was good reason to think that, after the agonies of the fifth century, the Balkans had a bright future within the Empire. The optimism prevailing in official circles was shown by a law promulgated in 535, in which Justinian spoke of his having increased the size of the Empire, and named towns to the north of the Danube that had been brought under his sway, perhaps through the efforts of Chilbudius. It was the very time at which conquests in the West were advancing with great speed, and the remarkable successes of Belisarius doubtless encouraged positive thinking about the prospects of the Empire elsewhere. Yet there are signs that the Balkans were not flourishing. In another act of 535, Justinian established a new position, that of quaestor of the army. His headquarters were at Odessos (the modern Varna), but he had responsibility for an oddly shaped area: the two provinces along the lowest reaches of the Danube, Caria in south-western Asia Minor, Cyprus and the islands in the Ionian Sea. So awkward did the unit prove that Justinian later transferred the judicial functions of the office to the capital. The rationale for such an agglomeration of territories is not clear, but it could well be that the grain being grown in the region was no longer enough to supply the needs of the army on the Danube, which made it necessary for the quaestor to draw on the production of a wider area. If the grain grown in the Balkans did not suffice for the needs of the army, perhaps there had been a loss of control over productive areas. But despair was on no one's mind. Decades later, the emperor Tiberius made a gesture of confidence when, in 580, he supplied funds for the renovation of an aqueduct at Serdica. By then, however, the situation had changed. In a way no one could have foreseen, developments that were just beginning at the end of Justinian's reign had started to transform the history of the region for ever.[15]

SLAVS AND AVARS

During the sixth century, our written sources mention for the first time the Slavs, speakers of a language that was the ancestor of the modern Slavonic speech, of which there are now more speakers in Europe and Russia than there are of either the Romance or Germanic language families. Their speech has undergone wide dispersion, much of which occurred during the period we are concerned with in this book. This was a time of great migration among the Slavs, of which their moving southwards into imperial territory was only a part; by the seventh century, others had arrived at the site of Szczecin (Stettin), on the Baltic coast. The origin of these people, while it has been fiercely debated, has remained elusive. Perhaps, as with the Germanic peoples, it would be well not to probe deeply into the ethnogenesis of the Slavs. It is certainly interesting that the first author to deal with the origin of the Slavs, who wrote in Russia in the twelfth century, associates the early Slavs with a tribe called Norics, a term that suggests the inhabitants of the old province of Noricum, and has them moving to land on both sides of the Danube, into an area where Hungarians and Bulgarians lived when he was writing. It was from there, according to this author, that they later scattered far and wide.

Most modern scholars believe this report to be false, although it is possible that the Slavs who entered the Empire, like most of the newcomers to Roman soil in late antiquity, and the overwhelming majority of those who made a lasting impression, travelled a short distance to get where they finished up.[16] Be this as it may, in the sixth century people named Slavs fought in Justinian's armies and came to the serious attention of the Empire.

Authors writing in Constantinople around the middle of that century describe them residing in swamps and forests rather than cities, and living not under one man but in a situation of 'democracy', a word whose connotations for ancient and medieval authors were not necessarily positive. They sacrificed to a god they believed to be responsible for lightning, probably to be identified with the deity Perun, known to have been worshipped by Slavs centuries later, and to rivers, nymphs and other deities. These people were said to have come to occupy most of the northern side of the Danube.[17] About 50 years later, a handbook of military strategy written for the benefit of imperial commanders gave advice on how to deal in battle with such folk, whom it describes as free people who refused to be enslaved or governed. They had proved to be tricky opponents, living as they did among forests, rivers, lakes and marshes, from which they were given to ambushing their enemies. Such was their skill in watery terrains that, when threatened, they dived to the bottom of bodies of water and breathed through reeds until their enemies went away. The best way to deal with them, according to this text, was for armies to take plenty of material for building bridges and rafts. Attacks in winter were recommended, for they could not easily hide among trees that had lost their leaves, or conceal themselves when the snow would reveal their footsteps. Moreover, when the rivers among which they lived were frozen, they could be crossed on foot.[18]

Such are our first references to a people who were destined to play a major role in European history. But before long the history of the Slavs was bound up with that of another, and very dissimilar, people.

The entry of the Avars on to the stage was far more dramatic than that of the Slavs, yet they were a less substantial people. Whereas the Slavs, from their first appearance, could be seen as an ethnic group with a distinctive set of cultural practices and, presumably, language, the picture presented by the Avars is much less clear. Scarcely anything is known about an Avar language, and we can only speculate as to the origin of the word 'chagan', which they used for their leader. They were a warrior group, doubtless not large, who rapidly emerged from the steppes, perhaps having been driven from their homes by other groups; an emperor is represented as having taunted them with being refugees. Doubtless, as happened with successful groups of warriors, they would have been joined by others, who would have diluted whatever ethnic specificity they originally had. The Avars conducted themselves much as the Huns had under Attila, and it was with good reason that Greek and Latin authors sometimes called them 'Huns'; by the tenth century, the process of identification had gone far enough for a Byzantine author to make the mistake of calling Attila 'king of the Avars'. They were formidable horsemen, their cemeteries characterised by horse burials, who made a point of terrifying their opponents by howling before battles. Their chagans supplied strong leadership. Such was the power inherent in this office that Greek authors generally refer to 'the chagan' without supplying a name; we know the personal name of only one chagan, Bajan, who flourished in the late sixth century.[19]

The Slavs and Avars, who intruded upon the Empire at almost exactly the same time and were often linked by contemporaries, were very different, yet possessed of complementary skills; when the Avars made their definitive crossing of the Danube, it was in ships that the Slavs built at the command of the chagan.[20] They fought differently. Whereas the Avars excelled at the use of horses, the original Indo-European root for 'horse' was lacking in Slavonic; whereas Slavic society lacked centralised leadership, and archaeology indicates its relative lack of social differentiation, the principle of command was strong among the Avars. Not surprisingly, the Slavs feared the other group, and in the Slavonic languages now spoken in regions where the Avars once held sway, a word for giant is based on 'Avar'. But the political system of the Slavs was a good recipe for survival, for it meant that they could not be destabilised by the removal of a single leader. The power of the Huns scarcely survived Attila, and a few centuries later Charlemagne would find the disorganised Saxons far harder to deal with than the politically more developed Lombards. Indeed, as we shall see, the characteristics of Slavic society may have lain behind their ability to turn other peoples into Slavs.

For some time, however, it was the Avars who made the running. In 558 an embassy arrived in Constantinople, where their long hair, plaited and tied with ribbons, seemed so sinister that those who saw them were reminded of snakes. They were bought off with money. When, a few years later, another embassy was unsuccessful in seeking land south of the Danube, they sought to take it by force, and the authorities used subtle diplomacy to prevent this occurring. Just as the Huns had in similar circumstances, the Avars turned their attention to the west. In 562 they attacked the Franks, and a few years later they captured a Merovingian king, who had to buy his way out of captivity; later, there were rumours that the fierce queen Brunhild had invited them to attack her enemies. But the Avar heartland was by the Danube. In 567, in alliance with the Lombards, they defeated the Gepids, and the withdrawal of the Lombards to Italy in the next year gave them control of the middle reaches of the river. After the Avars defeated an imperial army, the emperor bowed to necessity and ceded to them land around Sirmium. This did not suffice, for in 582 they took the city itself, which the Empire had been able to reoccupy following the defeat of the Gepids, although the absence of coins minted during the immediately preceding years suggests that Sirmium had been isolated prior to its capture. Its last bishop left in 582. Not contented with this, within a few years the Avars were again causing trouble for the Empire, which found it necessary to buy them off with generous subsidies. From 574–5 the chagan Bajan was receiving 80,000 solidi annually. It was easy money, and the emperors were vulnerable, especially when, as also occurred in the time of Attila, they had to deal with Persia at the same time.

Nevertheless, the year in which Sirmium fell saw the Empire gain a strong emperor in the person of a military man, Maurice (582–602). The conclusion of an advantageous peace with Persia enabled him to commit more resources to the Balkans, where some successes were won by generals such as Comentiolus, who had returned to the east from his tour of duty in Spain. But the Avars were able to keep the good times coming. As the years passed, they steadily increased their demands, until in 623–4, 200,000 solidi flowed to them. By these standards, the demands of Attila had been modest. The wealth that the Avars gained is abundantly evident in the archaeological record in the Carpathian area. Scarcely a single free Avar was placed in a tomb without gold. At one site, Kunbábony, a person was buried with a sword, its sheath fitted with gold, a sabre with a golden handle, a bow with a golden quiver, and six daggers with golden ornamentation. Several golden belts, golden drinking horns, tumblers and a jug made of gold were also present in the burial; all in all, he was laid to rest with some 3 kg of gold. While his family and friends may have hoped that such equipment would add to his comfort in the after-life, an important motive in providing such a rich burial was the wish to display the wealth that his associates could afford to give away, and among the Avars such displays were lavish. The warriors of Charlemagne could not believe their eyes when they came upon the wealth of the Avars at the end of the eighth century. The ruler of a society accustomed to the display of wealth on this scale could disdain gestures of goodwill. The possession of elephants seems to have been an imperial prerogative, so when the emperor Maurice sent the chagan an elephant it was a sign of distinction, but the recipient simply sent it back, as he did a bed made of gold. Unlike the subsidies paid in the days of Attila, the largesse that the Byzantines paid the Avars was on a scale that hurt the donors. So reduced were the circumstances of the Empire that in the early seventh century an emperor was forced to sell church plate and alienated some of the property of the cathedral in Constantinople; despite this, the stipends of the soldiers had to be reduced.[21]

The Avars settled among the native population, centred on the Danube basin upstream from Singidunum. No less than the Franks and the English who settled in Northumbria, they straddled the old imperial frontier; in all three cases, the units that were established may have maintained border zones that had developed in the Roman period. But the greater number of the Avars continued to live to the north of the Danube, a circumstance that may account for their failure, unusual among the newcomers to imperial territory, to accept Christianity. The early years of their settlement saw a spectacular retreat of imperial power in the Balkans. The sequence of coins at Nikopolis ends with those of Tiberius, and the city was destroyed by fire; by the beginning of the seventh century its inhabitants had retreated to a fortress built along one of the walls of the old city. The last coin found on the site of Justiniana Prima was minted in 615, by which time Slavs seem to have been living in the city. Displaced persons were beginning to appear, and pope Gregory used the patronage at his disposal to find posts for bishops who had been forced to flee from their sees. One such was bishop Sebastian, who had moved to Constantinople. He had turned down a see that the bishop of Antioch offered him, and Gregory wondered whether he would be interested in one of the sees that were then vacant in Sicily.[22]

Others seem to have found their way to Italy by a more direct route. So close are the extreme south-east of Italy and what is now Albania that the author of the *Expositio totius mundi*, a text of the fourth century, began his discussion of Italy with Calabria, immediately after treating Dyrrachium, and it is possible that the arrival of refugees from the Balkans contributed to a Hellenisation of southern Italy in the early middle ages. Be this as it may, the Empire was hard pressed. When the general Comentiolus arrived at Novae, a town south of the lower Danube, and asked for a guide to conduct him and his forces along an old pathway across the Haemus Mountains to Constantinople, the townspeople attempted to dissuade him, but told him of a man, 112 years old, who lived 12 miles away and would be able to do the job. But the old man was unwilling, claiming that no one had made the journey for 90 years, and Comentiolus wintered in Plovdiv. Whatever the degree of truth in the details of the story, communications across the Balkans were clearly parlous.[23] Worse was to follow.

THE SEVENTH CENTURY

In November 602 Maurice was murdered. Part of the army had spent the preceding summer north of the Danube, where it had done well against the Slavs, but an order to winter there, perhaps given in accordance with the perception that the Slavs were vulnerable to attack when the trees were bare, the ground covered in snow and rivers frozen over, led some of the troops to mutiny. A force under a non-commissioned officer who had already had a bitter dispute with the emperor, Phocas, marched on Constantinople, where its leader was proclaimed emperor (602–10). Maurice was executed, together with many of his supporters, including Comentiolus. This was good news for the Avars and Slavs. The Empire had managed to hold its own while Maurice was alive, but its defences collapsed in the decades following his death. Caričin Grad was abandoned. In its last years it became still less like a classical town, for ceramics then in use were hand-turned and there is evidence for building in wood, phenomena reminiscent of developments that had taken place over much of western Europe. As so often, developments in one area were mirrored in another.

News of these developments reverberated from one end of the Mediterranean to the other. Isidore of Seville reported laconically that 'the Slavs took Greece from the Romans', while towards the end of the century an Egyptian author wrote:

> It is recounted that the barbarians and foreign nations and the Illyrians devastated Christian cities and carried off their inhabitants captive, and that no city escaped save Thessalonica only; for its walls were strong, and through the help of God the nations were unable to get possession of it.

Sources closer to the events add little to these general reports. Centuries later, a chronicler told how Avars occupied a broad swath of territory from which they expelled the former inhabitants, and stayed without submitting to anyone from the reign of Maurice till the early ninth century. It was within this perspective that the chronicle located the founding of Monemvasia, a fortified city perched on a rock in the Aegean, just off the most eastern of the southern prongs of the Peloponnesos: we are told that when enemies pursued and destroyed the Greek inhabitants of the Peloponnesos, the survivors went to live in Italy or the islands, and among them were the founders of Monemvasia, where they settled with a bishop.[24] Such reports, distant from the events in place or time, paint a picture which recalls, in general terms, that given by our literary sources for the English occupation of much of Britain.

But we have seen this to be to be seriously flawed, and in the Balkans as well the reality was more complex.

The incompetent Phocas did not last long, for he was overthrown and replaced by the son of the exarch of Carthage, Heraclius (emperor 610–41), who was raised on a shield by soldiers and crowned by the patriarch Sergius, a Syrian who may have been named after the Arab saint Sergius. The first decade of the new reign saw an extraordinary series of disasters, as the power of Persia was felt in the eastern Mediterranean as it had not been for nearly a millennium. Persian forces occupied Antioch, and in 614 they captured Jerusalem, from which they removed the relic of the True Cross. In 615 they penetrated as far as Chalcedon, just across the Bosporus from Constantinople, and by the end of the decade Egypt, which provided the grain consumed by the people of Constantinople, was occupied. Heraclius despaired, and had to be talked out of returning to Africa. In the face of challenges on such a scale, the resources that would have been needed to shore up the Empire's position in the Balkans could not be spared. To free himself for offensive operations against Persia, Heraclius negotiated a peace with the chagan of the Avars, which enabled him to transfer troops from Europe to Asia. Their evacuation is reflected in the disappearance of stray coin losses along the frontier at about the beginning of the seventh century; as with the end of Roman rule in Britain, the withdrawal of troops and the end of a money economy occurred together. Just as Britain had been 200 years earlier, the Danubian provinces were effectively abandoned. Not feeling bound to keep the peace, the Empire's old enemies made merry. Thessaloniki and other cities were attacked; Slavs, competent at naval activities, launched raids on the islands of the Aegean which saw them penetrate as far south as Crete in 623; while an Avar force broke through the Long Wall and ravaged the suburbs of Constantinople. The treasure that they stole from churches was taken across the Danube.

The crunch came in 626 when the chagan led the Avars, their forces boosted by Slavs and warriors of other peoples, in an attack on Constantinople by land and sea. At the same time a Persian army, led by a general whose keen and successful involvement in recent victories against the Empire had earned him the nickname 'Wild Boar', established itself at Chalcedon on the Asian side of the Bosporus. Constantinople was threatened as it had never been since its foundation, at a time when Heraclius had been absent for some years campaigning against the Persians. The assailants set up siege engines outside its massive walls, and an aqueduct named after the emperor Valens, who was responsible for much work on it late in the fourth century, was cut, only to be restored in the eighth century. But in August an attack by sea was defeated, and the humiliated chagan ended the siege. And while this defeat and one that followed in the next year were enough to destabilise the government of Persia at a time of imminent danger, the raising of the siege turned out to be important for all who had been involved in it.

For the Avars, it was the beginning of the end. Never again did they mount such a threat, and the cessation of the payments from the Empire on which their power had been based weakened their hold over the Slavs. All they could do was slide into obscurity and await the *coup de grâce* administered by Charlemagne late in the eighth century. While the archaeological record does not point to a dramatic impoverishment after 626, and indeed the burial at Kunbábony may have taken place after this date, they had become much less of a force to be reckoned with. When Arab ships withdrew from a siege of Constantinople in 678, the once mighty Avars were among the peoples who sent ambassadors with gifts, seeking the peace and friendship of the emperor. The nature of their society was such that the weakening of their elite entailed their disappearance. An emperor of the tenth century was obscurely aware of there once having been Slavs who were also called Avars. Writing to a Bulgarian prince early in the tenth century, a patriarch of Constantinople could observe that the Avars, of whom he thought his correspondent's people were offshoots and slaves, had attacked Constantinople and been destroyed; 'not a vestige of the race survives'.[25]

For the Slavs, on the other hand, the defeat was their liberation. They were in the same position as the Goths had been following the death of Attila, but their future was to be brighter than that of the Goths. In increasing numbers they settled within what had been imperial territory, much as the Franks and English had, in the process removing large parts of it from the effective control of the distracted authorities in Constantinople. Other Slavs moved a long way to the west. In about 642 a force turned up at Siponto, a town on the Adriatic coast which was controlled by the Lombard dukes of Benevento. They killed the duke, but were later disarmed by his brother, who spoke to them in their language and drove them away. The brother's ability to speak Slavonic is a minor puzzle. Perhaps he had learned it when, decades earlier, he had been a captive of the Avars, or perhaps there were enough Slavs in the north-east of Italy to make it natural for a Lombard from Friuli, where he had been brought up, to speak their language.[26] In any case, the range of activity implied by a raid on the south of Italy and the ease with which a Lombard communicated with Slavs in their own tongue indicate an impressive spread on the part of the Slavs. It is possible that the Danevirke, a defensive wall built across the south of Denmark, the oldest part of which has been dated by tree-rings to about 737, was erected to keep the Slavs out, although Saxons or Franks may have been the enemies its builders had in mind.

A curious story that begins before the events of 626 allows us to see something of the process by which one group of Slavs broke away from the domination of the Avars. In 623 a Frankish merchant, Samo, joined a group of merchants trading with the Wends, a Slavic group who seem to have settled in Bohemia, when they were beginning to rebel against the Avars. Our source for these events, a Frankish author, describes the Avars as having forced the Slavs to fight on their behalf in risky and exploitative ways, to allow their women to sleep with them, and to pay tribute, details that may reflect relations between the two peoples not made so explicit by our eastern sources. Samo threw himself into the struggle, and in recognition of his ability the Wends made him their king, a position he used to advantage, for he took 12 Wendish wives, by whom he had 37 children. Some years later he ordered the Wends to ravage Frankish territory. In such ways did the Slavs prosper.[27]

The inhabitants of Constantinople, for their part, never forgot their deliverance in 626. They knew whom to thank. The mood in the Empire was becoming increasingly religious. Before leaving to wage war against Persia, God, his Mother and the patriarch Sergius had been among those to whom Heraclius committed the city, and in 641 a new emperor dedicated to God the crown of his father, just as Visigothic kings of the time were doing.[28] It was therefore not surprising that stories circulated which attributed the saving of the city to supernatural intervention, particularly that of the Virgin Mary. Her role in the events of 626 was commemorated in a stanza added to the 'Akathistos', a famous hymn in honour of the Theotokos, the 'God-bearer', as the Byzantines called Mary, perhaps written in the time of Justinian:

> Mother of God, Constantinople chants its thanks to you
> in a victory paean. You are my champion, my commander.
> You have rescued me from the terrors of the siege.[29]

The patriarch Sergius, who had been left holding considerable power in the besieged city, paraded about its walls displaying an icon of Mary holding Jesus in her arms, and the chagan was said to have been perturbed at the sight of a woman in stately dress going about the walls by herself.[30]

The behaviour of the Virgin Mary on this occasion resembled that of the goddess Athena who, when Athens had been attacked by Alaric in 396, was said to have been seen walking around the walls of the city that she was reputed to protect, while a column erected in Constantinople by the

Christian emperor Arcadius a few years later shows a female figure denying Goths entry into the city. Sometimes, to be sure, such defenders disappointed those who looked to them. When the Persians attacked Jerusalem in 614, angels were seen guarding the walls of the city, but when the Lord heard of the evil of its inhabitants, another angel was sent to tell them to desist, so that the people might be killed and made captive, whereupon they departed, unable to stand in the way of the command of the Lord. Even more alarming was the vision of a holy man, who saw himself on Golgotha, where Mary stood before Christ interceding for the people. But the Lord turned his face away, so as not to hear her prayer, an extraordinary act, for the art of the period depicted Christ on the cross looking towards his Mother. Such a visual apprehension of Mary's intercession, characteristic of Byzantine Christianity, was associated with the contemporary cult of icons, which carried all before it until, just a century after the victory of 626, the emperor Leo III would set under way the great iconoclastic movement. Turning towards the saints in this way was a recent development in Byzantine piety, there being scarcely a sign of it in the reign of Justinian, but it was firmly established in the seventh century, towards the end of which the emperor Justinian II could refer to the enemies of St Demetrius who were also his own.[31]

Memories of the siege of Constantinople, especially as transmitted by the Akathistos, were to take on contemporary relevance in the Balkans during the sixteenth century. It was then that frescos were painted on the walls of various churches in Moldavia, now part of northern Romania, which among other things illustrated various sections of the hymn. They include a scene hitherto unknown, which depicts a walled city, identified as 'Tsarigard', the Slavonic name for Constantinople, under attack.[32] People are shown processing around its walls, one group of them carrying the mandylion, a cloth that was believed to have been imprinted with an image of Christ when he pressed it against his face on the way to Golgotha. An inscription in one of the churches identifies the scene as occurring when Persians and others attacked Constantinople in the days of Heraclius. It is wildly anachronistic. The mandylion did not arrive in Constantinople until the tenth century, and, more worryingly, cannon are shown firing on the city, the assailants of which are dressed as Turks. But the appearance in the frescos of this scene, the representation of which cannot be securely documented anywhere else, answered to the situation of Moldavia at the time they were executed, when the power of the Turks threatened. The Avar attack on Constantinople in 626 has been blended into that of the Turks in 1453, and shown to be relevant to the needs of Christians in the sixteenth century. Doubtless the art is provincial, but even in this circumstance it suggests something of the long historical memory of the peoples of the Balkans, and the significance they attributed to the siege of 626.

THESSALONIKI

Placed on the northernmost point of one of the gulfs of the Aegean Sea, at the westernmost point where the Via Egnatia met the sea, Thessaloniki was strategically located. As was Aquileia, a similarly placed town at the north of the Adriatic in Italy, it was one of the success stories of late antiquity. By the end of the third century it had a mint, and towards the middle of the fifth century the headquarters of the praetorian prefect of Illyricum were trans-ferred thither from Sirmium, a move that exactly paralleled the transfer of the headquarters of the prefect of the Gauls from Trier to Arles; in both cases, a location that had been chosen because of its proximity to a border was evacuated as the border proved impossible to defend, and the administrative headquarters were moved towards the sea. Not surprisingly, Thessaloniki was a target for attacks.

The first siege probably occurred late in the sixth century. It was led by an Avar, whose force included Slavs and members of other peoples. They proved unnervingly competent at siege-warfare, and it was only after St Demetrius, a martyr whose cult had become strong in the town, appeared before the enemy in military guise that they retreated. Another attack took place in 604, cleverly timed to coincide with the celebrations that marked the feast of St Demetrius, but again the assailants withdrew. The enemy returned in 618, after refugees from Niš and Serdica had found their way into the city. On this occasion Thessaloniki was besieged for 33 days, but again it held out. According to a collection of miracle stories compiled by a later bishop of the city, John, this was owing to the intervention of its patron, St Demetrius. Just as, in Rome, pope Gregory wrote a book of miracle stories that effortlessly collapsed distinctions between high and low culture, so in Thessoloniki John did the same.

John's work left its readers in no doubt that the city was in safe hands. It tells of a man holding important rank who, in the course of one siege, had a vision in which he saw two men who looked like bodyguards sent to St Demetrius. They announced that the Lord had ordered him to leave the city, which was to be handed over to enemies. The saint wept and, having confirmed the truth of the message, told the messengers to inform the Lord that he was not going to leave the city. Not unnaturally, they were uneasy, but

Demetrius, who knew that the Lord's love of humanity was stronger than his wrath, closed the discussion. When the people of the city were told of the vision, they regained their boldness. The story is meant to be read on more than one level. Just as the mosaics at San Vitale in Ravenna and at Parentium show Christ and his angels in poses and garb that make them resemble the emperor and his officials, so in John's account there is an ambiguity in the reference to the Lord, for the word used for him (*despotes*) is one that could refer to either God or the emperor. The word used for the bodyguards (*somatophulakoi*) who did his will is appropriate to agents of the emperor, yet love of humanity (*philanthropia*) is a quality frequently attributed to God in the liturgy.[33] Such ambiguity in the text precisely reflected doubt as to where the people of the city could expect help to come from, raising as it did the possibility that someone other than the earthly lord could be looked to.

In hard times the people of Thessaloniki, no less than those of Constantinople and Jerusalem, hoped for supernatural defenders, and St Demetrius was made of stronger stuff than the angels who left the walls of Jerusalem at God's command. Two mosaics still to be seen in the church dedicated to him at Thessaloniki, where they were placed in just this period, show how people thought of their youthful protector. In one, which seems to have been installed soon after 620, he stands between two figures, a bishop to his right and an officer of the state to his left, performing a gesture of patronage as he places an arm around a shoulder of each of them. An accompanying inscription reveals that these two were responsible for the mosaic: 'You see the donors of the glorious house on either side of the martyr Demetrios, who turned aside the barbarous wave of barbarian fleets and was the city's salvation.'[34] In the other he stands between two children, the hand on the shoulder of one of them again showing his lasting care for the people of his city.

Perusal of John's collection of the miracles worked by St Demetrius can give the impression that Thessaloniki was constantly harassed by the Slavs, but even here there is evidence that points in a different direction. One story tells how, probably in 677, the emperor ordered that a resident of the city, king Perbundus of the Rynchini, was to be arrested and brought to Constantinople in chains. But when he was arrested, an embassy comprising people from Thessaloniki and Slavs went to the royal city to intercede with the emperor on his behalf. Perbundus, who is described as wearing Greek clothing and speaking Greek, twice attempted to escape. On the first occasion he was discovered in Thrace on the estate of an imperial functionary described by a term which means that he was involved in foreign affairs and may have been an interpreter; perhaps he was a Slav. But when he was captured a second time, Perbundus admitted that he planned to make war and spare not a single Christian, whereupon he was executed.[35] While the story has a sad end, it reveals a tolerably assimilated and popular Slav living in Thessaloniki, and perhaps more generally suggests that towns may have remained centres of Greek ways and Hellenisation while the countryside was increasingly becoming Slavicised. If this were the case, it would be reasonable to suppose that a degree of economic interdependence continued to exist between the Greek towns and the rural areas where Slavs were settling.

To the west, the situation was more grim. Pope John IV (640–2), who had been born in Dalmatia, just across the Adriatic Sea from Italy, sent an agent, abbot Martin, throughout Dalmatia and Istria to redeem captured people, and built a chapel for the martyrs whose relics Martin brought back. The names of three of these martyrs are recorded. Little is known of the first of them, Venantius, although curiously enough the pope's father bore that name. The second, Anastasius, was a fuller who had been martyred at the coastal town of Salona, the modern Solin, where in the sixth century his relics had been deposited beneath the altar of a new basilica. But his town faced a bleak future. In later centuries it was believed that its inhabitants abandoned it for the nearby Split, perhaps in the hope that what remained of Diocletian's palace would afford them protection. As it happens, there are signs from the period that parts of the palace were being demolished so that the material could be reused elsewhere, and there is evidence for a modest expansion at Split in the seventh century; that artefacts of that time show Slavic influence suggests assimilation between newcomers and indigenes. The third martyr whose name we know, Maurus, was one of the figures depicted in the mosaic commissioned by bishop Euphrasius at Parentium.[36] Isolated as they were from Constantinople, these regions faced an uncertain future following the withdrawal of their saintly protectors.

THE EMPIRE FIGHTS BACK

Even though the position of the Empire had weakened considerably since the time of Justinian, some of the traditional ways of dealing with unwelcome people remained open to it. A source written several centuries later tells how Heraclius brought other peoples into play against the Avars. Under his auspices Croats moved into Illyricum, where they defeated the Avars and settled, while Serbs were settled in the territory they occupy today, both groups being converted to Christianity by clergy sent from Rome. Our source for these events claims that the Serbs received their name because they were the 'slaves' of the emperors. While the word it uses for slaves is Greek (*douloi*), the point relies on the unstated Latin word for slaves, *servi*, for the pronunciation of the consonants 'b' and 'v' was easily confused.[37] Modern scholarship inclines to see the Serbs and Croats as being of Iranian origin, but ultimately they intermarried with the more numerous Slavs in the region and were assimilated into them. We shall see the same thing happening to the Bulgars.

Another response to enemy intruders was making direct assaults on their territory. In 656–7 the emperor Constans, taking advantage of internal warfare between Arabs who had hitherto been attacking the Empire in the east, made a successful expedition against territory to which our source, written in the ninth century, for the first time applies the term 'Sklavinia'. Just as, in the west, the word 'Francia' came into being to denote the land that the Franks had occupied, so now the use of a similar term signalled a degree of recognition of the newcomers. In 688 a later emperor, Justinian II, made an expedition against 'Sklavinia and Bulgaria', the first use by this author of the second word. Justinian advanced as far as Thessaloniki, and after a solemn entry into the city presented gifts to the church of St Demetrius. It is a measure of how low the stocks of the Empire had fallen that an army had to make its way by force between two of its main cities. Worse, on the way back Justinian was defeated by Bulgars, and when, a few years later, he settled a group of Slavs whom he had armed in Asia Minor and named them the Chosen People, the biblical term for the Jewish people, they defected to the Arabs. Some of the members of their families were killed and others sold as slaves.[38]

These were not the only responses that the Empire offered to the newcomers. Late in the seventh century, the emperor Constantine IV, the successor of Constans II, placed the administration of Thrace on a new footing, which may have involved the establishment of an institution familiar in later Byzantine history, a 'theme'. Unlike the kingdoms that had emerged in the west, the Empire continued to raise considerable revenue from taxation, and the loss during the seventh century of its wealthiest provinces, which we shall consider in the next chapter of this book, made the payment of the army difficult. This situation seems to lie behind the founding of the themes, the term used a few centuries later by the Byzantines to denote blocks of territory under the control of generals, within which troops were settled on the land and provided for themselves. For some time the Empire had been moving in this direction. There is evidence from the early fifth century of frontier troops in the East cultivating land, and it was taken for granted in Italy after Justinian's reconquest that members of the army would be landholders, while the authority delegated to the exarchs shortly afterwards in Africa and Italy clearly anticipates that of the generals in their themes. By the end of the seventh century, there seem to have been two themes in the Balkans, that of Thrace, not far from Constantinople, and that of the Helladoi, which is difficult to locate.

So it was that, just as was the case in Italy at the same time, even areas that remained unconquered in the Balkans saw great change. One reason for this was that in both areas the newcomers entered a society that was already changing. We know that hand-thrown pottery was coming into use in the Balkans during the second half of the sixth century, and old systems of authority were being replaced by new ones: 2,000 troops stationed at Thermopylae were maintained by the transfer of funds raised in Greece for other purposes.[39] Indeed, we may ask whether the newcomers caused, or benefited from, the end of the ancient world over much of the Balkans. In Athens, which enemies of the Empire never succeeded in holding for long, despite apparently having sacked it, houses were being subdivided, and only four of some 15 wells that were used in areas around the schools in the sixth century were still used in the seventh century, while tile kilns and olive presses were installed in the agora. The evidence from other towns is puzzling. In Corinth, an Italian bishop on his way to Constantinople and his entourage occupied a large deserted house that turned out to be inhabited by the devil, while a bath built early in the early sixth century soon passed out of use, but the hypocaust of its tepidarium was still being heated early in the next century. Tombs of the seventh century contain grave goods that have been identified as Avar or Bulgar, but it may well be that they were the property of Slavs who were holding the town on behalf of the Byzantine government. At Split, the sequence of imported African pottery came to an end in the sixth or seventh century; thereafter locally produced pottery was used, its styles being similar to those found in Slavic cemeteries in the region.[40] In this shaded world, cultural, ethnic and political zones overlapped. In any case, it would be wrong to envisage a sharply defined line between imperial and non-imperial territories, for the emperor certainly laid claim to territories into which his soldiers, and still less his tax collectors, would not care to venture.

Evidence from a later period makes it clear that realities on the ground were sometimes ambiguous. In the ninth century, when the Byzantines were invited to send missionaries to the Moravians, a Slavic-speaking people who had recently established themselves in the former province of Pannonia, the emperor chose two brothers, Cyril and Methodius, who had been born in Thessaloniki. While their father was an officer in the army, the brothers had at their command not only Greek but also excellent Slavonic, which suggests that they were the products of a bilingual home in which their mother was a native speaker of Slavonic, just as Ulphilas, who centuries earlier had translated the Bible from Greek into Gothic, may have been the product of what we may loosely think of as a mixed marriage. During the same period Danielis, a wealthy woman who played an important part in the political life of the Empire, owned large estates in the north of the Peloponnesos, in an area where Slavs had settled. The position of the indigenes in the Peloponnesos and elsewhere in Greece can be compared to that of those in Britain when the English settled. While modern Greece has a good number of place-names of Slavonic origin, particularly in its western areas, there are very many places whose names have remained virtually unchanged for millennia, and, whatever linguistic perturbations may have occurred in the early middle ages, Greece has remained Greek speaking. Moreover, the Slavs left few archaeo-logical indications of their presence in Greece, far fewer than the Franks or English settlers did in the territories where they settled. The main changes within the Balkans took place to the north of Greece.

BULGARS

A Turkic people whose settlement stretched from the Black Sea far up the Volga, the Bulgars, sometimes referred to by modern scholars as 'Proto-Bulgarians', became involved in the affairs of the Balkans in a minor way as early as the fifth century. Thereafter they were widely diffused. Narses, the general responsible for the final defeat of the Ostrogoths in Italy, had a Bulgar swordbearer who spoke the Bulgar language. In about 630 a number of Bulgars estimated at 9,000, with their families, were driven out of Pannonia by the Avars, and asked the Frankish king Dagobert to take them in. He determined that they were to winter among the Bavarians, but later ordered that they were to be killed. We are told that only 700 men and their families, led by one Alcioc, survived. Some decades later, a man named Alzeco, perhaps identical with Alcioc, arrived in Italy with his people. He was allowed to settle in the duchy of Benevento; a little over a century later, Bulgars were still there, speaking both Latin and their own language. A group that may have been connected with that of Alzeco settled in Byzantine ter-ritory near Ravenna.[41]

Other Bulgars, who lived to the north of Constantinople, were cultivated by the emperors as a counter to the expanding power of the Avars and the Khazars, a people who had settled north of the Caucasus whose rulers, like those of the Avars, are referred to in Greek texts as 'chagans'. In the early seventh century Kuvrat, described as the ruler of Great Bulgaria – that is, the territory of the Bulgars who were independent of the Empire – took the same step as the king of the Heruls a century earlier when he was baptised in the royal city. He went on to do useful work against the Avars, following which he was made a patrician, the same rank as that held by the leaders of an allied Arab tribe at the time. A wonderful treasure of gold and silver discovered in 1912 at Malaja Pereščepina, a site on the river Vorskla, a tributary of the Dnieper at the extreme north of the great steppes, may have been associated with him. The great deposit of treasure, which may have been assembled for a burial, is reminiscent of the nearly contemporary treasure laid down at Sutton Hoo. The items it contained were made by Byzantines, Persians, Avars and probably others. They included a silver patten for use in celebrating the Eucharist, which had been the property of Paternus, bishop of Tomi on the Black Sea, and control stamps indicate that it was made during the reign of Anastasius I, the very emperor whose control stamps are found on the great silver dish that formed part of the Sutton Hoo treasure; whatever the means by which these goods found their way so far from their place of origin, their spread indicates how desirable Byzantine goods were found over a wide area. Various other goods were included in the treasure, among them coins, the latest of them minted during the reign of the emperor Constans II. The treasure included two seal rings, and the monogram on one of them has been interpreted as 'Of Kuvrat the patrician'.[42]

But the Bulgars were too strong to be controlled, and in the 670s their leader Asparuch, apparently taking advantage of the Arab naval attacks on Constantinople which were then under way, established a base north of the mouths of the Danube. The emperor Constantine IV responded by sailing with a large fleet across the Black Sea, and disembarked north of the Danube. But the terrain was difficult, and before long the imperial forces were staging an ignominious retreat, which turned into an unambiguous defeat as the Bulgars attacked them. A treaty was concluded in which the Byzantines agreed to pay an annual tribute to the Bulgars, who promised not to attack imperial territory. The imperial authorities may have seen the newcomers as a useful counter to other groups, and as early as 717, when Constantinople was besieged by Arabs, they were to intervene in support of the Empire. Nevertheless, for the first time the Byzantines had been forced to acknowledge by formal treaty the existence of an independent state within the Balkans.[43]

While most of the lands of the Bulgars, like those of the Avars, were still to the north of the Danube, the treaty of 681 effectively marked the founding of the Bulgarian state, the position of which was strengthened in a second treaty concluded in 705, after Bulgars and Slavs had helped Justinian II regain the throne a decade after he had been deposed. Its first headquarters were located at Pliska, in the middle of a plain in the north-east of the modern Bulgaria. Such a location indicates that the Bulgars were unconcerned about the possibility of being attacked. The town grew, and by the early eighth century a small royal complex was functioning. Steadily, the Bulgars extended their power southwards into imperial territory. Serdica, now the capital of Bulgaria, remained in Byzantine hands until the beginning of the ninth century, while Philipopolis, the modern Plovdiv, located as it was closer to Constantinople, remained an imperial stronghold for centuries, as did Diocletianopolis, where the traces of a great hippodrome and other buildings were still to be seen in the twelfth century.[44]

Yet before long the Bulgarians who were to play a major role in the Balkans thereafter had become very different to the original Bulgars. When they settled to the south of the Danube, they found themselves among an indigenous population of Thracians, by then largely Hellenised, and the recently arrived Slavs. It was the latter who came to dominate in the region, and through their influence the Bulgars were quickly transformed into a Slavonic people.[45] Such a process of Slavicisation, as we have seen, may also have occurred among the Serbs and Croats, and it is a tribute to the thoroughness of the process that scarcely anything is known of pre-Slavonic speech among the Bulgars. When their ruler Boris was converted to Christianity in the ninth century, the church established among his people used Slavonic for its liturgy. Whereas the newly arrived English, at a time when they were beginning to develop strong monarchies, turned the Britons into people like themselves, the loosely organised Slavs were able to absorb the newly arrived Bulgars. Yet it is the name of the non-Slavic group responsible for the establishment of the state that lives on in the Bulgaria of today.

The events we have considered in this chapter severely curtailed the reach of the Empire. It remained in control of most of the coastline from Constantinople to the south-eastern tip of the Peloponnesos, and intermittent pockets as far west as Italy, but nowhere did this control extend far inland; just as occurred in Italy and Africa, as Byzantine territory contracted it did so towards the coastline. One index of the authority that remained to it towards the end of the seventh century is the attendance of bishops from the Balkans at church councils then held in Constantinople. This was very thin, and all the bishops who managed to attend were from the coast, with the exception of the bishop of Stobi, a town that enjoyed the advantage of being located in the valley of a major river, the Vardar, which flowed into the sea near Thessaloniki. Stobi had been a prosperous town, as could be seen from its cathedral, which may have been built shortly after the sack of the town by Goths in 479. Yet by the late seventh century even it had fallen into ruins, and little would be heard of the town for centuries. Perhaps its demise was caused by invasions; perhaps environmental factors were at work. As the centuries passed, the Empire would regain some of the territory it had lost in the Balkans, while the lands that remained beyond its grasp would come under its influence as they adopted orthodox Christianity, the religion of the Empire. But by 700 the map of the Balkans had been withdrawn.

This had involved the working out of various factors, among which were the coming of new peoples into the region. Some of these, dramatic players such as the Huns and Avars and Germanic groups such as the Goths and Lombards who went on to great things in western Europe, turned out to be insubstantial epiphenomena in the Balkans, minor tracks that led nowhere. But the arrival of the Slavs, a people whose very name was unknown to the ancient world, and their settlement in the Balkans, was one of the major events of the period. They put down deep roots that were destined to last. By the tenth century, the Byzantines remembered the ancient Singidunum as having a tower of the emperor Constantine. But by then even they were calling it by the Slavonic name 'Belegrad', 'white town', which has lasted almost unchanged until this day as the name of the capital of Serbia.[46] Of the fault lines that had run through the zone in Roman times, that between the northern and southern areas remained, although the extent of the latter was diminished, while those that divided the region into units looking eastwards or westwards disappeared or were reconfigured. Henceforth, the greater part of the Balkans would constitute a new zone, intermediate between east and west, dominated by Slavs. So it was that these centuries saw the creation of a situation that still exists today.

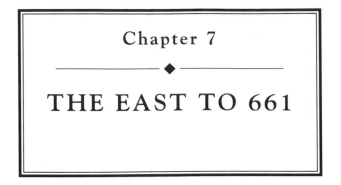

Chapter 7

◆

THE EAST TO 661

A CITY AND ITS EMPIRE

While the Empire lost its western provinces in the course of the fifth century, those in the East flourished. More and more they found their centre in its capital, the great city of Constantinople. Paradoxically, the city remained central even to the western territories that had been lost to the Empire. When the future pope Gregory lived there, he developed a great network of acquaintances that included other westerners also residing in the city, such as the future bishops of Milan and Seville. Whether by choice or force, many popes of the period had ample occasion to become familiar with the city. It was from there that Justinian sent complaisant clerics to occupy the sees of Rome and Ravenna, and there that members of the Vandal, Ostrogothic and Visigothic royal families, whose presence could conceivably be of future use to the Empire, were made welcome. Indeed, despite the trend away from the use of Latin in Constantinople, for a while the city was the centre for writing in that language. It was there that Cassiodorus worked on his long exposition of the Psalms, that Jordanes wrote his history of the Goths, and that various African authors wrote. And within what remained of the Empire, the royal city was a magnet. In 539 a law was issued dealing with provinces being despoiled of their inhabitants, especially farmers, who made their way to Constantinople. While the inhabitants of the great Hellenistic cities of Alexandria and Antioch may have despised the royal city as a johnny-come-lately, they were within its sphere of influence. A story in a collection of miracles performed by a saint in Constantinople which was written in the seventh century suggests the regions from which people travelled to it. It tells of a man with a swollen testicle who was not immediately healed on visiting the saint's shrine. But he was told not to worry, for many people who departed without being healed were later visited by the saint, whether in Alexandria, Africa or Rhodes.[1] The city remained buoyant in a way that the ancient capital in the west did not; in the sixth century, many churches were built in Constantinople, but few in Rome.

One reason for the eminence of the capital was its ability to draw upon the services of the competent people who made their way there from the provinces. Such a person was Anthemius, a product of the town of Tralles in Lydia. An architect and the author of a still surviving work on mathematics, he collaborated with another author of scientific works, Isidore, originally from the ancient town of Miletus, in designing the capital city's grandest building, the great cathedral of Hagia Sophia (532–7). The son of a doctor, Anthemius belonged to a generation whose members did extraordinarily well for themselves. One of his brothers, Metrodorus, taught grammar to the children of the nobility in Constantinople; another, Alexander, wrote books on medicine and travelled widely in the west before settling in Rome; a third, Olympius, was an expert on legal matters, while Dioscorus practised medicine at Tralles, just as his father had. The brothers would have had every reason to look on their careers with satisfaction, and for most of them success meant moving away from their home town. Miletus was similarly productive of talent. Isidore's near contemporaries there included Hesychius, a historian and biographer of non-Christian authors, fragments of whose works survive; his mother bore the beguiling name Philosophia. After an earthquake in 558 caused the dome of Hagia Sophia to collapse, another man from Miletus known for his skill in erecting buildings, a nephew of Isidore also named Isidore, saw to its restoration. Loyalties to one's home town could survive a rise to eminence in the capital. During the sixth and seventh centuries, a small village in northern Syria, Kaper Koraon, came to boast a treasure of at least 56 silver objects, which had been produced in Constantinople towards the end of the reign of Justinian, doubtless for liturgical use in its church, which was dedicated to an Arab saint popular in Syria, St Sergius. Some of the items bear the names of donors. They included an official, Megas, who was a person of some note in the royal city. In 584, an embassy that the Frankish king Childebert II sent to the emperor Maurice brought with it a series of letters to influential men in Constantinople. Among those Childebert thought could help his cause was Megas, whose office made him directly responsible to the emperor. A local man who made good in the capital, Megas did not forget his provincial origins.[2]

The treasure of Kaper Koraon, which was discovered near the southern coast of what is now Turkey in 1963, is a pointer to the wealth of Syria. Weighing over 22 kg, it seems to have belonged to one church, which would have had more silver liturgical apparatus than that with which Constantine had endowed the great basilicas of Rome. A patriarch of Antioch had no hesitation in firmly asking his congregation, some of whom ate their meals off silver plates and were lavish users of silver goods in their daily lives, for donations of silver to embellish the church, and the shah of Persia found it worth his while to mount what were little more than great plunder- and tribute-raising expeditions in Syria. Silver was being put to good use else-where in the Empire. Early in the seventh century, nine exquisite plates of remarkably classical style were produced, showing scenes from the life of the biblical king David. They were probably made in Constantinople, although they were buried in Cyprus. 'Who does not know that easterners are extremely wealthy?' asked a westerner of the time.[3]

With all its wealth, the East was much more regionally diversified than the late-imperial West had been. It was an immensely fertile breeding ground for Christian heresies, and as we have seen, linguistic variation was much greater there than in the West. Two languages in particular enjoyed regional pre-eminence. In Syria, Syriac (or 'Christian Palestinian Aramaic', as it is some-times called) was a language of theological scholarship and of one of the greatest poets in the Christian tradition, Ephrem the Syrian. In a nice illustra-tion of the influence of the provincial on the metropolitan, two centuries after Ephrem wrote, another Syrian, Romanos Melodos, would go to Con-stantinople and, having received a miraculous gift, write famous hymns of a kind later called *kontakia*, which draw on the works of Ephrem in both form and content. In Egypt, Coptic was a language in which Christians, especially monks, wrote, and into which both Christians and Gnostics translated texts from Greek. Syria and Egypt were key areas in the East in late antiquity, and it will be worth our while considering them.

In late antiquity, the intellectual life of the East was often most lively far from the capital. So it was that the oldest known illustrated Gospel book, the Rossano Gospels, seems to have been produced in Syria in the sixth century, as was a beautiful manuscript of Genesis, the Vienna Genesis. The text of these works was in Greek, but the text accompanying a superbly illustrated volume of the Gospels completed in 586 by the monk Rabbula in a monastery by the Euphrates was in Syriac. Speakers of this language were keen to translate Greek works into it. Their interests were largely theological, but from the sixth century they were also involved with secular texts. Sergius of Resh'aina translated Galen and wrote an introduction to Aristotle's works on logic, and some key texts, such as Aristotle's *Organon* and Porphyry's *Eisagoge*, received more than one translation; such endeavours recalled those of Boethius in Italy at much the same time. The town of Harran, near Edessa, remained an eccentric centre of polytheistic intellectual life until well into the Islamic period. The monasteries of Syria produced significant theology, and while the monasticism of Egypt had a popular, demotic feel, Alexandria was a city with a distinguished history of intellectual achievement. Its continuing importance was manifested in the distinguished work of a scholar of the sixth century, John Philoponos, who moved beyond the scientific teaching of Aristotle; the dialogue across the centuries would be continued when his own work was criticised by an Arab scholar, Alfarabi. In the midst of so much excellence, the contribution of Constantinople was second rate; the greatest theologian of the sixth and seventh centuries, Maximus the Confessor, was a pupil of the schools of Palestine, not those of the capital, as was his successor of the eighth century, John of Damascus. Intellectual life in the capital was quiet, for which the narrow views of Justinian were partly to blame.

In various ways, the Egyptians were unique. People who built their houses in neither stone nor wood, but of bricks, they were utterly distinct within the empire. The age-old culture of Egypt had surprised the ancient Greeks; the artistic traditions of the Fayum were mightily to influence portraiture in Christian icons; and Egyptians were responsible for a rich crop of Christian heresies. Not only had Arius been an Egyptian, but the great mass of Egyptians defied the teaching of the council of Chalcedon and, together with some Syrians, held that Christ had only one nature. The capital, Alexandria, was known for the turbulence of its populace as well as its unparalleled intellectual liveliness. A series of murdered high officials and churchmen testified to the difficulty that the Empire found in imposing its will. Such people felt that the west had little to teach them. For every papyrus of the Roman and Byzantine periods containing a Latin author found in Egypt, where the great bulk of such papyri have been found, over ten have been found in Greek. Perhaps more significant is the overall decline in papyri. Their production peaked in the third century; by the fifth century only a sixth as many were being produced, and further decline was to follow. East and west both participated in a move away from the production of books in late antiquity.

But whatever the fate of its literary culture, Egypt remained rich. Its wealth was based on its agriculture, a gift of the Nile, and the yield of the sowing was the subject of astonished exaggerations by ancient authors. Christian authors conjectured that the pyramids had been constructed as storehouses for grain by Joseph, while he was serving the Pharaoh.[4] For centuries, the bread of Constantinople was baked from the grain of Egypt; in 563 the people of the capital rioted when contrary winds delayed the grain fleet from Alexandria. The export of grain, while on terms favourable to the government, was a sure source of income to Egypt, and at some stage Egypt became the only part of the Mediterranean world to cultivate hard wheat, with superior qualities. The church of Alexandria was also a major landlord, and the ability of its most famous patriarch, Cyril, to encompass the ruin of his theological opponents by bribery owed as much to the wealth of his see as to the strength of his convictions. Alexandria, located as it was half way between Britain and Sri Lanka, sat astride trade routes. Cosmas, a merchant of the sixth century whose nickname, 'Indicopleustes', registered his claim to have sailed as far as India, wrote a geographical treatise.

Large estates had grown up, the possessions of families such as the Apions, whose holdings were based on a town in the Nile valley, Oxyrhynchus, although they also owned property in the Fayum. They produced grain, wine, oil and more exotic foodstuffs such as asparagus. Surviving papyri tell a good deal about the scale of the enterprises of this family, and the self-sufficiency of their estates. A blurring of the lines between its authority and that of the state took place. The Apions maintained their own prisons, in which were detained not only criminals but also unfortunate people whom the family sought to use for its own purposes, and they forwarded taxes collected from their tenants on behalf of the state directly to Alexandria. An Apion held an important office in Constantinople, that of praetorian prefect, at the beginning of the sixth century. One of his sons was forced to become a deacon, but another became an honorary consul and state treasurer. He in turn was the father of the Apion who, in 539, was one of the last people other than an emperor to hold the old Roman office of consul. The family maintained a home in the royal city; one of its members had wine sent there from the estates. Writing to a correspondent in Constantinople, pope Gregory asked her to pass on his regards to an Apion.[5]

Families such as the Apions had their counterparts, perhaps modest ones, in the west. A different model was provided by Syria. There, independent small farms organised around villages, often of two-storeyed houses, were the norm. Between the mid-fourth and the mid-sixth centuries, agriculture in the limestone massif of northern Syria was in full expansion. Houses were being built with more rooms, better constructed and more richly adorned. The region seems to have owed its prosperity to the production of olive oil for the market, particularly to satisfy the needs of the large city of Antioch and, further afield, Constantinople itself. And while, from about 550, new houses, and even new rooms, were no longer being built, the construction of churches continued unabated. Many of these, like the synagogues that were also being built in the area, were erected by local people who, in other endeavours, were also often responsible for the construction of bath houses. In the Holy Land, more churches were built in the sixth century than in any preceding century. The vitality of towns in the east was responsible for the continuing use of copper coins. People living in towns, who often need to make small purchases, find small coins more useful than do country dwellers, whose purchases are fewer but larger. In the west, they ceased to circulate in the seventh century; in the east, they were not only minted but, as finds in urban sites such as the military town of Amorium indicate, remained in common use. In the Transjordan, a large number of water mills supported intensive cultivation. As far as we can tell from animal remains, there were coming to be fewer camels in the region. Perhaps an expansion in farming was forcing the nomads, to whose lives the camel was central, into more arid lands, which may have been an ominous development at a time when the great victories of the Arabs were just around the corner.[6]

Yet there were signs that all was not well in Syria. Problems occurred, although the extent to which they resulted from contingent circumstances rather than structural weakness is unclear. We may take the case of Antioch, the capital of Syria. Dated inscriptions in the city peaked in the fourth and fifth centuries, and remained strong in the sixth, while in the fifth century its walls were extended to enclose buildings that had sprung up. Later, however, it experienced at least six earthquakes. After the first, which occurred in 526, Justinian ordered that the city be renamed 'Theopolis', the City of God. Perhaps the change of name was the fruit of desperation, but it may have represented confidence in divine assistance, and hence optimism. Alas, such a feeling would have been misplaced, for Antioch's run of bad luck continued. It was burned by the Persians in 540, the first occasion in a millennium that they reached the Mediterranean, and plague, which may have had a devastating demographic impact, struck the city in 542 and again in 560. If this was not enough, in the early seventh century Antioch was captured and held for some years by the Persians. Interesting in another way are developments in a town in an adjacent part of the Empire, Aphrodisias, the capital of Caria. It is noteworthy for its inscriptions, of which there is an abundance from the mid-fifth to the mid-sixth centuries, many of them recording the generosity of private citizens who continued to patronise various works. But by about 600 formal public inscriptions disappeared. In the seventh century

Aphrodisias adopted the name 'Stauropolis', City of the Cross, a gesture that may have been positive, for the cross is pre-eminently a sign of victory in eastern Christianity. But as with Antioch, the future would belie optimism.[7]

The economy of the east was marked by interregional trade. Boats that sailed along the Nile can be distinguished from those that sailed the Mediterranean in graffiti at Alexandria. The monks of a poor monastery in Syria planted a vineyard, and sold the wine it produced to people from Cappadocia. And although John the Almoner, a patriarch of Alexandria who made a career of being abstemious, refused to touch expensive Palestinian wine and made a point of drinking the cheaper wine produced on the out-skirts of the city at Lake Mareotis, strong wine from Gaza was used at mass in Gaul, where it could also be found with Italian wine in the cellar of a king's high official. Towards the end of the sixth century, wine from Laodicea and Gaza was available in Tours. A ship that went down in the Aegean Sea off the modern Turkish town of Bodrum in the early seventh century was carrying a cargo of perhaps 900 amphorae, containing both red and white wine as well as oil, perhaps for the use of the army.[8] The contrast between the economy of the east, orientated towards producing goods for the market, and that of the west, apart from Africa, is marked. Moreover, the surviving parts of the Empire were plugged into networks which meant that its trade with peoples to its south and east was at least as important as that it conducted across the Mediterranean. Its policy in the Red Sea was aimed at keeping the trade routes from the Indian Ocean, which brought luxury goods into the Empire, out of the hands of Persia; its coins have been discovered in Sri Lanka; and Arab caravans plied their way to and from the Mediterranean area. Two great caravans left the town of Macca each year, one to Yemen in the winter and the other to Syria in the summer. One of the latter was attacked by some of the earliest Muslims at the battle of Badr fought near Madina in 624, and such was the reliance of Macca upon its trade that this was the turning-point in its difficult relationship with Muhammad. But the trade route was very old. Some 1,500 years earlier, when the queen of Sheba, apparently a native of the south-west of Arabia, had visited king Solomon in Jerusalem, she came with a camel train bearing spices, gold and precious stones.[9]

In such ways the Empire was locked into economic relationships with peoples beyond its frontiers in the east which were stronger than those across its old western borders had been. Religious relationships also strad-dled the frontiers in a way unparalleled in the west. While Jews remained numerous in the Empire, they had come to settle over a wide area in the east, especially Persia; late antiquity saw the compilation of the two great Talmuds, that of Palestine in the Empire and that of Babylon in Persia. Monophysite Christians were another religious group with large numbers of adherents on both sides of the frontier. By 600 they not only encompassed Egypt and much of Syria, but were also numerous in Persia, Arabia and Armenia. Nubia, to the south of Egypt, had become largely Monophysite following the success of missionaries sent by Theodora, while further to the south the church of Axum, a kingdom that had already been evangelised, went the same way. There were therefore many Monophysites both within and without the Empire, while Nestorian Christianity, despite being named for a former patriarch of Constantinople, quickly found its centre of gravity in Persia, and established offshoots in Arabia. By the end of the fifth century, Nestorians had founded an institute of higher study at Nisibis, just across the Persian frontier, and their theology was later systematised by the learned Babai the Great, an exact contemporary of Muhammad. The extraordinary growth they enjoyed, which took them to China by the seventh century, was almost entirely outside the Empire.

The Middle East constituted a unit within which stories easily passed from group to group. The Qur'an tells of a group of men who, at a time of religious persecution, entered a cave where they lay for a long time, before one of them went out to buy food with a coin. The tale, presumably of Syrian origin, is recognisably the same as the story of the seven sleepers of Ephesus which Gregory of Tours had told a few decades previously. Elsewhere, the Qur'an preserves traditions about the Virgin Mary which had grown up in the Christian East. The wife of the shah Chosroes II, the beautiful Shirin, was a Christian, whose husband believed she had conceived because of the intercession of the martyr Sergius, whose cult was popular among Arabs.[10] If the old frontiers in the west had been porous, those in the east remained so, but in different ways.

The East also differed from the west in the enduring strength of its cities. There are few signs of wealthy people leaving them for the country, as they did in the west. Yet in the midst of strength, change was taking place. About half way through the sixth century, the building of peristyle houses seems to have ended in the royal city, and the public baths and theatres so central to the communal life of antiquity were being used less. Christian leaders were to the fore in this movement. In 538, a bishop on his deathbed at a remote place in the Egyptian desert was advised to bathe, and when he replied that he had never seen his body since becoming a monk he was persuaded to bathe in his clothes. When a holy fool was prevailed upon to take a bath in the Syrian town of Emesa, he subverted proceedings by placing his garment on his head and making his way into the women's bath, whence he was speedily ejected.[11] Moreover, cities were beginning to be laid out differently. Justinian extended the main road in Jerusalem, the broad cardo, 12 m wide, and a slightly later representation of the city, still to be seen in a mosaic in the floor of a church at Madaba, in Jordan, shows this road, broad and straight, with rows of columns on both sides. While Justinian's undertaking accorded with the ancient principles of town planning, such streets were coming to replace the old forum, or agora, as markets, and before long the constructions of private individuals were encroaching on to the public space of the roads. The atrophy of central market-places may have been connected with a redirection of energies towards churches, then emerging as rival poles of civic life, but secular life was coming to be conducted in new ways. It was into this changing world that invaders made their way in the seventh century.

THE ARABS

According to a historian of the fourth century, the Arabs were a destructive race, desirable neither as friends nor enemies. But relations between Arab bedouin and settled peoples had been difficult for millennia:

> And so it was, when Israel had sown, that the Midianites came up, and the Amalekites, and the children of the east . . . And they encamped against them, and destroyed the increase of the earth, till thou [*sic*] come unto Gaza, and left no sustenance for Israel . . . For they came up with their cattle and their tents, and they came as grasshoppers for multitude; for both they and their camels were without number: and they entered into the land to destroy it.

In the ninth century, a patriarch of Antioch looked back on the days when the Arabs had existed on the margin of the civilised world, 'the most despised and disregarded of the peoples of the earth, if indeed they were known at all'.[12] But such judgements need not have been universal, for a daughter of an emperor of the sixth century, Justin II, was named Arabia, and they were certainly unfair. Relations between Arab bedouin and settled peoples were awkward in the same way as those between the Berbers of Africa and nearby farmers. Moreover, while the Arabian peninsula could appear marginal to the peoples round about it, it could equally be seen as central. Facing as they did the Empire in the north-west, Africa in the west and Persia to the north, the Arabs could borrow freely from others. The polytheism characteristic of their society at the time of the prophet Muhammad may not have been a purely Arab development; when Muslims later looked back on the pre-Islamic period as the time of ignorance (Jahiliyah), it may have been cults inspired by the Greeks that they had in mind.

Theirs was a society made up of disparate elements. Some Arabs were nomadic bedouin, who drew their livelihood from their flocks and the transport of goods. Others, particularly those who lived in the south-east of the peninsula, which enjoyed limited rainfall in summer, or around oases, cultivated grain and dates, and maintained an interdependent relationship with the bedouin. Some of the Arabs were merchants, and during the sixth century the oasis town of Macca became more important as a centre of trade. It contained a religious shrine, the ka'ba, around which existed an inviolable zone (*haram*, the Arabic word from which 'harem' is derived) where fighting was forbidden. A town offering a religiously sanctioned peace was a good place for the development of commerce, and with the encouragement of the dominant tribe in Macca, Quraysh, trade boomed.

Relations between the Arabs and the Empire were variable. Sometimes they were hostile; in 410, the year in which Rome was sacked by the Visigoths, people described as barbarians of whom it could be said they were 'people from Barca wandering widely' and to whom could be applied what Scripture said of Ishmael, 'he shall live against the face of all his brothers', are said to have run like a torrent through the paths of Egypt, Palestine, Phoenicia and Syria.[13] But more significant than such raids was the steady migration of Arabs into the adjacent parts of the Empire and Persia, in a movement across frontiers similar to that of the Franks across the Rhine. The oldest surviving inscription in Arabic, from the time of Constantine, is from Namara, in southern Syria.[14] In the sixth century, the great monastery founded by St Sabas near Jerusalem relied on grain conveyed to it from the Dead Sea by camels driven by an Arab. An inscription recording the building of a shrine dedicated to the martyr St Sergius, at Zabad, south-east of Aleppo (Halab), in 512, is trilingual, in Arabic, Greek and Syriac; of the people commemorated in Arabic, three bore the name of the martyr. An Arab poet of the sixth century, 'Amr ibn Kulthum, boasted of having drunk in Baalbec, Damascus and Qasirin; the grandfather of Muhammad, Hashi, had received his name from the bread and cakes that he brought to Macca from Syria, and was said to have died at Gaza; while the Prophet himself traded in Syria. The general who took Alexandria, Amr, was believed to have met, on an earlier trading trip to Jerusalem, a monk from Alexandria who took him there on a visit, while the second caliph, 'Umar, was said to have made his fortune in Gaza, a port through which goods from Arabia were consigned. The Arab armies that invaded Syria in the seventh century encountered Arabs already living there, and others had interests there; Abu Sufyan, a prominent member of Quraysh whose son Mu'awiyah became a caliph, owned property near Damascus. The Arabs were by no means strangers to the Empire; no less than the Roman frontier on the Rhine, that in Syria was porous.[15]

Historically, the Arabs had been for the Romans an irritant who occasionally became a problem. Each side tried to use the other. The force that defeated the Goths and their allies outside Constantinople in 378 had been sent there by an Arab queen, Mavia. On succeeding her husband, she had made war on the Romans, but having obtained the consecration of an Arab hermit, Moses, as bishop for her people, she made peace and married her daughter to a general in imperial service, Victor, the member of an Iranian-speaking group, the Sarmatians, who had so advanced as to hold a consulship in 369. Roman policies towards the Arabs varied. The early Empire relied on the services of client states, but from about the late third century fortifications were erected along the eastern frontier. Over the centuries, those in the northern sector, which faced the formidable Persians, were maintained and improved. The fortress of Zenobia, the modern Halabiyya, by the Euphrates was strengthened at the time of Justinian or shortly before; of eight coins that have been discovered there, six are from the sixth century. To the south, however, the fortresses came to be abandoned. But this need not have foreshadowed a Roman withdrawal, for from about 400 the system of fortifications in the Julian Alps in Italy had also been allowed to lapse, and the changes in the east can be seen as part of a new way of managing some border areas. Hereafter, the interests of the Empire would be seen to by an allied tribal group of Arabs at the north-western end of the peninsula, the Ghassanids.

They were incorporated into imperial structures. By the early sixth century they had become *foederati*, formal allies of the empire, led by their own officials who held the title phylarch. In addition to being effective allies against the Persians, who cultivated another group of Arabs, the Lakhmid dynasty, the Ghassanids kept an eye on the bedouin of Arabia. They were Christians, whose adhesion to Monophysitism recalled that of many of the German peoples who settled in the west to Arianism, another deviant belief in imperial eyes. Just as Huneric and Theoderic were interested in the welfare of Arians living within the Empire, the Ghassanid phylarchs intervened with emperors on behalf of Monophysites. They were keen builders of churches, for a cathedral complex erected at Bostra at the end of the fifth century or the beginning of the sixth rivalled in size the great cathedral that Justinian would soon build at Constantinople. The Ghassanids had a penchant for living in stylish residences in or adjacent to the desert which was later displayed by the Umayyad caliphs. And just as the Empire benefited from them, so they gained from their connection with it. Arabs referred to the Ghassanids as 'al-bitriq', a term based on the office of patrician that the emperors bestowed on some of them. Their dealings with the Empire were not always smooth, and towards the end of the sixth century there were major ructions in the relationship. But they remained loyal. They were among those who fought for the Empire at the decisive battle against the Muslims in Syria, after which some settled within the Empire. An emperor of the early ninth century was believed to have been of Ghassanid descent.

The recognition and status accorded to the Ghassanids was a sign that Arabia was being increasingly drawn into the surrounding world. Inescapably, people living further into Arabia than the Ghassanids became exposed to Christianity. A trading town in north Yemen, Najran, had come to have a sizeable Christian element following the introduction of the faith by one Hayyan, not surprisingly a merchant, and one of the leaders of the Monophysite movement, Philoxenos of Mabbug, consecrated bishops for it. But there were Jews as well in Arabia, and in about 520 Najran fell to a remarkable figure, Dhu Nuwas, a Yemeni who, having accepted Judaism, adopted the name Yusuf and set about the Christians. It was said he burned a church where 2,000 people were assembled. The leader of Najran, Harith (Greek Arethas), and other townspeople who refused to deny Christ and the Cross were martyred. They included a group of women who proclaimed 'Christ is God and the son of the Merciful', the last word foreshadowing one of the main attributes accorded God by Islam.[16] The Christian powers could not stand idly by. The Empire and the Ethiopian king Elesboas sent a force that killed Yusuf and established a protectorate in the south of Arabia; before long there was a cult of Arethas and his fellow martyrs. In the south of Arabia, the Christian ruler Abraha restored the great dam at Marib, the ruins of which can still be seen. Before long, however, the dam was in ruins, and the failure to rebuild it may reflect a decline in political authority.[17] Muslim authors later wrote at length of a mysterious building, 'al-Qalis', which Abraha erected at San'a, the name of which may have been derived from *ekklesia*, the Greek word for 'church'. According to later Arab traditions, the emperor of the time sent experts to help beautify it. It was later believed that Abraha attempted to make the church a place of pilgrimage to rival the ka'ba at Macca, which would have had economic consequences. In 570 he led an expedition to Macca, believed on the evidence of the Qur'an to have been destroyed when birds dropped stones on it.[18] Abraha received ambassadors from Ethiopia, Byzantium and Persia, and in about 570 part of Arabia was subject to an invasion by the last of these powers. As the sixth century progressed, the Arabian peninsula was becoming increasingly open to influences.

In some ways the Arabs resembled the Germans in the West, so that the invasions which followed were partly a speeding up, by military means, of a process long under way. Yet there were differences. The cultivation of clients by the Empire and Persia, the strength of long-distance trade, the spread of Christianity and Judaism, and the military intervention of foreign powers all suggested a possible internationalisation of the peninsula. But as it turned out, the Arabs had nothing to fear. With remarkable speed, the tables were turned.

MUHAMMAD

The Arabs owed their great prominence in world affairs to religion. There is tantalising evidence for an indigenous Arabic tradition that claimed a place apart from Judaism and Christianity within a monotheistic framework derived from the patriarch Abraham. A Greek historian of the fifth century, writing of people he termed 'Saracens', explained that, while they took this name from Abraham's wife Sarah, they were really descended from Ishmael, his son by his wife's handmaid Hagar, whence the name Ishmaelites, by which they were commonly called. Indeed, he continued, they retained practices very similar to those of the Jews. Hence two names by which they were widely known, Saracen and Ishmaelite, both pointed to their descent from Abraham, the father of the Chosen People. It is hard to know what weight to put on this report, but it distinctly foreshadows some of the emphases of the Qur'an. This text sees Abraham and Ishmail as hanifs, people who, neither Jews nor Christians, did not ascribe partners to God and built the Holy House, or Ka'ba, at Macca. When it credits Abraham and his immediate descendants with 'submission' to God, it applies to them a word derived from the same Semitic root (*slm*) as the word 'Islam' is. An odd echo of the association of Saracens with Abraham occurs in a Christian author of the sixth century, who told the story of a Saracen whose son was paralysed down one side by a demon. In response to a vision, he took his son from Arabia to a monastery near Jerusalem, where the boy was healed. The party of Arabs was baptised, and departed 'no longer Agarenians and Ishmaelites but now descendants of Sarah and heirs of promise, transferred through baptism from slavery to freedom'. The formulation owes something to St Paul, according to whom Abraham's lineage from Hagar, symbolising the Jews, stood for bondage, whereas that from Sarah, which he took to mean the Christians, meant freedom (Gal. 4:22–31). Christian authors could therefore use the terms Saracen, Hagarene and Ishmaelite interchangeably for the people who called themselves Arabs.[19]

It was into this world of associations that Islam advanced.[20] Its teachings were expressed in the Qur'an, believed by Muslims to have been a series of revelations from God delivered in Arabic to a merchant of Macca, Muhammad, from about 610 until shortly before he died in 632. The revelations commenced with a command from an angel to recite, and despite his asserting that he could not, he began to recite the words of the Qur'an.[21] The series of messages he went on to receive was definitively committed to writing while 'Uthman was caliph (644–56). The teachings of the Qur'an concerning one God, the creator of all things other than himself, are similar to those of the preceding monotheistic religions, Judaism and Christianity, whose adherents it politely refers to as 'people of the book', and early Islamic tradition emphasised the point in a number of stories that cluster around Bostra, the Syrian town that had produced the emperor Philip the Arab and which was a stronghold of Christianity among the Arabs. It was said that when Muhammad's mother was pregnant with him, she saw a light come forth from within her by which she could see the castles of Bostra. Muslims told of how Muhammad, when a boy accompanying a trading caravan, had encountered at Bostra a monk, Bahira, who was able to identify him as a prophet on the basis of books he had read. The story, as told by Muslim authors, tended towards the validation of Islam; when it was told by Christian authors, the monk, whom they identified as a heretic, was blamed for the flaws in Islam.[22]

Not only major themes but many of the incidentals of the Judeo-Christian scriptures recur with minor variations in the Qur'an: whereas the Old Testament has the chosen people missing cucumbers, melons, leeks, onions and garlic when they left Egypt, the Qur'an represents them as pining for green herbs, cucumbers, grain, lentils and onions. Even at a verbal level, the striking image of a camel passing through the eye of a needle, which Jesus used to indicate the difficulty that the rich would find in entering the kingdom of heaven, recurs in the Qur'an, where it is applied to the difficulty some would have in entering heaven. In other respects, the doctrine of the Qur'an reflects post-biblical notions. Its teaching that Satan was banished from God's presence after refusing to bow down before Adam agreed with that first expressed in a Hebrew text of the first century CE, later translated into Greek and Latin, *The Life of Adam and Eve*, while its understanding that Jesus only appeared to suffer on the cross expressed the teaching of an early Christian heresy, Docetism, and its Mariology reflects that expressed in apocryphal gospels; a passing reference in the Qur'an to a stream that God made flow at the feet of Mary recalls the wonderfully sweet water flowing from a rock near Jerusalem which an Italian visitor of the late sixth century was told Mary had drunk from while fleeing to Egypt. We have also seen that the Qur'anic description of God as the 'merciful' (*rahman*) repeats a word already in use among Christian Arabs.[23]

In such ways, the Qur'an takes its place among expressions of monotheistic belief already current in the Middle East. But in other, very important ways the Qur'an sets itself against Jews and Christians, whom it accuses of falsifying the texts of their scriptures. While Muhammad is placed in a line of biblical 'prophets' beginning with Adam, he was also a member of the narrower group of 'messengers'. Hitherto this had extended to Jesus, but it is clear that Muhammad was the last and greatest of them. Furthermore, its strong teaching on the unity of God excluded any notion of the Christian Trinity and the incarnation. The Qur'an was therefore both eirenic and combative in its stance towards the earlier monotheistic religions.[24]

The teachings that Muhammad placed before the people of Macca irritated the ruling elite of the town. This was not simply because they disagreed with what he said; in that his message threatened the cult which had grown up around the shrine of the ka'ba, with its 360 'idols', to the city's great benefit, it endangered its prosperity. After a period of growing harassment, the prophet and his followers fled north to the oasis town of Madina, or Yathrib as it was known in pre-Islamic times, in 622. He had been invited there by the town's population of Jewish and polytheistic Arabs, and concluded a treaty with them. This emigration (*hijra*) was decisive in the history of Islam. Within a few decades it had become the base from which the years were, and still are, counted in the Islamic calendar, and those who took part in it, the *muhajirun*, were later accorded special status. At Madina the importance of the community of Islam, and by implication the danger of being excluded from it, became clear. Increasingly, as an Islamic community developed there, the revelations received by Muhammad concerned its governance. Western readers can find the long suras revealed at Madina, which are placed at the beginning of the Qur'an, heavy-going; for the Arabs, they offered the first clearly expressed system of law they had known. Beyond this, the rudiments of a system of taxation were introduced. In these ways, during Muhammad's years at Madina, Islam took long strides towards being the vehicle by which the apparatus of a state would be introduced into

Arabia. These years also saw Islam turn away from Judaism, a movement symbolised by a change in the *qibla*, the direction Muslims faced when praying, from Jerusalem towards Macca, the home of the ka'ba, which was now seen as having been founded by Abraham and Ishmail. The Prophet had hitherto enjoyed close relations with the Jews of Arabia, some of whom, perhaps horrified at the treatment their co-religionists were receiving at just this time from Christians, had acknowledged him as Messiah.

Gradually the reach of Muhammad lengthened, particularly after the battle of Badr (624), in which the Muslims of Madina defeated the troops protecting a large caravan on its way from Syria to Macca. In 630 the Prophet entered Macca as the master of the city, and, at the cost of admitting into his innermost councils members of Quraysh who had converted at the last possible moment, the Islamicisation of Arabia proceeded. Ultimately the peninsula was to become entirely Islamic. The Byzantine town of Ayla, at the north-eastern tip of the Gulf of Aqaba, submitted peacefully to Islam in 630; before long a new, Islamic town was functioning alongside the old one. Early in the Islamic period a great mosque was built at San'a, bearing crosses on two of the capitals; perhaps the qalis had been pillaged for building materials. By the time Muhammad died, in 632, he had been generally accepted as prophet by the polytheistic Arabs.

Muhammad is certainly the most important individual to have lived in the period covered in this book; that he lived in a land generally regarded as a backwater can only heighten one's sense of amazement at his achievement and that of his followers. But it occurred in tandem with events that were taking place elsewhere, to which we shall now turn.

PERSIANS AND JEWS

The decades during which Muhammad preached coincided with significant developments in the relations, by then more than a millennium old, between the Greek speakers of the eastern Mediterranean, the Persians and the Jews. Whatever evaluation modern scholars place on the various wars fought at Justinian's behest, when Photius, an intellectual of Constantinople in the ninth century, summarised the eight books that Procopius had written on those wars, he dealt only with the first two, those concerning Persia; for the Byzantines, these were the most significant. Intermittently, Persia had caused anxiety since the Sasanid dynasty came to power in the third century. The usurpation of Phocas gave the shah Chosroes II (590–628) a wonderful opportunity to intervene in the affairs of the Empire. A victim of insurrection at the beginning of his reign, he had regained his throne with the help of Maurice, whose overthrow at the hands of Phocas he felt gave reason for war. Antioch, Damascus and Jerusalem fell as his forces penetrated deep into imperial territory. Not surprisingly, Jews were on hand to help them, for the anti-Jewish sentiments that Christianity was held to entail were foreign to the Zoroastrian religion of the Persians. The preparedness of Jews to support the assailants of Christian towns was almost a topos,[25] and their doing so reinforced the deterioration in relations between the existing monotheistic faiths in the region.

The Jews had long been a nuisance for the Roman state, which fought a bitter war culminating in the destruction of the Temple and much of Jerusalem in AD 70, and following the suppression of a revolt in 135 they had not been allowed to live in Jerusalem. Only then did the church there gain its first gentile bishop. Hadrian gave the city a new name, Aelia Capitolina, a remarkably arrogant one, for its first component referred to the name of his own family and the second, which alluded to a temple on the Capitoline Hill in Rome, was an epithet of Jupiter. The city's role was changed for ever in 326 when Constantine's mother, Helena, identified the True Cross on which Christ had been crucified. Suddenly, it gained a standing among Christians which little in the preceding centuries had foreshadowed. Jews continued to be excluded. They only returned officially under the auspices of Julian the Apostate, who, seeking to encourage non-Christians, gave permission for the rebuilding of the Temple, which remained unfinished at his death. The patronage that the apostate emperor bestowed on the Jews did nothing for the opinion in which church leaders held them. Ambrose of Milan and Symeon the Stylite triumphed in encounters with emperors whom they deemed soft on Jews, and it was generally true that the leadership of the church took a firmer line towards Jews than the secular authorities.

Most Jews in the ancient world practised the same occupations as gentiles did, and despite the odd figures they often cut in our texts, it must sometimes have been hard to distinguish them from the people among whom they lived. But it became increasingly necessary for Christians and Jews to define themselves against each other, and the coming to supremacy of the younger religion turned out to be one of the most important events in the history of the elder. It led Judaism to rework itself. This it did by turning away from the standard translation of the Jewish Bible into Greek, the Septuagint, which was now seen as having been compromised by the uses to which it had been put by Christians. The great Palestinian and Babylonian Talmuds were formed, legal texts worthy of being set beside the codes of Roman law produced under Theodosius II and Justinian in the same period. Jewish identity was becoming more concerned with observance of the Law and increasingly expressed in the Hebrew language. Needless to say, these developments in turn made it all the easier for Christians to feel uneasy at that which they could not understand.

At the turn of the seventh century, the trajectory of relations between the adherents of the two religions turned steeply downwards. We have already seen how they worsened in Spain, when the Visigothic king Sisebut turned against the Jews, and although Isidore of Seville looked on this step with disquiet, a century of persecution followed. Across the Pyrenees, a synagogue was destroyed in Clermont in 576, and the bishop of the town told the Jews that, while he did not compel them by force to confess the Son of God, but rather preached and conveyed the salt of wisdom, they had the choice of being baptised or leaving! More than 500 were baptised, and the recalcitrants went to Marseilles, already the home of a sizeable Jewish community. In Antioch, the Jews were said to have murdered the patriarch and placed his genitals in his mouth. Far away on Mt Sinai, a hermit, in a vision that Christians felt sure was sent by the Devil, saw the throng of the apostles, martyrs and other kinds of Christians looking wretched in the deepest darkness, while Moses, the prophets and the Jewish people lived joyously, bathed in bright light. He left the monastery and went to Palestine, where he was circumcised, took a wife and began to attack Christianity.[26] The Persian invasions of the Empire occurred at this time, and the enthusiastic Jewish response gave Christians little cause to like them. But the Jews had good reason for welcoming the armies of Persia, for their co-religionists who lived there, not being defined in terms of a refusal to accept the Messiah, enjoyed a higher legal status and social standing than did those in the Empire. That the Talmud of Babylon was accorded more weight than that of Jerusalem suggests that the centre of gravity of Jewish civilisation had moved outside the Empire. For many Jews, the sudden incorporation of Jerusalem within the Persian Empire was a historical moment, and they sought to make the most of it.

The new regime in the Middle East showed itself determinedly anti-Christian. After Zacharias, the patriarch of Jerusalem, had been tortured, he and many others were taken to Persia with the True Cross that Helena had discovered. When the sad group came to the ancient town of Babylon, the patriarch appropriated the sentiments of Jewish exiles from Jerusalem in biblical times, saying with conviction the words of Psalm 137, 'By the waters of Babylon, there we sat down, yea we wept, when we remembered Zion. If I forget thee, O Jerusalem, let my right hand forget her cunning.' When Alexandria fell, the new regime was reported to have put to death almost every monk in 600 monasteries, the inmates of which had made the mistake of mocking the Persians; at the monastery of Nikiu, 700 monks were said to have been slain. Egypt had been under Persian power during the period of the Achemenid shahs in the sixth and fifth centuries BC, and again for a few years before Alexander arrived; now it was again abruptly pulled away from its orientation towards the Mediterranean. The Jews of the conquered territories made the most of their chance, and it may be to the years of Persian occupation that a curious story belongs. A rumour spread that the 4,000-strong Jewish population of Tyre planned to murder the Christians of the town on Easter Eve, and asked Jews from other cities to be on hand then. When the plot came to light, the Jews of Tyre were imprisoned, and as other Jews came from elsewhere and began to harm the churches outside the city, they were methodically put to death. Finally, the visiting Jews fled.[27] In Jerusalem, people described as 'malign Jews, enemies of truth and haters of Christ' were said to have offered to redeem Christians taken captive by the Persians, and, when their offer met with no response, to have bought the captives and promptly killed them. During the Persian occupation a Jewish leader, Joshua, produced a lead bull with an inscription in Hebrew in which he was referred to as an *archon*, or leader.[28] Astonishingly, there is evidence that Jews revived Temple worship during the Persian period. This had not taken place for over 500 years, and may have been interpreted in the light of apocalyptic notions of a return of the Jews to Jerusalem at the end of time.

The Jewish revival was to be short-lived. The Persian authorities could not favour them without alienating the majority population in the conquered lands and an important minority elsewhere in their domains. In any case, it was not long before the Byzantines bounced back. Under the emperor Heraclius they staged a rapid recovery, the more impressive for its having commenced at the time when the Avars were posing their greatest threat. The great victory over the Persians, Avars and their allies before the walls of Constantinople in 626 marked the turning of the tide. The Empire was supported by new allies, the Khazars, a people then living around the northwestern part of the Caspian Sea. Campaigning culminated in a battle fought towards the end of 627 at the biblical city of Nineveh, near the upper Tigris, at which the Persian army was virtually obliterated. Heraclius celebrated Christmas on the estates of Iesdem, a Christian of Syrian origin who held high office under Chosroes. Early in the new year, Byzantine troops occupied Chosroes' palace at Dastagerd, where they found countless ostriches, gazelles, wild asses, peacocks and pheasants, and a hunting park with lions and tigers; they had stumbled upon a late example of the old pleasure garden or *paradeisos* of the shahs.[29] Their traditional competence at organisation had served the Byzantines well, and it is pleasant to think that the ship that went down near Bodrum may have been carrying supplies for troops. In 629 Heraclius entered Jerusalem, the only emperor ever to visit the holy city, and the True Cross was returned. The cult of the Cross, a symbol of both the victory of Christ and that of the emperor, was growing at that time; a portion of it had been sent to Radegund at Poitiers, in Gaul. Its solemn restoration was the high-water mark of Heraclius's reign. At the same time, Heraclius and Sergius, the patriarch of Constantinople, himself a Syrian and the son of Monophysite parents, who had been feeling their way to reconciling Monophysite Christians with those who adhered to the council of Chalcedon, promulgated the doctrine of monothelitism, which attributed only one will to Christ. The notion met with an encouraging response, from Alexandria to Rome.

Such disasters placed the political system of Persia under immense strain. Chosroes was imprisoned and put to death shortly after the defeat at Nineveh, to be replaced by his eldest son, who sued the Empire for peace. But the cure was worse than the disease, for during the five years after Chosroes was deposed, the throne of Persia was claimed by eight men, among them the Empire's old enemy 'Wild Boar', whose daughter, in a sign of the changing times, had married a son of Heraclius. Stability only returned with the accession of Yazdigird in 632, the very year in which the Prophet of Islam died. But the glorious victory that the Empire had won came at a price. Even the temporary loss of the food-producing areas of Syria and, more importantly, Egypt, was a heavy blow to a state whose capital was located in an area of low agricultural productivity. In 618 the food dole for the inhabitants of Constantinople was abolished. In its diminished situation, the city could live with the destruction of the aqueduct named after Valens; it would be over a century before the aqueduct was restored. As the Empire moved into the seventh century, it faced a grim future. Prior to their defeat the Avars had been milking the Empire shamelessly, and the Persian war, expensive in manpower, was fought at a time when the tax-base of the Empire had been severely narrowed by the loss of wealthy provinces. Such an empire would have a clouded future.

Inevitably, the defeat of the Persians entailed a swift reversal of the fortunes of the Jews, who had supported them so fervently. Heraclius decided to deal with the problem that he thought they posed by having them baptised, and orders to this effect were dispatched. In France it was believed that Heraclius had discovered, by astrology, that a circumcised people would devastate his empire, and he wrote to Dagobert, telling him to have all the Jews baptised. The king complied immediately. Coming as it did not long after the beginning of the Visigothic kings' long campaign against Judaism, the previous situation in which the attitudes of church authorities towards the Jews were more hostile than those of the state had now been reversed. As the Christian world moved further into the seventh century, secular governments would set the pace in moves against Jews. Even in Italy, tolerant policies that the papacy had advocated at the beginning of the century were overthrown when the Lombard state offered Jews the alternatives of baptism or being put to the sword. Such legislation failed; henceforth, the figure of the Jew who had made an insincere profession of Christianity would be a familiar one in the Christian world. But the early decades of the seventh century had irreparably worsened relations between Christians and Jews. The latter could have been forgiven for thinking that they would be better off under non-Christian governments. According to one report, after the Persians evacuated Edessa in the face of the Byzantine reconquest, the Jews who had congregated there took the road to the desert and went to Arabia, where they explained to the Arabs that they were related by blood. It was the very time that Muhammad was preaching.[30]

PREPARATION FOR EXPANSION

The death of the Prophet left the community he had founded in a quandary. He had left no instructions as to its future leadership, and while the Qur'an has a good deal to say on the preaching of the various prophets and messengers, it is virtually silent on the periods lying between them. It certainly made no provision for succession. Rivalry existed between the *muhajirun* who had supported Muhammad in his early years in Macca prior to the *hijra*, the *ansar* who had helped him in Madina, and the Quraysh, the old ruling elite of Macca who had embraced Islam very late, perhaps when there was no alternative. Beyond this, it might have been thought that the claims of family would be significant, in which case Muhammad's son-in-law and cousin, 'Ali, who had been taken into the Prophet's house as an orphan at the age of five and was one of the very first to acknowledge him as prophet, would have had a good claim to authority. The matter was settled when a group of the *muhajirun* met and elected one of their number, Abu Bakr, to be the caliph of the Prophet. The term was one with complex resonances, which include the ideas of being the successor or deputy of someone else; the Qur'an describes Adam as having been the 'caliph' of God. Abu Bakr's claims to authority were substantial. He was a respected man whom Muhammad was later believed to have compared to Abraham, Jesus, Noah and Moses,[31] and one of his daughters had married the Prophet. But his hands were full, for some of the Muslims almost immediately sought to break away from the community that Islam had suddenly created in Arabia. So it was that Abu Bakr spent the two years of his caliphate (632–4) in the apostasy (*ridda*) wars, which culminated in the victory of the Muslims and the firm incorporation of Arab tribes within the framework of Islam. A considerable military momentum among the Arab Muslims lay behind this success, and what would be more natural than its prolongation? The next caliph, 'Umar (634–44), was another of the *muhajirun*, perhaps the first holder of the office to be called 'Commander of the faithful'.[32] Under him, the great wars began.

It is hard to determine just why they did. Inevitably, Christian authors outside Arabia connected the beginning of the wars with things they were familiar with. A Byzantine historian writing two centuries later mentions attacks on Christian Arabs, and it may be significant that the Qur'an presents itself as a specifically Arabic scripture and that the first attack on an area with a large population of non-Arabs, Egypt, seems to have been undertaken without the approval of the caliph. But this author represents the wars as beginning with a single incident. On one occasion, he tells us, Arabs being paid by the Empire to guard approaches to the desert were denied their customary stipend, and, apparently in revenge, led their fellow tribesmen towards Gaza. That stipends to the Arabs were denied is certainly plausible, for imperial resources had been overextended during the disastrous early decades of the seventh century. But this account confronts us with an extreme version of a phenomenon we have encountered more than once in this period, that of people on the receiving end of attacks offering explanations for them in ignorance of the situation of the people launching them. The Byzantine author seems to have been unaware of the extraordinary changes in Arabia that occurred immediately prior to the outpouring of the Arabs.[33]

Later Arab traditions move in the opposite direction, by locating the origin of these wars with Muhammad himself. He is said to have written to Heraclius, urging him to accept Islam, and Arab historians who later wrote about the wars that ensued saw them as being bound up with religion. But a precise connection between Islam and the wars of conquest is elusive. The wars were not launched to convert non-Muslims, with the possible exception of Arabs living outside Arabia, and some texts of the Qur'an that are often taken to legitimate war on non-Muslims had, in fact, a much more restricted application. The teaching that Muslims were to 'fight them till persecution is no more' may seem bellicose, but an early Arab historian saw it as part of a revelation directed against the pagan Arabs of Macca, and it could hardly have been extended to justify the making of war on the Christian Empire. Yet before long the injunction 'Whether unarmed or well-equipped, fight on and fight for the cause of God' was applied to warfare in Byzantine Africa.[34]

The very early wars may have been seen by some of their participants as a form of *jihad* or virtuous striving, and to the extent that the wars were seen as holy wars, the promise of Paradise for Muslims who fell would have added to their appeal. An author of the ninth century has Abu Bakr describe the war he planned to wage in Syria, the first of the great wars of conquest, as a 'holy war', whereupon he enticed some people actuated by greed and attracted others by hope of divine renumeration,[35] and doubtless there was a mixture of secular and religious motivations among those who participated. The new society that Islam created among the Arabs both provided the cohesion necessary to wage wars and prompted them, for widespread conversion to Islam among the Arabs made the sustained low-level *razzias*, or raids, which had been a feature of their society, out of the question, and stimulated their redirection against wealthy targets beyond Arabia. There may also have been a wish to replace income lost because of disruption to trade during the wars between Byzantium and Persia, while at a more general level it is possible that overpopulation encouraged Arabs to leave home. But clear evidence is lacking. Even the extent to which the early expeditions were centrally controlled cannot be established. To make matters still more obscure, whatever motivations the Arabs had for launching the first wars must have changed, for before long, tentative expeditions had turned into unprecedented wars of conquest.

EXPANSION BEGINS

Some of the Arab conquests were to the north, against Persia. After overstretching itself at the beginning of the century, this state had been severely weakened in the course of its war with Heraclius, and virtually fell apart after the murder of Chosroes. Its capacity to resist attacks from Arabia was minimal. Moreover, Arabs had been nibbling at Persian territory before the coming of Islam, and a high proportion of the population in the south was Arab. Several years of fighting came to a head in 637 at a battle fought at Qadisiyya, to the west of the Euphrates, where the Persian army, despite disconcerting its opponents by the use of elephants, was decisively defeated. The shah and his upper officials left for the Iranian plateau, allowing the Arabs to occupy Mesopotamia, where they were supported by taxes. A subsequent victory at the battle of Nihavand, an upland town in the Zagros Mountains, opened up the great plateau to the invaders. The shah, Yazdigird, sought safety in flight and alliance with the Turks, but he was ingloriously killed, probably in 652, at a mill near Marv, in the modern Turkmenistan, nearly 2,000 km from his old capital city. Thereafter, it only remained for the Arabs to mop up pockets of resistance.

At the same time, Arabs were moving against the Byzantine Empire. They first attacked Syria, perhaps seeking to bring its large Arab population into the fold of Islam; in this case, they would have been continuing the process of Islamicisation that had taken place in Arabia. Initially, they confined their activities to the countryside, but the scale of attack changed after the general Khalid made a daring crossing of the desert, which culminated near Damascus. On Easter Day 634 he defeated Heraclius's Ghassanid allies. Damascus and Hims subsequently fell, and an Arab victory at the battle of the Yarmuk, a watercourse flowing westwards into the Jordan, in August 636, was decisive. Thereafter, the Byzantines being unable either to put an army in the field or to rely on their Arab allies, the newcomers were unbeatable in Syria.

Of the cities they took, the most important was Jerusalem, so recently retaken from the Persians. Sophronius, an old friend of John Moschus and Maximus the Confessor, who had become patriarch in 634, had led the resistance. Before long he was unable to go to Bethlehem to celebrate the birth of Christ, being in dread, as he put it, of the cruel sword of the Saracens and the dagger of the Hagarenes. The situation reminded him of the flaming sword that kept Adam from entering paradise after he had been expelled from it.[36] The city fell in 637. Our sources describe 'Umar, who had succeeded Abu Bakr as caliph (634–44), making a special journey from Macca to the city, which, displaying the modesty that endeared him to his followers, he entered wearing dirty clothes. When Sophronius pressed the caliph to accept clean clothes he refused, but finally a compromise was reached: 'Umar would wear a clean set of clothes while his own were being washed.[37] The Muslims and the Christians of the city concluded an agreement, the more generous for its having surrendered rather than been taken by force, for the Arabs treated the cities taken by capitulation more harshly – a practice that may have had the consequence, annoying to modern historians, of influencing the descriptions of their capture by later Arab historians in ways that we cannot now detect. The people of Jerusalem would keep their property, there would be no forced conversions, the poll tax (Arabic *jizya*) would be paid as usual, those who wished to depart would be able to, and Jews were not to live in the city. The provisions of the treaty were respected, save that very shortly Jews resumed residence there. It is hard to determine the nature of relations between the Muslims and Christians in the newly conquered holy city, for here again the sources may reflect no more than what their authors wanted to be believed, but it would be reasonable to assume a degree of tension.

In 637 the garrison at the port city of Gaza also surrendered. Its members were sent to Jerusalem where, after refusing to abjure Christianity and being encouraged by Sophronius, 60 Christian soldiers were martyred. Yet religion does not seem to have been a major issue in the Arab advance; indeed, it may have been less important than it had been a few decades earlier, when Byzantines were fighting Persians. Before long Antioch, the old Hellenistic capital of Syria, and Damascus fell. Elsewhere, desperate steps were taken. John, the officer left at Edessa when Heraclius withdrew in 636, negotiated an agreement to pay the Arabs annually 100,000 solidi, a sum which invites comparison with the payments that had been made to the Avars, provided that they did not cross the Euphrates. Heraclius speedily sacked him, but the town was forced to surrender. Just as occurred elsewhere, Byzantine power in Syria contracted towards the coast. The last town to fall was Caesarea. Orientated towards the sea, it had imported fine pottery from Cyprus and Africa; time would tell what the future of such towns, looking towards the sea as they did, would be. As Heraclius made his dejected way towards Constantinople, he paused at a pass in the Taurus Mountains, where he was reported to have uttered the words, 'Peace unto thee, O Syria, and what an excellent country this is for the enemy!'[38] Before long, he had turned a band of territory to the south of the range into scorched earth, so creating a frontier of a new type. Whereas the borders of the Empire had traditionally been areas of meeting and integration, that which Heraclius established with the world of Islam heightened the natural barrier of a range of mountains so as to make the frontier as impermeable as possible. In later centuries, the Christian and Muslim parts of Spain would be similarly divided.

The loss of Egypt followed shortly upon that of Syria. After the recapture of Alexandria from the Persians, Heraclius had determined upon a radical concentration of power in the city, by appointing someone who would not only have both civil and military authority, as the exarchs did in the west, but lead the church as well. His choice for the post was Cyrus, the bishop of a diocese in one of the extremities of the Empire, to the east of the Black Sea. Heraclius knew him as a supporter of his ecclesiastical policies and as someone likely to provide a firm hand at the wheel, although once in office Cyrus tempted fate by persecuting the Monophysite majority. But at the end of 639 the Arab general 'Amr, probably on his own initiative, invaded Egypt. It fell to Cyrus to deal with the invaders, and according to a tradition preserved in one Byzantine author he did this in an inventive way, by proposing that 'Amr become a Christian and marry a daughter of Heraclius. According to other traditions, he paid tribute to the Arabs to keep them at bay.[39] For whatever reason, Cyrus was relieved of office, and when he was sent back to Alexandria there was no alternative to negotiating the surrender of the city. In the autumn of 642 'Amr entered Alexandria, and Egypt came under Islamic power; in the following year an Arab force reached Tripoli, half way across the northern coast of Africa.

It proved impossible for the Arabs to sustain the initial pace of conquest in the following decades, although rapid advance occurred under the caliph 'Uthman (644–56) when, in defiance of any expectations, the Arabs built a fleet and showed themselves expert at naval warfare, launching attacks on the large islands of Cyprus and Rhodes. The set of nine silver plates decorated during the reign of Heraclius with scenes from the life of David was part of a treasure buried in a coastal area of the former island, apparently at the time of an Arab raid in the middle of the century. By that time, people described in a contemporary source as Saracens were living in Sicily. Armenia was taken, the caliph wrote to the emperor inviting him to renounce Christianity and rule as his subordinate, and an attack was launched on Constantinople itself.[40] Developments within the world of Islam gave the Empire a breathing space. A rebellion broke out against Uthman, who seemed to favour unduly the Quraysh, the old pre-Islamic elite of Macca. The caliph was murdered while reading the Qur'an in his house at Madina, and those who committed the deed nominated as his successor 'Ali, the son-in-law and cousin of the Prophet. The manner of his coming to power, and deep-seated tensions within the Islamic community, made his task as caliph difficult, and he proved unequal to it. In 657 two Muslim armies, one led by 'Ali and the other by Mu'awiya, the governor of Syria, confronted each other by the upper Euphrates. A decision to put the issues that separated them to arbitration was a blow to the standing of the caliph, who came to be thought of as the leader of a party (*shi'a*), the group from which the modern Shi'ites trace their origin. His position continued to weaken, and by the time he was assassinated near a mosque at Kufa in 661, Mu'awiya had become caliph. Such distractions among the Muslims gave the Empire a welcome breathing space.

THE INITIAL IMPACT OF THE ARABS

It is not clear what immediate difference the Arabs made when they brought territories under their sway. The troops who settled in them give the impression of keeping out of harm's way. In Iran, garrison towns such as Basra, on a bank of the Euphrates, and Kufa, not far inland from the Gulf, were established at a distance from existing towns. Within decades, the tents and reed huts of soldiers' camps were replaced by buildings appropriate to dignified cities, and each had a population of over 100,000, probably larger than any city still under Christian power except Constantinople. Kufa quickly gained a sizeable mosque, with a paved floor, the installation of which had been necessitated by the worshippers' habit of throwing stones at the preacher. Such explosive growth foreshadowed the urban orientation that would distinguish the world of Islam from Christendom for most of the medieval period. In Egypt, 'Amr established a garrison town by the Nile at Fustat, a name that preserved the Greek form of the Latin word for a ditch around a military camp, *fossatum*. The town flourished to such an extent that by the eighth century Copts, as the Christian Egyptians came to be called, were living there; from these origins the modern Cairo developed. The exception was Syria. Apart from Jabiya, where the leaders of the Ghassanids used to reside, and Ramla, established some 200 km inland from the Mediterranean in the early eighth century, the Arabs who found their way there tended to settle in towns that already existed. Late in the seventh century, a rectangular house of prayer that the Muslims had built in Jerusalem was capable of accommodating 3,000 worshippers. Such an urban predilection was made easier by the presence of an existing Arab population, and by abandoned houses that had been left by local elites as they fled, as many of the people of Damascus were said to have done when they departed to Antioch.[41] The newcomers proved creative in the adaptations they made to existing appurtenances. In the town of Scythopolis, to the west of the river Jordan, the *vomitoria*, as the Romans tastefully named the entrances to theatres, were turned into housing. Such was the settlement in Syria that a hadith, one of the prophetical traditions attributed to Muhammad, has him saying 'The building of Jerusalem is the destruction of Madina.'

Centuries later, people looked back on the coming of the Arabs as having been a dramatic event. A famous story attributes the destruction of the great library of Alexandria, which had been the centre of learning of the Hellenistic world, to an order issued by 'Umar, although the tale is not known before the thirteenth century. More significant is a passage in a Christian

Egyptian author of the early tenth century, in which he purports to reproduce a letter written by 'Amr to 'Umar:

> I have conquered a city, the contents of which I am unable to describe! Among other things, I have found 4,000 buildings with 4,000 baths, 40,000 Jews who have to pay tribute, 400 royal places of pleasure, and 12,000 vegetable dealers, who sell greens. I have conquered it by force, without a pact and without a treaty.[42]

Whatever sophistication the Arabs had picked up in earlier visits to lands to their west, it cannot have been easy coming to terms with Alexandria. The conquerors of such a city would have been well advised to leave existing systems in place.

This they did. In all the lands that the Arabs occupied, they wisely maintained the established systems of taxation. The Arabic word *kharaj*, usually taken to refer to a tax on land, came into the language from a Syriac word that was itself based on the Greek word *choregia*, which originally referred to providing or paying for a chorus. Similarly, the Arabs' gold coin, the dinar, took its name from a Roman coin of silver or gold, the denarius, and their silver dirham from a Greek silver coin, the drachma. The precise nature of the tax regimes that the Arabs established is unclear, as is the exact meaning of the terms *kharaj* and *jizya*, a poll tax. But the lands conquered by the Arabs had formerly paid the greater part of the taxes raised by the Empire, and their new masters were keen taxers. Already, the caliph 'Umar ordered a census to be taken in the inhabited territory under his rule, which was said to have enumerated beasts and plants as well as humans. Some taxpayers fled to monasteries, whereupon early in the eighth century a governor of Egypt ordered that monks were to be branded, and that people travelling without 'passports', perhaps to be taken as receipts for taxes they had paid, were to be arrested.[43] Such efficiency in raising taxes did little to endear the new regime to the indigenous people, but it gave it the luxury of having large sums of money to spend. In this respect the caliphate was very different to most of the states that emerged in the post-Roman west.

Some of its income was directed towards maintaining the army. In general, the early Muslims in the conquered territories were supported by taxes paid by non-Muslims. From the time of 'Umar a pension ('*ata*, literally 'gift'), organised by a bureau called the *diwan*, was paid to Muslims outside Arabia. Not everyone received the same pension, a circumstance that was to lead to trouble later; those who had fought at the battle of Badr received five times as much as those who had become Muslims after the battles of Qadisiyya and Yarmuk. The Arabs did not farm the land, as the Franks and English did; no

land changed hands, as it did when the Vandals took Africa. The closest ana-
logue with the provisioning made for them would be with the system of
'thirds', understood as involving revenue sharing, which was practised in
parts of the west. The dependence of the Arabs on the state for stipends, and
their practice of living together, prevented their being diluted among the
indigenous populace, and this would have great consequences. But the
caliphate, no less than the preceding regimes, could use its revenues for non-
military purposes. A carefully worded inscription in Greek records that
in 662, when Mu'awiya was caliph, a bath house in Syria was restored by a
governor with an Arab name, through the care of an official with a Greek
name.[44] Public works had, in late antiquity, come to be largely the responsibility of the state rather than of local people, and the caliph was operating
within that tradition.

The inscription in the bath house also reveals continuity of administrative
personnel. It did not occur to the Arabs, any more than it did to the newcomers in Italy or Africa during the fifth century, to dismiss civil servants
from their posts. In Egypt they retained the services of officials such as
Menas, who had been placed in office by Heraclius, and appointed other
indigenes, such as Senuthius, who occupied under the Arabs what had been
an office of military command in the Empire since the fourth century, that
of duke of the Thebaid. The names of these men were those of native
Egyptians, but an appointee to high office in the Fayum, who saw to the
delivery of grain ordered by an amir in 642, Philoxenos, bore a Greek name.
In Syria, as we shall see, a family that held important office when the Arabs
took Damascus maintained its position for generations after they came. For
most people, the transition from Byzantine to Arab power would not have
been abrupt.

In one important way, however, the coming of the Arabs brought about
great change. During late antiquity, religion had become much more important in the societies around the Mediterranean than it had been previously,
and now an explicitly non-Christian government was settling in for what
turned out to be the long haul. Oddly enough, the coming of Islam initially
made little difference to the religious pursuits of the local people. In Jordan,
mosaic floors were installed in churches at Rihab in 635, while elsewhere
similar floors date from 637 and 639, right across the period of the Arab conquest. The chief immediate significance of the non-Christian views of the
new regime lay in their upsetting the balance of power between the religions
already established. Jews came to enjoy more dignity; a few decades after
the conquest, when the Christian inhabitants of Tripoli caused trouble, many

Jews were settled there to counter them. Relations between the various Christian groups altered. Hitherto, the adherents of the council of Chalcedon, despite being in a minority in Egypt, had enjoyed the support of the state against the Monophysites. During the last decade of Byzantine power in Egypt, the Monophysite patriarch of Alexandria, Benjamin, had frequently had to retire to Upper Egypt. Suddenly, what had resembled an underground church was liberated. Benjamin found himself consecrating a new church in the region of the lower Nile. The author of an account of this event, who represented himself as Agathon, Benjamin's successor, has the bishop thanking Christ for accounting him worthy to see the boldness of the orthodox faith, as he termed Monophysitism, the opening of holy churches, and the destruction and elimination of the godless heretics. He gave thanks for the freeing of his soul from the hands of the tyrant and apostate dragon.[45]

There is no mistaking the rejoicing at the end of Byzantine power. Later, some remembered the coming of Islam as a delivery from oppression. It was believed that when the people of Hims were threatened by Heraclius, they said to the Muslims: 'We like your rule and justice far better than the state of oppression and tyranny in which we were.' When the Byzantines were defeated by the Muslims, the townspeople opened the gates of the city and went out with singers and musicians.[46] It does not follow from this that, as has sometimes been thought, the invaders owed their success to the support of the people who occupied the lands they invaded, for even if it were accepted that the attitudes of civilians were important in the warfare of the period, the prospect of being ruled by a folk whom the people of the Empire tended to despise cannot have been attractive. As late as 717, the Egyptian crew of two fleets besieging Constantinople deserted and acclaimed the emperor.[47] Nevertheless, the two Christian churches, as they had effectively become, now had to deal with a government that had no interest in the validity of their positions, and were thus vulnerable to manipulation by the authorities.

The expansion of the Arabs that followed the death of Muhammad is one of the most significant events in the history of the world during the last few millennia. Yet its sheer contingency stands out. The enfeebled state of Persia and the Empire, which provided a window of opportunity such as had not existed for centuries, the impact of Islam on both the beliefs and society of the Arabs, the successful establishment of the caliphate, the skill of its generals, the impulse that took the Arabs far beyond their homeland, and 'Amr's private decision to invade Egypt were things that could not have been foreseen. Before long, the Empire and the caliphate were edgily treating each other as superpowers of equal status. The early frontier between the Arabs and Byzantines in northern Syria was marked by a column, atop which was a portrait of Heraclius, shown sitting on a throne. On one occasion a Muslim warrior, galloping towards the column, accidentally poked the emperor's eye, and honour was only restored when an image of the governor of Syria was similarly defaced.[48] The expansion of the Arabs to such a position is staggering. Within a decade of the death of Muhammad, Persia, one of the greatest empires of the ancient world, had been brought to its knees and would soon disappear, while three of the five patriarchates of the Christian church had ceased to be in Christian territory. It was then that one of the seven wonders of the ancient world, the colossus of Rhodes, met its end. Some people believed that it was thrown into the sea; others thought that it was sold to a Jewish merchant from the distant town of Edessa, who loaded the metal on to a caravan estimated to have comprised 900, or 980, camels.[49] Whatever the means by which it met its sudden fate, it is hard not to see the end of the colossus as emblematic of the end of the ancient world in the east.

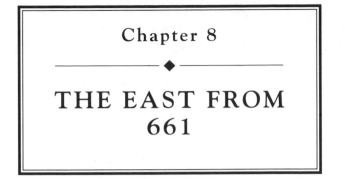

Chapter 8

◆

THE EAST FROM 661

THE NEW REGIME

The first four caliphs, traditionally known as 'rightly guided', hold a special place in Islamic history. The coming to power of 'Ali's antagonist Mu'awiya, the founder of the Umayyad dynasty, in 661, was a decisive turning point. No longer would the faithful be led by one of the ageing associates of Muhammad. Indeed, the parents of the new caliph had been two of their most bitter enemies, for his father, Abu Sufyan, had led military operations against the Muslims of Madina and only embraced Islam when there seemed to be no alternative, while according to some later traditions his mother had been condemned to death by the Prophet. The company that Mu'awiya kept gave offence to the pious, who were scandalised at such people as al-Akhtal ('the loquacious'), effectively the court poet for much of the Umayyad period (661–750). A heavy drinker and womaniser, he not only disdained efforts to convert him from Christianity, but looked back with nostalgia on the pre-Islamic past.

The Umayyad order marked the partial return of those whose authority had been eclipsed by the advent of Islam. But whatever doubts may have been entertained about the piety of the new regime, it set to work changing the principles of governance in Islam. Decades earlier, 'Umar, famed for his austere life, had drawn attention to Mu'awiya's partiality for his retinue, and to a report that petitioners were waiting at the door of his home at the beginning of the day. Mu'awiya is said to have replied:

'O Commander of the Faithful, our enemy is close to us, and they have scouts and spies, so I wanted, O Commander of the Faithful, for them to see that Islam has power.' 'Umar answered, 'This is the ruse of an intelligent man or the deception of a clever man.'

Mu'awiya retained the practice of 'Uthman, whereby the leader of the Islamic community was referred to no longer as 'caliph of the messenger of God' but simply as 'caliph of God'. If this were not enough, he groomed his son to succeed him, thereby introducing into Islam the principle of hereditary succession which, while familiar in non-Islamic states, had been unknown to the earlier caliphs.[1]

The massive conquests had altered the centre of gravity of the lands controlled by the Arabs in a way that made it appropriate for Mu'awiya to establish his headquarters at the ancient town of Damascus, where he moved into the former palace of the Byzantine governor. To be sure, he retained affection for the land of his origin. A surviving inscription records his building a dam near Ta'if, in an area far more fertile than it is now, a few years before he died; interestingly, its text contains early usages of the terms 'servant of God' and 'commander (amir) of the faithful'.[2] But, as victory followed victory, Madina had become a backwater; the town that the Prophet had referred to as 'the sweet smelling' was, for the Umayyads, 'the dirty'. In any case, Mu'awiya's family, like so many in Arabia, had been connected with Syria prior to Islam. His father had traded there and owned a village south of Damascus prior to the Islamic period,[3] and he himself had succeeded his brother as governor of the town. When he settled into the residence formerly occupied by Byzantine governors, it must have seemed that Islam was one occupying power in succession to another.

The changing role of Damascus pointed the way to the future. The establishment of a capital with no religious importance was itself significant, for it was a big step for the Arabs from being a people united by a culture and religion to a people who were also members of a state, one whose officials began at this time to keep copies of outgoing official correspondence. When a later caliph, 'Abd al-Malik, levelled a difficult pass on a road near the village of Fiq, to the east of the Sea of Galilee, he was improving the main road between Jerusalem and the capital; in Umayyad times, all roads led to Damascus. 'Abd al-Malik also demonstrated his power by erecting milestones, some of which survive, giving a distance from Damascus or Jerusalem. Damascus was also important for being where it was. An old Hellenistic and Byzantine city just 100 km from the Mediterranean, it was full of temptations for people who had quickly emerged from the Arabian desert. But in the long run, Damascus would be changed more than the Arabs who adopted it as their capital. Almost a thousand years earlier, its capture by Alexander the great had forced the city to orientate itself towards the Mediterranean; now, a process that would see it rejoining the Semitic world of the Middle East was under way.

EXPANSION TO THE WEST

The cause of 'Ali was not extinguished by his assassination, and some Muslims remained opposed to the rule of Mu'awiya and his successors. But in 680 'Ali's son Husain, a grandson of Muhammad, was killed in the act of rebellion; his brother Hasan had already died in suspicious circumstances. The theme of martyrdom that was to give the understanding of Islamic history held by 'Ali's party, the Shi'ites, such an emotionally compelling form was already in place. But the Umayyads had other things on their minds, and under them the great conquests resumed.

Some years after becoming caliph, Mu'awiya decided to take in hand the conquest of Africa. While the chronology of the campaigns that followed is unclear, we know that the initial advances were made inland. This was doubtless with strategic intent, for the Arabs were impressed by the Roman forts. Modern African towns with names like Kastiliya, no less than English places-names with the component 'chester', witness the impact that Roman *castra* made upon Arab and English newcomers. A desire to avoid confrontation with the Byzantines may lie behind the location of the Arab city of Kairouan. While it was built on the site of an old Roman town, its function was implicit in its Arabic name, literally 'garrison camp'. Since 682 it has occupied a site some 50 km inland from Sousse. As Carthage was not to fall for another decade, the Arabs must have been advancing within territory notionally controlled by the Byzantines, much as the expansion of the Slavs sometimes occurred in areas nominally under imperial control, without battles being fought. By the end of the century, the old capital was definitively in Arab hands. After its fall, the Byzantines, lacking a fleet in the western Mediterranean, dispatched one from Constantinople which succeeded in retaking the city. But before long the Arabs had received larger reinforcements, and they were able to regain the city for good. Justinian II, the emperor who had sought to regain the city, was overthrown in a coup, and although his successor did useful work against the Arabs nearer the royal city, distant Carthage was remote from his concerns. By the end of the seventh century, the entire north African littoral was effectively in Arab hands.

The Arabs' conquest of Africa allowed them to acquire allies. The Berbers, who had caused so much trouble to the Vandals and the Empire, were still there, and the Arabs found them no less of a problem. After the first capture of Carthage, their resistance was led by a spirited widow nicknamed al-Kahina, 'the sorceress', who operated from headquarters in the Aurès Mountains. Although she was said to have been a Christian and to have married a

Byzantine, Arab authors describe her in terms which suggest that she may have been an exponent of indigenous religious traditions, and she may have been similar to the woman who had advised the Berber leader Guenfan some two centuries earlier. Their adoption of Islam did nothing to stem the resilience of the Berbers, whose language is still vigorously spoken. In this respect their future was unlike that of the indigenous peoples of Syria and Egypt under Islam, whose Syriac and Coptic tongues became moribund over the centuries, and also that of the large number of speakers of Latin in north Africa. Patchy evidence allows us to trace, in some measure, the destiny of the classical inheritance there. After a gap of some two centuries, inscriptions in Latin reappeared in about the mid-ninth century and lasted until the mid-eleventh, during which period we know of bishops in Africa. But both Latin and Christianity were destined to become extinct there. While there are signs of the influence of Latin in dialects of Arabic spoken in Africa, the language died, as did the religion, which in its African guise had successfully resisted so many hostile regimes. Yet the Berbers flourished. They reminded the Arabs of themselves. Ibn Khaldun, the great philosopher of history who wrote in the fourteenth century, attributed to the peoples of Syria, among them the Jews and the peoples of Egypt, Yemen, Iraq and Spain 'sedentary culture'. The Berbers, on the other hand, lacked such traditions, and in this they were were similar to the Bedouin.[4] Before long, Berbers had become the first non-Arab people to join the victorious armies.

Just as had occurred in the time of Justinian, a conquest of north Africa opened the way to involvement in Spain. Legends developed that conceal the circumstances of its invasion. Behind them lie various interpretations of the interface between the Arabs, the Visigoths and any pockets of Byzantine authority that may have survived in the extreme west of Africa into the early eighth century. Stories were later told of how Julian, an officer in charge of Ceuta, invited the Muslims into Spain to avenge himself after king Roderic had debauched his daughter. On the other hand, king Witiza had died in 710, hoping to be succeeded by one of his sons, but the seizure of power by Roderic and his defeat of the sons of the late king in battle may have prompted disgruntled members of the family to invite the Muslims to Spain. Be this as it may, conditions in Spain were unsettled; not for the first time in their career of conquest, the Arabs profited from circumstances. In the spring of 711 a force of Arabs and Berbers made its way to Spain by way of the shortest crossing, the name of which still preserves that of Tariq, the leader of the army, for the word 'Gibraltar', in use at least as early as the ninth century, is derived from the Arabic for 'the rock (*jabal*) of Tariq'. They disembarked at

Tarifa, the port from which the Vandals had sailed to Africa some three centuries earlier. That summer the army of Roderic was defeated in battle, and Tariq wintered in the centre of the peninsula at Toledo, the Visigothic capital. In 712 his superior, Musa, came to Spain and quickly took Seville and Cordoba. Success on such a scale made the caliph al-Walid uneasy, and in 714 he recalled both generals to Damascus. Thereafter it fell to others to mop up the resistance. As early as 716 the Arabs were issuing bilingual coins that referred to Spain not only by its old Roman name, 'Hispania', but also by the name that would be used for it in the following centuries, 'al-Andalus'.

The Arabs did not take the northernmost parts of the peninsula. The Asturias and the Basque lands remained independent, although rather than seeing them as having survived the wreckage of the Visigothic state, it may be more accurate to see them as continuing to enjoy a *de facto* independence that they had already possessed as outlying regions in the time of the Goths. When, towards the end of the eighth century, a bishop of Toledo mocked a monk who accused him of heresy by calling him a sickly sheep, he was demonstrating the disdain of one dwelling in a metropolitan city for a provincial living in a backwoods part of the peninsula that happened to be independent. Moves that the Arabs made across the Pyrenees into the Frankish possessions were raids rather than invasions, and had no lasting impact. One such raid was defeated by Charles Martel, probably at Poitiers in 732, and while his victory may not have been as important as has sometimes been thought, it was soon clear that the immediate future of most of Spain was as part of the world of Islam, while France was to remain a Christian state; just as the Taurus Mountains did in Asia, the Pyrenees came close to being a frontier in Europe.

The collapse of the Visigothic state had been spectacular. But, as was their wont, some local elites adjusted themselves to the changed circumstances with surprising agility. The widow of king Roderic married Musa's son, who some believed adopted Christianity, and a regional governor took as his wife the sister of Pelayo, sword bearer of the last Visigothic kings who went on to lead Christian resistance. Centuries later, elements in Spain attempted to draw status from alleged links with the Visigothic past. In the tenth century, the historian Ibn al-Qutiya, 'Son of the Gothic woman', claimed descent from Sara, the granddaughter of king Witiza. It was said that, having gone to Damascus to place a case before the caliph, she married an Arab with whom she returned to Spain and by whom she had two sons, Ibrahim and Issac. In Murcia the local Gothic ruler Theodemir was confirmed in his privileges, to become in Arabic texts 'Tudmir'. The text of the treaty that he concluded with Musa in the spring of 713 survives. It shows him recognizing the new regime, agreeing that he and his subjects would pay a fixed sum of tribute annually in both money and produce, and surrendering seven strongholds.[5] Given that authority within the Visigothic state had been largely devolved locally, for many it must have seemed that little had changed with the coming of the Arabs. The transition from Gothic to Islamic power in Spain involved the displacement of one central government by another, but also a large number of accommodations locally made. All over the conquered regions, Spaniards settled down to a *convivencia*, the happy term for 'living-together'.

A small number of its elite, however, had left Spain. The bishop of the hitherto proud church of Toledo, Sinderid, characterised later as a hireling rather than a shepherd of Christ, abandoned his flock. In 721 he was in Rome, where he fixed his name to the proceedings of a council. Indeed, the occupation of so much territory by the Arabs had as a consequence a flood of refugees that washed over the surviving parts of the western church. The problem went back to the time of the Persian invasions, when a council in Spain dealt with a heretical Syrian who claimed to be a bishop. But with the coming of the Arabs it assumed far greater proportions. The narrative of their expansion written by al-Baladhuri proceeds to the sound of slamming doors: the emperor sent many ships to Tripoli which took away people whose houses were occupied by Jews; most of the inhabitants of Balu and Qasirin, and some of the Greek inhabitants of Alexandria departed, it having been agreed that those who wished to leave could do so. Doubtless such people were resettled within the Empire, but when an Arab force came to Carthage, it was said to have encountered only a small number of lower-class people, and it was said that some Christians sailed for Sicily and others for Spain. Presumably, as in the case of the departure of the Romans from Noricum, our sources underestimate those who stayed behind, but those who departed quickly made their presence felt at the highest levels of the western church. From 687, when Sergius, whose family came from Antioch although he was born in Sicily, became pope, until the middle of the following century, every pope but one was of eastern origin, and Theodore, the distinguished archbishop of Canterbury, had been born in Tarsus. A warning that pope Gregory II (715–31) sent to the Thuringians, of all people, against receiving Africans in holy orders who might turn out to be Manicheans or people who practised rebaptism, indicates how widespread the diaspora was.[6]

While these developments were under way in the west, a series of attacks that the Arabs launched on islands in the Aegean was bringing them steadily closer to Constantinople. The rapidity with which they took to the waters of the Mediterranean rivalled that displayed by the Vandals. The defeat of a Byzantine fleet in 655 opened the way for attacks on Rhodes and Crete. Before long the capture of Constantinople could be contemplated, and in 674 it was besieged. Yet again, its walls proved too strong for its assailants, and after some years the siege was terminated. The Byzantines had deployed for the first time Greek fire, an intensely flammable substance fired through tubes. Later, a treaty was concluded on terms favourable to the Byzantines: it was said that the caliph agreed to pay 1,000 gold pieces, a horse and a slave each day.[7] The two parties also agreed to share the revenues of Cyprus, with each to enjoy access to its ports. It was a major check for the Arabs, but the royal city retained its allure, and a second siege was begun in 717, under the command of Maslama, the brother of the caliph of the time. But the Arabs were confronted by an able emperor, Leo III, who was able to turn the siege in the following year, enjoying on this occasion the aid of a new ally, the Bulgar chagan. A time of population decline, very limited building activity and a severely debilitated intellectual life, the seventh and early eighth centuries were a dismal period in the history of Constantinople. But in just under 100 years the city saw off three attacks of a scope unprecedented since its foundation, and the way lay open to a glorious future.

So it was that the expansion of the Arabs slowed down, approximately a century after the death of Muhammad. They had completely redrawn the map. Sitting in his distant monastery in the north of England, Bede contemplated the scale of their victories. When writing a commentary on Genesis in about 720, he came to some words describing Ishmael, the putative ancestor of the Arabs: 'And he will be a wild man; and his hand will be against every man, and every man's hand against him; and he shall dwell in the presence of his brethren.' He was happy to reproduce the exposition of Jerome: the seed of Ishmael, the Saracens, would live in the desert, attacking peoples living nearby and being subdued by them. But then he then went beyond Jerome, adding his own words:

> But these things are of former times. For now his hand is against all and the hands of all against him to the extent that they weigh down all the length of Africa with their dominion, and also hold the greatest part of Asia, and some of Europe, odious and hurtful to all.[8]

Bede's impression, while it exaggerated the scale of the Arabs' expansion, gives a feeling of how immense an intelligent contemporary saw their conquests as having been. But, however impressive these were, they need not have been historically significant; the vast domain of Attila came to nothing.

That the Arab conquests were important is because of the new society that was soon to emerge throughout the lands they won.

CONTINUITIES

Just as had been the case over most of western Europe in the fifth century, in many ways life in the conquered territories remained recognisably the same. As we have seen, the administrations of Syria and Egypt continued to be staffed by indigenes, who presided over an apparatus largely unchanged. The official Arab post, the barid, which is known to have operated from the Umayyad period, took its name from the post horses of the Byzantine state, the *beredoi*, and Roman provincial law may have been one of the elements that entered into the Shari'a, the system of Islamic law that is chiefly based on the Qur'an and hadith. Some of the early Arab rulers were men of ecumenical sympathies, such as Khalid, a governor of Iraq early in the eighth century, who built a church for his Christian mother, called upon a priest to bless a fountain installed in a mosque, and ventured to assert the superiority of Christianity over Islam. In the short term, the coming of Islam made little difference to many people. The building of churches continued. At one site in Jordan, an inscription of 785 records the completion of a mosaic of St Stephen, undertaken under the auspices of a deacon, an official and 'all the Christ-loving people'. The word used for 'official', *archon*, could be a military title, and a camp of the Roman army had previously been located on the site; perhaps an auxiliary tribe that had served the Romans and Byzantines remained in Arab service. That only 16 of the 56 names mentioned on inscriptions there are Graeco-Roman suggests that a local Semitic population remained Christian. In the eighth century, Syrian artists, working in a tradition that continued to observe classical style, created a fine series of ivory plaques, perhaps designed to be fixed to the doors of churches.[9]

We now know that a new civilisation was to grow up in the world of Islam. Nevertheless, that the lands conquered by the Arabs are now so obviously Islamic may incline us to overestimate the role of Islam, and indeed that of the Arabs, in determining their future. Just as the Qur'an looked back to preceding scriptures while moving beyond them, so the society that developed in the conquered lands displayed continuity with what came before it in some ways and sharp discontinuity in other ways. Some practices now identified with Islam were current in the region before its advent. The veiling of women is depicted in bas-reliefs of the first century which can still be seen at Palmyra, in the Syrian desert. A Byzantine text describes a Christian woman who covered her face when she went about the streets of a town doing good,[10] while the Virgin Mary is shown wearing a veil in icons, and few respectable women in Byzantine society would appear out of doors without wearing a veil. The practice adopted by Muslim women was therefore not specifically Islamic. The world of Islam took to Roman baths with gusto, and the *hammam*, which corresponded to them, quickly became a feature of life. Its layout followed classical precedent, according to which the bather would progress from a cold bath to a warm one and finally a hot one, and until the tenth century the Arabs often referred to these complexes as 'Roman baths'. Indeed, the atrophy of bathing in the Empire from about the sixth century suggests that the Arabs were more enthusiastic for this aspect of classical life than the Byzantines themselves. Little had changed in the commercial life of towns such as Apollonia (Arsuf) when a market street, some 2.5 m wide and at least 65 m long, was built in the time of the caliph 'Abd al-Malik (685–705). In accordance with Byzantine practice of the period, it had shops along both sides, and the site was littered with pig bones, which suggests that it was a Christian street, or one in which the Islamic prohibition on the eating of pork was not strictly enforced.[11]

In many ways the basic infrastructure of society continued unchanged. That the Arab society of the Middle East invested in camels for transport rather than vehicles with wheels can be readily deduced from the layout of streets in such places as the Old City of Jerusalem, but a bishop from France who visited the Christian holy places some decades after the Arab conquest found that camels were used to convey wood to Jerusalem, and commented on the absence of waggons and chariots.[12] His experience suggests that, just as with the coming of the English to Britain, so the Arabs moved into a society already experiencing change. Similarly, the turning away from the representation of the human body which was so powerfully to characterise the art of Islam had been foreshadowed in the conquered territories, where a strong preference for geometric over figurative decoration can be detected in Syrian mosaic art of the Byzantine period. Such an emphasis already looks away from such art as the mosaics of Ravenna and towards the art of Islam and that of Byzantium during the iconoclastic period. Such were the continuities between the Christian and Islamic periods in the Middle East.

DISCONTINUITIES

But in reality the Christians and Jews of the conquered territories, despite their status as 'people of the book', were not as privileged as the Muslims, and their long-term future would be clouded. 'Umar is said to have offered the inhabitants of the conquered territories three choices, those of accepting Islam, paying the poll tax, or flight, and those who availed themselves of the second option doubtless thought they had chosen wisely. But their condition was not fixed, and developments a few decades after the conquests would prove decisive.[13]

One important change concerned coinage. Having no tradition of minting, the Arabs maintained the monetary systems of the Byzantines and Persians, based respectively on gold and silver, in the territories they conquered from them. Islamic coins remained imitations of Byzantine and Persian issues until developments among the Christian powers triggered change. From the reign of king Erwig (680–87) the head of Christ sometimes replaced that of the sovereign in Spanish coinage, and in about 692 the Byzantine emperor Justinian II issued coins depicting on the obverse Christ, in a powerful portrayal that anticipates the intimidating figure of Christ Pantokrator of later Byzantine art, and on the reverse himself carrying a cross and the legends 'Servus dei' and 'rex regnantium'. Yet again, disparate parts of the Christian Mediterranean world were acting similarly; it is no surprise that the earliest known depiction of Christ pulling Adam out of his tomb, which was to become the standard Byzantine representation of the resurrection, first occurs in Rome at that time. But portrayal of Christ on coinage had its greatest impact beyond Christendom. The innovation inevitably caused dismay in the world of Islam, and the response was not long in coming. In the last decade of the seventh century, gold and silver coins minted in Damascus, and bronze issues minted more generally, came to show different things. On some coins, in what might be thought of as a typically Umayyad gesture, the figure of the emperor was replaced by that of the caliph. But some Islamic opinion opposed the portrayal of the caliph, so in 697 'Abd-al-Malik introduced coins that were purely epigraphic. Not merely did they contain no portraits, but the religious texts that they now displayed were anti-Christian in tendency. Dinars minted by 'Abd al-Malik reproduced a Qur'anic text (9:33) with additions, here enclosed in brackets: 'There is no god except Allah alone [he has no partner]; Muhammad is the apostle of God whom he sent with guidance and the religion of truth [that he may make it victorious over every other religion].'[14] In Africa, where the conquests were finalised at about this time, the earliest Islamic coins bear busts of the emperor and an inscription in Latin: 'There is no god but God, and he has no associate'. But shortly afterwards they too became purely epigraphic, and Arabic was the only language used. The Islamic coinage of Spain, which began a little later, was from the beginning purely epigraphic and in no language other than Arabic. So it was that a lasting change, of a kind to make the coinage assertively Islamic, was introduced at the end of the seventh century.

Another series of reforms which began in 697 saw the languages that had traditionally been used for government in the conquered territories replaced by Arabic. In Iraq, the governor al-Hajjaj ordered that registers be kept in that language rather than Pahlavi; in Damascus, 'Abd al-Malik ordered that Arabic was to be used instead of Greek; and shortly afterwards the governor of Egypt ordered its use for all official documents. Henceforth the servants of the state, whatever their background, would have to know Arabic. Whereas Cassiodorus, a Roman who served the Goths during the sixth century, had written to Goths in his own language, his counterparts in the world of Islam would have to learn the language of the conquerors. The reform was later attributed to an unfortunate incident when a Geek scribe urinated into an inkwell, but it may more plausibly be associated with other moves under way at the time which reduced the standing of the cultures that were in place when the Arabs arrived. One authority associates the reform in Persia with rivalry between a Persian and an Arab in the bureaucracy in the time of al-Hajjaj. Initially, the reform could not be enforced universally, and the chance survival of some papyri of the early eighth century from the Egyptian village of Aphrodite allows us to see the system in operation at that time. Some of them are letters from the governor of Fustat to the prefect of the region of Aphrodite, who had a Greek name, others from him to the taxpayers of the village, and there are registers of taxes and requisitions, impressive testimony to the thoroughness of the administration of the Arabs. Contrary to what the reform would have led one to anticipate, the documents are almost entirely in Greek. The Arabic name of the governor, Qurrah ibn Sharik, is rendered into Greek, while the qualities attributed to God in the formula 'In the name of God the merciful and compassionate' are given in words fundamental to Christian Greek. But the pressure to use Arabic would be irresistible.[15]

In such ways did life in the conquered territories become Arabised. But the movement of power in society away from those who had traditionally held it towards newcomers is most clearly to be seen in other developments, which were under way at the very period when the coinage and languages of state were being changed. These were made clear in buildings that still survive.

BUILDINGS

The Ummayads devoted a lot of attention to Jerusalem, being responsible for a series of palaces, work on various gates, the rebuilding of the walls of the city near the Damascus Gate, the reconstruction of fortifications in the area of the Armenian Garden, and work on the citadel.[16] One of the greatest buildings in the world of Islam, and the oldest that survives, the Dome of the Rock, was built by 'Abd al-Malik in Jerusalem in the early 690s. It consists of a large dome, some 20 m in diameter, built over an octagon, a shape exceptional in Islam which recalls the similarly sized church of San Vitale in Ravenna, and was presumably the work of a Christian architect. Non-figural mosaics, the significance of which is unclear, decorated it. The proportions are pleasing, the Dome's diameter being the same size as its height and almost the length of each of its walls. Erected in what is now the Haram ash-Sharif, it occupied a religiously sensitive site, for not only had the area formerly been occupied by Solomon's Temple, but it was believed to be the place where, in even earlier times, Abraham had prepared to offer his son Isaac as a sacrifice. But, at least by the ninth century, Muslim scholars thought of the site as significant in another way, holding that the rock over which it was built bore a footprint left by the Prophet when he took a mysterious night ride, and it may be that a wish to emulate a Christian site on the Mount of Olives, where marks on another rock were held to be the footprints left by Christ when he ascended into heaven, lay behind the selection of this site.

But the construction of the Dome was more significant than its location. Its inner diameter is almost exactly the same as that of the church of the Holy Sepulchre. This building had been the chief Christian structure in Jerusalem since Constantine had erected it where Jesus Christ was thought to have been buried and risen from the dead. Only a few decades before the Arabs took the city, the mosaicist responsible for the map still preserved in a church at Madaba in Jordan indicated its standing by the care he took to represent it, although the circumstance that it is shown upside down can prevent casual observers of the map from realising this, and the dome of the church had been restored early in the seventh century following damage inflicted by the Persians. The near coincidence of the diameters of the domes of the Christian and Islamic buildings suggests conscious emulation on the part of the builders of the latter. Writing late in the tenth century, Mukaddasi pointed out that its builders 'had as a rival and comparison the great church (of the Holy Sepulchre) belonging to the Christians at Jerusalem, and they built this to be even more magnificent than that other'.[17] Moreover, inscriptions ran around the rim of the dome. There were good precedents for this in the Christian Empire, for such an inscription could be found in the church of SS Sergius and Bacchus erected at Constantinople towards the beginning of the reign of Justinian. But those in the Dome of the Rock, written in gold letters against a blue background in a difficult form of Kufic script with few diacritical marks, respects in which it recalls early manuscripts of the Qur'an, are polemical. They comprise religious texts, the wording of which is very similar to passages in the Qur'an, which assert the teachings by which Islam could be distinguished from Christianity. Presumably intended to be read by Muslims, the inscriptions provided an assertive view of Islam in a city that was still overwhelmingly non-Islamic.

Early in the eighth century 'Abd al-Malik's son, the caliph al-Walid (705–15), began the building of a great mosque in Damascus, the capital of the caliphate. As with the Dome in Jerusalem, the mosque was erected on a site sacred in pre-Islamic times, having been occupied successively by temples dedicated to Hamad, the god of storms, and to Jupiter, and finally by a church that Theodosius I erected in honour of St John the Baptist. Doubtless the site was desirable on its own merits, but a point was being made, as it frequently was when houses of worship were erected on sites occupied by those of displaced cults. Over the door of the church was an inscription which read 'Thy kingdom, O Christ, is an everlasting kingdom and thy dominion endureth throughout all generations' (cf. Psalm 145:13, Septuagint), but the words were no longer appropriate. The new reality was expressed in the words of a contemporary poet, addressing himself to al-Walid:

> Thou hast torn their churches from the middle of our mosque, pulled up its foundations from the entrails of the earth,
> Whilst the faithful stood in prayer, the bishops did not cease to reply from the church,
> Cries of barbarians celebrating their liturgy, like swallows cry in the morning;
> Today the word of truth triumphs and the call of the Book of God.[18]

Later texts emphasise the great expense to which the caliph went, and while a tradition that artisans were summoned from Persia, India, Africa and the Byzantine Empire, and that the entire land tax from Syria for seven years was devoted to the project may have overstated that matter, the scale suggests the resources that an Islamic government of the early eighth century could command.[19] A tradition that al-Walid removed columns from the church dedicated to Mary at Antioch, the former Byzantine capital of Syria, which were to be placed in the mosque, is interesting. This will have been the church built there by Justinian; the work of an emperor was being recycled by one who, in his capacity of builder, was himself acting as an emperor. Imperial associations occur on the façade of the mosque. It recalls the design of Theoderic's palace at Ravenna depicted in a mosaic in the church of Sant'Apollinare Nuovo, and it is reasonable to suppose that imperial palaces in Constantinople furnished a common archetype. Imperial echoes were also to be heard in the use to which it was put in 714, when al-Walid used the mosque to welcome back Musa after his victories in Spain.

The mosque is particularly noteworthy for the vast expanse of its wall mosaics, which can still be seen in restored form. They show scenes that include palaces, rivers and gardens with slender trees; it is unclear whether the pictures are to be taken realistically or as symbols, perhaps representing things mentioned in the Qur'an. In some ways they sit comfortably within the traditions of late antique art. Towns and buildings are represented in a two-dimensional way, just as they are in mosaics at Sant'Apollinare Nuovo in Ravenna, while the depiction of rocks and mountains is similar to that in the mosaics of San Vitale. In other ways, however, the mosaics have the characteristics of a specifically Islamic art. In their avoidance of empty space and the absence of any notion of a horizon, they foreshadow tendencies, later displayed in Persian carpets, which would be expressed across the centuries in the art of the world of Islam. More importantly, the scenes shown in the mosaics at Damascus are unpopulated by humans.

From their earliest days, works of art commissioned by Muslims but presumably created by local indigenes showed a willingness to rework items familiar in the art of the area for new purposes. People entering a room displaying a mosaic of the Umayyad period at Qasr al-Hallabat, in what is now Jordan, would be confronted with depictions of familiar things. But these were organised in an odd way: fruit-bearing trees, a bull, a ram and birds were to be seen on their right, while to the left were bare trees, a lion, a snake and a goat, and a man could be seen leading an ostrich from left to right. Items familiar from the repertoire of classical art had been used to suggest a religious theme, that of the passage from evil to good.[20] As time passed, figurative art came to be frowned on in the world of Islam. At Gerasa (the modern Jerash), for example, during the seventh century the representation of human figures on pottery became increasingly abstract, until in the eighth century pottery was decorated with stylised floral patterns or design that was completely abstract. Quite quickly, the potters had turned their backs on over a millennium of western tradition. In a way, the dematerialising of the content of Graeco-Roman art by the Arabs recalled that of the Germanic peoples; in its lack of interest in the human form and its horror vacui, the Franks Casket reflects tendencies similar to those that inform Islamic art. But whereas western art would always be able to regain contact with the classical past, and Islamic thinkers made fruitful use of classical learning, Islamic art turned its face against the traditional art of the area, so that westerners seeking to appreciate Islamic art have to unlearn things that the last 3,000 years of western art have encouraged them to take for granted.

There was no escaping the theme of the strength of Islam, enunciated with such clarity after the second generation from Muhammad. An inscription that was placed in the mosque at Damascus reads in part:

> There is no god but God alone, without associate, and Him alone do we adore. Our Lord is God alone, our religion is Islam, and our prophet, Muhammad . . . The construction of this mosque and the destruction of the church that was formerly here were ordered by the servant of God, the commander of the faithful, al-Walid.

A thirteenth-century Arab writer tells a story that is probably apocryphal but suggests what Muslims believed of the mosque at Damascus. It was said that when ambassadors from Constantinople visited it, their chief began to hang his head and his colour became yellow: 'Verily, I had told the assemblies of the people of (Byzantium) that the Arabs and their power would remain but a brief space; but now, when I see what they have built, I know of a surety that their (dominion) will reach to length of days.'[21] Mukaddasi later provided an explanation for the building of both the mosque at Damascus and the Dome of the Rock:

> Al-Walid believed Syria to be a country that had long been occupied by the Christians, and he noted therein the beautiful churches still belonging to them, so enchantingly fair and so renowned for their splendour, even as are the Kumamah (the church of the Holy Sepulchre) and the churches of Lydda and Edessa. So he sought to build for the Muslims a mosque that should prevent their regarding these, and that should be unique and a wonder to the world. And in like manner is it not evident that the khalif 'Abd al-Malik, noting the greatness of the dome of Al Kumamah and its magnificence, was moved lest it should dazzle the minds of the Muslims, and hence erected above the Rock the Dome which is now seen there?[22]

Similarly, the excellence of a mosque that al-Walid erected near the Dome, al-Aqsa ('the furthest'), the title of which recalled the furthest place Muhammad visited during his night ride, was due to a wish to display superiority:

> This mosque is even more beautiful than that of Damascus, for during the building of it they had as a rival and comparison the great church belonging to the Christians at Jerusalem, and they built this to be even more beautiful than that other.[23]

This is not to say that the traditions of Islamic art fell into place overnight. During the first half of the eighth century, the Umayyads, who may never have reconciled themselves fully to living in Damascus, built a number of residential complexes in the Syrian desert. They shared some characteristics with a 'palace', or country residence, previously erected in southern Syria, conceivably by a Ghassanid prince, while the audience halls that some of them contained, perhaps built in imitation of those erected at Bostra in the sixth century, were of a type one would have thought suitable for a caliph as that office had developed under the Umayyads.[24] The complexes have been described in English as palaces, forts and castles, but no one word suffices for them, just as there is no consensus as to the purpose for which they were erected. Given that they do not seem to have been intended for permanent occupation, they cannot have been villas of the kind familiar in western Europe; rather, they were probably meant to be used for recreation. But the kinds of recreation pursued there would have caused eyebrows to be raised in pious circles, for the statues of semi-nude girls offering wine flagons at one of them suggest that those who occupied it were liberal Muslims in more than one respect. The complex at Qasr 'Amra, to the east of Amman, was built with a set of Roman baths, frescos depicting hunting and nude bathing, and a formal hall where the caliph, like Roman emperors in late antiquity, sat behind a curtain. There were even places for images of him. The ambience was distinctly pleasure-loving and imperial. A poet described his experience:

> Al-Walid invited me to his residence. As I entered it, a servant told me the Commander of the Faithful was behind the curtain. I greeted him and sang some songs. Then I saw the exquisitely formed hand of a girl reaching me a goblet from behind the curtain, and, by God, I don't know which was the more beautiful, the hand or the goblet.[25]

A badly damaged fresco at Qasr 'Amra showed six figures. Four of them are named: the fragment 'sar' would have been the last part of the word 'kaisar', which we know the Persians, but not the Byzantines themselves, used for the emperor; 'Chosdrois' represents the name of the long-lived Persian shahs Chosroes I (531–79) and II (590–628), the first of whom was long remembered by the Arabs; 'Rodorik' is a form of the name of the last Visigothic king, Roderic; and 'Nigo' will have been the negus, or ruler, of Ethiopia. Two unnamed figures may have represented the emperor of China and a Turkish or Indian ruler. The six may have stood for enemies alleged to have been defeated during wide-ranging conquests in the time of al-Walid I (705–15). The figures imply perceptions of political grandeur that we shall consider later; for the time being, the secular art of the early eighth century was happy to depict human figures. Indeed, as if this were not enough, at Qasr 'Amra there are also frescos representing Poesy, History, Philosophy and Victory, identified as such in Greek!

ICONOCLASM

But such art was marginal to the developing world of Islam. As it turned out, attitudes to the kind of art appropriate to Islam were connected with a crisis that preoccupied Christians as well as Muslims in the eighth and ninth centuries. No less than the status of Jews had in the seventh century, that of images became a burning religious issue in the eighth.

Since the late sixth century, the cult of images, 'icons' as they were called in Greek, had been becoming increasingly prominent, particularly in eastern Christianity, as images depicting the saints, the Mother of God and Christ himself proliferated and received more intense devotion. It was a sign of the times when, in 692, the council of Trullo decreed that the lamb, under which guise Christ had sometimes hitherto been shown, as for example on the throne of Maximianus of Ravenna, was to be replaced by representations of him in human form, at about the time when the emperor Justinian II placed a picture of Christ on coins. A little earlier, hostility to Christian symbolism had been displayed within Islam. In the 680s the governor of Egypt ordered the destruction of crosses, together with the affixing to churches of inscriptions bearing the words 'Muhammad is the great Apostle of God and Jesus also is the Apostle of God. But verily God is not begotten and does not beget.'[26] It was a straw in the wind.

More significantly, the caliph Yazid II (720–24) ordered the destruction of images and statues. The impact of his command, or that of another issued shortly earlier, is visible in a church at Ma'in, where a lion and ox shown grazing together were destroyed in an operation that can be seen to have been a response to the government's wish rather than the work of fanatics, but Christian iconography was scarcely affected by it. Yazid's edict accurately reflects the main tendency of Islamic art across the centuries, which has been cool towards representations of living creatures. Already, the mosaics on the walls of the great mosque at Damascus depict a variety of landscapes devoid of human life. As we have seen, the kind of art that has developed in the world of Islam, which makes much of abstract, often patterned designs, may owe something to tendencies at work in the Middle East before the Arabs arrived. But little in early Islamic teaching supports a turn against images, and the period could accommodate the decidedly un-Islamic decoration of the desert dwellings of the Umayyads; indeed, it was said that Muhammad himself had allowed a picture of Jesus and Mary to remain in the Ka'ba at Macca.[27] Perhaps the turning of Islam away from representational art was linked with moves under way in Christianity at the time.

Yazid issued his edict at a time tantalisingly close to the beginning of the iconoclastic controversy in the Byzantine Empire. Launched by Leo III in 726, this was to see the cult of images forbidden in territories under imperial sway. When the church of St Irene in Constantinople was rebuilt after an earthquake in 740, its apse was decorated with a plain cross rather than a scene with people in it, such as had long occupied such places, while nearby, in the small sekreton of the cathedral of Hagia Sophia, images of saints were unpicked and the tesserae replaced. The defenders of the icons included the able John of Damascus, who, thanks to his residence in the caliphate, was beyond the reach of the emperor, and an ecumenical council held at Nicaea in 787 justified their veneration, which was solemnly made definitive in 843. But the position taken at Nicaea was not acceptable to some Christians in the west. Charlemagne and his advisers argued against the degree of veneration that Byzantines offered icons, holding that it was close to idolatry. A few years after the council, its teachings were attacked in a work later called the *Libri Carolini*, which seem to have been written by a Spaniard who had come to Charlemagne's court, Theodulf, later bishop of Orléans. Not far from Orléans he built a chapel at Germigny-des-Prés, where the mosaic in the apse shows angels guarding the ark of the covenant, a sober scene illustrating a portion of the Bible discussed in the *Libri Carolini* which was unlikely to have aroused the kind of devotion of which Theodulf disapproved. Similar tendencies operated across the Pyrenees, where works commissioned by the Christian monarch Alfonso II of Oviedo depicted a heavenly Jerusalem whose absence of inhabitants recalled the mosaics of Damacus.[28]

So it was that religious art became a difficult issue in the eighth century, in both the eastern and western parts of Christendom and in Islam. Among Christians it would stage a triumphant return, to produce in the east works that are among the glories of world art. In the world of Islam, on the other hand, for official purposes artistic energies would be channelled in other directions.

THE BALANCE OF POWER

Developments in coinage, the status of Arabic, places of worship and art reveal a sharpening of the self-identification of Islam. As this occurred, the non-Islamic indigenes of the conquered territories found their position worsening. In the late seventh century, a Monophysite historian expressed the hope that God would deal with the Ishmaelites as he had with Pharaoh, and shortly afterwards a Monophysite patriarch of Alexandria prayed that God would make 'gentle the hearts of those who oppress us, and abate the disturbing storms that lower over us, and break in pieces our sufferings at the hands of the mob'. Such attitudes were quite different from the views such people had of the Arabs when they arrived.[29]

The period was later remembered as a time of change. 'Umar II (717–20) was said to have forbidden Christians to dress as Arabs, a sign that the accommodation of indigenes to the dress codes of newcomers that was familiar in the West would not operate in Arab-controlled lands, and enjoined that Islamic law was to be followed in cases between Muslims and non-Muslims, and between members of different non-Islamic groups. The preceding caliph was believed to have forbidden the drinking of wine in cities and put pressure on Christians to convert. Doubtless, as has often been the case, there was room for uncertainty as to the degree to which Islamic teachings were to be applied to non-Muslims, but it was clear with whom power lay. A story was told that 'Abd al-Malik, when he heard of the beauty of the women of one town, ordered the local commander to send him all suitable virgins. The people fasted and prayed for three days, after which the bishop received a revelation that the tyrant had died, and so it turned out. The author who preserved this tradition in the thirteenth century was unsure of the time when these events happened, and the tale may reflect the position of Christians of later periods, but it conveys a vivid sense of disempowerment. Christians found themselves on the back foot, and members of groups that until recently had devoted themselves to polemic against Jews and other Christians were advised to seek common ground in discussions with Arabs, by anathematising those who said that there were two gods or that God bore a son according to the flesh, and those who adored creatures in place of God. Even indications of Muslim interest could be double-edged, as when an early ruler ordered that the Gospel be translated into Arabic omitting the word 'God' when applied to Christ and the words 'baptism' and 'cross'.[30]

Not surprisingly, conversions to Islam began to occur more frequently. This is not to say that there were no conversions in the opposite direction. In the middle of the eighth century, a Muslim in Alexandria, seeing a picture of Christ on the cross being pierced in one side by the spear of a soldier, took a rod and pierced the other side of the picture, whereupon he was transfixed and could not move. Only when he asserted that he was a Christian was he able to move, and he made his way to a monastery where he was baptised. Christian symbols could be valued by Muslims. While he did not convert, a leader of the rebellion that was to allow the Abbasids to displace the Umayyads in the middle of the eighth century, Abu Muslim, saw in the midst of battle an angel carrying a golden rod surmounted by a cross, and enemies falling dead wherever the cross went. He therefore had his followers place crosses on their breasts, observing 'by means of this sign God had given us the victory and it has conquered the empire for us'. Has there ever been so unlikely an appropriation of the example of Constantine?[31]

But the main flow of interest and conversion was in the opposite direction. Arabia itself quickly became Islamic, as the conversions of polytheists were supplemented by those of Christians. As early as the caliphate of 'Umar I, the Christians of Najran, whose community had produced so many martyrs in earlier days, were ordered to evacuate the city and moved to Iraq, although there is some indication of a bishop continuing to function in the town as late as the tenth century, and our evidence may conceal the continuing presence of Christianity in the peninsula. Elsewhere, a clear lesson could be drawn from the events of the seventh century: Islam was the religion of winners. Moreover, whereas the Arian newcomers who succeeded in founding kingdoms in the west during the fifth century tended not to seek the conversion of Catholics and over time adopted Catholicism themselves, Islam was hospitable to converts. Like Catholicism in the west, it offered a plausible means of assimilation into what was clearly going to be the dominant group in society, and it was this added to conviction, rather than any desire for remission of taxes, which led people to embrace Islam. There were some very early converts, such as John, one of the monks of Mount Sinai, a group that seems to have been prone to apostasy in this period; he accepted Islam and, taking the sword, persecuted his erstwhile co-religionists. The author of an apocalyptic text of the second half of the seventh century written in Syriac under the name of Methodius, a martyr of the early fourth century, was already concerned at Christians who denied Christ and separated themselves from the Christian community, making the telling point that such conversions occurred without people being subject to compulsion.[32] But it seems to have been a good century after Arab conquest that widespread conversions began, these being part of a move towards assimilation, one of many we have seen in these centuries. Thereafter the Christian communities went into irreversible decline. In Egypt and Syria they diminished so as to constitute the small minorities they remain today, while the African church, the former powerhouse of Christianity in the West, which had conducted itself so vigorously when persecuted by the Vandals in the fifth century and in polemic against emperors in the sixth and seventh centuries, ceased to exist in the middle ages.

Adherence to Islam involved more than a mere switch in private belief, for it was a matter of public loyalty and practice. Unlike Christianity, the language of its scripture was itself sacred, and attendance at Islamic worship involved exposure to Arabic, a living language, unlike the liturgical Latin of the Christian West. Of the five pillars of the religion, those of prayer and fasting committed one to public practice, whether in the mosque at the appointed hours of prayer or during the month of Ramadan, when communal fasting was practised from sunrise till sunset, and alms were collected by the state. Jesus, on the other hand, had taught that the disciplines of alms-giving, prayer and fasting were to be undertaken in secret,[33] and while it would certainly be false to anticipate that his followers at any time would have adhered with particular fidelity to his teachings, Islam quickly expressed itself as a religion of public and communal practice, adherence to which entailed not only a change of religious opinion but also incorporation into a new community.

The liturgical space within which Muslims worshipped pointed in the same direction. The basilica of the ancient world, on which the layout of most of the great Christian churches was based, was rectangular in shape; one entered through a doorway and immediately faced the apse, where the judge or high official sat. Christian architects worked within this model, so that the entry and the apse were at opposite short sides, and the attention of worshippers in the basilica was drawn towards the altar at the east end where the clergy officiated. In a mosque, on the other hand, the worshippers look towards one of the long sides of the building, making it easy for them, massed in rows, to perform the prescribed movements of prayer at the same time. In such ways did Islam become not only an attractive choice but a weighty one.

CO-EXISTENCE AND APOCALYPSE

Just as elite groups in the West adjusted to Germanic occupation, many people in the East initially found it easy to reconcile themselves to the new reality. A series of papyri allows us to trace something of the history of a leading family that acted its part for some generations on the modest stage of Nessana (the modern Auja Hafir, in the Negev). We know of one Patrick, the son of Sergius, who was alive in about 560. His son, Sergius, became a priest and the abbot of the monastery of St Sergius, dying in 592. He was succeeded in these offices by his own son, Patrick, who died in 628 and may have been the father of George, a money-lender who was still alive in 684. The last member of the family known to us, Sergius the son of George, was a substantial landowner and payer of heavy taxes who held the office of abbot in about 689. Clearly a wealthy family that exercised power within the church, it was flourishing under the emperor Justinian and continued to do so, while remaining explicitly Christian, under the caliph 'Abd al-Malik.[34] For such people, the coming of Islam took a long while to have an impact; no major change in their activities occurred during the period for which they can be documented.

This was not true of a more substantial family that was much closer to the seat of power. A generation before the coming of the Arabs, the emperor Maurice had appointed to collect taxes in Damascus a man whose name is known to us in the Arabic form Sarjun, and we may take it that the family was one of Christian Arabs. At the time of the Arab conquest, the commander in charge of Damascus was Mansour, his son (ibn Sargun). He must have already held this post during the Persian occupation of Damascus, for during this period he is said to have forwarded the tax receipts to Persia. When Heraclius regained Damascus, he had Mansour flogged and imprisoned, and made him pay a hefty fine before reinstating him in office. On a subsequent trip to the city, Heraclius extorted more money from Mansour. As it turned out, Mansour was the last person whom the emperor would have wished to harbour a grudge against him. Some sources identify him as the person who saw to it that the Byzantine army fled from the Arabs, and the negotiations into which he entered with the Arab commander Khalid caused the church hierarchy to declare him anathema.[35] In 691 one 'Sergius the son of Mansour', presumably his son, was the official in charge of the business of the caliph 'Abd al-Malik, raising taxes that would have been spent against the Byzantines. But his situation was more difficult. He is reported to have been among a group who persuaded the caliph not to use columns from Christian buildings in Jerusalem for work in Macca, and to have been dismayed at the adoption of Arabic in state documents. When 'Abd al-Malik informed him of his plan, Sergius is said to have told Greek clerks, 'Seek your livelihood in any other profession than this, for God has cut it off from you.'[36] He in turn was succeeded in this office by his son, Mansour, who was said to have been a childhood friend of the future caliph Yazid in his young days.

But with this Mansour the fortunes of the family changed, in a way important for Christian thought. Letters were forged which gave the impression that Mansour had been seeking to betray the caliph to the emperor, and at some time he retired to the great monastery of St Sabas, where he took the name John and, as John of Damascus, became a great theologian. There he wrote against the contemporary Byzantine practice of iconoclasm, in works of an intellectual depth which suggests that orthodox thought in the Middle East continued to repose on deeper intellectual foundations than that of

Constantinople, just as the freedom of utterance that John enjoyed when living beyond the reach of the emperor under Islam recalls the freedom from imperial control that the papacy enjoyed when Italy was governed by Arians. He also wrote on heresies, among them the heresy of Islam, in works which reveal first-hand knowledge of this subject. He calls several suras of the Qur'an by their proper names, and he is one of the earliest sources we have for the teaching of Islam other than the Qur'an itself. But with John the accommodations that his most adaptable family had made with Byzantines, Persians and Arabs in Damascus came to an end. His withdrawal to a monastery symbolises the distance between the Muslim and Christian Arabs that was opening up by his time.

Some of the indigenous populace of the conquered territories looked coolly on the Arabs from an early date. Writing several decades after the occupation of most of Spain, the author of a chronicle took a long-term view. He opined that the disaster which had befallen Spain could be compared to others that had occurred since the time of Adam: the fall of Troy, the burden imposed on Jerusalem, the sufferings of Babylon and what occurred at Rome were now being experienced by Spain, a place of delights that had been made wretched.[37] Elsewhere, people engaged in speculation about the end of the world.

Among the Jews who submitted to baptism in accordance with the command of the emperor Heraclius was a merchant, Jacob, and a text of the time, the *Teaching of Jacob the Newly-baptised*, purports to contain a discussion he had with some former co-religionists in Carthage. At one point the group turned to the prophecy of Daniel, who foresaw that the fourth beast, understood to denote the Empire, would at the end fall, that ten horns would prevail and the Little Horn come (cf. Dan. 7:7f). Arguing that this disquieting prophecy would shortly be fulfilled, Jacob pointed out that the sway of Rome, that is, the Empire, had diminished: in former times, the peoples of Ireland, Britain, Spain, France, Italy, Greece, Thrace, lands as far as Antioch, Syria, Persia, the entire East, Egypt, Africa and its hinterland had all been subject to Rome, but this had ceased to be the case. His antagonist in the debate, a Jew named Justus, was compelled to agree that the end was at hand:

My brother Abraham has written to me from Caesarea that a false prophet has appeared. 'For when the bodyguard (*candidatus*) Sergius was killed by the Saracens', Abraham said, 'I was in Caesarea, and I went by boat to Sycamina, and they said "the bodyguard has been killed", and we Jews were full of joy. And they say that a prophet has appeared coming with the Saracens and proclaims the arrival of the anointed, the Christ who is going to come. And when I [Abraham] came to

Sycamina I went to an old man very learned in the Scriptures, and said to him: "What do you say about the prophet who has appeared with the Saracens?" And he said to me, groaning deeply: "He is false, for surely the prophets do not come with sword and chariot. Verily the troubles of today are works of confusion, and I fear lest the Christ who came first, whom the Christians worship, was himself the one that was sent by God . . ." And I Abraham made enquiry and learned from those that had met him, that there is nothing true to be found in the so-called prophet; there is only the shedding of human blood; for he says that he holds the keys of paradise, and that cannot be true.'

So it was that Justus joined Jacob in confessing his belief in Christ, born of St Mary.

While it is unlikely that Muhammad ever claimed to hold the keys of paradise, Abraham's information was generally sound, for a Sergius holding the rank of *candidatus* was indeed killed by Arabs shortly after the death of Muhammad, and it may well be the earliest source for Islam and its Prophet other than the Qur'an itself. But its most interesting characteristic is its looking back to the Old Testament to suggest the collapse of the Roman Empire, this being the fourth and last of the great kingdoms predicted by Daniel. An author of the preceding century had argued that, while the sins of the Empire may have caused barbarians to enjoy some successes, it would last until the end of the world. The evidence provided by Abraham suggested that the end was at hand.[38]

Such themes concerned people in the seventh century. It was then that 'Fredegarius' based a story that indicated the decadence of the later Merovingians on a passage of Daniel. When the Armenian historian known as Sebeos came to write his history in the second half of the seventh century, he thought of the four beasts that the prophet Daniel had seen rising from the sea (Daniel 7). He superimposed the four directions on this vision, suggesting that the first, a human, was the kingdom of the west, that of the Greeks; the second, a bear in the east, was that of the Sasanids, which included Medes, Persians and Parthians; the third, which looked like a leopard, was the kingdom of the north, that of Gog and Magog. But the fourth was 'fearful and amazing, and its teeth were of iron and its claws of bronze. It ate and broke in pieces, and crushed the remnants under foot.' Its identity was clear:

The fourth, arising from the south, is the kingdom of Ismael [*sic*], just as the archangel explained: 'The fourth beast, the fourth kingdom, shall arise, which shall be greater than all [other] kingdoms; and it will consume the whole earth.'[39]

It was an ominous prospect. Writing at about the same time, the Syrian author of a text purportedly written by Methodius, an eastern bishop who became a martyr in about 312, predicted that the children of Ishmael would rise up and cause great devastation and destruction before they were defeated by the 'king of the Greeks', or Byzantine emperor.[40] The prophecy touched a raw nerve. It was speedily translated into Greek, and thence into Latin, in which language a manuscript from as early as the eighth century survives; later it was translated into Slavonic. By the end of the seventh century, the imagination of many Christians had become remarkably bleak.

STRUCTURAL CHANGE

What future was there for such people? Some adopted a jaunty, if not subversive tone, mocking the muezzin's call to prayer in the mosque. According to the poet al-Akhtal:

I am never standing calling out
Like an ass 'Come to salvation!'

Such a description of the muezzin could be thought offensive, and the text occurs in another form:

And I am never crying out in the night
Shortly before the dawn: 'Come to salvation.'

When the grandfather of Eulogius, a Spanish author of the ninth century, heard the call to prayer being uttered, as if by a donkey with loose jaws, he made the sign of the cross and sang the words of a psalm: 'God, who is like unto thee? Do you not be quiet or silent, God, since your enemies, Lord, have given the sound, and those who hate you have lifted up their heads.'[41] Some lines of communication with the Christian world beyond the world of Islam remained open. A representative of the see of Jerusalem seems to have attended the ecumenical council in Constantinople in 680–1, while the patriarch of Jerusalem was present at the Quinsext council of 691–2. Macarius, the patriarch of Antioch, was certainly there; he was condemned. More surprising is a document written in the ninth century.

There has come down to us what purports to be a letter to the Byzantine emperor Theophilus (829–42), written in the names of the patriarchs of Alexandria, Antioch and Jerusalem.[42] It represents its origin as having been a council held in Jerusalem in 836, which had been attended by 185 bishops, 17 abbots and 1,153 monks. The document provides various arguments in favour of the veneration of icons, the arguments being backed up by a good number of interesting stories. The holding of a council bringing together so many ecclesiastics from within the world of Islam seems unlikely, although the fact that the letter is extant in a manuscript of the ninth century indicates that, if it is a forgery, it was confected at a time not far removed from that at which it represents itself as having been written. But in it the patriarchs are made to represent themselves persistently as the loyal subjects of Theophilus, and use the formal language of imperial intitulature to indicate his status. Moreover, they assert that they found themselves under tyranny, and were the hostages of barbarian enemies. Whoever wrote this text thought that Christians under Islam remained the subjects of the emperor, and this person, if writing within the world of Islam, was certainly not reconciled to the contemporary reality. But by then, some 200 years after the Islamic conquest, it should have been becoming clear just how anachronistic such views were. Islam was not going to go away.

Throughout the parts of the Middle East which, at the beginning of the seventh century, had been subject to Constantinople, enormous change took place following the Arab conquest. This did not happen overnight. As we have seen, mosaics continued to be installed in churches, and work continued to be done on synagogues. Ganei-Hamat (Tiberias), on the west coast of the Sea of Galilee, was a village that boasted a synagogue, first built in the third century. Alterations were made in the early Islamic period, and at some time after the coming of Islam two new floors were installed. In the seventh century, a workshop for the glazing of Islamic pottery was produced, which was rebuilt after the earthquake of 747. Both the synagogue and the workshop remained in use until the tenth or eleventh century, when the village was abandoned. In the late fourth century, the Jewish community at Qasrin, a village 13 km north-east of the Sea of Galilee, built a synagogue, which was replaced by a slightly larger one, probably in the early sixth century. It in turn was remodelled early in the seventh century, in ways that suggest a more difficult economic situation. The synagogue was destroyed by an earthquake, probably that of 747.

So life flowed on across the divide represented by the coming of the Arabs. But changes did occur, and one is left to speculate as to why they did. One obvious reason is the impact of contingent and fortuitous events, such as the earthquake of 747. But these were probably not of great moment. The century before the coming of the Arabs, when the plague had caused a high incidence of mortality and the Persians wreaked great havoc, particularly in the very decades before the arrival of the Arabs, had produced disasters of a magnitude that would not occur again for centuries under Islam, and by then a very different society had emerged. The explanation for the degree of change under Islam must be sought elsewhere.

The Arabs arrived in a part of the world that was already changing. The city of Antioch, one of the centres of Christianity, faded into obscurity under their rule, but it could be held that the fate of the city had been sealed in the sixth century (see above, p. 191). More generally, towns in the Middle East were already assuming an appearance that one would associate with Islam. Whereas towns declined in the west during late antiquity, in the east the economic and social functions of cities were not diminishing but taking different forms. The complex change from the classical *polis*, with wide, straight streets laid out in the form of a grid, an impressive set of public buildings and a central forum, to what we think of as a medieval Islamic town with its narrow and winding streets, relative lack of public amenities and absence of a forum, was already under way when the Arabs arrived. The classicising nature of some written sources for the period masks such change. Take for example, Procopius's description of the way in which Justinian restored Antioch after the city was sacked by the Persians in 540. He states that, after the site had been cleared of rubble, the emperor

> laid it out with stoas and market-places, and dividing all the blocks of land by means of streets, and making water-channels and fountains and sewers, all of which the city now boasts, he built theatres and baths for it, ornamenting it with all the other public buildings by means of which the prosperity of a city is wont to be shown . . . Thus it was brought about that Antioch has become more splendid now than it formerly was.

But a law that was issued at Constantinople in 383 forbidding the erection of structures in fora and other public places responded to a development that would later be characteristic of Islamic cities. At Scythopolis, we know of a curved street of the early sixth century, and by the early seventh century public space was increasingly being exploited by private citizens. Of the public buildings in the Byzantine period, while one bath house fell out of use, the other was extended; the theatre went out of use during the sixth century; the odeon was destroyed in the early years of that century; and the hippodrome was converted into a smaller amphitheatre, the entrances to which were in time blocked.[43] These tendencies were already operating in the Empire, and were reflected in the towns of what remained of the Empire in the seventh and eighth centuries. It is true that in the world of Islam they were strengthened by an unexpected development, as the camel drove out wheeled transport over the lands conquered by the Arabs, but as we have seen, this development was well under way a few decades after the coming of the Arabs, and was presumably not the result of their arrival.

A parallel development occurred in another field. One of the world's greatest scholars of the ancient world, Theodor Mommsen, offered a harsh evaluation of the relationship between Islam and preceding intellectual culture in the Middle East when he described Islam as the executioner of Hellenism. Doubtless Islamic civilisation was based on premises very different from those of the Greek world, but in important ways its intellectuals were able to develop much of the work of the Greeks, and it was largely on the basis of their achievements that the Latin west would later enter into serious dialogue with the thought of the Greeks. Moreover, as we have seen, by the seventh century the intellectual life of the Byzantine Empire was at its strongest in precisely those areas taken by the Arabs. Again, we may see the kind of civilisation that developed in Islam as owing much to a situation that was developing in the lands it conquered.

A further consideration is relevant. Doubtless society underwent important changes as a result of the arrival of the Arabs, but these need not have been connected with Islam. Muslims came to govern Persia, but few Arab Muslims settled there, and Persian became one of the great languages of Islam. Where Arabs settled more densely, as in Syria, their impact was greater. It cannot be denied that many of the Christian and Jewish villages of the Levant were to decline under the Arabs; the sad account of a pilgrim of the mid-eighth century describes Bethlehem as having been destroyed, apart from a few houses, and surrounded by olives and vines.[44] But the coming to power of a people familiar with different economic practices, and perhaps the return into Syria of pastoralists who had recently been displaced by the expansion of agriculture, may have accounted for this. Towns that had flourished in accordance with the needs of one economy found their *raison d'être* threatened as new systems developed. Cities such as Alexandria and Carthage, the prosperity of which was bound up with Mediterranean trade, suffered as trade across the sea rapidly declined. No less than in Italy, towns that lost their economic function faced a grim future, but there may have been deeper reasons than the arrival of newcomers. In any case, the early Islamic centuries saw the establishment of towns which boomed, and witnessed what has been called an 'agricultural revolution', which entailed new crops and ways of farming, and while some areas fell back, new settlements were established in the early Islamic period around Aqaba, as they were in the Negev desert.

One index of the changing world is provided by languages. A steelyard with notches indicating the weight, which must have been in use before the middle of the eighth century, has been discovered at Scythopolis, marked on one side with Greek letters and on the other in Arabic. It must have been the property of a business that dealt with the speakers of both languages. But one of these languages would come to predominate. The intellectual energies that had distinguished Christianity in Syria were not extinguished by the coming of Islam. In the orthodox tradition, John of Damascus was followed by James of Edessa (c.640–708). A native Syriac speaker born just outside Antioch, he travelled to Alexandria for higher education and became highly competent in Greek. He wrote on an extraordinary variety of subjects, including history, but his specialty was the exegesis of Scripture; his occupancy of the see of Edessa may have overlapped with the period when another distinguished biblical commentator from the region, Theodore of Tarsus, was archbishop of Canterbury, just as it coincided with the pontificate of Sergius I, a pope of Syrian origin. But the times were changing. An Egyptian text, of perhaps the eighth century, suggests that considerable cultural loss had already taken place:

> They have abandoned the beautiful Coptic language in which the Holy Spirit spoke through the mouths of our fathers; they teach their children from infancy to speak Arabic and glory in it . . . All at this time are abandoning this [Coptic] language to speak Arabic and glory in it, up to the point where one would not even know them for Christians any more, but would take them for barbarians.

A person who wrote, in the name of its author, a preface to a later historical work, represents himself as seeking help in translating texts from Greek and Coptic into Arabic, which was then spoken among the people of Egypt, most of whom did not know Coptic or Greek.[45]

Increasingly, Christian works became available in Arabic. While the 'Ladder of divine ascent', written in Greek by John 'Climacus', an abbot of Mt Sinai during the first half of the seventh century, seems to have been translated into Syriac by end of the century, an Arabic translation had been made by the beginning of the tenth, by which time John of Damascus's 'Exposition of the faith' had been translated from Greek into Arabic; only in the twelfth century did it become available in Latin. These translations answered to the needs of Christians who read in Arabic, the descendants of people who, not many generations previously, had been unfamiliar with the language. The theologian Theodore abu Qurrah (c.750–c.825), who was born in Edessa, wrote in Arabic as well as Syriac and, perhaps, Greek; that he, and other writers of the time, were beginning to address works to fellow Christians in Arabic as well as the traditional languages of Christian discourse showed where the future lay. Before long, the content of the Islamic scriptures was influencing both the form and content of Christian writings: a Christian text written in Arabic in the eighth century praises God in terms drawn from the Qur'an, and fleshes out its narrative of biblical events with detail drawn from that source.[46] Already, the assimilation of Christian indigenes into Muslim Arabs is foreshadowed, together with the marginalisation of those who did not take the step of conversion. By the tenth century, the patriarchs of Alexandria and Antioch seem to have written to each other in Arabic. In some respects, the process of Arabisation mirrored that of Romanisation that we considered at the beginning of this book. But to the degree that it was bound up with the adoption of a new religion that was both universal in its message and specifically Arabic in its linguistic expression, its impact was deeper than that of the earlier process.

In Africa, Latin passed out of use, by a process that eludes our under-standing. In the ninth century a writer saw Kabis (Gabes, the classical Tacape) as 'the town of the foreign Africa' – that is, as not being Arabic in population – but the language of Arabia would become universal. The medieval Arab writer el-Bekri described the ruins of a number of cities. At one of them, Arzao, visitors gaped in astonishment at what they saw, and at another, Tlemcen, where Christians still worshipped, hidden treasure was often found in ruins. But Africa was losing touch with its pre-Islamic past. El-Bekri attributed the building of Carthage, which he placed 72 years before the foundation of Rome, to king Didon, a contemporary of king David, and when he placed the building of a citadel at Badja in the time of Jesus, he was wildly inaccurate, for its surviving dedicatory inscription attributes it to a count Paul, one of Justinian's officers. In Spain, Romance speech remained strong, a phenomenon also reflected in the nomenclature of old towns, which kept their names, and the atypical failure of the newcomers to found important new ones; while Madrid was an Islamic foundation, it only became important some centuries into the Christian period. There were unexpected linguistic survivals from Visigothic times: German ambassadors who came to Spain in the tenth century reported that they were escorted to church by officers named *saiones*, the very word used for policemen in Gothic times, and as late as the fourteenth century an Arab author referred to 'Rakabil', so did the name of Recopolis linger. But the beginnings of the general use of Arabic can be discerned even in Spain, a process that may have been con-nected with intermarriage. By the late eighth century, some three generations after the taking of Spain, disturbing reports were reaching pope Hadrian of Christian women marrying non-Christian men. The issue appeared in another light to a Muslim jurist of the mid-ninth century, faced with the problem of Muslims celebrating Christian feasts, particularly when relatives and in-laws were involved. A process of intermarriage seems to lie behind the names of some Christians who became martyrs in Cordoba during the ninth century. Perfectus and Servusdei, unusual names in Spain, are Latin versions of common Arabic names with religious content (al-Kamil, 'Abd-Allah), a circumstance which suggests that the martyrs were the products of mixed marriages.[47]

Hence, the coming of the Arabs into imperial territory had consequences for the lands they occupied far greater than the coming of the Germanic peoples, or indeed the Slavs, had elsewhere. But their impact was also important in another way. Whereas the centre of gravity of most of those who occupied the European provinces of the Empire came to rest firmly within the territories they conquered, this was not true of the Arabs. Not merely did the religious centre of Islam remain beyond the former borders of the Empire, its importance emphasised by pilgrimage thither, but the territory that the Arabs conquered included lands which the Empire had never made its own. In particular, their conquest of Persia allowed them to bring together a large block of territory that had hitherto never been a unit. Suddenly, the lands taken from the Byzantines and Visigoths were part of a world that included Mesopotamia, and before long they were dancing to unfamiliar rhythms. That these included the economic powerhouses of the Mediterranean had inevitable repercussions on the lands that remained under Christian authority.

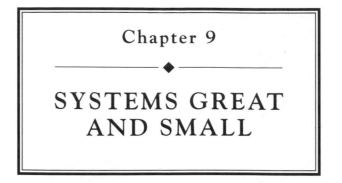

Chapter 9

♦

SYSTEMS GREAT
AND SMALL

THE PIRENNE THESIS I

The changes we have considered in this book took place across some centuries over a wide area. Many of the things that happened were obviously specific to regions, and as time passed local particularism generally became stronger within such regions. But other developments involved wider areas and interactions between different regions, and it would be satisfying if as many of them as possible could be bound up in a single explanatory framework. Over 50 years ago a Belgian scholar, Henri Pirenne, proposed such a framework. He argued that the Mediterranean Sea had been central to the Roman Empire, and that it remained central after the Germanic peoples took the western part of the Empire in the fifth century. Indeed, according to Pirenne their advent was of little significance, for the importance of the Mediterranean, and more generally the ancient civilisation that had continued around its shores, only ended in the seventh century with the coming of the Arabs, particularly Arab pirates, who put an end to Christian trade on its waters. Pirenne saw this as having caused four major products, papyrus, gold, luxury clothing and spices, hitherto widely imported into western Europe, to cease to be available there. Deprived of its trans-Mediterranean connections, the West became closed in on itself, and turned into a self-sufficient economy with no outlets. Pirenne's view that the coming of Islam was responsible for the state of western Europe for much of the middle ages led to the book in which his ideas were most fully expressed being given the provocative title *Mohammed and Charlemagne*.[1]

A lot of water has flowed under the historiographical bridges since the posthumous publication of Pirenne's great work. In some respects his views

must be queried. We have already seen that more change was occurring in the
fifth century and those immediately preceding it than he thought, although
his intuition in separating the newcomers from much of the change that was
taking place was sound. When Pirenne thought of trade, it was in terms of
commerce conducted over long distances rather than locally, but the tendencies for towns to diminish in significance and for regions to become
self-sufficient, as we have seen happen in more than one area in the case of
pottery, may have interacted with any disruption to trade across the sea in
complex ways. Changes in demand as well as alterations in supply could
account for some of the fluctuations in the west's imports of clothing and
foodstuffs, for as we have seen, a large part of Gaul was becoming culturally
Germanic at this time, and such a change would have been reflected in con-
sumer preferences. It is also possible that climatic and ecological changes
were occurring at the time that made the north more independent of the
south. Moreover, that the papal chancery was still using papyrus in the
eleventh century suggests that the four disappearances may not have been as
total as Pirenne thought they were, although when the English began in the
seventh century to generate written documents that have come down to us,
parchment was the only material they used. And while the build-up of trade
in the north-east of the Merovingian state began at the time when the Arabs
were gaining control of much of the Mediterranean coastline, its early stages
must have occurred independently of developments in the south. Indeed, it
is not easy to extrapolate from the Arabs' control of much of the coastline,
which can scarcely be doubted, to the widespread piracy envisaged by
Pirenne. Yet despite its deficiencies, Pirenne's theory remains a useful con-
struct around which other ideas can be framed. It will be worth our while to
consider various classes of evidence unknown to Pirenne, with a view to
establishing the extent to which they can be accommodated with his views.
We may begin by examining patterns in the trade of three commodities.

One important way in which progress has been made in the last few decades
is in the establishment of a chronology of the exports of a kind of pottery
known as African red slip-ware.[2] It had come during Roman times to dominate
the pottery markets of first the western and then the eastern Mediterranean,
and in the fourth century penetrated far up the Nile and into western Spain.
Annoyingly for historians who prefer to work from written sources, such
pottery is alluded to in not a single text, and our knowledge of it is entirely
derived from the artefacts themselves. But material that survives in such
bulk, items of which can be broadly dated on stylistic grounds, provides a
very useful guide to fluctuations across the centuries in the export of one of

the most widely traded commodities in the Mediterranean. At about the time that the Vandals came to Africa, exports declined, especially those to the east, although this development may reflect changing patterns in the export of goods that accompanied the pottery. But there are indications of a revival at the end of the fifth century, and one definitely occurred at about the middle of the sixth century. Early in the seventh century, however, exports to Syria, Palestine and Egypt dried up, perhaps because of disruptions caused by the Persian conquest of those territories. In the Aegean and the region of Cyrenaica, to the west of Egypt, exports continued to arrive in large volume until they suddenly ceased at about the middle of the century. In the west there was a steady, although not uninterrupted, decline in exports. In Italy, for example, African red slip-ware became less widely available, while its import into Spain seems to have ceased in about 625. Nevertheless, production in a minor way apparently continued at Carthage until the Arabs took the city, towards the end of the century. In other words, the coming of the Vandals seems to have coincided with a decline in trade, at least in the short term, while the seventh century saw its end, although its progressive diminution can only in part be correlated with the coming of the Arabs.

Such global patterns can be tested by local findings. Excavations at a site in Constantinople with an exceptionally rich quantity of pottery, that connected with a church erected by the wealthy Juliana Anicia in the sixth century, indicate that from the fifth century Phocaean ware produced in the west of Asia Minor predominated there, but from the middle of the sixth African ware became more common, coming to comprise a quarter of the total of fine wares. In the seventh century, Phocaean imports suddenly declined, to be replaced by African and local products, and direct trading contacts with Africa seem to have remained in place until the very end of the seventh century, whereupon wares of apparently local manufacture were used. At Anemourion, the modern Eski Anamur on Cape Anamur, 65 km north of Cyprus, large quantities of pottery were imported from the fifth to the seventh centuries: Cypriot, which was the most popular; African, which became scarcer in the seventh century; and Phocaean, which seems to have ceased in about 600. During the seventh century a type of pottery known as 'piecrust rim-ware' was being produced locally, and by the end of the century the site was no longer occupied. Its abandonment can be connected with fear of Arab raids, such as those which were launched by land across the Pyrenees in the eighth century, but there is no reason to associate earlier developments in pottery use with such raids. Evidence from the great trading port of Marseilles suggests that amphorae continued to be imported in large numbers as the seventh century advanced, many of them from Africa, imports from which came to displace those from the east and Italy. In the Aegean region, where African wares first appeared in the second half of the third century, they seem to have fallen away in the fifth century, yielding ground to Phocaean wares.[3]

Some tentative conclusions can be drawn from this body of data. Exports of pottery from Africa seem to have declined at about the time the Vandals arrived, but this development need not have been connected with the Vandals; rather, it may have been caused by the increased competitiveness of Phocaean wares, especially in the east, which suggests that happenings offstage, as it were, may have been important in the fortunes of African exports. Similarly, the demise of African exports in the seventh century certainly occurred at about the time of the expansion of the Arabs, but apparently predated it in territories briefly occupied by Persia. And while an export trade may have continued within what survived of the Empire until the final capture of Carthage, the atrophy of the city towards the end of the Byzantine period tells against the survival of a major industry there.

The pattern of trade in another, more expensive commodity that was pro-duced in a different part of the Empire points in a broadly similar direction. Some 200 km south-west of Constantinople lay the island of Prokonnesos, where the great quarries of marble from which the modern Sea of Marmara takes its name were located. The industry was commercially important; when the government granted a remission of unpaid taxes early in the fifth century, the Prokonnesos was one of the places with mines and quarries to which it was explicitly not extended. Marble produced there was distributed far and wide during the reign of Justinian, for not only was a large amount employed in the rebuilding of Hagia Sophia in Constantinople, but it was also used to decorate the church of the monastery which that emperor erected in the dis-tant Mount Sinai, and in churches built in Ravenna. One of the Ostrogothic sovereigns of Italy received a present of marble from Justinian, and at about the same time a pre-fabricated church prepared from marble produced there went down in a shipwreck off the east coast of Sicily. But the trade was not to last. A legendary account of the building of Hagia Sophia, written in the ninth century, makes much of the collecting of marble from old buildings, so it could be recycled in the great cathedral; it does not seem to have occurred to the author that it could have been produced from quarries. Indeed, Byzantine builders had for some time been content to recycle spolia from old buildings, even for their most prestigious projects: some of the columns used in the great cathedral of Hagia Sophia had been removed from older buildings. The Arabs cannot be blamed for this, and we have already seen that the decline of the Italian town of Luni may have been connected with the difficulties faced by nearby marble quarries, which it would be equally implausible to attribute to Arab pirates. It therefore looks as if trade was declining in the seventh century, but as part of a longer process that was independent of the coming of Arab power.[4]

The same was true of trade in another commodity of high status. In the ancient world, ivory had been freely used for diptychs, statues and inlays, and while prized it was not particularly rare; towards the end of the fourth century, a law was issued forbidding private persons to distribute presents of gold or ivory tablets. Everyone knew where ivory came from: the Barberini diptych, a diptych leaf of the sixth century itself made of ivory, shows a figure meant to represent a barbarian carrying a tusk walking behind an elephant, while a picture in another work of that century, the *Vienna Genesis*, which would not be out of place in a modern children's Bible, shows a pair of elephants with splendid tusks, dominating the procession of animals walking two by two out of Noah's ark. It remained plentifully available in the Mediterranean area after the fall of the Empire in the west, being used for the diptychs of consuls until that office effectively ceased in the mid-sixth century. One of the most impressive works of that century, the throne of Maximian, the bishop of Ravenna who is depicted in a mosaic in the church of San Vitale, was made out of ivory, with carvings depicting the life of Christ and that of the Old Testament figure Joseph. Ivory combs were widely used to comb the hair of bishops before they celebrated the Eucharist, with a view to deterring demons. While comparisons in the use of ivory in different regions in the following centuries are difficult, the western Islamic lands had plenty of it, and elephant ivory seems to have been freely available in Byzantium, where it was used in the tenth century to produce triptychs. Some fine pieces were executed in the west during the Carolingian period, but in circles close to the court, and ivory passed out of widespread use in western Europe for some time. The Franks Casket, a work produced at about the turn of the eighth century, was made of whalebone, and an inscription on its front which has been interpreted as concerning a fish becoming sad when it swam on to shingle may refer to the origin of the material from which it was made. Given the superiority of ivory over the whalebone and walrus tusks which replaced it in the west, the decline in its use may be attributed to a lack of supply.[5] Again, the date at which this came about was approximately that of the Arab expansion, and Byzantium, where it continued to be used, did not depend on trans-Mediterranean shipping for its supply.

On the basis of trade in the commodities we have considered, we may deduce that such shipping became rare. As it happens, there is a rough-and-ready indication that this was so. It is possible to tabulate century by century the numbers of ships wrecked in the Mediterranean and Roman provinces, which provide a useful indication of how the volume of shipping was changing over time. Fifty-four wrecks of the fourth century have been discovered, and only 25 from the fifth. However, 34 ships that went down in the sixth century have been found, 10 from the seventh, only two of them clearly in its second half, and one from the eighth, although this century is no more than the median date of the very long period within which the wreck could have taken place, and there is no particular reason to believe that the ship was wrecked then. Again, there is clear evidence for a decline in shipping during the fifth century. However, a large part of the shipping at the beginning of the century had probably been generated not by private commerce but by the carriage of goods between the provinces of the Empire on behalf of the state, particularly because of the needs of the army and major cities. As the reach of the Empire steadily contracted over that century, such cargoes would have disappeared, despite the odd later survival; the sending of grain ships from Egypt to Rome by an emperor during the 570s is the last known occasion of a shipment to Rome. The impact of the newcomers will therefore have been indirect, the decline in shipping occurring because of the new political situation they created, rather then their direct action. The sixth century emerges as a relatively active period, a situation that may have been connected with Justinian's wars in the west, while the seventh century witnessed catastrophic decline. One well-laden ship that went down near Yassi Ada, in Turkey, at some time after 625 carrying a cargo of at least 900 amphorae may have been a merchant vessel, or it may have been carrying goods to supply Byzantine troops; if it was the latter, it was a vessel of the kind for which the west had little need after the fifth century. But in either case, such shipping had a very limited future. To judge by the evidence of shipwrecks, Mediterranean trade involving Christian shipping had effectively died by 700.[6]

While its interpretation is difficult, another body of evidence, the Byzantine coins that have been found in Gaul, seems to point in the same direction. From the reign of Phocas (602–10), 25 such coins have been discovered there. That 42 coins minted during the long reign of Heraclius (610–41), many of them minted in Constantinople, have been found there suggests a diminished impact, which continued during the almost equally long reign of Constans ii (641–68), from which only 12 coins, many of them minted at the much closer centre of Carthage, have been found, while just one is known from the periods when Justinian II reigned (685–95, 705–11). Only one coin minted in the eighth century has turned up in the west; a stray solidus of Leo III found its way to Kent.[7] It must be said that this pattern could be held to measure things other than interaction between Francia and the steadily contracting Empire. Few coins have been found in Ravenna, which remained under Byzantine control throughout this period, from about 640, and it is likely that the diminishing finds in Gaul are partly to be accounted for by a lower production of coins overall. But the scale of the decline in coins found in Gaul is, prima facie, evidence for a steady lessening of contact between it and the Empire during the seventh century.

It is possible to draw on other kinds of evidence bearing on this question, although they run the risk of being impressionistic. Nevertheless, it can be suggested on grounds other than those we have considered that relations between Gaul and the east were still strong at the end of the sixth century. It is clear from his various works that Gregory of Tours (bishop 573–94) was fascinated by the east, and that he had good sources of information concerning it. He tells a funny story about how Justinian was outwitted when he tried to take over the treasure of Juliana Anicia; provides details about the coronation of two emperors of the sixth century which are unknown from eastern authors; tells of having learned from a deacon how the star of Bethlehem appeared to the pure in heart who visited a well from which Mary had taken water; describes the coming of relics of the True Cross from eastern lands to a convent at Poitiers; is an early witness to the legend, later found useful by the church of Constantinople, that St Andrew had sailed to that city; and seems to be the first western author to show awareness of a doctrine that had become known in eastern Christianity, the assumption of the Virgin Mary. It comes as no surprise that the relics such a cosmopolitan man placed in a baptistery he built at Tours included those of the Arab saint Sergius.[8]

Writing a few decades before the expansion of the Arabs began, Gregory, the bishop of a see just north of the river Loire, was fascinated by the East, concerning which he was in some ways surprisingly well informed. Yet nowhere in his works has he anything of substance to say about Britain, which enjoyed close contacts with the north of Gaul at the time. In many ways, the Christian world to which he saw himself as belonging was still bound together across the Mediterranean. A few decades after Gregory wrote, two monks, John Moschus and Sophronius, later to become patriarch of Jerusalem, left Bethlehem on travels which, over the course of decades, took them to Egypt, Palestine and Rome. Some visitors from the south of Ireland who were in Rome for Easter in 631 found themselves sharing accommodation with people described as a Greek, a Hebrew, a Scythian and an Egyptian.[9] One of our earliest sources for aspects of the expansion of the Arabs in Syria, and the earliest text to mention the mistaken action that Heraclius undertook against a circumcised people that he failed to identify correctly, the chronicle attributed to Fredegarius, was written in Gaul. Such evidence suggests the openness of the Mediterranean early in the seventh century.

But even at that time this situation was ceasing to obtain. For centuries, Christian historians had made a point of supplying in their works the names of important bishops and the dates of their episcopates, and it is possible to gain an idea of when historians ceased to be in possession of such data for distant sees. The information available to the Byzantine historian Theophanes, when he wrote early in the ninth century, only allowed him to supply the names of popes until Benedict I, who became pope in 575. Thereafter the names of popes are not given until that of Gregory III, who took office in 731; perhaps the iconoclastic crisis that broke out at about that time made the see of Rome more significant to some Byzantine observers. With the eastern patriarchs, his knowledge of the patriarchs of Jerusalem ceases with Sophronius, who occupied the see when the city was taken by the Arabs; those of Alexandria with Peter II, the successor of Cyrus under whom the Arabs took the city; while his knowledge of the patriarchs of Antioch derives from a list compiled before the Persians occupied the city early in the seventh century. The Egyptian historian Eutychius, who wrote in the early tenth century, explicitly stated that he did not know the names of the patriarchs of Rome after Agatho, who died in 681, and of Constantinople after one Theodore, whom he confusingly dates to the caliphate of Marwan and believed was a contemporary of Agatho. Here again, it is important not to place too much weight on such evidence, for the council in Trullo held in Constantinople in 692 included representatives of the sees of Rome, Alexandria, Antioch and Jerusalem. But it implies that the lines of communication were becoming longer.[10]

Taken together, such evidence suggests that the Pirenne thesis largely works. Economic activity was certainly sustained in the Mediterranean following the fall of the Empire in the west. Doubtless it was at a lower level than it had been, but it remained significant, and such decline as occurred need not have been directly caused by the incoming Germanic peoples. Moreover, such developments occurred in the face of a tendency towards regionalism that must have interacted with diminishing sea-borne trade in ways more complex than simply being a response to it. Similarly, the seventh century experienced what turned out to be a disastrous decline. Trade around the Mediterranean certainly continued into the century. Jacob, the Jewish merchant whose conversation in Carthage showed him so aware of the lessening of Roman power, is said to have had dealings with weavers in Rhodes, and went to Constantinople, where he was entrusted with clothes to sell in Africa, and he promised to go there, or to Gaul for that matter. It may be that Jewish merchants provide the strongest evidence for continuity in trade around the Mediterranean in the following period, although the coming to prominence of a marginal group may indicate that the enterprise with which its members were involved was itself marginal. Again, when the Arab general 'Amr took Tripoli, he carried away many fine loads of silk brocade from its merchants.[11] Yet the northern coastline of Africa was then ceasing to be part of the Christian world, and whatever diminution in its trade across the sea had occurred prior to the seventh century accelerated markedly within it, until little was left.

We may take it, then, that Pirenne was correct in identifying the seventh century as crucial. Nevertheless, it is not clear that his theory explains this, for the reasons he adduced for the change in the seventh century are unsatisfying. While it is certainly true that the Arabs took to the water and gained command of much of the Mediterranean with astonishing ease, the pirates whom he alleged drove Christian shipping off the Mediterranean are difficult to detect during the period; that the Devil may be described as turning himself into an Ishmaelite pirate in the *Life* of a saint which may have been written in the seventh century indicates that such people may have been known, but firmer evidence would be welcome.[12] Perhaps Pirenne, for all he did to widen the horizons of scholars accustomed to accounting for change in western Europe with reference to purely internal developments, was nevertheless less broad than he could have been. The role that the Arabs play in his account is that of a kind of *deus ex machina*; it may be that the importance they had for the west will be able to be understood more clearly when their activities are located against the background of their own circumstances.

WORLD SYSTEMS

As we have seen, the situation of Arabia could be understood very differently, depending on from where it was viewed. From the perspective of the Mediterranean peoples it was utterly marginal, but seen from within it was a central place. On its north-west it abutted the Empire, across the Persian Gulf and around its terminus it looked northwards to Persia, Africa lay close by across the Red Sea, while some parts of Arabia were closer to India than they were to Macca. Its contacts with its various neighbours were of long standing. An Egyptian who probably wrote in the first century AD knew of a port in Africa, perhaps near Dar-es-Salaam, which Arab trading vessels frequently visited. Arabs had come to marry the local women and learned the speech of the region, a development that foreshadowed the subsequent growth in the area of Swahili.[13] But their rapid expansion in the seventh and eighth centuries brought the Arabs into contact with members of other civilisations, as graphically indicated by the fresco at Qasr 'Amra, and before long they were benefiting from what such civilisations had to teach them. Such developments suggest that the Mediterranean, the chief area of interaction between Muslims and Christians, may have been an area of only secondary importance for the former. For them, their most important conquest was that of the old antagonist of the peoples of the eastern Mediterranean, Persia. Its incorporation into Islamic territory opened to the Muslims a world of unimaginably broad horizons.

Islam, entirely Arab in its origin, found Persia difficult to digest. Whereas the languages used in territory taken from the Byzantines became marginal or disappeared under Islam, Persian, far from being displaced by Arabic, went on to become one of the great languages of Islam. Even among Christians, the headquarters of the patriarch of the Church of the East, the body of Christians often called Nestorians, were moved from Seleucia-Ctesiphon, where they had been located for centuries, to Baghdad, where the Abbasid caliphs established their capital, in the middle of the eighth century. The history of early Islam was written in Baghdad. It was thither that Ibn Ishaq went from Madina to work on his biography of Muhammad, while the great historian al-Tabari, who had been born near the Caspian Sea, lived there for decades. But in some ways it resisted Islam. While the caliph al-Mansur bestowed on the new city the Arabic, indeed qur'anic name Dar as-Salam (home of Peace), it became universally known by an old pre-Islamic name, Baghdad. Indeed, pre-Islamic influence proved hard to shake off. Stories were told that Charlemagne's great contemporary, the caliph Harun al-Rashid, had sought to tear down a great reception hall erected by the shah Chosroes I, but was unable to do so.[14] Such was the awe with which Chosroes was regarded that an Islamic tradition had Gabriel inform Muhammad that there was no need for him to think of the shah as being in hell.

Moreover, Persia was a large unit. The writers of classical antiquity, reasonably enough, made much of its dealings with the Mediterranean area, and its sustained importance there cannot be doubted. The teachings of the Persian religious teacher Mani (c.216–76) were rapidly diffused around the sea. Within a few decades of his death Manichean missionaries arrived in

Egypt, and in the late fourth century Augustine attended their meetings in both Africa and Italy. By the early fifth century, the elite of the eastern Empire were playing a ball game similar to polo on horseback, which had been introduced from Persia. But modern historians, like ancient authors, can easily over-emphasize the importance of the Mediterranean for Persia. Based as it was on the Iranian plateau, Persia also looked eastwards, towards both India, where Mani spent some time, and China. Justinian's contemporary, Chosroes I, kept empty thrones for the emperors of China and Rome and the king of the Khazars, and the building in which Chosroes II was imprisoned after being deposed in 628 was known as the House of the Indian.[15] Planning to convert the world, Mani had undertaken a missionary journey to India, and by the end of the seventh century Manichean missionaries had arrived in China. Missionaries dispatched by the Church of the East similarly fanned out far from Persia. In 781 a stele was erected in China, recording the planting of Christianity there by missionaries who had come from Syria in about 635.

The centrality of Persia was shown in other ways, none more important than the arrival there of a system of numerals that had been devised in India. The Syrian monk Severus Sebokht (ob. 666/7), who lived in a monastery by the Euphrates, was a translator from Greek and Persian into Syriac. In one of his works he pointed out ways in which the Indians were superior to the Greeks, a comparison that people in his part of the world were better qualified than most to make. As evidence for their superiority he could cite 'the logical method of their calculations and the way of counting which surpasses description (I refer to the method which uses nine signs.)'[16] The use of a special set of signs for numerals, and their deployment in a series of ten, beginning with zero, which could be reused to denote units, tens, hundreds and other, higher sequences of numbers, marked an immense advance on systems that employed letters of the alphabet to represent numbers. Another arrival in Persia was chess, which had almost certainly come there from India in Sasanid times; together with a system of numerals based on those of the Indians, chess would later be diffused from Persia into the broader Islamic world, and thence into Christendom. The origins of medical teaching at the great Christian centre of Jundishapur were later traced to the arrival of a visitor from India, appropriately enough, in view of its location in the modern Khuzestan. And it was this interconnected world based on Persia of which the Arabs suddenly found themselves masters in the seventh century.

The central position that Arabia enjoyed and the broadening of horizons that followed the conquests, especially that of Persia, meant that the world of

Islam, politically one entity until well into the eighth century, operated as a unit of exceptionally wide dimensions. Shortly after they captured Egypt, the Arabs excavated a canal originally built by the emperor Trajan, with the aim of linking Babylon, the site of a fortress on the eastern bank of the Nile opposite the pyramids, and the Red Sea.[17] A later text states that, early in the eighth century, people using the road between Antioch and al-Massisah, the ancient city of Mopsuestia which now found itself at the edge of the Arabs' domain, were often molested by lions. The caliph al-Walid (707–9) dealt with the problem by sending there 4,000 buffaloes, 'by which the required result was attained through Allah's help'. He had been able to act in this way because thousands of buffaloes had come into the possession of al-Hajjaj, the powerful governor of Iraq, who gave al-Walid 4,000 of them and set the others free in a jungle. In 711 an Islamic army made its way into the Indian subcontinent, and by 714 it had come to control the lower Indus Valley. Among the towns it took was Daibul, famous for its Buddhist stupa; before long it had been destroyed and a mosque erected. As we have seen, the great mosque at Damascus was said to have involved workers from Persia, India, Africa and Byzantium.[18]

But the clearest sign of the reach combined with unity which distinguished the world of Islam is the diffusion of foods, particularly those of south Asian origin. Cosmas Indicopleustes, the Egyptian voyager of the sixth century, seems to have been personally responsible for the original of the drawings of two banana plants found in later manuscripts of his work.[19] These would have been fruits of the utmost exoticism in his day; 300 years later they were cultivated in Egypt. Crops of Asian origin spread to the far end of the world of Islam: by the tenth century, oranges, rice, sugar cane, aubergines and water melons had been introduced in Spain, all having originated in lands with warmer climates. For practical purposes, Spain had ceased to be a part of Europe, and found itself plugged into a much larger and more prosperous part of the world.

The changing relationships of different areas were revealed by the movements of goods originally from Jerusalem. When the emperor Titus captured the capital of the ancient Jewish state in AD 70 he is said to have removed the treasures of king Solomon, and when Alaric besieged Rome in 410 he in turn took them with him. This cannot have been true of all of them, for some of the treasure was carried off by Geiseric the Vandal, to be forwarded at a later time to Constantinople by Belisarius after his defeat of the Vandals. But some remained with the Goths, for Arab traditions describe Tariq acquiring the table of Solomon when he came to Spain, and sending it to Damascus.

The journeyings of the table show the chief developments in the political history of these centuries: the expansion of Rome's authority, the later breaking up of its power around the Mediterranean, and finally the passage of power inland, away from the sea.[20]

The breadth of the world of Islam could be seen in many ways. Caliphs in Damascus ordered the execution of officials in Spain. In 751 the Arabs encountered a Chinese force in a battle fought in the southern region of what is now the Kazakhstan republic; by the end of the century, paper mills had been built in Baghdad in accordance with technology borrowed from China. Eleven years after the battle, a Chinese captive went home by junk from the Persian Gulf, and when he arrived he boasted of the role that his compatriots played in crafts among the Arabs. Before long, ceramics had replaced silk as the main Chinese export to western Eurasia. In the middle of the ninth century, a sailor wrote an account of China and India in Arabic. He described such curiosities as the use of toilet paper rather than water by the Chinese on the basis of first-hand knowledge. We can trace precisely the route that he took eastwards, via Sri Lanka, where the port of Mantai had recently begun to attract international maritime trade, and Sumatra, unlike that of the best-known long-distance traveller of the early Byzantine Empire, Cosmas Indicopleustes, whose claim to have reached Sri Lanka is suspicious. The Arab author asserted that the inhabitants of India and China agreed that there were four important kings in the world, among whom the king of the Arabs was universally agreed to be foremost, followed by the kings of China, the Romans (i.e. Byzantines) and those who pierced their ears, as he thought of the Indians.[21] Such notions, already centuries old in the Middle East, where the Persian teacher Mani was said to have taught that there were four great kingdoms, those of Babylon or the Persians, the Romans, the Axumites (or Ethiopians) and Chinese, quickly made their presence felt in the world of Islam, for something very similar lay behind the fresco at Qasr 'Amra.

Views of such breadth were beyond the imagination of Christians of the period. Towards the end of the ninth century, a biographer of Charlemagne described Persian envoys to his court at Aachen laughing and clapping their hands at its magnificence, and reporting that all the peoples of the east were in awe of Charles's power. Such tact would have done credit to the most accomplished diplomats. On one occasion the caliph Harun al-Rashid sent Charlemagne an elephant as a present, which a Jewish merchant, Isaac, conveyed by way of Africa and Italy. The animal lived for some years in its new home, before dying on campaign against the king of Denmark. Harun's gift to Charlemagne may have been a put-down, for it recalls one made by the emperor Maurice who, some two centuries earlier, had sent the barbarous and troublesome Avar chagan an elephant. But with a staggering Eurocentricity, one of our sources represents the caliph as sending his only elephant, simply because the king had asked for it. Little did Charlemagne know, but the name of the elephant, represented as Abul Abaz, was the same as that of the first caliph of the Abbasid dynasty, Abu l-'Abbas.[22]

People like Harun were not disinterested in Europe, but it did not seem very important to them. When, in the tenth century, the learned Arab scholar al-Mas'udi considered ancient nations that had their own languages, he came up with seven: the Persians, the Chaldeans, among whom the Hebrews and Arabs found their place, the Greeks, who included the Byzantines and Europeans, the Libyans, who seem to include Africans in general, the Turks, the Indians and the Chinese. The amplitude of this view is thrown into stark relief when it is compared to the confined intellectual world inhabited by the scholars of the period in western Europe. Mas'udi's work contains some information about western Europe, from which we may excerpt one particular. While in Egypt, he came upon a book that a bishop of the northern Spanish town of Gerona had written for the son of one of the Spanish caliphs. Astonishingly, Mas'udi reproduced from it in one of his own works a partial list of the kings of the Franks, starting with Clovis – whom he describes as having been converted from paganism to Christianity under the influence of his wife, who is named – by way of Charlemagne up to the king who ruled when he was writing, Louis IV.[23] It is doubtful whether any writer in Christian Europe could command such information about the world of Islam. But for Mas'udi, the Franks whose kings he was able to list were of far less consequence than the Indians and the Chinese. The rise of Islam had relegated western Europe to being an unimportant backwater, from which it would take centuries to emerge.

THE PIRENNE THESIS II

Our discussion has taken us far away from the Mediterranean. But it suggests how the sea had become, for the areas around its shores with the most lively economies, a backwater. In some cases, goods that earlier would have been consigned to the west now found outlets within the wealthy, spacious and interconnected world of Islam; in other cases, new lines were developed for the markets that had opened up. In either case, the vast cities that sprang up needed to be supplied. In the late sixth century, as we have seen, the wine of Gaza was finding its way to Gaul. It was a sign of changing times that, late in the eighth century, Palestine was sending the treasury at Baghdad 300,000 lb of raisins annually. In Africa, Kairouan became the centre of a web of trade routes, just as Carthage had in earlier centuries. But whereas the roads of Roman Africa had converged on a port, from which pottery and other goods were dispatched northwards by ship, Kairouan was a great slave market, linked eastwards by inland roads to Fustat and, beyond it, Syria. Some naval trade continued, but it took place within the world of Islam; a geographer of the eleventh century reported that the Moroccan port of al-Madhiya was frequented by ships from Alexandria, Syria, Sicily, Spain and other lands. In his time, pistachio nuts were sent from Cafsa, an inland town in what is now Tunisia, to all parts of Africa, as far away as Egypt, Spain and the east of Morocco. Caravans are described as coming to another African destination from Iraq, the Hijaz, Egypt, Syria and all parts of the Maghreb. Hippo, the town where Augustine had been bishop, which was now known as Annaba because of its jujube trees, was frequented by merchants, who came in particular from Spain. No less than the Middle East, Africa had become unplugged from the Christian shores of the Mediterranean and looked to other parts of the world of Islam.[24]

Evidence from western Europe confirms that such a reorientation occurred. In late antique Gaul, much trade was in the hands of people described in the texts as 'Syrians', such as the Eusebius who bribed his way to becoming bishop of Paris in 591 and installed his compatriot cronies as servants in the episcopal household. References to such merchants dry up in the seventh century. Similarly, evidence for colonies of eastern merchants in Spain disappears during the second half of the seventh century. This is not to say that the west was totally deprived of goods from the east, but those that were still known there were of a marginal and exotic kind, such as the 'treasures' that Bede is described in a moving scene as distributing among his friends as he lay dying in the north of England in 735: pepper, the stoles that members of the clergy wore, and incense. Domitian, a bishop of Tongres in the sixth century who resided at Maastricht, was laid to rest not long after his death at Huy. Among the contents of the treasure that accumulated there was a silk textile with a note in Soghdian script stating that it was made in what is now Uzbekistan. The writing is similar to that used on inscriptions in a site destroyed by Arabs in 722, and the silk has therefore been dated to the late seventh or early eighth century. Some of the influence that the world of Islam tenuously exerted on the west was mediated by Byzantium. From the time of Leo III at the end of the eighth century, popes were making altar cloths and vestments from silks decorated with types of motif common in Persian art, while a little earlier Pippin, the first Carolingian king, had received from the Byzantine emperor a silk with pictures of an emperor hunting a lion; in all cases we may be dealing with Byzantine imitations of Arab imitations of Persian originals.[25] But such items and imitations were not the fruit of major trade. Moreover, given that the parts of the Mediterranean which the Arabs had taken had provided not merely goods that were exported to the west but also many of the merchants who traded them, the disappearance of the latter from the west was doubly damaging to trade in that area. The economies of the lands that had made up the old Empire were therefore moving in very different directions. Those remaining in Christian hands were devolving into regions that usually had a high degree of self-sufficiency, while the lands that had been part of the Byzantine Empire generated trade which took place over longer distances than it had previously. And while the developments were divergent, they both involved a turning away from the Mediterranean.

There is therefore no need to invoke pirates to explain the fate of shipping in the Mediterranean during the seventh century; rather, this answered to a massive reconfiguration of trade. The atrophy of shipping across the Mediterranean and the location of political power in the world of Islam were reflected in the decline of ports and the growth of inland centres. The old, coastal centres of power and population that had for many centuries been an immovable feature of the ancient world found themselves in reduced circumstances. In Syria, Antioch declined as Damascus grew, while in place of the old Hellenistic and Byzantine capital of Egypt, Alexandria, the Arabs founded the garrison town of Fustat, at the point on the Nile just upstream from where it turns into a delta, which supplanted it and developed into Cairo. In Africa, the role that Carthage had formerly played was divided between the new inland foundation of Kairouan and the smaller coastal town of Tunis, which was occupied by troops. The sea had been displaced.

THE MEDITERRANEAN

If we wish to appreciate the state of shipping in the Mediterranean in the period after the seventh century, there is no better evidence than the experiences of a group of English travellers, which are known from a biography written towards the end of the eighth century.[26] In the spring of 724 an Englishman, Willibald, set out from Rome with two companions to visit Jerusalem. Their journey turned out to be protracted. They made their way to Naples where, after a delay of two weeks, they boarded a ship from Egypt that took them to Reggio in Calabria. There they waited for three weeks before boarding a ship to Syracuse, whence they sailed to Monemvasia, the fortress on the south of the Peloponnesos, which the author of the account described as being in Slav lands. Finally they arrived in Cyprus, which they found divided between Greeks and Saracens. Leaving it at the feast of the birth of John the Baptist, 24 June, in 725, they sailed into the 'region of the Saracens'. This leg of their journey was a short one, for they disembarked at Tartus (Arwad), whence they proceeded to Emesa (Hims). The birthplace of the poet Romanos Melodos, the town was decidedly inland, and a curious way station for people on their way to the Christian holy places.

There, however, people described in the biography as pagan Saracens suspected them of being spies. They were arrested and brought before a wise old man who recognised them as being similar to other people whom he had seen engaged in fulfilling their 'law', or religious obligation. But when they went to the palace to enquire as to the road to Jerusalem, they again fell under suspicion of spying and were imprisoned. Nevertheless, their conditions were not onerous, for a kind merchant sent them meals twice a day, his son escorted them to the baths twice a week, and on Sunday he took them to church. They owed their release to someone from Spain whose brother was one of those in attendance on the king. He spoke to them, and the person who had imprisoned them, the Spaniard and a man from the ship in which they had sailed from Cyprus came before the king of the Saracens, Myrmummus. Matters were smoothed over, it being explained that the captives came from the furthermost west, beyond which was nothing but water, and they resumed their journey, passing by way of Damascus and Nazareth to Jerusalem. There Willibald experienced blindness for two months, before regaining his sight at the basilica built by Constantine. Having obtained from the king, who had gone to Emesa because of high mortality, a letter allowing them to proceed, they made their way to Tyre where, after a long delay, they took ship to Constantinople. Willibald spent two years there, before sailing to Syracuse with legates of the pope and the emperor, the iconoclast Leo III, whence he made his way back to Rome. He reached the city seven years after he had departed on his travels.

It had been a long trip. Doubtless Willibald and his friends did not aim for speed, and the narrative of their journey suggests that they were happy to linger in interesting places. But the coming of Islam roughly coincided with a great slump in the number of pilgrims visiting the Holy Land. The town that had grown up to service the pilgrims venerating the site of Symeon the Stylite's ascetic labours at Qal'at Sem'an fell into decay as early as the seventh century, while Bethlehem fell into a sorry state in the following century.[27] We may conjecture that the sheer difficulties in mounting expeditions to such sites, rather than acts of positive harassment, contributed to their decline. The future of pilgrimage in the world of Islam lay elsewhere, for *hajj*, the undertaking of pilgrimage, was incumbent upon Muslims who could afford it, and the pilgrimage to Macca came to attract great numbers; the wife of Harun al-Rashid was responsible for preparing a way for pilgrims from Baghdad to Arabia. By Willibald's time, the tourist infrastructure for Christians was remarkably primitive. He and his companions spent an inordinate amount of time waiting for boats to turn up, and in prison. No less than the archaeological evidence for trading patterns, the experiences of Willibald and his companions show that the volume of shipping in the Mediterranean, particularly that involving its Christian parts, and the numbers of people who travelled to strange lands was a shadow of what it had been earlier. The people living around the sea had decisively turned their backs on it.

What was true of trade and travel was also true politically, for the realities encountered by Willibald were reflected in political changes in the decades that followed his journey. The Byzantine Empire, whose territory had shrunk to less than a third of the size it had been after the conquests of Justinian, had become irrelevant. In 751 the last Merovingian king of the Franks was deposed and replaced by Pippin, the first king of the Carolingian dynasty. The new ruling family, which had emerged from the mayors of the palace of Austrasia, was from the north-east of Francia, where its estates were based in the Rhineland, and it soon brought swathes of southern Europe under its domination. The papacy, which had for centuries seen itself as part of the Mediterranean world centred on Constantinople, sought an alliance with the rising power to the north, in accordance with which Pippin's son Charlemagne marched to Italy against the Lombards in 773. Their capital, Pavia, fell in the following year, and with it the Lombard monarchy. Henceforth, the destiny of Italy and the papacy would be bound up with the politics of northern Europe. The understanding of Rome as the head of the world, which survived into the fifth century, was now impossible, and could only be understood with reference to the past, as people came to think of Rome as having formerly had the status of being the head of the entire world.[28]

At precisely the same time as Pippin acceded to the kingship, the world of Islam was turning away from the Mediterranean. Its reorientation found political expression in the replacement of the old Umayyad capital, Damascus, by Baghdad when the Abbasids came to power. Damascus seemed increasingly far from the centre of gravity of the large section of the world that the Arabs had brought under their sway, and work was begun on the new city, designed in the form of a circle with a diameter of 2,300 m. If the growth of Kufa and Basra, the early Arab foundations in Persia, had been surprising, that of Baghdad was explosive. The Abbasid caliph al-Mansur moved there in about 762, and by the turn of the century, Baghdad may have been the largest city in the world; its population certainly surpassed that of Constantinople. The ability of the world of Islam to support such an enormous city, and its staggering growth in its early decades, is yet another sign that its economy operated at a different level from that of the Christian lands. But no less significant was its location, in the former Mesopotamia. Built *de novo* at a point on the Tigris where the river is still navigable and not far distant from the Euphrates, it was a mere 30 km upstream from the old Persian capital, Ctesiphon, where Chosroes I had erected his great palace.

The city of Baghdad looked down the Tigris towards the Persian Gulf and the great Indian Ocean beyond. After centuries during which those living around the eastern, and indeed, southern, shores of the Mediterranean had been orientated towards the sea, they suddenly came to be configured around the ancient Fertile Crescent, which came to form a political unit for the first time in centuries. In just the same way, after centuries during which power in western Europe lay in the south, the second Carolingian monarch, Charlemagne, established towards the end of the eighth century his headquarters at Aachen, a location almost exactly as far away from the Mediterranean as was the capital of the Abbasids. Everywhere, energies had passed from the sea, as could be seen even from the distribution of architecture: the finest Christian buildings erected during the seventh century may well have been the wonderful stone churches of inland Armenia.

THE WEST LOOKS BACK

We may therefore accept that the east, together with the west, knew greater change in the seventh and eighth centuries than in the fifth. It was in the later period that people in the west came more strongly to feel that they were living in a period that could be sharply defined from the ancient world, an understanding which, curiously enough, was expressed in a misinterpretation of the events of the earlier century. In many parts of the Empire, it was possible to live through the fifth century without feeling that it was a time of great change. It was eastern authors writing some decades later who first attributed significance to the deposition of the last emperor of the West in 476. Similarly, it was a Greek author of the mid-sixth century who felt that the invasion of Alaric at the beginning of the fifth century had caused Italy to be depopulated up until his own time. But as we have seen, depopulation was under way for other reasons, and contemporaries were not inclined to make much of the events of Alaric's sack of Rome in 410. The version that Jerome offered of this event was remarkably literary, while it suited Augustine's apologetic purposes and those of his follower Orosius to minimise its impact. A similar tendency was shown in the early sixth century by Cassiodorus, who made light of the actions of the Goths by mentioning that they were clement in their victory. When, about a century later, Isidore of Seville reached the year 410 in his history of the Goths, he gives the impression of relishing the deeds of Alaric, to whom he attributes the words that he was waging war on the Romans, not the apostles, as if this made everything all right. Doubtless the circumstance that Cassiodorus and Isidore both wrote under Gothic governments encouraged circumspection in descriptions of the sack, but they found no difficulty in integrating the events of 410 into their narratives in a way which suggested that they had been harmless. No one reading them would have gained the idea that anything significant had taken place, just as no reader of the chronicle that Cassiodorus wrote covering events up to 518 would have thought that any important caesura had occurred in the immediately preceding period.[29]

Later, however, the events of the fifth century appeared in a very different light. While one author of the early seventh century described Medard, a bishop in the north of Gaul, as having had a Frankish father and a Roman mother, a distinction that may still have been valid but that was starting to become anachronistic, another writer of that century represents the mother of a Vandal king as telling her son to gain a name for himself by destroying what others had built and killing the people who were still alive. A text of the early eighth century describes a king of the Burgundians as using gladiators to dispatch those Romans who did not flee; by the end of the century, the learned scholar Alcuin believed that nearly all Europe had been made empty by the swords and flames of the Goths and Huns. A book on the history of the Franks written early in the eighth century has Clovis cross the Rhine with a great army and kill the Roman people, and in the ninth century an unknown person annotated this text in a way that heightened the impact of the Franks:

> Clovis exterminated all the Romans who then lived in Gaul, so that one could scarcely be found. And the Franks seem to have learned in those times the Roman tongue which is used today from those Romans who had lived there. What their native tongue had been in those parts is not known.

At about the same time, a biographer of Charlemagne has the Goths and Vandals throwing the quiet of mortals into confusion, leaving the whole of the west empty. Such a perspective left no room for positive interactions between Romans and the newcomers. It found expression in a prologue added to the Salic law of the Franks towards the end of the eighth century, which described the Franks as a strong people who threw off the harsh yoke of the Romans from their necks in battle. When they had been baptised, they adorned with precious stones the bodies of the holy martyrs whom the Romans had burned by fire, butchered with iron or thrown to be torn by wild beasts. This colourful view flew in the face of the realities: the people of the area into which the Franks moved thought of Catholic Christianity as being, explicitly, the religion of the Romans, and far from doing battle with the Romans, the Franks were their old allies who can be discerned as having operated on their behalf.[30] Just as the Anglo-Saxon Chronicles imposed on the past of Britain a reading that saw the fifth century in terms of massive discontinuity, so did thinkers on the Continent. Their view has found echoes among later historians, but it was the product of a time when people found it necessary to explain changes that had really taken place at another time and for other reasons.

RETROSPECT AND PROSPECT

It has been our purpose in this book to examine the process of change across some three centuries in the territory of the old Roman Empire. Historians of the eighth and ninth centuries were correct in their belief that great change had occurred in the period preceding their own. No one contemplating the developments that took place in such fundamental areas of human activity as the production and exchange of goods, the environments in which people lived and the names they gave their children, systems of law, the uses to which writing can be put, and more generally the location of power within society, could doubt that important changes had taken place. Yet the historians who accounted for the change in the west in terms of the arrival of violent newcomers, and those who in later centuries accepted this explanation, were wrong. To be sure, in many respects the dismemberment of the western parts of the Empire by Germanic peoples in the fifth century was an important development. It was responsible for Britain acquiring a very different identity, and elsewhere the newcomers elbowed aside groups that had previously been potent in society. In some areas, important changes in the ownership of land occurred. But over most of the territory that they occupied, these newcomers sought to accommodate themselves within the existing structures, and assimilated without great difficulty. The border between the zones of Romance and Germanic speech in the continental part of western Europe today runs not far within the old borders of the Empire.

At least as significant as the direct impact of the newcomers were the unforeseen results of their arrival in various areas. The establishment of a number of separate states within what had hitherto been a single political unit entailed the collapse of the enormous infrastructure of the empire, and the atrophy of the economic and cultural systems that had held its disparate regions together, although there were already clear signs of regionalisation towards the end of the Roman period. But more significant still were other trends, and that many of them can be seen in Byzantine as well as western society indicates that they were not caused by the arrival of newcomers. The movement away from towns and the increasing importance of religion in society, a process within which the conversion of Constantine marked no more than a hesitant beginning, struck at the heart of the ancient world. Moreover, when the impact of the Germanic peoples who settled in the fifth century is compared with that of the peoples who later occupied other regions of the old Empire, it emerges as having been relatively slight. They changed western Europe far less than the Slavs changed the greater part of the Balkans, which quickly became thoroughly Slavonic and has remained so to this day. And, significant as the impact of the Slavs was, it was less than that of the Arabs, whose activities made the seventh century the crucial period it was.

The Arabs were the great changers of society. Across the vast swathe of territory they took from the Empire, the indigenous people came to adopt their language, religion and social practices. Moreover, those lands, which included those that had been the wealthiest within the Empire, were speedily integrated into a gigantic economic unit that offered them far more than trade with the remnants of the Christian world could promise. It is true that the greater part of economic activity in pre-modern times was agricultural and occurred at a local level, with most communities consuming food that they had produced. But to the extent that society was configured around the exchange of goods and ideas, which in our period tended to flow from the east towards the west, the loss of the east had grave consequences for the west.

Indeed, the subject matter of this book has described a steady movement of political power in the opposite direction, which led to the west becoming a sideshow by the end of the period. This was another movement already under way before the fifth century. The Roman Empire had grown up around a city located in a fairly central position on the northern shores of the Mediterranean. In the fourth century Rome came to share its power with Constantinople, towards the eastern end of the sea, and in the fifth century the latter city became the sole centre of authority. The rise of the Arabs in the seventh century was almost immediately followed by the emergence of Damascus as the most important city within the post-Roman world, while in the eighth century it in turn lost this position to Baghdad in Mesopotamia. This move in political power across and then away from the Mediterranean was faintly echoed in the west by the rise of inland Aachen. What was true of political power was also true of economic power, something that is readily demonstrated by the ability of societies to use surplus wealth for non-utilitarian purposes. The buildings erected by the Romans occupy a place in the landscapes of Europe far more significant than those which were built in the immediately succeeding centuries. Yet this was not true of the lands that passed under Islam. It would be the work of western Europe in succeeding centuries to regain the ground it had lost relative to those lands. But at the end of the period with which we have been concerned, the marginality of the west is indisputable.

NOTES

———◆———

Chapter 1: The Empire

1. Cosmopolitan poet: Meleager, in *Greek Anthology*, 7.419.11.6f. Historian: Procopius, *Wars*, 3.1.
2. Pliny, *Natural History*, 15.20.75.
3. Narbonne to Africa: Sulpicius Severus, *Dial.*, 1.3.1. Constantinople to Alexandria: Priscus, ed. and transl. Blockley, 28.1; a message takes nine days in Theophylact Simocatta, 8.13.10–14. Constantinople and Arles: *MGH Ep.*, 3:13–15. Lynching in Alexandria: Leo, *ep.*, 144f.
4. Few sailings in winter: Vegetius, *Epitome rei militaris*, recommends that sailings not be made from 11 November until 10 March because of the roughness of the sea (without specific reference to the Mediterranean). Anastasius's letters: *Collectio Avellana*, nos. 107, 109. Justin's letter: ibid., no. 212. Gregory's congratulations: *Reg.*, 13.32. Codex: Weitzmann and Keesler (1986), who note among other texts in the same tradition four Carolingian manuscripts and two Anglo-Saxon biblical paraphrases of the eleventh century.
5. Cassius Dio, *Roman History*, 68.29.1.
6. Occupation of Britain: Tacitus, *Agricola*, 21. Claudius: *Ann.*, 11.24. British leader: *Agricola*, 30.
7. 'Urbem fecisti quod prius orbis erat': Rutilius Namatianus, *De reditu suo*, 1.66. A similar pun in Ovid, *Fasti*, 2:684.
8. Armenians: Cyril of Scythopolis, *Vitá Sabae*, 20, 32. Italian visitor: *Antonini Placentini Itinerarium*, *CCSL*, 175:148. Late second century: Irenaeus, *adv. haer.*, praef. 3 (*SChr*, 264:24). Ausonius: epic.9f, with Green's note *ad loc*).
9. Septimius Severus: *Liber de caesaribus*, 20.8. Philip's celebrations: Cassiodorus, *Chronica*, s.a. 248 (*MGH AA*, 11:147).
10. Howling nations: Vegetius, *De re militare*, 6.1. Augustus: Herodian, 2.11.5, Loeb transl. Rhine: *Panégyriques latins*, 10(2).7.3; Ambrose: *Exameron*, 2.3.12; Festus: *Abrégé*, 8.1.
11. 360s: Ammianus Marcellinus, 27.5.7. In 369 trade with the Goths, which had until then occurred wherever the Goths wished, was restricted to two cities: Themistius orat. 10.135, transl. P. Heather and J. Matthews, *The Goths*, p. 4. Rugians and Romans: *Vita Severini*, 9.1.3, with 6.4. Persian frontier: Procopius, *Buildings*, 3.3.10. Roman law: Justinian, *cod. iust.*, 4.63.4, of 409. Peace treaty: Menander the Guardsman, *History*, 6.1. (ed. Blockley; 11 ed. Müller-Dindorf), of 561.
12. Ammianus Marcellinus, 31.4.8.
13. Limitanei: *nov. theod.*, 24.1.4; the novels of fifth-century emperors are published in *cod. theod.* 'Barbarians' given land: *cod. theod.*, 7.15.1, of 409. *Laeti: cod. theod.*, 13.11.10, of 399. Alamanni: Ammianus Marcellinus, 28.2.15. The word 'Germans' is used

loosely. Its application was unclear in late antiquity. Procopius thought it was an old word for Franks (*Wars*, 3.3.1), apparently to be distinguished from Goths, the term he used for Ostrogoths, Vandals, Visigoths and Gepids, whom he considered to be identical apart from their names (*Wars*, 3.2.2–6). Yet his near contemporary John the Lydian regarded the Vandals as a Germanic people (*Powers*, 3.55).

14. Kent and Painter (1977): 123f.

15. Prudentius: *contra Symm.*, 2:816–19; the categories recall those of an author of the first century AD, Velleius Paterculus, according to whom there was nothing human about the people of Germany other than voice and limbs: *History*, 12:117.3. 118.1. Cassiodorus: *Expositio psalmorum*, 113:1 (*CCSL*, 98:1029). Victor: *History*, 3.62. Symmachus: *ep.*, 2.46 (*MGH AA*, 6/1:57); he was the very Symmachus against whom the work of Prudentius cited at the beginning of this note was directed.

16. Victor: 3.62. Salvian: *Gubernatione dei*, esp. 5.4, 7.23. Jordanes: *Origo*, 152. Julian's teacher: *Misopogon*, 352. Zeno: *Vita Danielis*, 84 (*Saints stylites*, ed. Delehaye p. 79, 1.12f; misleadingly translated in *Three Byzantine Saints*, p. 58). Burgundians: Sidonius Apollinaris, *carm.* 12, with *ep.* 1.11.3f on the addressee.

17. Writing in the late sixth century, Gregory of Tours has the Christian wife of the Frank Clovis, attacking the gods he worships, mention Saturn, Jupiter, Mars and Mercury (*History*, 2.29). It is highly unlikely that Clovis would have worshipped Roman deities in his pre-Christian days, but in Gregory's mind ancient Roman gods and those whom Clovis would have known amounted to the same thing. It is extraordinary to find the Persians, traditional enemies of the Greeks, described as 'Hellenes' in a Greek text of the early seventh century: *Pasch. Chron.*, 614. Only fear of appearing pedantic has prevented me from enclosing the word Arian in quotation marks throughout this book.

18. Jordanes, *Origo*, 4.25, for migration from the island of Scandza in the time of king Berig; 60.313 for the evidence on which chronology is based. That a text of the seventh century has the Lombards originating in an island named Scadanan (*Origo gentis Langobardorum, MGH SRI*, 2), and in the following century Paul the Deacon saw the island of Scandinavia as their place of origin (*History*, 1.1) suggests the survival of a topos rather than independent evidence. A similar story was told of the Burgundians: see below, p. 69 with n. 6.

19. Paul the Deacon, *History*, 2.26. But not all these terms are ethnic, for Pannonians and Noricans would have been the people living in the old Roman provinces of Pannonia and Noricum.

20. 'Roman' as Catholic: Gregory of Tours, *Glory*, 24, 78. Gotones and Gothones: Tacitus, *Ann.*, 2.62; *Germania*, 43.6. Gutones: Pliny, 37.1.35.

21. Graphic examples in Klein-Pfeuffer (1993): 180–3.

22. Classical author: Tacitus, *Germania*, 23; similar sentiments in Ambrose, *Helia*, 15.24. King's letter: Procopius, *Wars*, 8.19.16f.

23. First reference to soap: Pliny, 28.191. Constantine: Silvius Polemius, in *MGH AA*, 9:547. Law of 400: *cod. theod.*, 12.19.2 (addressed to officials in Gaul). Colloquialism: Orosius, *Adversum paganos*, 7.32.12. A few centuries later, a poem in English on a ruin speaks of a 'bright city' (*beorhtan burg*; see below, p. 95, for this poem). The origin of the word may be the Greek *purgos*, a tower.

24. Theodosius: Ambrose, *ep.*, 74.22; Sozomen, 7.24. 'Bandion' in the sixth century: Procopius, *Wars*, 4.2.1; in the seventh: Theophylact Simocatta, 3.4.4,6.4.

25. Branding: *cod. theod.*, 10.22.4.

26. Synesius, *De regno*, 14 (*PG*, 66:1089–92). Law of 364: *cod. theod.*, 15.15.

27. Julian: Ammianus Marcellinus, 20.4.17. Hariulf: Heinen (1985): 325f, with *CIL*, 13:3683. Panegyric: Pacatus, *pan.*, 32 (=*Panégyriques latins* 3:99). Ambrose: *ep.*, 75a.2.

28. Maximus and Ambrose: Ambrose, *ep.*, 39. Augustine: *PL*, 43:362.

29. The biographies of the people mentioned in this paragraph can be followed via the relevant articles in *PLRE*, vols. 1 and 2.

30. Ambrose, *ep.*, 76.9.

31. Constantine's consuls: Ammianus Marcellinus, 21.10.8. Serapion: ibid., 16.12.26. Erelieva: Anonymus Valesianus, 58. Theoderic's daughter is named Ostrogotho by Jordanes, *Origo*, 297, Areagni by Anonymus Valesianus, 63. Lupus and family: *PLRE*, 2:798; see further below, p. 79. Barbara: Ennodius, *MGH AA*, 7:315.18; see further the case of Genevieve, below, p. 72. Gothigus: Procopius, *Wars*, 7.35.10, although his real name was Cethegus.

32. Catholics dressed as Vandals: Victor of Vita, 2.8. Shirts and trousers: ibid., 1.39. Young man of Corinth: *PL*, 74:336. Shirts vulgar: Jerome, *ep.*, 64.11. Barberini ivory: Weitzmann (1979): no. 28. Arian bishop: *Gesta conc. Aquil.*, *ep.*, 2.9 (ed. Ambrose *Opera*, 3, p. 346). Country people: *Panégyriques latins*, 2.4. Piazza Armerina: Rinaldi (1964f). Laws: *cod. theod.*, 14.10.2–4; cf. 1. Eastern consul: Claudian, *In Ruf.*, 2.78–85. Yet the eastern author Procopius believed that the dress of Roman soldiers could be distinguished from that of the Franks: *Wars*, 5.12.19. Lombards: Paul the Deacon, *History*, 4.22.

33. Dressed in Roman style: Olympiodorus, frag. 24 (ed. and transl. Blockley). Cranial deformation: Buchet (1988). Jordanes, *Origo*, 127, may refer to the practice.

34. Poet of Gaul: Ausonius *Mosella*, 318ff. Montaubin: Fouet (1969). Piazza Armerina: Gentili (1959), with Weitzmann (1979): no. 91 for the Circus Maximus.

35. Constantine's legislation: *cod. iust.*, 8.10.6. Desert a city: *Life of Antony*, 14 (where categories mentioned by St Paul at II Cor. 11:46 may be relevant); cf Aristotle *Polit.* 1253a. John: *PG*, 60:147f; compare an observation that cities, despite having courts of justice and laws, suffer from injustice and lack of law, whereas the desert abounded with the fruit of philosophy (*PG*, 47:328; the comments on justice and law echo categories that Aristotle went on to employ at *Polit.*, 1253a). Augustine: *Confessions*, 8.6.15 (similarly, continence is by no means sterile, but fecund: 8.9.27). Gregory: *Reg. past.*, 2.5 (transl. Henry Davis, p. 58).

36. Law of 400: *cod. theod.*, 12.19.1. Writer in Gaul: Sidonius Apollinaris, *ep.*, 7.15, 8.8. Italy: Cassiodorus, *Var.*, 8.31.8, transl. Hodgkin; the counters refer to a game like draughts.

37. Naboth: I Kings 21, a story concerning which Ambrose wrote a book. Contemporary account: Salvian, *Gubernatione*, 5.8.38f, 43; for the meaning of 'pervasores', cf. *cod. theod.*, 2.4.5. Thugs in Africa: Augustine, *ep.*, *10, ed. Divjac. Impoverished freedom: Orosius, *Adversum paganos*, 7.41.7; Isidore of Seville, *De origine*, 16, is similar. The situation in the east was very different; in Syria, farmers were mobilising the army and, occasionally, holy men against landlords and tax collectors.

38. *Cod. theod.*, 11.1.4; cf. *cod. iust.*, 11.48.20.

39. Pamphylia: Zosimus, 5.15.5. Spain: Orosius, *Adversum paganos*, 7.40.5; Sozomen, 9.11.4; Zosimus, 6.4.3. Law of 440: *nov. val.*, 9. South of Italy: Cassiodorus, *Var.*, 8.33. Barbegal: Bellamy and Hitchner (1996); Leveau (1996).

40. Latin and Greek: John the Lydian, *Powers*, 2.12, 3.42. Cyrus made enemies and was consecrated bishop of an obscure diocese; *Vita Danielis*, 31, provides a sympathetic account of his troubles.

41. Boethius found it difficult to translate into Latin the word *logikos*, doing his best with 'an iron tool and, as it were, paraphernalia' (*In Porphyrii Isagogen commentorium*, 1.4, *CSEL*, 48:9f). Yet Cicero had insisted that Latin was richer than Greek (*de fin.*, 1.10, 3.51).

42. Melania: *PLRE*, 1:593.

43. Augustine on Antony: *Confessions*, 8.6.15.

44. Attila: Agnellus of Ravenna, 37. Ambrose: *ep.*, 75a.10; what the martyrs offered was very similar to what *coloni* sought.

45. Cult of Symeon: Théodoret, *Histoire*, 26.11. Theologian: Maximus the Confessor, *Mystag.*, 1 (*PG*, 91:665); the biblical quotation conflates Gal. 3:28 and Col. 3:11. John Chrysostom saw a person at Rome as being a member of the same body as Indians: *PG*, 59:362.

46. Church of Rome: *Liber pontificalis*, 34 (Silvester). Churches of Constantinople and Alexandria: *cod. theod.*, 11.24.6. S Vitale: Deichmann (1969–89) copiously illustrates the mosaics of Ravenna. An idea of the success of churches in obtaining grants of land a few centuries later can be obtained from Sawyer, *Charters*. Rome in 400: Jerome, *ep.*, 107.1; a highly rhetorical text, however.

47. *Commentaire sur Isaie, SChr.*, 304:124.

Chapter 2: The western Mediterranean till the mid-sixth century

1. This is the perspective of Procopius, *Wars*, 3.2.6; for legendary accounts that invoke Scandinavia, see above, p. 14f with n. 18.

2. Černjachov: Bierbrauer (1994): 105ff.

3. Origin of Huns: *Origo*, 24.121f. Suicide of Ermaneric: Ammianus Marcellinus, 31.2.1f. In a fine piece of evasion, Jordanes attributes his death to a wound and his inability to bear the incursions of the Huns, and mentions that he was 110 years old: *Origo*, 130. At about the time he was writing, an Eormenric was king in Kent: Bede, *Ecclesiastical History*, 2.5. Entry of Goths: Ammianus Marcellinus, 31.4.

4. Citizens and lords: Jordanes, *Origo*, 26.137; cf. Lev. 25:35, 47, and elsewhere. Adrianople: Ammianus Marcellinus, 31.13. Move towards Constantinople: 31.16.

5. Zosimus, 5.6.4f.

6. Alaric's demand: Zosimus, 5.41.4. Hun woman: Priscus, ed. and transl. Blockley 11.2 (transl. p. 263); at the end of the sixth century, pepper, Indian cloves and cinnamon were among the goods that Avars were happy to receive from an imperial general: Theophanes, *Chronographia*, AM 6092. Slaves: Zosimus, 5.42.3.

7. Jerome: 'In una urbe totus orbis interiit', *CCSL*, 75:3; compare 'the whole world falls down . . . the famous city and head of the Roman empire is consumed in a single fire' (ep.128.5). Rutilius Namatianus: see above p. 9 with n. 7. Ovid: *Fasti*, 2.684.

8. *Civitate Dei*, transl. Bettenson, 4.7 fin. Orosius's History: *Adversum paganos*.
9. *Cod. theod.*, 14.1.6 (assuming a date of 25 September 410; 409 is possible). 15.1.48 was definitely issued in November 411.
10. *Siliquaticum: nov. Val.* 15; it was retained in Italy into the sixth century. Leo: *Tract.*, 82.1.
11. Jordanes, *Origo*, 254.
12. *Liber pontificalis*, 45, 47.
13. Malchus, frag. 10 (ed. and transl. Blockley).
14. Coins: Grierson and Blackburn (1986): 28. Report on senate: Malchus frag. 14 (ed. and transl. Blockley).
15. Joshua the Stylite, *Chronicle*, pp. 67–73.
16. Thirds: Procopius, *Wars*, 5.1.4f, 28; Cassiodorus, *Variae*, 2.16; Ennodius, *ep.*, 9.23.
17. Ennodius, *pan.*, 29; cf. Gen. 22:17.
18. Ammianus Marcellinus, 27.5.1, 31.12.8f.
19. Peace and war: Cassiodorus, *Variae*, 6.1.5. Poor and well-to-do: Anonymus Valesianus, 61. In the centuries that followed, however, it may have been poor rather than wealthy Romans who remained entrenched in their identity (see below, p. 144).
20. Agnellus of Ravenna, 94.
21. The notion of an imperial 'adventus' may be implied by Cassiodorus' words 'Theodericus Romam . . . advenit' (chron. s.a. 500; *MGH AA*, 11:160). The chief source for the visit to Rome is Anonymus Valesianus, 65–70.
22. Truly an emperor: Procopius, *Wars*, 5.1.26, 29. Quaestor to be as Pliny: Cassiodorus, *Variae*, 8.13.4. Theoderic as Trajan: Anonymus Valesianus, 60. Columns and stones: *Variae*, 3.9. Panegyric: Ennodius, *pan.*, 56 (*MGH AA*, 7:210).
23. Coins: Grierson and Blackburn (1986): 32. House in Constantinople: *Chron. pasch.*, 623, where the description of Symmachus as a former consul would be appropriate.
24. 26,000 solidi: Agnellus of Ravenna, 59. San Vincenzo: Hodges and Mitchell (1993–).
25. Throughout this book, the word 'Africa' indicates the old Roman prefecture. This did not include Egypt, which classical geographers tended to see as part of Asia, with which it had much in common. Africa extended inland to a variable degree; a medieval Arab writer saw Ifrikiya as extending from the Sea to the sands that marked the beginning of the land of the Blacks (el-Bekri, p. 49).
26. Oil: *Expositio*, 61. Pottery: Hayes (1972, 1980).
27. Jerome, *ep.*, 123.15 refers to Spain being about to perish while the Vandals engaged in atrocities in Gaul. Boniface: Procopius, *Wars*, 3.3.22–6, with Marcellinus, *Chronicle*, s.a. 432 on his wife.
28. *PLS*, 3:259f. Compare the report of cruelty and destruction in another early source, Possidius, *Vita Augustini*, 28.
29. Vergil, *Aeneid*, 4.624–9.
30. Command from God: Salvian, *Gubernatione*, 7.13; cf. Huneric's referring to the provinces entrusted to him by God: Victor of Vita, *History*, 2.39, cf. 3.14 and Jordanes, *Origo*, 169. God is angry: Procopius, *Wars*, 3.5.24f.
31. *Anglo-Saxon Chronicles*, s.a. 885 (884) (Wendel sæ); *Hildebrandslied*, line 43 (wentil sêo; ed. H. Mettke, p. 52).
32. Victor of Vita, *History*, 1.1–14; Procopius, *Wars*, 3.5.11ff. See further *nov. val.*, 34 (of 451), and Justinian, *nov.*, 36.

33. Wealthy Africans: Victor of Vita, *History*, 1.48, 3.27. Family of Fulgentius: Ferrandus, *Vita Fulgentii*, 1, 4. The *Tablettes Albertini* are edited by Courtois (*c*.1952).

34. See, in particular, Anselmino *et al.* (1989); also Mattingly and Hayes (1992). Tipasa: Victor of Vita, *History*, 3.30.

35. Victor, *History*, 1.13, 3.60.

36. Carthage: *Excavations at Carthage* (1984): 44–7. Cherchel: Potter (1995).

37. Fulgentius at the baths: *Vita Fulgentii*, 2. Merchants at Carthage: Procopius, *Wars*, 3.20.22, 3.20.5ff.

38. Monasteries at Memphis: Theodosius, *De situ terrae sanctae*, 14 *(CCSL*, 175:120). Augustine's letter: Possidius, *Vita Augustini*, 30. See for the reigns of Geiseric and Huneric Victor, *History*, and for that of Thrasamund, *Vita Fulgentii*. Barbas: Victor of Tunnuna, *chron.*, s.a. 500 (*MGH AA*, 9:193), a story copied in Italy and Spain.

39. Arrest of monks: *Vita Fulgentii*, 6. Huneric's rage: Victor, *History*, 2.1, 13, 16.

40. Tipasa in the reign of Huneric: Victor, *History*, 3.30, a story well known to Byzantine authors; in the reign of Julian, Optatus of Milevus, *schism. Don.*, 2.18f (*PL*, 11:969–74).

41. Cathedral of Carthage: Victor, *History*, 1.15. Huneric's legislation: ibid., 3.3–14.

42. Iugmena: *PLRE*, 2: 634. Masties: ibid., 734. Masuna: ibid., 734f. Guenfan: Corippus, *Iohannidos*, 3.107f, 116f; cf. Procopius, *Wars*, 4.8.13 on women as the utterers of oracles among the Moors.

43. Procopius, *Wars*, 3.8.17–24.

44. *Vita Fulgentii*, 28.

45. Invaders of 429: Possidius, *Vita Augustini*, 28. Early history of Alans: Ammianus Marcellinus, 31.2.13, 17 (where there is nothing to support Procopius' description of them as a Gothic people, which rather reflects what they had gone on to become: *Wars*, 3.3.1). United in the name of Vandals: Procopius, *Wars*, 3.5.21.

46. The names of Vandal clergy are recorded by Victor of Vita. Inscriptions: Ennabli (1975). Fulgentius: *Vita Fulgentii*, 7. Arianism a requirement: Victor, *History*, 1.43, 2.10, 2.23. Catholics dressed like Vandals: ibid., 2.8f.

47. By the end of their time: Procopius, *Wars*, 4.6.6–9. Last king: ibid., 3.17.8–10.

48. Inscription at Carthagena: Vives, *Inscripciones* no. 362. City overthrown: Isidore of Seville, *Etymologiae*, 15.1.67. Advice sought: *PL*, 53:847–9.

49. Spain as mother: *Pan. Lat.*, 12.4 (vol. 3:72). Horace: *Sat.*, 2.8.46.

50. Italy: Cassiodorus, *Variae*, 5.35. Marseilles: Gregory of Tours, *History*, 9.22.

51. Jerusalem: Hydatius, *cont. chron.*, 40; edge of world: praef., 7; signs and wonders: 253.

52. Archaeology: Bierbrauer (1994). Romans on Toledo: Livy, 35.22.7.

53. Taxes, Theudis: Procopius, *Wars*, 5.12.50–4. Aspidius: John of Biclaro, *cont. Vict.*, s.a. 575.

54. Euric's law: *Leges Visigothorum*, 8.4.9. Burgundian law: *Leges Burgundionum*, 4.8. For the Farmer's Law, #36, I follow the translation of Ashburner.

55. Gregory of Tours, *History*, 3.30.

Chapter 3: From Gaul to France

1. Happy combination: Tacitus, *Agricola*, 4. Compared to Athens: Strabo, *Geography*, 4.179–81. Vineyards and olive trees: Gregory of Tours, *History*, 2.31 ad fin. Abbot

in Paris: ibid., 6.9; cf. the case of Sulpicius, who became bishop of Bourges, ibid., 6.39. Distinction: Cassius Dio, *Roman History*, 46.55.5.

2. *Panégyriques latins*, 7.6.

3. *Ep.*, 123.5.

4. Another author: Orientius, *Commonitorium*, 2, transl. J. Hillgarth, *Christianity and Paganism*, p. 70. Africa: Victor of Vita, *History*, 1.3. Britons: Bede, *Ecclesiastical History*, 1.14, although Bede follows the unreliable Gildas, *Ruin*, 20.2, whose 'montibus, speluncis' is lifted from the Bible, Heb. 11:38.

5. *Poème*, ed. Moussy.

6. *Passio Sigismundi*, 1, perhaps of the eighth century; *MGH SRM*, 2:333.

7. Fredegarius, *chron.*, 2.46; Marius of Avenches, *chron.*, sa 456 (*MGH AA*, 11:232). Senators remained a force: Gregory of Tours, *History*, 2.33 ad fin.

8. The etymology of the word 'Alamanni' was known to Agathias (*Histories*, 1.6.3).

9. Gall: Gregory of Tours, *Life of the Fathers*, 6.2. Yet bishop Audoin of Rouen found many relics when he went there in the seventh century: *Vita*, 13 (*MGH SRM*, 5:562, transl. Fouracre and Gerberding, p. 162).

10. Sidonius Apollinaris, *ep.*, 8.9.5 mentions Saxon, Sicambrian, Herul, Burgundian, Ostrogoth, Roman and, surprisingly, Persian representatives.

11. Sons as consuls: Sidonius, *ep.*, 5.16.4. Military capacity: Gregory, *History*, 2.37; Avitus, *ep.*, 51. Bishop: Gregory, *History*, 3.2.

12. Agrippinus: *V. Lupicini*, 11 (*MGH SRM*, 3:149). Seronatus: Sidonius, *ep.*, 7.7.2. Leo: ibid., 4.22. Height of church: Gregory of Tours, *Glory*, 91.

13. Tomb: Brulet and Ghenne-Dubois (1984). Story: Fredegarius, *Chronicae*, 3.11 (*MGH SRM*, 2:96); cf. Procopius, *Wars*, 5.12.16f. The holy man Leo lived such an ascetic life that he died: *Vita Danielis* (ed. Delehaye), 60–3. Allies: for example, count Paul led an army of Romans and Franks against the Goths: Gregory, *History*, 2.18.

14. *CCSL*, 117:408; transl. Hillgarth, *Christianity*, p. 76. The letter implies that Clovis knew Latin, which is also indicated by a letter that Cassiodorus wrote to him, mentioning 'verbo vobis aliqua dicenda' (*Variae*, 3.4.5).

15. Cf. Cassiodorus, *Variae*, 7,1,4f, 12,5,8,

16. Sea-monster: Fredegar, *Chronicae*, 3.9. Long hair: Agathias, *Historiarum libri*, 1.3.4; Gregory of Tours, *History*, 3.18.

17. Campus Martius: Gregory, *History*, 2.27; Gregory describes Valentinian III speaking to the people in the Campus Martius in Rome: ibid., 2.8. New Constantine: *History*, 2.31 implies a legend similar to that found in the Donation of Constantine, written in about 800; part of it is already in John Malalas, *Chronographia*, 317. More fancifully, Gregory used of Clovis language that recalls words applied to Christ in the Bible: *History*, 2.12, cf. Luke 1:31f. 'Consul or augustus': Gregory, *History*, 2.38.

18. Voulon: Gregory, *History*, 2.37. Caesarius: *Vita Caesarii*, 13, 21, 24, 29–31, 36–8.

19. Trial by ordeal: *Pact. Leg. Sal.*, 16.5 Harp player: Cassiodorus, *Variae*, 2.40.17. Human sacrifices: Procopius, *Wars*, 6.25.9f. Views in Constantinople: Procopius, *Wars*, 5.5.9, Agathias, *Historiarum libri*, 1.2.3.

20. Coins: Grierson and Blackburn (1986): 115–17, with Procopius, *Wars*, 7.33.5f. Letter to Justinian: *MGH Ep.*, 3:133; cf. below p. 133 for Justinian's ambition to

regain territory to the edges of the ocean. Fear in Constantinople: Agathias, *Historiarum*, 1.4.1–6. Duke being applauded: Venantius Fortunatus, 7.8.63f. Famous hymn: Venantius's 'Pange lingua gloriosi proelium certaminis' (hymn 2.2, ed. and transl. Reydellet). Theology and alphabet: Gregory, *History*, 5.44 (the fathers whose teaching he was thought to have rejected, Hilary of Poitiers and Eusebius of Vercelli, both confronted heretical emperors, and are also mentioned together as having been active against heresies at *Glory*, 3); for reform of the alphabet, compare Claudius, in Suetonius, *Claud.*, 41). Circuses: Gregory, *History*, 5.17; cf. Totila, see below, p. 133f. 'Most clement': Childebert, in *MGH Leg.*, 1:1.

21. Gregory of Tours: *History*, book 5, preface. Saxons: Fredegarius, *Chron.*, 4.74. Thuringia: ibid., 4.87.

22. Isidore: *Etymologiae*, 9.2.101, although he notes the possibility that the Franks were called after a person. Passion of Christ: *MGH SRM*, 2:101; surprisingly, the author asserts that by these words he showed himself a true Christian. Similarly, when the letters of Theoderic mention 'our Goths' it is in a military sense. Water mills: *Pact. Leg. Sal.*, 22.3.

23. Childebert decr. 8, *MGH Leg.*, 1:10.

24. Lupus and relatives: *PLRE*, 3:798. Gundulf: ibid., 568. Ninth century: *AA SS*, Sept. II, 782–84.

25. Frénouville: Pilet (1980). Houses of Franks: *Pact. Leg. Sal.*, 16.1; Gregory, *History*, 2.9, quoting Sulpicius Alexander. See on the archaeology, Van Ossel (1992): 183, with 297–300.

26. Data summarised in Périn (1980).

27. Gregory of Tours, *History*, 4.14, 4.16, 9.20, cf. earlier usage of the word in passages quoted from Sulpicius Alexander at 2.9 for lands across the Rhine where Franks lived.

28. Land of the Franks: *Vita Eligii*, 1.4f (*MGH SRM*, 4:671); Eligius 'Roman': 2.20 (712). Council of Vaison: can. 3 (*CCSL*, 148A:79), yet at the end of the century pope Gregory observed that the practice of Rome in saying the Kyrie was different to that of the Greeks: *reg.* 9.26(=12). Council of Narbonne: can. 4 (*CCSL*, 148A:254). Einhard: *Vita Karoli*, 2. Romans exterminated or expelled: see below, p. 267.

29. Descendants of Trojans: Fredegarius, *Chron.*, 2.4–6. Ship in Rome: Procopius, *Wars*, 8.22.5ff. Fourth century: Ammianus, 5.9.5. A participant in the first crusade knew a story that Franks and Turks were of common stock.

30. Council of Orléans, can. 1, *CCSL*, 148A:4. Council of Tours: ibid., 186, quoting fairly accurately from both the Interpretatio of a law and a law itself. Bonitus: *MGH SRM*, 6:119. Praejectus: *MGH SRM*, 5:240 (transl. Fouracre and Gerberding, p. 289); the legislation had also formed part of Alaric's Breviarium.

31. Frankish general: see above, p. 38. Bishop of Toul: *PL*, 61:1006. Sidonius: *ep.*, 4.17.1f, Loeb transl. In the reign of Theudebert a priest named Arboast, presumably a relative, was active at Trier: Gregory of Tours, *Glory*, 91.

32. Leontius: Venantius Fortunatus, *carm.*, 1.18.5, with *PLRE*, 3:774. Mass at Rion: Gregory of Tours, *Glory*, 86. Gregory's family: *History*, 10.31.

33. Fredegarius, *Chron.*, 3.12; *MGH SRM*, 2:97. The story has biblical echoes; cf. Daniel 7.

34. Murder of Brunhild: Fredegarius, *Chron.*, 4.42. Byzantine official: *Chron. pasch.*, 696, a passage in which numerous other murders, most by beheading, are mentioned;

more atrocities at 694 and 700f; see further Nicephorus, *Short History*, 1, for the mutilation of the emperor Phocas and his allies.

35. Edict of Paris: can. 12 (*MGH Leg.*, 2/1:21). Pragmatic Sanction: no. 12, ed. *Corpus iuris civilis*, 3. Heraclius's son: Nikephoros, *Short History*, 17, 25.

36. Einhard: *Vita Karoli*, 1.1. Constantius: Ammianus Marcellinus, 16.10.6. Cassiodorus: *Inst. div.*, 32.5; cf. *Variae*, 6.15.2, 18.2. Patricians: Iohannes Lydus, *Powers*, 1.18.

37. Note the words of Sidonius Apollinaris: 'militia . . . clericali potius quam in palatino decursa': *ep.*, 7.2.3.

38. Cassiodorus, *Variae*, 12.27.

39. Nicetius: Venantius Fortunatus, *carm.*, 3.12. Desiderius: *ep.*, 1.13, to a bishop of Clermont (*MGH Ep.*, 3:200f).

40. Remigius: *CCSL*, 117:409f; transl. Hillgarth, *Christianity*, p. 79. Bishop of Auxerre: Fredegarius, *Chron.*, 4.19. Edict of 614: can. 1, *MGH Leg.*, 2/1:21, cf. Hillgarth, *Christianity*, p. 114 (can. 2). Desiderius: *PLRE*, 3:398, with references.

41. Gregory, *History*, 5.48f, 6.32.

42. Gregory, *History*, praef; yet elsewhere he writes of a 'rustic' who lived in the town of Saragossa: ibid., 3.29; 'rustic' speech was frowned upon by Cicero (*de Orat.*, 3.42, *Brut.*, 180). Bishops disquieted: the council of Châlons-sur-Saône (can. 14, *CCSL*, 148A:306). Dagobert: Fredegarius, *Chron.*, 4.53, 78. Councils met at Clichy in 626 or 627, and 636; cf. Fredegarius, *Chron.*, 4.55. Certain villa: *CCSL*, 148A:321.

43. Chilperic: Gregory, *History*, 6.46, amended transl. Thorpe, whose translating 'eclesias' [*sic*] by 'the Church' reflects a common misconception. Theoderic: *Edictum Theodorici*, no. 32. Frankish queen: Gregory, *History*, 9.36. Roman lands: Gregory of Rome, *reg.*, 4.8. Italy: *Liber pontificalis*, 73. English bishop: Bede, *ep. ad Ecgbertum* 11, ed. Plummer p. 414, transl. Hillgarth, *Christianity*, p. 164. Tithes: can. 5 of the Council of Mâcon (*CCSL*, 148A:241), with Gregory, *History*, 6.6.

44. Remigius: *CCSL*, 117:409 (transl. Hillgarth, *Christianity*, p. 76). The narrative of Clovis given by Gregory of Tours makes much of treasure: *History*, 2.37, 2.40, 2.41, 2.42; compare for the seventh century Fredegarius, e.g. 4.38, 42. Franks and taxation: Gregory, *History*, 3.36, 7.15. The Salic law distinguishes between Romans who were courtiers of the king, landowners and those subject to tax (*Pactus legis salicae*, 41.8–10).

45. Tours: Gregory of Tours, *History*, 9.30; cf. 5.34, 28. Roman law: *cod. theod.*, 11.12. Lyons: Gregory of Tours, *Glory*, 62. Pope Gregory: *reg.*, 9.215.

46. Symmachus: *ep.*, 5.62, 65. Cargoes of papyrus: *Vie des pères du Jura*, 142 (*SChr*, 142: 390–2).

47. I regret not having been able to consult Bayard (1993).

48. The fullest source of data remains Salin (1949–1959).

49. *Regula*, 1.10–11.

50. Fara: Guerout ed., 'Le testament'. Agilbert: Bede, *Ecclesiastical History*, 3.7, 4.1; Eddius Stephanus, *Vita Wilfridi*, 12.

51. Slaves in forum: Bede, *Ecclesiastical History*, 2.1. Not long before, a merchant in Gaul had been killed by his two Saxon slaves: Gregory of Tours, *History*, 7.46. Wearmouth: Bede, *Historia Abbatum*, 5 (ed. Plummer). Balthild's Life is edited *MGH SRM*, 2, transl. Fouracre and Gerberding. Accusation: Eddius, *Vita Wilfridi*, 11 (according to

his biographer, Wilfrid was prepared to be a martyr as well, but the executioners would not touch him as he was English); Bede, *Ecclesiastical History*, 5.19. Some copyists of these texts replaced Balthild's name with that of the more sinister Brunhild.

52. Bertila: *Vita Bertilae*, 6, *MGH SRM*, 6:106. Amandus: *Vita S. Amandi*, 9 (*MGH SRM*, 5:435; transl. Hillgarth, *Christianity*, p. 142). Gregory's agent in Gaul: *reg.*, 6.10; the observation that the solidi of Gaul could not be spent in Italy recalls the situation of the mid-fifth century, when the Gallic solidus was not worth as much as solidi minted elsewhere: nov, Maj, 7.14, in *cod. theod.*

53. Bede, *Ecclesiastical History*, 4.1; Eddius, *Vita Wilfridi*, 25.

54. Bede, *Ecclesiastical History*, 4.22.

55. Procopius, *Wars*, 8.20.10. Gregory the Great wrote to Frankish rulers in terms which implied that the Angles were their subjects (*reg.*, 6.49).

56. *Glory* [incip].

57. Pronunciation: *PL*, 83:781. Forms of Latin: *Etymologiae*, 9.1.6–7.

58. At Bar. 6:5 the Vulgate reads: 'visa itaque turba de retro et ab ante'. Oath of Strasbourg: Nithard, *Historiarum libri IIII*, 3.6 (ed. Pertz and Muller, p. 36).

59. As did Gregory of Tours, although he spelt the word so that it began 'ab'.

60. Gregory, *History*, 2.37, 4.24, although the initial response of the Frank in the story to the words of Isaiah, 'Incongruae hoc', does not suggest strict Latin; cf. 4.15 for a Frank reading the Bible.

Chapter 4: From Britain to England

1. Infrastructure: Roman cities, lighthouses, bridges and paved roads were still to be seen in the eighth century, Bede *Ecclesiastical History* (hereafter *HE*), 1.11. Cities can be seen: Shippey, *Poems*, p. 77. Splendid this rampart: 'The Ruin', in R. F. S. Hamer, *A Choice of Anglo-Saxon Verse*, (Faber, 1970), p. 27; the phrase 'works of giants' (*enta geweorc*) occurs in both poems. Italy: see below, p. 145, for a poem on Aquileia. Carlisle: Colgrave ed., *Two Lives*, pp. 242–5.

2. Trouble makers: Sidonius Apollinaris, *carm.*, 7.369–71. Unexpected measures: Vegetius, *Epitome rei militaris*, 4.37; its applicability to Britain is indicated by Vegetius' giving the British name for these boats. A problem of nomenclature raises its head. Gildas, a Briton writing in the sixth century, speaks once of 'Saxons, a word not to be spoken' (*Ruin*, 23), and indeed this is the only occasion on which he gives the newcomers a name. When Bede used this passage as the basis for a section for his *History*, he reproduced the term used by Gildas, but went on to refer to them as 'the people of Angles or Saxons', and confusingly proceeded to describe them as 'Saxons, Angles and Jutes' (*HE*, 1.14f). Gallic authors spoke of the newcomers as 'Saxons', but in the sixth century Procopius and pope Gregory knew of them as Angles. I shall call them Saxons in contexts beyond Britain and when they are so called by sources; otherwise, I shall call them English.

3. Maximus a Briton: *Anglo-Saxon Chronicles*, mss A and E, s.a. 381. Honorius: Zosimus, 6.10.2; this author believed that the Britons had cast off Roman authority a short while before: 6.5.2f.

4. Littlehampton hoard: reported in the *Daily Telegraph* (London), 9 July 1997; cf. for burials of gold *Anglo-Saxon Chronicles*, mss A and E, s.a. 418.

5. Germanus: Constantius, *Vita Germani*, 12–18 (ed. *MGH SRM*, 7, where the first-quoted phrase is at 261.9 and the second at 265.7; when Bede inserted this material in his *History* he omitted 'most wealthy': *HE*, 1.20).

6. Roman policy: Tacitus, *Agricola*, 21. Hoard at Coleraine: Kent and Painter (1977): 125–7.

7. Bede, *HE*, 1.15, on their 'segnitia'; Bede's rebuke of the Britons is similar to the eastern critique of fifth century emperors (see below, p. 126).

8. Gildas, 23.5.

9. Hengist and Horsa: Bede, *HE*, 1.15, with *Beowulf*, 1068ff on Hengist. Goths: Jordanes, *Origo*, 94; cf. *Anglo-Saxon Chronicles*, ms F, s.a. 448; mss A and E, s.a. 477; ms F, s.a. 511; it is not surprising that the first Vikings to arrive in Britain are said to have turned up in three ships, *Chronicles*, mss A, E, F, s.a. 787 [789].

10. Bede, *HE*, 1.15.

11. Bede, *HE*, 5.9. A Greek author also associates the Angles with the Frisians in Britain: Procopius, *Wars*, 8.20.7, writing long before Bede.

12. Landing at Ebbesfleet: *Chronicles*, mss A and E, s.a. 449. Caesar: *Bellum Gallicum*, 5.13.1; see too Ammianus Marcellinus, 20.1.3, 27.8.6. Fifth-century author: Orosius, *Adversum paganos* 1.2, followed by Bede, *HE*, 1.1. Metropolis: ibid., 1.25. The other names preserved like that of the Cantii are those of the Cornovii (Cornwall) and Dumnonii (Devon). Queen: Bede, *HE*, 1.26. Archaeology: Everitt (1986), against *Chronicles*, ms E, s.a. 456.

13. West Stow: West (1969). Bede's description: *HE*, 3.16. Wasperton: Crawford (1983). Stretton-in-Fosse: Clarke (1979): 329, 406–8.

14. Gildas, 24.3f. Bede, *HE*, 1.15.

15. *Chronicles*, ms A, s.a. 937.

16. Johns and Bland (1993).

17. *HE*, 1.22, 2.5, 2.9, 3.6.

18. Bede's description of the English, 'plebem suam quam praescivit' (*HE*, 1.22) almost exactly reproduces 'plebem suam quam praesciit' (Rom. 11:2). Yet Ireland shares with the Promised Land the characteristic of being rich in milk and honey (Bede, *HE* 1.1; an explicit parallel is not drawn).

19. *Vita Samsonis*, 16, ed. Fawtier p. 116f; cf. Gregory of Rome, *Dialogues*, 2.8 for Benedict; Cyril of Scythopolis, *Vita Sabae*, 48.

20. Candidates for priesthood: Gildas, *Ruin*, 67.5. Tintagel: Thomas (1982).

21. Bede, *HE*, 1.1 (cf. 3.6); *Anglo-Saxon Chronicles* ms. E, transl. Swanton, p. 3, although the distinction may be between Cornish and Welsh.

22. Bede, *HE*, 2.2.

23. Bede, *HE*, 3.28.

24. Lament: see above, p. 95f. Baths: Bede, *HE*, 1.1.

25. Caedmon: Bede, *HE*, 4.24. Gildas on 'cyuls': *Ruin*, 23.3; compare the modern English 'keel'. Guthlac: Felix, *Life*, 34. Provide shelter: *Vita Wilfridi*, 18. Gathered soil: Bede, *HE*, 3.10; perhaps the house (*domus*) where the party was held was like the *domus* of king Edwin: *HE*, 2.13.

26. Holy places abandoned: Eddius *Vita Wilfridi*, 17. See on the Chiltern Hills, Rutherford-Davis (1982). Shrine: Bede, *HE*, 1.7, ad fin.

27. See above, p. 45.
28. Procopius, *Wars*, 4.20.11–41, assuming the Angili of Brittia to have been English in Britain.
29. Bede thought that glaziers were unknown in Britain until Benedict Biscop brought some over from France (*Historia Abbatum* 5, ed. Plummer p. 368, transl. J. F. Webb p. 189).
30. Bastien and Metzger (1977): 177–86.
31. The initial publication by Bruce Mitford (1975–83) remains basic, but see too Carver (1992).
32. *Gallic War*, 6.28.
33. Mackeprang (1952).
34. On the casket, see Webster and Backhouse (1991): 101–3; its title commemorates the name of a nineteenth-century collector, and has nothing to do with the Frankish people.
35. Edwin's baptism in the kingdom of Rheged: *Welsh Annals*, s.a. 626; cf. Nennius, 63; baptism by Paulinus: Bede, *HE*, 2.14. Somewhat later, an English priest is described as having received baptism 'in Brittania': Felix, *Life of Guthlac*, 48. No stone churches of the seventh century survive in the north, but such stone buildings as St Peter's Bradwell (Essex, of the mid-seventh century) give an idea of what Paulinus's church may have looked like: Webster and Backhouse (1991): 185.
36. Bishops and dogs: Council of Mâcon, 585, can. 13 (*CCSL*, 148A:245); one wonders whether the dogs were hunting dogs. Death of Aidan: Bede, *HE*, 3.17; rarely dines with the king, ibid., 3.5. Finan's church: ibid., 3.25.
37. Augustine in Kent: Bede, *HE*, 1.25ff. Gospel book: Webster and Backhouse (1991): 17–19. Biography: *Earliest Life*. Presents: Bede, *HE*, 2.10f.
38. Benedict Biscop: Bede, *Historia Abbatum*, 5f, 9 (ed. Plummer p. 368ff, transl. Webb p. 189ff); cf. Aldhelm, *carm. eccl.*, 3.66f for glass in a church in Wessex at much the same time. Runes carved: Carletti (1984f): 141f.
39. Aldhelm: *MGH AA*, 15:202.5. Codex Amiatinus: Webster and Backhouse (1991): 123–6. Lindisfarne Gospels: ibid., 111–14.
40. Whitby: Bede, *HE*, 3.25; Eddius, *Vita Wilfridi*, 10. Holy communion: Ep ad Ecg15 (ed. Plummer p. 419, transl. Hillgarth, *Christianity*, p. 167). Expressions of universality are recurrent in Bede; cf. *HE*, 2.2, 2.4, 5.23.
41. Aldhelm, *De Virginitate*, 58 (*Opera*, p. 318; transl. Lapidge and Herren, p. 127f). Visitors to Charlemagne: Alcuin, ep. 230 (*MGH Ep.*, 3:375).
42. Cucumbers and melons: Bischoff and Lapidge, p. 375. Theodore not able to attend: *PL*, 87:1224D.
43. London: Bede, *HE*, 2.3, but it had been known as a commercial centre in the early Empire (Tacitus, *ann.*, 14.33); Vince (1990). Mancuses to pope: Jaffé, 2494, 2511. Imitation: Grierson and Blackburn (1986): 330.
44. Grants of land: Sawyer, *Charters*, e.g. 7f; Aldhelm, *carm. eccl*, 3.6. Yeavering: Hope-Taylor (1977). Its abandonment: Bede, *HE*, 2.14, easily read in the light of Bede's description of Edwin sitting with his followers in a hall, ibid., 2.13.
45. Tolls on ships: Sawyer, *Charters*, nos. 86–8, 91. Æthelberht on compensation: Attenborough, *Laws*, p. 5. Gregory: Bede, *HE*, 1.27, quest. 3. Earthly kingdoms and kingdom of heaven: e.g. Bede, *HE*, 3.1, 3.6, 3.7, 3.12, 3.18, 3.22.

46. East Anglia: Dumville (1976). The scene is depicted, surrounded by an inscription in runes, on a bracteate of the fifth century found in Suffolk, as it also was on coins elsewhere in England. Compare the carvings in whale bone on the Franks Casket, an English but not East Anglian work of the early eighth century, one of which shows this scene, with the inscription: 'Romulus and Remus, two brothers, a she-wolf nourished them in Rome, far from their native land.'

47. Bede, *HE*, 3.22.

48. Worldly monasteries: Bede, *ep. ad Ecgbertum*, 10–14 (ed. Plummer, pp. 413–18). Hereditary succession: *Historia abbatum auctore anonymo*, 16 (within Bede ed. Plummer, p. 393).

49. The material that follows is drawn from the *Vita Wilfridi* by Eddius; specific chapters are cited only when compared to other sources.

50. Gospel book: 17; its splendour is confirmed by Wilfrid's epitaph, in Bede, *HE*, 5.19. Wide door: 'Saeculi huius lata ianua . . . aperiebatur' (cap. 8) recalls the 'lata porta' that leads to destruction (Matt. 7:13), while the expression 'of this world' is frequently used in a negative sense in the New Testament. Adoption: compare Hrothgar's adoption of Beowulf, *Beowulf*, 1175f. Similar values were displayed by a bishop who reminded his abbots that people of the world who deserted lords whom they had loved in time of prosperity were universally despised: Aldhelm, in *MGH AA*, 15:502.

51. Bede, *HE*, 4.25.

Chapter 5: The western Mediterranean post-Justinian

1. Zeno a barbarian: see above, p. 14, n. 16; see further on the Isaurians, *Expositio totius mundi et gentium*, 45. His name: *PLRE*, 2:1200 (s.v. Zenon). Aspar declines honour: *MGH AA*, 12:425. Simeon's relics: John Malalas, 369. Dagalaif: *Vita Danielis*, 80 (ed. Delehaye). Basiliscus: ibid., 84, perhaps a metaphorical usage.

2. Justin's walk: Procopius, *Anecdota*, 6.2f. Last Germanic general: *PLRE*, 2:1176, s.v. 'Vitalianus 2'.

3. The indolence ($\dot{\rho}\alpha\theta\upsilon\mu\acute{\iota}\alpha$) of earlier emperors is blamed by John the Lydian (*Powers*, 3.55; the quality is explicitly attributed to Arcadius and Honorius (2.11) and to emperors prior to Justinian (2.16)). See too Justinian, *nov.*, 30.11.2, for acts of negligence on the part of the old Romans. Honorius and Rome: Procopius, *Wars*, 3.2.25f; Malalas has him inviting Alaric to sack Rome (349; cf. Zonaras, *PG*, 134:1181–4).

4. Diptychs: Weitzmann (1979), no. 48 (pp. 48–50), the diptych of Clementius, eastern consul in 513, now in Liverpool Museum. Rome the centre: the historian John Malalas describes Theodosius as leaving Constantinople for Rome on his last trip to the West, although this was certainly not his destination (348), and he saw the emperors and kings who ruled in Italy thereafter as having ruled from, or in, Rome, allotting Ravenna a very secondary role in his narrative. Marcellinus: s.a. 476, transl. Croke.

5. Pope Hormisdas to Avitus of Vienne, Avitus, *ep.*, 42 (*MGH AA*, 6/2:71). Report from Greece: *Liber pontificalis*, 49, 50. Procopius: *Wars*, 4.18.40 (cf. 7.9.12, 21.12), 4.29.11 (cf. 7.21.4), 8. 23.25. 'Greek emperor': Sidonius, *ep.*, 1.7.5. 'Little Greek': Ennodius, *Vita Epiphani*, 57.

6. His addressing a letter 'The basileus Gelimer to Justinian the basileus' (Procopius, *Wars*, 3.9.20, misleadingly translated in the Loeb edition) was a remarkable *faux pas*.

7. Procopius, *Wars*, 1.22.17; the word used to describe its intended duration, ἀπέραντον, was also used of a peace concluded between Zeno and Geiseric in about 476 (3.7.26), which lasted for as long as the Empire wished.

8. Justinian's law: *cod. iust.*, 1.27.1,5f. Shipwreck: Kapitän (1969). Caput Vada: Procopius, *Buildings*, 6.6.15f. Elsewhere: Evagrius, *HE*, 4.18.

9. Epitaph: 'Valarit qu[i et . . .]telus': Ennabli (1991), no. 512. Senate of Rome: Cassiodorus, *Variae*, 11.13.5; cf. e.g. Justinian, *inst.* 1.27.1, *nov.* 78.4.1. Slave: Paul the Silentiary, *Ekphrasis*, 16 (*PG*, 86:2120).

10. Vigilius not vigilant: Columban, *ep.*, 5.5. Theodosius: Facundus, *Ad Iustinianum*, 12.5.9f, 14 (*CCSL*, 90A:395f). Sweet Justinian: *MGH Ep.* 3:119.2.

11. Coins: Camps (1984): 200f. Refugees: Procopius, *Wars*, 4.23.28f. Yet the force that Heraclius led to Constantinople in 610 included Africans and Moors: Nikephorus, *Short History*, 1.

12. Charges against Maximus: *CCSG*, 39:13–17.

13. Ibn 'Abd al-Hakam, p. 77.

14. Vergil quoted: Marrou (1953); the quotation is from *Aeneid*, 7.53.

15. *Const. omnem*, 7 (Justinian, *Corpus*, 1:11).

16. Agent in Ceuta: *cod. iust.*, 1.27.2.2. Regaining of territory: *nov.*, 30.11.2, of April 535. Procopius felt that the limits of Roman dominion were the eastern boundaries and the setting of the sun (*Buildings*, 6.7.17).

17. Franks: Gregory of Rome, *Reg.*, 9.214; Gregory of Tours: *History*, 3.32, 'lesser Italy' would have been a term like 'Asia Minor', indicating a nearby, politically subordinate part, rather than lower Italy in apposition to upper Italy (so Thorpe, p. 189); cf. the description of Kuvrat the Bulgar, below p. 183. Milan: strongly worded accounts in Procopius, *Wars*, 6.21.39; Marius of Aventicum, *chron.*, s.a. 538 (*MGH AA*, 11:235); Marcellinus comes, *chron.*, s.a. 539 (*MGH AA*, 11:106).

18. Totila prays: Procopius, *Wars*, 7.20.22. Presides at races: *Wars*, 7.37.4.

19. Opinion in 540: Cyril, *Vita Sabae*, 74 (power in Italy is again falsely associated with Rome, as also at 72). Mosaic: conveniently in Lowden (1997), ill. 80f.

20. Judges: Justinian, *nov. app.*, 7.12; weights and measures: ibid., 19.

21. *Liber pontificalis*, 63. Pelagius: ibid., 62; *PL*, 69:402f.

22. Earliest source: *Liber pontificalis*, 63 (although the invitation is presented as an act of revenge); similarly Paul the Deacon, *History*, 2.5. Migration rather than invasion: Gregory of Tours, *History*, 4.41, with 5.15.

23. Difficulties in communication: Gregory of Rome, *Reg.*, 5.15. Nocera Umbra: Paribeni (1918). Private persons: an inscription of 556 records the building of a castrum at Como by a subdeacon, 'by his own industry and toil, and not without great expense' (*CIL*, 5:5418). Cassiodorus' home town: *Variae*, 12.15.5. Manuscript: Schiavone (1993): 333. Such tendencies were not confined to Italy; in Byzantine Greek, 'castron' was often used of towns.

24. Baptism: *Reg.* 8.29; drink: 7.37; timber: e.g. 6.58.

25. Paul the Deacon suspected a desire to take Italy from the Lombards: *History*, 5.6; Theophanes was remarkably brusque: *Chronicle*, AM 6153.

26. Depiction as lamb forbidden: Council of Trullo, can. 82 (Mansi 11:978–80). Sly rejoinder: *Liber pontificalis*, 86.

27. Interpreter: Gregory of Tours, *History*, 6.6. Two centuries later: Paul the Deacon, *History* 2.32, 3.16. Gregory: *Reg.* 1.3, 1.8, 2.13, etc.

28. Adaloald lifted up: Paul the Deacon, *History*, 4.30. Phocas: Theophylact Simocatta, 8.7.7.

29. Marcelli (1989).

30. Romans for sale: Gregory, *Reg.* 5.36. Where is the senate: *Hom. Ez.*, 2.6.22 (*CCSL*, 142:311f.); see too on the disappearance of the Roman senate from the time of the coming of the Lombards, Agnellus of Ravenna, 95. Prophecy: *Hom. Ez.*, 2.6.23, oddly recalling the sentiments attributed to enemies of Rome by Tacitus, see above p. 8. Augustine: *PL*, 38:505, quoting Ps. 103:5. Power of barbarians: Gregory, *Reg.*, 5.37(= 20) trans. Barmby, addressed to the emperor Maurice.

31. Authari: Gregory, *Reg.*, 1.17.

32. Ravenna: Agnellus, *Liber pontificalis*, 111 (ed. Deliyannis, 561f.).

33. Gregory, *Hom. Ez.*, 1.10.34 (*CCSL*, 142:161f.).

34. Surrounded by luxury, the plain-living Attila had already eaten from a wooden plate and drunk from a wooden cup: Priscus, *frag.*, 13.1(= 8), transl. Blockley p. 285; compare the hermit in Gaul who cooked his food in a wooden pot: Gregory of Tours, *Glory*, 96.

35. Minting of coins: *Ed. Roth.*, cap. 243 (*MGH Leg nat Germ*, 4:160); the argument for this having been based on imperial legislation is based on the likelihood of its having had a common origin with similar Visigothic legislation (*Leges*, 7.5.1, 7.6.2)). Rothari and feud: *Ed. Roth.*, 45. The strongest evidence for taxation is the reissuing of a diploma of Charlemagne by Louis the Pious in 817, ceding to the pope the 'censum et pensionem seu ceteras dationes', which Lombard Tuscany and the duchy of Spoleto used to render the palace of the kings of the Lombards annually: *MGH Capit. reg. Francorum*, 2, no. 172. But it is unclear how much these vaguely described imposts were expected to yield.

36. Fifth century: Salvian, 5.5. Alaric: Zosimus, 5.42. Army of Totila: Procopius, *Wars*, 7.16.14f. Theoderic's observation: see above, p. 45. Ficarolo burial: Büsing *et al.* (1993). Droctulf: Paul the Deacon, *History*, 3.18.

37. Impressive tally: Paul the Deacon mentions Saxons, who later returned home (*History*, 2.6, 3.5–7) and Gepids, Bulgars, Sarmatians, Pannonians, Suevi, Noricans and others, names which lingered in those of villages where they settled: *History*, 2.26. Castel Trosino: Mengarelli (1902). Names: Jarnut (1972).

38. Totila is termed 'most unspeakable' (*nefandissimus*) in the Pragmatic Sanction (Justinian, *nov. app.*, 7.8), as is Agilulf by pope Gregory, for whom Lombard singing was unspeakable (*Reg.*, 1.17; *Dialogues*, 3.28.1). A letter of pope Pelagius describes the Lombard people as most unspeakable (*MGH Ep.*, 2:441); pope Gregory thought the same (*Reg.*, 5.38, 7.23).

39. Epiphanius: Ennodius, *Life of Epiphanius*, 47. Mosaic: Wilpert (1917), plate 9. Compare Gen. 13; needless to say, Isaac had not been born at that time.

40. Bishop of Velletri: Gregory of Rome, *Reg.*, 2.17. Bishop of Cagliari: ibid., 9.1, 11. Zeno: *cod. iust.*, 8.10, 12.5. Jewish merchants: Gregory, *Reg.*, 4.21. Monastery: ibid., 8.5. Eastern Mediterranean: see below, p. 194. International competition: see below, p. 251.

41. Sixth century: Gregory of Tours, *History*, 2.7; cf. Jordanes, *Origo*, 217ff (Attila so devastated the city that scarcely a trace of it could be seen). Ninth century: Paulinus of Aquileia (?), in Godman, *Poetry*, pp. 106–13. Compare the tenth-century Byzantine author who attributed the foundation of Venice to the attacks of the Huns: Constantine Porphyrogenitus, *De admin*, 28.

42. Milan: see above, n. 17. Bishop of Aquileia: Ennodius, *ep.*, 5.1 (MGH AA, 7:153f).

43. Fourth century: *cod. theod.*, 15.1.11, 15.1.19; cf. *nov. maj.* 1, of 458. Campus Martius: *cod. theod.*, 14.14. Cassiodorus: *Variae*, 11.39.1f, transl. Hodgkin).

44. Letter from Belisarius: Procopius, *Wars*, 7.22.9f (wild animals: Marcellinus, *Chronicon*, s.a. 547), 7.36.2. Forum and baths: Gregory, *hom. Ev.*, 1.6.6 (*CCSL*, 141:43). Litanies: Gregory: *Reg.*, 13.2. Sergius' donation: de Rossi (1870). Poem on Aquileia: see above, p. 145.

45. Gregory, *dial.*, 2.15.3; the pope felt that he could see the prophecy being fulfilled.

46. *Greek Anthology*, 4.3.77–96 (= 4.4.31–50).

47. Recopolis: Raddatz (1964) and articles in succeeding volumes of the same journal, with John of Biclaro, s.a. 578. Justiniana Prima: see below, p. 165. Coins: Grierson and Blackburn (1986), plate 12.

48. Marriage: 3.1.1, *MGH Leg nat Germ*, 1/1:121f. Claudius: *PLRE*, 3:316f (s.v. Claudius 2) John of Biclaro: Isidore of Seville, *De viris illustribus*, 44.66 (*PL*, 83:1105). *History*, 6.40. Names of bishops: data in Vives. Slate tablets: *Pizarras Visigodas*.

49. John of Biclaro on the synod: *chron.*, s.a. 590.1. Proceedings of the synod: Vives, *Concilios*, p. 116f. amended transl. Hillgarth, *Christianity*, p. 72f.

50. Isidore: *MGH AA*, 11:267.22–4. A work of history: Julian, *Historia*, 13, 19 (*CCSL*, 115:230, 234).

51. Morning gift: *Miscellanea wisigothica*, pp. 90–4. Visigothic legislation makes no mention of such gifts, although other codes, for example that of Rothari, do. Crowns: Palol, pp. 168–71. Earrings: Weitzmann (1979): 314f.

52. Isidore on Constantine: *chron.*, s.a. 334. Justinian accepts heresy: ibid., 379a. Lawgivers: *Etym.*, 5.1. Patriarchs: ibid., 7.12.5. Chief synods: ibid., 6.16.5–10. Council of 681: Vives, p. 385. Leo's letters: *PL*, 84:143Cf, 147A. Council of 684: Vives, p. 444f. Theodore's council: see above, p. 121.

53. It is instructive to compare Isidore of Seville's verdict on Sisebut, 'potestate enim compulit, quos provocare fidei ratione oportuit' (*Hist Goth*, 60), with Theoderic's 'religionem imperare non possumus, quia nemo cogitur ut credat invitus' (Cassiodorus, *Var.*, 2.27.2). Ravenna: Anonymus Valesianus, 81f.

54. *Leges Visigothorum*, 6.1.3.

55. Background: Julian, *Historia*, 2; the anointing of David is depicted on a Byzantine silver plate of the seventh century: Weitzmann (1979), no. 425. Treatment of rebels: Julian, *Historia*, 30. Deposition: 12th council of Toledo (ed. Vives, *Concilios*, p. 386f.).

Chapter 6: South of the Danube

1. Hence it has 'iobante' for 'iuvante'; for a slightly later use of the form 'victuria', an error in the opposite direction, see above, p. 139. The standard publication is Molajoli (1943).

2. The mosaics can be easily compared in Lowden (1997), ill. 79 (unfortunately back-to-front), 85.
3. Frantz (1988).
4. Cassius Dio, *Roman History*, 49.36.4.
5. Building of walls: *cod. theod.*, 11.17.4. Paulinus: *Eucharisticos*, 420–5.
6. Ioannes Lydus, *On Powers*, 3.43; Procopius, *Wars*, 3.6.1, doubles the amount of gold.
7. Fashion of the Danube: see, for example, Kazanski (1989). Historian's account: Priscus, frag. 8 (ed. and transl. Blockley); later, a Hun sitting next to Priscus at a feast passed on confidential information in Latin. Meleager: see above, p. 6.
8. His *Life of Severin*, edited *CSEL*, 9, is translated by L. Bieler, Washington, DC, 1965.
9. *Life of Severin*, 40.4 (transl. Bieler; note too the quotation of Ex. 14:14 at 4.3), 44.5.
10. Theoderic's letter: Cassiodorus, *Variae*, 3.50. Honorius' letter: see above, p. 97.
11. *Buildings*, 4.5.11ff.
12. *Buildings*, 4.4.
13. Feissel (1988).
14. See, in particular, *Caričan Grad* (1984+). Procopius' description: *Buildings*, 4.1.19–24.
15. Law of 535: *nov.*, 11. Quaestor of the army: Justinian, *nov.*, 41.
16. *Nikonian Chronicle*, p. 3, but against this see Jordanes, *Origo*, 35, of the sixth century. It has also been suggested that the word 'strava' used in connection with the burial of Attila is Slavic (Priscus, as followed by Jordanes, *Origo*, 258), while some scholars believe they can detect Slavic elements in the Černjachov culture (see above, p. 36).
17. Jordanes, *Origo*, 5.35; Procopius, *Wars*, 7.14.21–30. These texts, and the *Strategikon* attributed to Maurice, associate Slavs with an obscure people, the Antes.
18. Maurice, *Strategikon*, 11.4 (transl. Dennis, pp. 120–6.) Similarly, the absence of leaves on trees made winter a good time to attack the Franks around Cologne: Gregory of Tours, *History*, 2.9.
19. Avars as refugees: Corippus, *In Laudem*, 3.270–322, offers two very different accounts of recent Avar history. King of the Avars: Constantine Porphyregenitos, *De admin.*, 28; so too Fredegarius, *Chronicae*, 4.48, where the understandable error of treating the word 'chagan' as a proper name is committed.
20. Theophylact Simocatta, *Historiae*, 6.3.9–4.5.
21. Burial: Tóth (1972) with Pohl (1988), p. 181. Charlemagne's warriors: Einhard, *Vita Karoli*, 13. Elephant and golden bed: Theophylact Simocatta, *Historiae*, 1.3.8–12. Church plate: Nicephorus, *Short History*, 11, 19.
22. Gregory, *Reg.*, 5.40.
23. Theophylact Simocatta, 8.4.3–5; in Theophanes, *Chronicle*, AM 6093, the figure 90 is replaced by 'many'.
24. Isidore of Seville: *MGH AA*, 11:337. Egyptian author: John of Nikiu, *Chronicle*, p. 175f. Chronicle: *Cronica di Monemvasia*. The *Doctrina Iacobi*, a text of the seventh century, seems to envisage Greece and Thrace as lost to the Empire (see below, p. 239), while an English pilgrim of the eighth century described Monemvasia as being in Slavic territory: Hugeburc, *Vita Willibaldi*, p. 93.

25. Emperor: Constantine Porphyrygenitos, *De admin.*, 29. Patriarch: Nicholas Mysticus letter 10 (p. 71). A saying current in medieval Russia was 'They vanished like Avars': *Nikonian Chronicle*, p. 8.

26. Paul the Deacon, *History*, 4.44, with 4.37, 39.

27. Fredegar, *Chronicae*, 4.48, 75.

28. Nicephorus, *Short History*, 30; Maurice offers a crown to Hagia Sophia in Theophanes, *Chronicle*, AM 6093.

29. *Sacred Song*, transl. R. J. Schork (University of Florida, 1995), p. 209.

30. See, in particular, the account of Theodore Syncellos, transl. Makk. Chagan: *Chronicon paschale*, 725.

31. Athena: Zosimus, 5.6. Column of Arcadius: Weitzmann (1979), no. 68. Jerusalem: *Prise de Jérusalem*, 5.28–33, 6.6f; cf. 5.1–6 for confidence in divine protection. Justinian II: in Speiser, 'Inscriptions', at 156–60. Mary was later thought to have protected Constantinople against the Arabs: Constantine Porphyrogenitos, *De admin.*, 21 fin.

32. Henry (1930): text 238ff, album plates XLII.3, XLIII, XLIV.3.

33. Lemerle ed., *Recueils des miracles*, pp. 166–72. Bodyguards as *somatophulakoi*: Evagrius, *Hist. Eccl.*, 4.1, on Justin, before he became emperor.

34. Transl. Cormack (1985): p. 53, where also illustrations.

35. Ed. Lemerle, vol. 1, pp. 198ff (translation), 208ff (text); discussion 2, pp. 111ff.

36. Pope John: *Liber pontificalis*, 74. Split: McNally (1975).

37. Constantine Porphyrogenitos, *De admin.*, 32 (p. 152). By the ninth century the word *sclavus* was being used in Latin for 'slave'.

38. Sklavinia: Theophanes, *Chronicle* AM 6149. Sklavinia and Bulgaria: ibid., AM 6180; however, these terms could reflect usage of the ninth rather than the seventh century. Gifts to church: Speiser (1975). Chosen People: Theophanes, *Chronicle*, AM 6184.

39. Procopius, *Secret History*, 26.33.

40. Athens: Frantz (1988). Corinth: Gregory of Rome, *Dialogues*, 3.4; Weinberg (1974); Sanders (1999). Split: McNally (1975).

41. Sword bearer: Gregory, *Dialogues*, 4.27. Alcioc: Fredegarius, *Chronicae*, 4.72. Alzeco: Paul the Deacon, *History*, 5.29. Group near Ravenna: Theophanes, *Chronicle*, AM 6171.

42. Werner (1984); references to literary sources in *PLRE*, 3:763 (s.v. Koubratos). Great Bulgaria: Nikephorus, *Short History*, 35.

43. Defeat and treaty: Theophanes, *Chronicle*, AM 6171; Nikephorus, *Short History*, 35.

44. Diocletianopolis: Anna Comnena, *Alexiade*, 14.8 (Engl. transl., p. 463).

45. Note the location of Pliska, in a zone where cemeteries contained Bulgar rather than Slavic material: Fielder (1992), esp. 338f.

46. Constantine Porphyrogenitus, *De admin.*, 40.

Chapter 7: The East to 661

1. Law of 539: Justinian, *nov.*, 80. People visited by saint: *Miracles of Saint Artemios*, no. 44. Trade: Procopius, *Anecdota*, 25.2–5.

2. See on the family of Anthemius, *PLRE*, 3:88f (Anthemius 2) with cross-references; on that of Isidore, ibid., 724f (Isidorus 4 and 5); on Megas, ibid., 870 (Megas 2).

3. Kaper Koraon: Mundell Mango (1986); see Weitzmann (1979): 599ff. for an extraordinary variety of finds of silver in Syria. Perhaps the state's need of gold for coinage prevented its being similarly used. Patriarch of Antioch: Severus, *PO*, 20: 246–8. David plates: Weitzmann (1979): 475ff. Westerner: Gregory of Rome, *Mor. Job*, 1.6.8 (= *CCSL*, 143:28).

4. Gregory of Tours, *History*, 1.10; Isidore of Seville knew better (*Etymologiae*, 15.11.4). Procopius saw the pyramids as an example of 'useless show' (*Buildings*, 2.1.3).

5. Apions: *PLRE*, 3:96ff.

6. Syria: Tate (1992). Churches: Ovadiah (1970). Transjordan: LaBianca (1990).

7. Aphrodisias: Roueché (1989).

8. Boats: Rodiewicz (1984): 219–23. Sale of wine: John of Ephesus, in *PO*, 17:124ff. John the Almoner: *Life*, cap. 10 (even Cleopatra had apparently been content to drink Mareotic wine: Horace, *carm.*, 1.37.14). Gaul: Gregory of Tours, *History*, 7.29; see too 64 for Gaza wine in Lyons; Falernian wine from south of Rome was also available (83). See also above p. 137 for pope Gregory's enjoyment of imported wine. Ship's cargo: van Alfen (1996).

9. The annual caravans may be referred to in Qur'an sura 106, 'Quraish'. Battle of Badr: see below, p. 201. Queen of Sheba: i Kings 10:10, ii Chron. 9:1; cf. Is. 60:6, Jer. 6:20, and perhaps Song of Songs 3:6.

10. Sleepers in the cave: Qur'an sura 18, 'The cave', 9–26 (the account suggests that differing versions of the story were known); Gregory of Tours, *Glory*, 94. Mary: see below, p. 200. Shirin: Theophylact Simocatta, 5.14.

11. Modest bishop: *PO*, 2/3:259f. Holy fool: *Vie*, ed. Festugière, cap. 14.

12. Historian: Ammianus Marcellinus, 14.4.1. Difficult relations: Judges 6:3–5. Patriarch: Dionysius of Tell-Mahre, in *Seventh Century*, p. 141.

13. Jerome, *ep.*, 126, quoting Vergil, *aen.*, 4.42f, from a text reading 'vagantes' rather than 'furentes', and Gen. 16:12. Yet Barce was a town in Africa; Jerome's assimilating its people with Arabs may be significant.

14. *Répertoire chronologique*, no. 1, written in the Nabatean alphabet.

15. Grain from Dead Sea: Cyril of Scythopolis, *Vita Sabae*, 81. Inscription: *Répertoire*, 2. Arab poet: Lichtenstadter, *Introduction*, p. 149. Arabs at Caesarea in al-Baladhuri, *Origins*, p. 218 (where they need not have been prisoners), and near Aleppo, p. 224f. Father of Mu'awiya: al-Baladhuri, *Origins*, p. 197.

16. Shahid, *Martyrs*, noting evidence from inscriptions for the use of the term by Arab Jews and Christians in this period. Some early commentators on the Qur'an saw the events at Najran reflected in a graphic passage: sura 85, 'The constellations', 4–9.

17. Qur'an, sura 34, 'Sheba', 16, seems to refer to this.

18. Sura 105, 'The elephant'.

19. Sozomen, *History*, 6.38; that the author of this work was born near Gaza adds weight to his information. Compare the Book of Jubilees, a Jewish text of the second century BC, which has Abraham instructing all his sons and grandsons and predicting that they would all be a blessing on the earth. Qur'an on Abraham and Ishmail: see esp. sura 2, 'The cow', 125–33. Party of Arabs: Cyril of Scythopolis, *Vita Sabae*, intro. 10, transl. pp. 14–17. Interchangeable terms: e.g. Sophronius of Jerusalem: *PG*, 87:3207B.

20. The following account follows a traditional interpretation of the origins of Islam, the presuppositions of which some recent scholars question. But while the non-Islamic texts on which revision has been based are indeed very early, they need not have been well informed about affairs in Arabia; cf. a problem of dating created by a passage in Sebeos, below n. 30.

21. Ishaq, *Life*, p. 105f. Muhammad's experience recalls those of Romanos Melodos and Caedmon.

22. Muhammad's mother: Ishaq, *Life*, p. 69. Monk: Islamic tradition in ibid., pp. 79–81; a Christian version in John of Damascus, *PG*, 94:765.

23. Chosen people: cf. Num. 11:5 (explained by Theodore of Tarsus, see above p. 118) and sura 2, 'The cow', 61. Eye of a needle: cf. Matt. 19:24 and sura 7, 'The heights', 40. Satan and Adam: e.g. sura 15, 'Al-Hijr', 32ff. Christ appeared to suffer: sura 4, 'Women', 157. Mary and water: sura 19, 'Mary', 22ff; cf. the pilgrim's account in *CCSL*, 175:143. Non-Muslim readers of the Qur'an may find themselves prompted to speculate on the distance between the official teaching of the Christian church and the form it seems to have assumed in the milieu of the Prophet.

24. For example, eirenic sentiments occur in sura 5, 'The Table', 44ff, negative ones in sura 9, 'Repentance', 29–31.

25. As at Tella at the beginning of the sixth century (Joshua the Stylite, p. 47f); at Caesarea and Jerusalem later (Sebeos, *Armenian History*, 112, 115 (pp. 64, 68f).

26. Clermont: Gregory of Tours, *History*, 5.11, see further 6.17. Antioch: Theophanes, *Chronicle* AM 6101. Mt Sinai: Athanasius of Sinai, *PG*, 98:1689f. But the story may have been a topos: cf. John Cassian, *Conf.*, 2.8 (*SChr*, 42:119).

27. Zacharias: *Prise*, pp. 37–9. Alexandria: Severus, *History*, p. 221f. Tyre: Eutychius, *Amalenwerk*, Germ. transl. p. 101f. See further for anti-Christian sentiments *Chron. Pasch.*, 728.

28. Murders in Jerusalem: *La Prise*, 10. Lead bull: Dexinger and Seibt (1981).

29. On Heraclius, see Theophanes, *Chronicle*, AM 6118, with *PLRE*, 3:612, on Iesdem. *Paradeisos* of shahs: see, for example, in the Bible Nehemiah 2:8 (Septuagint). The same Greek word is used of Heaven in the New Testament, as is an Arabic word derived from it in the Qur'an.

30. France: Fredegarius, *Chronicae*, 4.65, where the 'circumcized people' are Arabs; a similar tradition was known in the east: Ishaq, *Life*, p. 654; Severus, *History*, p. 220. Papacy: Gregory, e.g. *Reg.* 1.34, 13.13. Lombard authorities: *MGH SRLI*, p. 190. Insincere Jew: see, for example, the eighth canon of the Second Nicene Council (787), Mansi, 13:1427–30. Arab armies: Sebeos, *Armenian History*, 134 (p. 95). Note, however, that the journey of the Jews is said to have occurred after Heraclius reoccupied Jerusalem, hence after 628, by which time Muhammad's career was well advanced.

31. Al-Tabari, *History*, vol. 7, p. 82f.

32. The title 'amir al-mu'minin' may owe something to Qur'an sura 4, 59, where obedience is enjoined on God, the messenger and amirs.

33. Single incident: Theophanes, *Chronicle*, AM 6123; Nicephorus, *Short History*, 23, has Saracens beginning to lay waste Roman territory because of restrictions on trade. Elsewhere, Theophanes suggestively mentions the rise of the Arabs after discussing

doctrinal deviancy among Christians, without explicitly stating that one caused the other: *Chronicle*, AM 6121.

34. Muhammad and Heraclius: Ishaq, *Life*, pp. 655–7. Muslims to fight: Qur'an, sura 8, 'The spoils', 39. Pagan Arabs: al-Tabari, *History*, vol. 6, p. 137. Injunction: Qur'an, sura 9, 'Repentance', 41. Africa: el-Bekri, *Description*, p. 50.

35. Al-Baladhuri, transl. Hitti, p. 165.

36. *PG*, 87:3205f.

37. Versions of this story in Agapios, 8.475; Michel le Syrien, *Chronique*, 2:425f; Theophanes, *Chronicle*, AM 6127, where further references. 'Umar was later said to have patched his sole garment with pieces of leather: Ibn Khaldun, *Muqaddimah*, 1, p. 419.

38. Baladhuri, p. 210, who explains that Heraclius referred to the pastures of Syria, a perspective that seems Arab rather than Byzantine; cf. Ishaq, *Life*, p. 657.

39. Marriage proposal and tribute: Nicephorus, *Short History*, 24, 26.

40. Saracens in Sicily: *Liber pontificalis*, 76. Caliph's letter: Sebeos, *Armenian History*, 169f (p. 144); the adjoining commentary defends the authenticity of the document.

41. Jeusalem: Adamnan, *De locis sanctis*, 1.1.14 (*CCSL*, 175:186). Damascus: al-Baladhuri, *Origins*, p. 189.

42. Eutychius transl. Breydy, p. 126f.

43. Passports: Severus, in *PO*, 5:68–71, where other instances of bad treatment are given.

44. Green and Tsafrir (1982), at 94–6.

45. *Livre de la consécration*, pp. 207–9; for 'boldness' the Coptic version of the text uses the Greek word *parrhesia*.

46. Al-Baladhuri, *Origins*, p. 211; Monophysite authors of later centuries saw the coming of the Arabs as a time of deliverance.

47. Theophanes, *Chronicle*, AM 6209 (De Boor, p. 397).

48. Eutychius transl. Breydy, p. 120f.

49. Colossus of Rhodes: Agapius, *PO*, 8:222, states that it was cast into the sea; variants of the other story are in Theophanes, *Chronicle*, AM 6145; Constantine Porphyrogenitus, *De admin. imperii*, 21.56ff; Michael the Syrian, 2:441.

Chapter 8: The East from 661

1. On Mu'awiya, see *Encyclopaedia of Islam*, 7:263–9; on his parents, Abu Sufyan and Hind bint 'Utba, ibid., 1:151, 3:455; on al-Akhtal, ibid., 1:331, on Mu'awiya's retinue, al-Tabari, *History*, vol. 18, p. 218.

2. Miles (1948).

3. Al-Baladhuri, *Origins*, p. 197.

4. Ibn Khaldun, *Muqaddimah*, 2, pp. 287–9. Another woman who was the focus for both military and religious Islam was the Arab prophet Sadjah (*Encyclopaedia of Islam*, 8, 738f); doubtless gender was significant.

5. Roderic's widow: *cont. hisp.*, 79 (*MGH AA*, 11:356). Pelayo's sister: *Christians and Moors*, 1, p. 27. Sara: *Historia de la conquesta*, p. 3ff. Theodemir/Tudmir: *Christians and Moors*, 1, pp. 11–13.

6. Sinderid the hireling: *MGH AA*, 11:352f (69). In Rome: Mansi, 12:265. Heretical Syrian: Vives, *Concilios*, p. 171. Al-Baladhuri: *Origins*, pp. 194f, 231f, 339, 348. Carthage: Ibn 'Abd al-Hakam, transl. Gateau, p. 77; Idhari, quoted by M. Talbi, in Gervers and Bikhazi (1990): p. 315. Letter of Gregory: *PL*, 89:502.

7. Theophanes, *Chronicle*, AM 6178.

8. Ishmael a wild man: Gen. 16:12; on Ishmael and the Arabs, see above, p. 198; Jerome describes sons of Ishmael engaged in just such activities, see above, p. 195 with n. 13. Bede: *CCSL*, 118A:201; a similar judgement in Alcuin, *ep.*, 7 (*MGH Ep.*, 4:32). For the Saracens as 'omnibus exosi', compare Bede's description of their people as 'exosa omnibus' (*CCSL*, 119B:195, on Song of Songs 1:5).

9. Khalid: *Encyclopaedia of Islam*, 4:927. Site in Jordan: Piccirillo (1987). Ivory plaques: Weitzmann (1979): 508f.

10. John of Ephesus, *Lives of the eastern Saints*, PO, 17:172; that it was shameful for women of high class to appear unveiled in public is indicated at *PG*, 85:1831A.

11. Roll and Ayalon (1987).

12. Adomnan, *De locis sanctis*, 2.12, *CCSL*, 175:211; it was cheaper to transport goods by camel than by wagon.

13. 'Umar's offer: Al-Baladhuri, *Origins*, p. 209.

14. Walker (1956).

15. Rivalry: al Baladhuri, *Origins*, p. 465. Papyri: Küchler (1991), where Qurrah ibn Sharik is represented as Κόρρα υἱός Σζέριχ and God is described as Τὸς ἐλεήμενος καὶ Φιλάνθρωπος (130, 134). See also above p. 178 on God's philanthropia.

16. Magness (1991); see also Küchler (1991). On the Dome of the Rock, Creswell (1989): 19–40.

17. Transl. Le Strange, *Palestine*, p. 98. See on the night ride Qur'an sura 17, 'The night journey', 1.

18. Nabigha, quoted in Creswell (1989): 188f, who observes (p. 189, n. 1) with reference to the third line that Greek poets compare the voices of barbarians to swallows. On the mosque: Bahnassi (1989); Creswell (1989): 46–73.

19. Le Strange, *Palestine*, p. 228.

20. Bisheh (1993): 53f.

21. Inscription: *Répertoire*, no. 18, p. 16f. Ambassadors from Constantinople: Le Strange, *Palestine*, p. 263f, quoting Yakut.

22. Le Strange, *Palestine*, p. 117f.

23. Le Strange, *Palestine*, p. 98; the building was destroyed in a great earthquake generally dated to 747.

24. Earlier structure: Gaube (1974). On the complex at Qasr 'Amra, discussed below, Almagro *et al.* (1975).

25. Hammad ibn Sabur, transl. Hillenbrand (1982): 10.

26. *History of the Patriarchs*, PO, 5/1, p. 25.

27. Ma' in: De Vaux (1938). Picture of Jesus and Mary: a tradition is reported in an addition by Ibn Hisham (ninth century) to the *Life of Muhammad* by Ishaq: p. 774.

28. Lowden (1997), ills. 88 (S Irene) and 93 (small sekreton). Theodulf's chapel: Grabar (1954), with discussion on architectural antecedents. *Libri Carolini: Opus Caroli regis*, p. 195ff. Oviedo: Bango Torviso (1989): 18ff.

29. Monophysite historian: John of Nikiu, *Chronicle*, p. 195. Monophysite patriarch: MacCoull, 'Paschal letter', p. 33f.

30. Drinking of wine and pressure: Theophanes, *Chronicle*, AM 6210. Beautiful women: Bar Hebraeus, *Chronicon*, pp. 140–2; compare the threats made against a Catholicus who compared Islam unfavourably to Christianity and Judaism, p. 136. Seek *rapprochement*: Anastasios of Sinai, *PG*, 89:41 (= *CCSG*, 8:9). Translation: Dionysius of Tel-Mahre, in Palmer, *Seventh Century*, 170f; baptism and the cross are elsewhere mentioned as causes of offence.

31. Conversion and Constantine: *History of the Patriarchs*, 5/1, pp. 149–53.

32. Najran: *Encyclopaedia of Islam*, 7:872. The monk John: John of Nikiu, *Chronicle*, 123.10f. Pseudo-Methodius: *Apocalypse*, 12.3,6, in Palmer, *Seventh Century*, p. 235.

33. Matt. 6:3–6, 16–18.

34. *Excavations at Nessara*, 3, *Non-literary Papyri*, ed. C. J. Kraemer, esp. p. 6f.

35. Eutychius, an Alexandrian author of the tenth century, makes Mansour, the enemy of Heraclius, the betrayer of Damascus: *Das Annalanwerk*, pp. 107, 109, 115–17. Al-Baladhuri, on the other hand, writing in the ninth century, attributes the taking of Damascus to its bishop (*Origins*, pp. 172, 186f, 189), while a Syriac text connects the fall of the city to the activities of a deacon named John, the son of Sargun, who was dear to the Saracens and well known to them: *Chronicum anonymum*, p. 194.

36. Al-Baladhuri, *Origins*, p. 301.

37. *MGH AA*, 11:353 (transl. Wolf, p. 132f).

38. *Doctrina Iacobi*, 3.16. Sergius: *PLRE*, 3:1134f. Preceding author: Cosmas Indicopleustes, *Topographie*, 2.75.

39. Sebeos, *Armenian History*, 142 (p. 105f).

40. Transl. S. Brock, in Palmer, *Seventh Century*, esp. pp. 230–8; a similar apocalypse of unknown date follows.

41. Al-Akhtal: transl. J. Bloom (Oxford University Press, 1989): 27, n. 37. Eulogius's grandfather: *PL*, 115:861f; cf. Ps. 83:1f.

42. Duchesne, 'Iconographie byzantine'.

43. Antioch: Procopius, *Buildings*, 2.10,22f. Law of 383: *cod. theod.*, 15,1,22. Scythopolis: Tsafrir and Foerster (1997).

44. Wilkinson, *Jerusalem pilgrims*, p. 205. The town may have done worse than many, for its fortunes were connected with those of pilgrimage, on which see below, p. 264.

45. Egyptian text in MacCoull (1985): 66. Preface: *PO*, 1:115.

46. Swanson (1998).

47. Kabis: *Encyclopaedia of Islam*, 5:338. Arzao: el-Bekri, *Description*, p. 143. Tlemcen: p. 155f. Carthage: p. 89f. Badja: p. 119, with Durliat, *Dédicaces*, no. 31 (pp. 78–80). Saiones: *Christians and Moors*, 1, p. 66; for saiones in Visigothic times, see for example *Leges Visigothorum*, 2.1.16,24. Isidore of Seville thought they were so named because they asked for things: 'saio ab exigendo dictus', *Etym.*, 10.263. Pope Hadrian: *PL*, 98:385, where other examples of interaction between Christians and Jews or 'pagans' are mentioned. Muslim jurist: *Christians and Moors*, 3, pp. 29–31.

Chapter 9: Systems great and small

1. Pirenne (1939).
2. The basic work is that of Hayes (1972, 1980). The following paragraphs do no more than attempt to synthesise a large amount of evidence.
3. Constantinople: Hayes (1992). Anemourion: Russell (1980). Marseilles: Bonifay and Piéri (1995). Aegean: Abadie-Reynal (1989).
4. Taxes: *cod. theod.*, 11.28.9,11. Shipwreck: Kapitän (1969). Ostrogothic sovereign: Cassiodorus *Var.*, 10.8. Luni: see above, p. 145.
5. Law of fourth century: *cod. theod.*, 15.19.1. Barberini diptych: Weitzmann (1979): 33–5. *Vienna Genesis*: Mazal (1980), plate 4. Maximian's throne: Weitzmann (1979): 450. Combs: ibid., 629. Franks Casket: Webster and Backhouse (1991): 101–3.
6. Parker (1992), with van Alfen (1996) on the Yassi Ada wreck. Grain to Rome: *Liber pontificalis*, 64.
7. Lafaurie and Morrisson (1987).
8. Justinian outwitted: *Glory*, 102. Coronations: those of Tiberius I in 578, *History*, 5.30, and Maurice in 582, ibid., 6.30. Star of Bethlehem: *Glory*, 1. True Cross: *History*, 9.40; the relic had been sent by the emperor Justin II to Radegund's convent. St Andrew: *Mir. And.*, 8, assuming that Gregory was the author of this text. Assumption of Mary: *Glory*, 4. St Sergius: *History*, 10.31; Gregory also knew of relics of this saint which a Syrian had brought to Bordeaux: ibid., 7.31. We have already seen that Gregory knew a version of the tale of the Seven Sleepers of Ephesus, also found in the Qur'an: see above, p. 193.
9. Cummian, *De controversia paschali*, pp. 93–5.
10. Theophanes: transl. Mango and Scott, pp. lxxi–lxxiii. Eutychius: *PG*, 111:1125; his estimate of the length of Theodore's episcopate is far too long.
11. Jacob: *Doctrina Iacobi*, 5.20. Tripoli: al-Baladhuri, *Origins*, p. 355.
12. *Vita S. Andreae Sali*, *PG*, 111:681C, following the translation 'Ismaelitæ', although the Greek text has Ἰσραηλίτου; similarly, at *PG*, 97:1045f. 'Ismael' is offered as a translation of Ἰσραήλ.
13. *Periplus*, 16.
14. Ibn Khaldun, *Muqaddimah*, 1, p. 356; 2, p. 242f.
15. Further to the west, the bodyguard of the emperor Justinian II is said to have kept an Indian cook: Nikephorus, *Short History*, 45.
16. Nau ed. 'La plus ancienne Mention'.
17. Canal: John of Nikiu, *Chronicle*, 20.29.
18. Buffaloes: al-Baladhuri, p. 259. Mosque at Daibul: Creswell (1989): 224, with al-Baladhuri transl. F. C. Murgotten, p. 217ff. Mosque at Damascus: above p. 229.
19. Cosmas: reproduction in Watson (1983): 53. The banana was known to Pliny as a sweet Indian fruit, its leaves shaped like birds' wings: Pliny, *nat. hist.*, 12.12.24.
20. Titus and Alaric: Procopius, *Wars*, 5.12.42. Geiseric and Justinian; ibid., 4.9. Tariq: *Christians and Moors*, 3, p. 7; Taha (1989): 93.
21. Ed. and French transl. Sauvaget, *Relation*. Four kings: p. 11f.
22. Laughing and clapping: Notker, *Gesta*, 2,8. Pet elephant: *Annales Regni Francorum*, s.a. 802, 810. Copyists of the text found it difficult to deal with the elephant's Arabic name, and provide variants, one turning it into 'ambulabat', 'it walked'; they were

more comfortable with the Arabic title 'amir al mumminin' (s.a. 801). But there is no doubt as to the correct Latin form. It is Einhard who has Harun, termed 'Aaron the king of the Persians' and described in vague terms as holding nearly all the east except for India, sending Charlemagne his only elephant in response to a request (*Vita*, 2.16).

23. Kings of the Franks: Mas'udi, p. 70f.

24. Raisins: Ibn Khaldun, *Muqaddimah*, 1, p. 365. Geographer: El-Bekri, pp. 67, 100f, 105, 117.

25. Eusebius: Gregory of Tours, *History*, 10.26. Bede: Cuthbert's letter, in Bede ed. Colgrave and Mynors, p. 584. Silk textiles: Blair (1998): 170f; Grabar (1968): 271–5.

26. For what follows, see Hugeburc, *Vita Willibaldi*. The name given the king, Myrmum-mus, must be an attempt to represent the Arabic title 'commander of the faithful' (above p. 290 n. 32).

27. Qal'at Sem'an: Biscop and Sodini (1989). Bethlehem: see above, p. 244.

28. Hence the expression of an Italian author, 'Roma quae aliquando totius mundi caput extitit' *CCSL*, 175:367(4).

29. Greek author: Procopius, *Wars*, 3.2.12. 410: Cassiodorus, *Chron.*, sa 410 (*MGH AA*, 11:155); cf. his *Variae*, 12.20. Isidore, HG 15–18 (*MGH AA*, 11:455). Jordanes asserts that the Goths of Alaric did not light fires, as *gentes* usually do: *Origo*, 156 (*MGH AA*, 5/1:98f).

30. Medard: *Vita Medardi*, 2.4. (ed. *MGH AA*, 4/2:168). Vandal king: Fredegarius, 2.60 (*MGH SRM*, 2:84). Kings of the Burgundians: *Passio Sigismundi*, 1 (*MGH SRM*, 2:333). Alcuin: *ep.*, 20 (*MGH Ep.*, 4:57). History of the Franks: *Liber historiae Francorum*, 5 (*MGH SRM*, 2:245). Annotation: *MGH SRM*, 7:773; it is not clear just who taught the Franks the Roman tongue. Biographer of Charlemagne: Notker, *Gesta Caroli*, 2.1. Salic law: *Lex salica*, p. 7f; transl. Hillgarth, *Christianity*, p. 93.

BIBLIOGRAPHY

———— ◆ ————

This bibliography is divided into three sections. The first lists the most important texts. The second, while it concentrates on archaeological reports and other kinds of non-literary evidence, also includes some discussions of data not directly available, and a small number of works noteworthy for illustrations or containing texts not easily obtainable elsewhere. The final section provides skeletal lists of modern works that is weighted towards books in English.

Encyclopaedias and works of reference

Dictionnaire d'Histoire et de Géographie Ecclésiastiques, Paris 1912+.
Encyclopaedia of Islam, 2nd edn. Leiden, 1960+.
Lexikon des Mittelalters, Munich and Zurich, 1980–98; Registerband, Stuttgart, 1999.
Oxford Dictionary of Byzantium, New York and Oxford, 1991.

I FONTES

Agathias, *Historiarum libri quinque*, ed. R. Keydell, Berlin 1967; transl. J. D. Frendo, Berlin/New York, 1975.

Agnellus of Ravenna, *The Liber pontificalis ecclesiae ravennatis*, ed. D. M. Deliyannis, University of Pennsylvania Ph.D. thesis, 1994.

Aldhelm, *MGH AA*, 15; *Poetic Works*, transl. M. Lapidge and J. L. Rosier, Cambridge 1985; *Prose Works*, M. Lapidge and M. Herren.

Ambrose, *Opera*, ed. and Ital. transl., Milan/Rome, 1977ff; *Hexameron*, transl. John J. Savage, New York, 1961; *Letters*, transl. M. M. Beyenka, New York, 1954.

Ammianus Marcellinus, ed. and transl. J. C. Rolfe, London, 1950–2.

The Anglo-Saxon Chronicles, ed. and transl. M. J. Swanton, London, new edn 2000.

Anna Comnena, *Alexiade*, ed. B. Leib, Paris, 1937–76; Engl. transl. E. R. A. Sewter, Harmondsworth, 1969.

Annales Regni Francorum, ed. G. H. Pertz and F. Kurze, Hannover, 1895.

Anonymus Valesianus, *MGH AA*, 9; transl. J. C. Rolfe, as under Ammianus Marcellinus, vol. 3.

Attenborough, F. L., ed. and transl., *The Laws of the Earliest English Kings*, Cambridge, 1922.

Augustine, *De Civitate Dei*, *CCSL*, 47f; transl. H. Bettenson, Harmondsworth, 1972.
　Confessiones, *CCSL*, 27; transl. H. Chadwick, Oxford, 1991.
　Epistulae nuper in lucem prolatae, *CSEL*, 87.

Ausonius, *Works*, ed. R. P. H. Green, Oxford, 1991; Engl. transl. H. G. Evelyn White, London, 1919–21.

Avitus of Vienne, *MGH AA*, 6.

al-Baladhuri, *The Origins of the Islamic State*, 1, transl. P. K. Hitti, New York, 1916; 2, transl. F. C. Murgotten, New York, 1924.

Bar Hebraeus, *Chronicon Ecclesiasticum*, ed. and Latin transl. J. B. Abbeloos and T. J. Lamy, Louvain, 3, 1877.

Bede, *Ecclesiastical History of the English People*, ed. and transl. B. Colgrave and R. A. B. Mynors, Oxford, 1969.

   Opera historica, ed. Ch. Plummer, Oxford, 1896.

el-Bekri, *Description de l'Afrique septentrionale*, transl. Mac Guckin de Slane, Algiers/Paris, 1913.

Benedict Regula, ed. R. Hanslik, *CSEL*, 75; ed. and transl. T. Fry, Collegeville, IN, 1981.

Bischoff, B., and Lapidge, M. *Biblical Commentaries from the Canterbury School of Theodore and Hadrian*, Cambridge, 1994.

Blockley, R. C., ed. and transl., *The Fragmentary Classicizing Historians of the Later Roman Empire*, Liverpool, 1983.

The Burgundian Code, transl. K. F. Drew, Philadelphia, PA, 1972.

Cassiodorus, *Institutiones*, ed. R. A. B. Mynors, Oxford, 1937; transl. L. W. Jones, *Introduction to Divine and Human Readings*, New York, 1946.

   Variae, ed. *MGH AA*, 12; partial transls Th. Hodgkin, London, 1886; S. Barnish, Liverpool, 1992.

Cassius Dio, *Roman History*, ed. and transl. E. Cary and H. B. Foster, London, 1914–27.

Christians and Moors in Spain, 1, transl. Colin Smith, Warminster 1988; 3, transl. Charles Melvile and Ahmad Ubaydli, Warminster, 1992.

Chronicon Anonymum ad annum 1234 pertinens, transl. J.-B. Chabot (= *CSCO SS*, 56).

Chronicon paschale, ed. L. Dindorf, 1832; transl. M. and M. Whitby, Liverpool, 1989.

Claudian, ed. and transl. M. Platauer, London, 1922.

Codex Iustinianus, ed. P. Krueger, Berlin, 1915.

Codex Theodosianus, ed. Th. Mommsen and P. N. Meyer, Berlin, 1905; transl. C. Pharr, *The Theodosian Code and Novels and their Sirmonian Constitutions*, Princeton, NJ, 1952.

Collectio Avellana, ed. O. Guenther, *CSEL*, 35.

Columban, *Opera*, ed. and transl. G. S. M. Walker, Dublin, 1957.

Colgrave, B., ed., *Two Lives of Saint Cuthbert*, Cambridge, 1940.

Constantine Porphyrogenitus, *De administrando imperio*, ed. G. Moravscik, transl. R. H. Jenkins, Washington, DC, 1967.

Corippus, *Iohannidos*, *MGH AA*, 3/2.

   In Laudem Iustini augusti minoris, ed. and transl. Averil Cameron, London, 1976.

Cosmas Indicopleustes, *Topographie chrétienne*, ed. with French transl., *SChr* 141, 159, 197.

Cronaca di Monemvasia, ed. I Duičev, Palermo, 1976.

Cummian, *De controversia paschali*, ed. and transl. Maura Walsh and Dáibhí Ó Cróinín, Toronto, 1988.

Cyril of Scythopolis, *Vita Sabae*, ed. E. Schwartz, *Kyrillos von Skythopolis*, Leipzig, 1939, pp. 85–200; French transl. A. J. Festugière, *Les Moines d'orient*, 3, Paris, 1962.

Deferrari, Roy J., ed., *Early Christian Biographies*, Washington, DC, 1951.

Delehaye, H., ed., *Les Saints stylites*, Brussels, 1923.

Doctrina Iacobi nuper baptisati, ed. and transl. V. Déroche, *Travaux et Mémoires*, 11, 1991, 69–219.

Duchesne, L., 'L'iconographie byzantine dans un document grec du IX siècle', ed. with Ital. transl. *Roma e l'Oriente*, 5, 1912–13, 222–39, 272–85, 347–66.

Dumville, D. N., ed., 'The Anglian Collection of royal genealogies and regnal lists', *Anglo-Saxon England*, 5, 1976, 23–50.

The Earliest Life of Gregory the Great, ed. and transl. B. Colgrave, Cambridge, 1985.

Eddius Stephanus, *Vita Wilfridi*, *MGH SRM*, 6; transl. Webb, *Age of Bede*.

The Edict of Diocletian, ed. Tenney Frank, *Economic Survey of Ancient Rome*, 5, Baltimore, 1940.

Edictum Theodorici regis, *MGH Leges*, 5.

Einhard, *Vita Karoli Magni*, ed. G. H. Pertz and G. Waitz, Hannover, 1911 (transl. L. Thorpe, *Two Lives of Charlemagne*, Harmondsworth, 1969).

Ennodius, *MGH AA*, 7.

Life of Epiphanius, transl. Deferrari.

Eugippius, *Vita Severini*, *CSEL*, 9; transl. L. Bieler, Washington, DC.

Eutychius, *Annalenwerk*, ed. with Germ. transl. *CSCO Scr Ar*, 44f.

Evagrius, *Ecclesiastical History*, ed. J. Bidez and L. Parmentier, London, 1898; French transl. A. J. Festugière, *Byzantion*, 45, 1975, 187–488.

Expositio totius mundi et gentium, ed. and French transl. J. Rougé, Paris, 1966.

'The Farmer's Law', ed. and transl. W. Ashburner, *Journal of Hellenic Studies*, 30, 1910, 85–108; 32, 1912, 68–95.

Felix, *Life of Saint Guthlac*, ed. and transl. B. Colgrave, Cambridge, 1956.

Ferrandus, *Vie de Saint Fulgence de Ruspe*, ed. G. G. Lapeyre, Paris, 1929; transl. R. B. Eno, in *Fulgentius selected works*, Washington, DC, 1997.

Festus, *Abrégé des hauts faits du peuple romaine*, ed. and transl. M.-P. Lindet, Paris, 1994.

Fouracre, P., and Gerberding, R. A., *Late Merovingian France*, Manchester, 1996.

Fredegarius, *Chronicae*, *MGH SRM*, 2; J. M. Wallace-Hadrill, ed. and transl., *The Fourth Book of the Chronicle of Fredegarius with its Continuations*, London, 1960.

Fulgentius of Ruspe, *CCSL*, 91 (partial transl. in Eno, as above under 'Ferrandus').

Gildas, *The Ruin of Britain and Other Works*, ed. and transl. M. Winterbottom, London, 1978.

Godman, Peter, ed. and transl., *Poetry of the Carolingian Renaissance*, London, 1985.

Gordon, C. D., transl., *The Age of Attila: Fifth-century Byzantium and the Barbarians*, Ann Arbor, MI, 1966.

Greek Anthology, ed. and transl. W. R. Paton, London, 1916–18.

Gregory of Rome, *Dialogues*, ed. with French transl., *SChr*, 251, 260, 265; Engl. transl. O. J. Zimmerman, New York, 1959.

Registrum, ed. *MGH Ep.* 1; *CCSL*, 140, 140A; partial English transl. J. Barmby, *Nicene and post-Nicene Fathers*, 2nd ser., 12f (with eccentric enumeration).

Gregory of Tours, ed. *MGH SRM*, 1.

Glory of the Confessors, transl. R. van Dam, Liverpool, 1988.

Glory of the Martyrs, transl. R. van Dam, Liverpool, 1988.

History of the Franks, transl. O. M. Dalton, Oxford, 1927, and L. Thorpe, Harmondsworth, 1974.

Life of the Fathers, transl. E. James, Liverpool, 1985.

Guerout, J., 'Le testament de Ste Fare', *Revue d'histoire ecclésiastique*, 60, 1965, 761–821.

Hamer, R. F. S., ed. and transl., *A Choice of Anglo-Saxon Verse*, London, 1970.

Heather, P., and Matthews, J., transls, *The Goths in the Fourth Century*, Liverpool, 1991.

Henry, P., *Les Églises de la Moldavie du nord*, 2 vols, Paris, 1930.

Herodian, ed. and transl. C. R. Whittaker, London, 1969–70.

Hillgarth, J. N., *Christianity and Paganism, 350–750*, Philadelphia, PA, 1986.

Historia de la conquesta de España de Abenalcotía el Cordobés, Span. transl. J. Ribera, Madrid, 1926.

Hugeburc, *Vita Willibaldi, MGH Scriptores*, 15: 86–106.

Hydatius, *Continuatio chronicorum, MGH AA*, 11.

Ibn 'Abd al-Hakam, *Conquête de l'Afrique du nord et de l'Espagne (Futuh' Ifriqiya wa'l-Andalus)* transl. A. Gateau, 2nd edn, Algiers, 1947.

Ibn Khaldun, *The Muqaddimah*, transl. F. Rosenthal, Princeton, NJ, 2nd edn, 1967.

Ioannes Lydus, *On Powers*, ed. and transl. A. C. Bandy, Philadelphia, PA, 1983.

Ishaq, *The Life of Muhammad: A Translation of Ishaq's Sirat Rasul Allah*, A. Guillaume, London, 1955.

Isidore of Seville, *Chronica, MGH AA*, 11.

    Etymologiae, ed. W. M. Lindsay, Oxford, 1911; ed. with Spanish transl., Madrid 1982–3; ed. with French transl., Paris, 1981+.

    De origine Getarum, ed. Th. Mommsen, *MGH AA*, 11; transl. G. Donini and G. B. Ford 2nd edn Leiden, 1970.

Jaffé, Ph., *Regesta pontificum Romanorum*, 1, Leipzig, 1885.

Jerome, *Lettres*, ed. and French transl. J. Labourt, Paris, 1949–63.

John Malalas, *Chronographia*, ed. H. Thurn, Berlin, 2000; transl. E. Jeffreys, M. Jeffreys, R. Scott *et al.*, Melbourne, 1986.

John Moschus, *Pratum spirituale*, ed. with French transl., *SChr*, 12; transl. *The Spiritual Meadow*, Kalamazoo, 1992.

John of Biclaro, *Continuatio Victoris, MGH AA*, 11.

John of Nikiu, *The Chronicle of John Bishop of Nikiu*, transl. R. H. Charles, London, 1916.

Jordanes, *De origine et actibus Getarum, MGH AA*, 5; transl. Chr. Mirow, *Gothic History*, Princeton, NJ, 1915.

Joshua the Stylite, *The Chronicle of Joshua the Stylite*, transl. William Wright, Cambridge, 1882.

Julian, *Works*, ed. and transl. W. C. Wright, London, 1913–23.

Julian of Toledo, *CCSL*, 115.

Justinian, *Corpus iuris civilis*, various eds, Berlin, 1870–93.

Küchler, M., ed. and Germ. transl., 'Moschee und Kalifenpaläste Jerusalems nach den Aphrodito – Papyri', *Zeitschrift des Deutschen Palästina-Vereins*, 107, 1991, 120–43.

Leges Burgundionum, MGH Leg nat Germ, 2/1.

Leges Langobardorum, MGH Leges, 4.

Leges Visigothorum, MGH Leg nat Germ, 1.

Lemerle, P., ed. and transl., *Les plus anciens recueils des miracles de saint Démétrius*, Paris, 1979, 1981.

Leo, pope, *Epistulae*, *PL*, 54; transl. E. Hunt, New York, 1957.

    Tractatus, *CCSL*, 138, 138A; transl. *Sermons*, J. P. Freeland and A. J. Conway, Washington, DC, 1996.

Le Strange, G., *Palestine under the Moslems*, London, 1890.

Lex Salica, *MHG Leg nat Germ*, 4/2.

Liber de caesaribus, ed. Fr. Pichlmayr, Leipzig, 1970.

Liber historiae Francorum, *MGH SRM*, 2, 215–328.

Liber pontificalis, ed. L. Duchesne, Paris, 1886–92; English transl. Raymond Davis, 1, Liverpool, 1989.

Lichtenstadter, I., *Introduction to Classical Arabic Literature*, New York, 1974.

Livre de la consécration du sanctuaire de Benjamin, ed. R.-G. Coquin, Cairo, 1975.

MacCoull, L. S. B., transl., 'The Paschal Letter of Alexander II, patriarch of Alexandria', *Dumbarton Oaks Papers*, 44, 1990, 27–40.

F. Makk, *Traduction et commentaire de l'homélie écrite probablement par Théodore le Syncelle sur le siège de Constantinople en 626*, Szeged, 1975 (= *Acta Antiqua et archaeologica*, 19).

Mansi, G. D., *Sacrorum conciliorum nova et amplissima collectio*, Paris and Leipzig, 1901–72.

Marcellinus comes, *Chronicon*, ed. *MGH AA*, 11; transl. B. Croke, Sydney, 1995.

Martinaus Capella, ed. James Willis, Leipzig; transl. W. H. Stahl, R. Johnson and E. L. Burge, New York, 1971–7.

Mas'udi (Maçoudi), *Les Prairies d'or*, ed. and French transl. C. Barbier de Menard and Pavet de Courteille, 3, Paris, 1864.

Maurice, *Strategikon*, ed. G. T. Dennis, Germ. transl. E. Gamillscheg, Vienna, 1981; Engl. transl. G. T. Dennis, Philadelphia PA, 1984.

Menander the Guardsman, *History*, ed. and transl. R. C. Blockley, Liverpool, 1985.

Mettke, H., *Altdeutsche Texte*, Leipzig, 1970.

Michael the Syrian, *Chronique de Michel le Syrien*, transl. J.-B. Chabot, 2, Paris, 1901.

The Miracles of Saint Artemios, Greek text with Engl. transl. V. S. Crisafulli and J. W. Nesbitt, Leiden, 1997.

Miscellanea wisigothica, ed. J. Gil, Seville, 1972.

Nau, F., ed., 'La plus ancienne Mention orientale des chiffres indiens', *Journal asiatique*, 10th ser., 16, 1910, pp. 208–28.

Nicholas Mysticus, *Letters*, ed. and transl. R. H. Jenkins and L. G. Westerink, Washington, DC, 1973.

Nikephoros, *Short History*, ed. and transl. C. Mango, Washington, DC, 1990.

The Nikonian Chronicle, 1: *From the Beginning to the Year 1132*, transl. Serge A. Zenkovsky, Princeton, NJ, 1984.

Nithard, *Historiae libri IIII*, ed. G. H. Pertz and E. Muller, Hanover, 1925.

Notker, *Gesta Karoli*, *MGH SS*, 2: 731–63; transl. Thorpe, as under Einhard.

Opus Caroli Regis contra Synodum, *MGH Concilia*, 2, suppl. 1.

Orosius, *Historiae adversum paganos libri vii*, ed. and French transl. M.-P. Arnaud-Lindet, Paris, 1990–1; Engl. transl. R. J. Deferrari, Washington, DC, 1964.

Pactus legis salicae, ed. *MGH Legum* 1, *Leg nat germ* 4/1; transl. K. F. Drew, Philadelphia, 1991.

Panégyriques latins, ed. and French transl. E. Galletier, Paris, 1949–55.

Paul the Deacon, *Historia Langobardorum*, *MGH SRLI*; transl. W. D. Foulkes, *The History of the Lombards*, repr. Philadelphia, PA, 1974.

Paulinus, *Poème d'action des grâces et prière*, ed. with *SChr*, 209; transl. H. G. Evelyn White, within *Ausonius*, 2, London, 1921.

Periplus maris Erithraei, ed. and transl. Lionel Casson, Princeton, NJ, 1989.

Pliny, *Natural History*, ed. and transl. H. Rackham, W. H. S. Jones and D. E. Eichholz, London, 1940–63.

Possidius, *Vita Augustini*, ed. M. Pellegrino, Alba, 1955; transl. Deferrari.

La Prise de Jérusalem par les Perses en 614, transl. G. Garitte, *CSCO*, 203 (*Scriptores Iberici*, 12).

Procopius, *History of the Wars, Anecdota, Buildings*, ed. and transl. H. B. Dewing, London, 1914–40.

Prudentius, *Contra Symmachum, CCSL*, 126: 215–88.

Poems, transl. M. Clement Eagar, New York, 1962.

The Holy Qur-an, ed. and transl. The Presidency of Islamic Researches.

Repertoire chronologique d'épigraphie arabe, 1, Cairo, 1931.

Rutilius Namatianus, *De Reditu suo*, ed. and Engl. transl. G. F. Savage-Armstrong, London, 1907.

Salvian, *De Gubernatione Dei*, ed. with French transl. *SChr*, 176, 220; English transl. J. F. O'Sullivan, New York, 1947.

Sauvaget, J., ed. and transl., *Relation de la Chine et de l'Inde*, Paris, 1946.

Sawyer, P., *Anglo-Saxon Charters: An Annotated List and Bibliography*, London, 1968.

Schork, R. J., *Sacred Song from the Byzantine Pulpit: Romanos the Melodist*, Gainesville, 1995.

Scripta saeculi VII Vitam Maximi confessoris illustrantia, with Latin transl., *CCSG*, 39.

Sebeos, *The Armenian History Attributed to Sebeos*, transl. with commentary R. W. Thomson, J. Howard-Johnston and T. Greenwood, Liverpool, 1999.

The Seventh Century in the West-Syrian Chronicles, transl. A. Palmer *et al.*, Liverpool, 1993.

Severus, *History of the Patriarchs of the Coptic Church of Alexandria*, ed. and transl. B. Evetts, *Patrologia orientalis*, 1.

Shahid, I., *The Martyrs of Najrâ: New Documents*, Brussels, 1971.

Shippey, T., ed. and transl., *Poems of Wisdom and Learning in Old English*, Cambridge, 1976.

Sidonius Apollinaris, *Poems and Letters*, ed. and transl. W. B. Anderson, London, 1936–65.

Sozomen, *Histoire ecclésiastique*, ed. J. Bidez, French transl. A.-J. Festugière, Paris, 1983+; Engl. transl. Ch. D. Hartranft, in *Select Library of Nicene and post-Nicene Fathers*, 2nd ser., 2 repr., 1973.

Speiser, J. M., 'Les Inscriptions de Thessalonique', *Travaux et Mémoires*, 5, 1975, pp. 145–80.

Strabo, *Geography*, ed. and transl. H. L. Jones, London, 1917–49.

Sulpicius Severus, *Dialogi, CSEL*, 1; Engl. transl. B. M. Peebles, New York, 1949.

al-Tabari, *The History of al-Tabari: An Annotated Translation*, Albany, 1985+.

Tablettes Albertini: actes privés de l'époque vandale, ed. Chr. Courtois, Paris, *c*.1952.

Tacitus, *Annales*, ed. and transl. John Jackson, London, 1931–7.

Agricola, ed. and transl. M. Hutton and R. M. Ogilive, and *Germania*, ed. and transl. H. Hutton and M. Warmington, London, 1970.

Théodoret de Cyr, *Histoire des moines de Syrie*, ed. and French transl. P. Cavinet and A. Leroy-Molinghen, Paris, 1977–9 (= *SChr*, 234, 257); Engl. transl. B. Jackson, *Select Library of the Nicene and post-Nicene Fathers*, 2nd ser., 3 repr., 1969.

Theophanes the Confessor, *The Chronicle*, transl. C. Mango and R. Scott, Oxford, 1997; ed. *Chronographia*, C. de Boor, Leipzig, 1883.

Theophylact Simocatta, *Historiae*, ed. C. de Boor and P. Wirth, Stuttgart, 1972; Engl. transl. M. and M. Whitby, Oxford, 1986.

Three Byzantine Saints, transl. N. Baynes and E. Dawes, Oxford, 1949.

Vegetius, *Epitome rei militaris*, ed. A. Önnerfors, Stuttgart, 1995 (Engl. transl. N. P. Milner, 2nd edn, Liverpool, 1996).

Venantius Fortunatus, *Poèmes*, ed. and transl. M. Reydellet, Paris, 1994– (partial Engl. transls J. George, Oxford, 1992; Liverpool, 1995).

Victor of Vita, *Historia persecutionis Africanae provinciae*, *CSEL*, 7; transl. John Moorhead.

Las Pizzaras Visigodas, ed. I. Vélaquez, Soriano, Murcia, 1989 (= *Antiquëdad y cristianismo*, 6).

Vie des pères du Jura, ed. and transl. F. Martine, Paris, 1986 (= *SChr*, 142).

Vita Antonii, ed. and French transl. G. J. M. Bartelink, Paris, 1994 (= *SChr*, 400); English transl. R. C. Gregg, 1980.

Vita Caesarii, *MGH SRM*, 3.

Vitae sanctorum Patrum Emeritensium, *CCSL*, 117.

Vita Samsonis, ed. R. Fawtier, *Bibliothèque de l'Ecole des Hautes Etudes*, 197, 1912, 93–172.

Vives, J., *Concilios Visigóticos e Hispano-Romanos*, Barcelona/Madrid, 1963.

  Inscripciones cristianas de la España romana y visigoda, Barcelona, 1942.

Webb, J. F., transl., *The Age of Bede*, Harmondsworth, 1983.

Welsh Annals ed. John Morris, London, 1980.

Wilkinson, John, transl., *Jerusalem Pilgrims Before the Crusades*, Warminster, 1977.

Wolf, K. B., transl., *Conquerors and Chroniclers of Early-Medieval Spain*, Liverpool, 1991.

Zosimus, *Histoire nouvelle*, ed. and French transl. Fr. Paschoud, Paris, 1971+; English transl. R. T. Ridley, Sydney, 1982.

II OTHER SOURCES

Abadie-Reynal, C., 'Céramique et commerce dans le bassin égéen du IVᵉ au VIIᵉ siècle', in *Hommes et richesses dans l'empire byzantine*, Paris, 1989, 143–59.

Almagro, M., Caballeco, L., Zozay, J., and Alamgro, A., *Qusayr 'Amra, residencia y baños en el deserto de Jordania*, Madrid, 1975.

Anselmino, L., *et al.*, *Il castellum del Nador storia di una fattoria tra Tipasa e Caesarea (I-Vi sec. d.C.)*, Rome, 1989.

Bahnassi, A., *The Great Omayyad Mosque of Damascus*, Damascus, 1989.

Bango Torviso, I. G., *Alta Edad Media de la tradición hispanogoda al románico* [no place], 1989.

Bastien, P., and Metzger, C., *Le trésor de Beaurains*, Arras, 1977.

Bayard, D., 'La céramique dans le nord de la Gaule à le fin de l'Antiquité (de le fin du IVᵉ au VIᵉ siècle). Présentation générale', in *La céramique du Ve au Xe siècle dans l'Europe du Nord-Ouest*, 107–28.

Bellamy, P., and Hitchner, R. B., 'The villas of the Vallée des Vaux and the Barbegal mill: excavations at La Mérindole villa and cemetery', *Journal of Roman Archaeology*, 9, 1996, 154–76.

Bierbrauer, V., 'Archäologie und Geschichte der Goten von 1–7. Jahrhundert: Versuch einer Bilanz', *Frühmittelalterliche Studien*, 28, 1994, 51–171.

Biscop, J.-L., and Sodini, J.-P., 'Travaux à Qal'at Sem'an', *International Congress of Christian Archaeology*, Rome, 1989, pp. 1675–93.

Bisheh, Gh., 'From castellum to palatium: Umayyad mosaic pavements from Qasr al-Hallabat in Jordan', *Muqarnas*, 10, 1993, 49–56.

Blair, S.S., *Islamic Inscriptions*, Edinburgh, 1998.

Bloom, J., *Minaret: Symbol of Islam*, Oxford, 1989.

Bonifay, M., and Piéri, D., 'Amphores du Ve au VIIe s. à Marseilles: nouvelles données sur la typologie et le contenu', *Journal of Roman Archaeology*, 8, 1995, 94–120.

Bruce-Mitford, R., *The Sutton Hoo Ship-burial*, London, 1975–83.

Brulet, R., and Ghenne-Dubois, M.-J., 'Autour de la tombe de Childéric', *Archeologia*, 189, 1984, 34–7.

Buchet, L., 'La déformation crânienne en Gaul et dans les régions limitrophes pendant le haut Moyen Age', *Archéologie médiévale*, 18, 1988, 55–71.

Büsing, H., Büsing Kolbe, A., and Bierbrauer, V., 'Die Dame von Focarolo', *Archeologia medievale*, 20, 1993, 303–32.

Camps, C., 'Rex gentium et rex Romanorum recherches sur les royaumes de Maurétanie des VIᵉ et VIIᵉ siècles', *Antiquités africaines*, 20, 1984, 183–218.

Carletti, C., 'I Graffiti sull'affresco di S. Luca nel cimitero di Commodilla', *Atti della Pontifica accademia romana di archeologia*, 57, 1984–5, 129–43.

Caričin Grad, 1, ed. N. Duval and V. Popovič, Rome and Belgrade, 1984; 2, ed. B. Bavant, V. Kondič and J.-M. Spieser, Rome and Belgrade, 1990.

Carver, M. O. H., ed., *The Age of Sutton Hoo: The Seventh Century in North-western Europe*, Woodbridge, 1992.

Clarke, G., *Roman Cemetery at Lankhills* (Winchester Studies 3/2), 1979.

Cormack, R., *Writing in Gold*, London, 1985.

Crawford, G. M., 'Excavations at Wasperton, third interim report', *West Midlands Archaeology*, 26, 1983, 29–35.

Creswell, K. A. C., *A Short Account of Early Muslim Architecture*, rev. J. W. Allan, Aldershot, 1989.

Deichmann, F. W., *Ravenna Haupstadt des spätantiken Abendlandes*, Wiesbaden, 1969–89.

De Rossi, G. B., 'Un insigne epigrafica di donazione di fondi fatta alla chiesa di s. Sussana dal papa Sergio ı', in his *Bullettino di archeologia cristiana*, Rome, 1870, 89–112.

Dexinger, F., and Seibt, W., 'A Hebrew lead seal from the period of the Sasanian occupation of Palestine (614–629 AD)', *Revue des Études Juives*, 140, 1981, 303–17.

Durliat, J., ed., *Les Dédicaces d'ouvrages de défense dans l'Afrique byzantine*, Rome, 1981.

Ennabli, L., *Les Inscriptions funéraires chrétiennes de la basilique de Sainte-Monique à Carthage*, Rome, 1975.

Les Inscriptions funéraires chrétiennes de Carthage, 2: *La Basilique de Mcidfa*, Rome, 1982; 3: *Carthage intra et extra muros*, Rome, 1991.

Everitt, A., *Continuity and Colonization: The Evolution of Kentish Settlement*, Leicester, 1986.

Excavations at Carthage, ed. H. P. Hurst *et al.*, Sheffield and Oxford, 1984–1994.

Excavations at Nessana, Princeton, NJ, 1950+.

Feissel, D., 'L'architecte Victorinus et les fortifications de Justinien dans les provinces balkaniques', *Bulletin de la Société nationale des antiquaires de France*, 1988, 136–46.

Fielder, U., *Studien zur Gräberfeldern des 6. bis 9. Jahrhunderts an der unteren Donau*, Bonn, 1992.

Fouet, G., *La Villa Gallo-Romaine de Montaubin*, Paris, 1969.

Frantz, A., *Late Antiquity* (= *The Athenian Agora*, 24), Princeton, NJ, 1988.

Fulford, M. G., and Peacock, D. P. S., *Excavations at Carthage: The British Mission*, Sheffield, 1984.

Gaube, H., *Ein Arabischer Palast in Südsyien Hirbet el-Baida*, Beirut, 1974.

Gentili, G. V., *La Villa Erculia di Piazza Armerina*, Rome, 1959.

Grabar, A., *Byzantine Painting*, London, 1979.

'Les Mosaïques de Germigny-des-Prés', *Cahiers archéologiques*, 7, 1954, 171ff.

Green, J., and Tsafrir, Y., 'Greek inscriptions from Hammat-Gader', *Israel Exploration Journal*, 32, 1982, 77–96.

Grierson, Ph., and Blackburn, M., *Medieval European Coinage with a Catalogue of the Coins in the Fitzwilliam Museum, Cambridge*, Cambridge, 1986.

Hamer, R., ed. and transl., *A Choice of Anglo-Saxon Verse*, London, 1970.

Hayes, J. W., *Excavations at Saraçhane in Istanbul, 2: The Pottery*, Princeton, NJ/Washington, DC, 1992.

Late Roman Pottery, London, 1972.

Supplement to Late Roman Pottery, London, 1980.

Heinen, H., *Trier und das Treverland in römischer Zeit*, Trier, 1985.

Hodges, R., and Mitchell, J., eds, *San Vicenzo al Volturno: The 1980–86 Excavations*, London, 1993, 1995.

Holum, K. G., 'Archaeological evidence for the fall of Byzantine Caesarea', *Bulletin of the American Schools of Oriental Research*, 286, 1992, 73–85.

Hope-Taylor, B., *Yeavering: An Anglo-British Centre of Early Northumbria*, London, 1977.

Jarnut, J., *Prosopographische und sozialgeschichtliche Studien zum Langobardenreich in Italien (568–744)*, Bonn, 1972.

Jayyusi, S. K., 'Umayyad poetry', in A. F. L. Beeston, ed., *Arabic Literature Towards the End of the Umayyad Period*, Cambridge, 1983, pp. 387–432.

Johns, E., and Bland, R., 'The great Hoxne treasure: a preliminary report', *Journal of Roman Archaeology*, 6, 1993, 493–6.

Kapitän, G., 'The church wreck off Marzameni', *Archaeology*, 22, 1969, 122–33.

Kazanski, M., 'La diffusion de la mode danubienne en Gaul (fin du IVe siècle–début du VIe siècle): essai d'interprétation historique', *Antiquités nationales*, 12, 1989, 59–73.

Keay, S. J., *Late Roman Amphorae in the western Mediterranean*, Oxford, 1984.

Kent, J. P. C., and Painter, K. S., *Wealth of the Roman World AD 300–700*, London, 1977.

Klein-Pfeuffer, M., *Merowingerzeitliche Fibeln und Anhänger aus Preßblech*, Marburg, 1993.

Lafaurie, J., and Morrisson, C., 'La pénétration des monnaies byzantines en Gaul mérovingienne et visigothique du VIe au VIIe siècle', *Revue numismatique*, 29, 1987, 38–98.

Leveau, P., 'The Barbegal water mill in its environment: archaeology and the economic and social history of antiquity', *Journal of Roman Archaeology*, 9, 1996, 137–53.

Lowden, John, *Early Christian and Byzantine Art*, London, 1997.

Mackeprang, M. B., *De Nordiske Guldbrakteater*, Aarhus, 1952.

McNally, Sheila, 'Diocletian's Palace Split in the middle ages', *Archaeology*, 28, 1975, 248–59.

Magness, J., 'The Walls of Jerusalem in the early Islamic period', *Biblical Archaeologist*, 54, 1991, 208–17.

Marrou, H.-I., 'Epitaphe chrétienne d'Hippone à réminiscenses virgiliennes', *Libyca archéologie-épigraphie*, 1, 1953, 215–30.

Mattingly, D. J., and Hayes, J. W., 'Nador and fortified farms in north Africa', *Journal of Roman Archaeology*, 5, 1992, 408–18.

Ma'oz, Z. U., and Killebrew, A., 'Ancient Qasin: synagogue and village', *Biblical Archaeologist*, 51, 1988, 5–19.

Mazal, O., *Wiener Genesis*, Frankfurt, 1980.

Mengarelli, R., 'La necropoli barbarica de Castel Trosino, presso Piceno', *Monumenti antichi della Reale Accademia dei Lincei*, 12, 1902, 145–380.

Miles, G. C., 'Early Islamic inscriptions near Ta'if in the Hijaz', *Journal of Near Eastern Studies*, 7, 1948, 236–42.

Molajoli, B., *La Basilica Eufrasiana di Parenzo*, Padua, 1943.

Mundell Mango, M., *Silver from Early Byzantium: The Kaper Koraon and Related Treasures*, Baltimore, MD, 1986.

Ovadiah, A., *Corpus of Byzantine Churches in the Holy Land*, Bonn, 1970.

Palol, Pedro de, *Arte hispanico de la epoca visigoda*, Barcelona, 1969.

Paribeni, R., 'La necropoli barbarica di Nocera Umbra', *Monumenti antichi*, 25, 1918, 136–352.

Parker, A. J., *Ancient Shipwrecks of the Mediterranean and Roman Provinces*, Oxford, 1992.

Piccirillo, M., 'Le inscrizioni di Um er-Rasa-Kastron Mefaa in Giordania I (1986–1987)', *Liber annuus studium biblicum fransiscanum*, 37, 1987, 177–239.

'The Umayyad churches of Jordan', *Annual of the Department of Antiquities (Jordan)*, 28, 1984, 333–41.

Pilet, Ch., *La Nécropole de Frénouville: étude d'un population de la fin du IIIe à la fin du VIIe siècle*, Oxford, 1980.

Pilet, Ch., *et al.*, 'Les nécropoles de Giberville (Calvados) fin du Ve siècle–fin du VIIe siècle après J.-C.', *Archéologie médiévale*, 20, 1990, 3–140.

'Le village de Sonnerville, «Lirosse» Fin de la période gauloise au VIIe siècle ap. J.-C.', *Archéologie médiévale*, 22, 1992, 1–189.

Rinaldi, M. L., 'Il costume romano e i mosaici di Piazza Armerina', *Rivista dell'Istituto nazionale d'archeologia e storia dell'arte*, 13f, 1964f, 200–68.

Rodiewicz, M., *Alexandrie III*, Warsaw, 1984.

Roll, I., and Ayalon, E., 'The Market street at Apollonia-Arsuf', *Bulletin of the American Schools of Oriental Research*, 267, 1987, 61–76.

Rouéché, C., *Aphrodisias in Late Antiquity*, London, 1989.

Russell, J., 'Anemurium: the changing face of a Roman city', *Archaeology*, 33(5), 1980, 31–40.

Salin, E., *La civilisation mérovingienne*, Paris, 1949–59.

Sanders, G. D. R., 'A late Roman bath at Corinth', *Hesperia*, 68, 1999, 441–80.

Schiavone, A., ed., *Storia di Roma*, 3, Turin, 1993.

Sondini, J.-P., 'La contribution de l'archéologie à la connaissance du monde byzantin (IVe–VIIe siècles', *Dumbarton Oaks Papers*, 47, 1993, 139–84.

Tate, G., *Les Campagnes de la Syrie du nord*, I, Paris, 1992.

Thomas, Ch., 'East and west: Tintagel, Mediterranean imports and the early insular church', in S. M. Pearce, ed., *The Early Church in Western Britain and Ireland*, Oxford, 1982, 17–34.

Tóth, E. R., 'Preliminary account of the Avar princely find at Kunábony', *Cumania*, 1, 1972, 143–60.

Tsafrir, Y., and Foerster, G., 'Urbanism at Scythopolis-Bet Shean in the fourth to seventh centuries', *Dumbarton Oaks Papers*, 51, 1997, 85–146.

Van Alfen, P. G., 'New light on the seventh century Yassi Ada shipwreck: capacities and standard sizes of LRA1 amphoras', *Journal of Roman Archaeology*, 9, 1996, 189–213.

Van Ossel, P., *Etablissements ruraux de l'antiquité tardive dans le nord de la Gaule*, Paris, 1992 (= *Gallia*, suppl. 51).

de Vaux, R., 'Une mosaïque byzantine à Ma'in (Transjordanie)', *Revue biblique*, 47, 1938, 227–58.

Walker, John, *A Catalogue of the Arab-Byzantine and post-reform Umaiyad Coins*, London, 1956.

Ward-Perkins, B., 'Two Byzantine houses at Luni', *Papers of the British School at Rome*, 49, 1981, 91–8.

Watson, Andrew, *Agricultural Innovation in the Early Islamic World: The Diffusion of Crops and Farming Techniques, 700–1100*, Cambridge, 1983.

Weinberg, G. D., 'A wandering soldier's grave in Corinth', *Hesperia*, 43, 1974, 512–21.

Weitzmann, K., ed., *Age of Spirituality*, New York, 1979.

'The ivories of the so-called Grado chair', *Dumbarton Oaks Papers*, 26, 1972, 43–92.

Weitzmann, K., and Keesler, H. L., *The Cotton Genesis*, Princeton, NJ, 1986.

Werner, J., *Der Grabfund von Malaja Pereščepina und Kuvrat, Kagan der Bulgaren*, Munich, 1984.

West, S. E., 'The Anglo-Saxon village of West Stow', *Medieval Archaeology*, 13, 1969, 1–20.

Wilpert, J., *Die Römischen Mosaiken und Malereien*, 3, Freiburg, 1917.

III MODERN WORKS

General

Brown, Peter, *The Rise of Western Christendom*, Oxford, 1996.

Fowden, Garth, *Empire to Commonwealth: Consequences of Monotheism in Late Antiquity*, Princeton, NJ, 1993.

Hauck, K., 'Von einer spätantiken Randkultur zum karolingischen Europa', *Frühmittelalterliche Studien*, 1, 1967, 3–93.

Herrin, Judith, *The Formation of Christendom*, Princeton, NJ, 1987.

Randsborg, K., *The First Millennium AD in Europe and the Mediterranean*, Cambridge, 1991.

Webster, Leslie, and Brown, Michelle, *The Transformation of the Roman World, AD 400–900*, London, 1997.

Wolfram, H., *Das Reich und die Germanen*, Berlin, 1990.

The Empire

Brown, Peter, *The World of Late Antiquity*, London, 1989.

Burr, V., *Nostrum mare Ursprung und Geschichte der Namen des Mittelmeers und seiner Teilmeere im Altertum*, Stuttgart, 1932.

Cameron, Averil, *The Mediterranean World in Late Antiquity AD 395–600*, London, 1993.

Jones, A. H. M., *The Later Roman Empire*, Oxford, 1964.

Western Mediterranean I

Amory, P., *People and Identity in Ostrogothic Italy, 489–554*, Cambridge, 1997.

Arce, J., *España entre el mundo antiguo y el mundo medieval*, Madrid, 1988.

Collins, Roger, *Early Medieval Spain: Unity in Diversity, 400–1000*, 2nd edn, Basingstoke, 1995.

Courtois, Ch., *Les Vandales et l'Afrique*, Paris, 1955.

Goffart, W., *Barbarians and Romans*, Princeton, NJ, 1980.

I Goti, Milan, 1994.

Heather, Peter, *The Goths*, Oxford, 1996.

  Goths and Romans, 332–489, Oxford, 1991.

Magistra barbaritas: I barbari in Italia, Milan, 1984.

Moorhead, J., *Theoderic in Italy*, Oxford, 1992.

Orlandis, J., *Historia de España época visigoda (409–711)*, Madrid, 1987.

Vallejo Girves, *Bizancio y la España tardoantigua (ss. V–VII): un capitulo de historia mediterranea*, Alaca de Henares, 1993.

Wickham, Chris, *Early Medieval Italy: Central Power and Local Society, 400–1000*, London, 1981.

Wolfram H., *History of the Goths*, Engl. transl., Berkeley, CA, 1988.

Wolfram, H., and Schwarcz, A., ed., *Anerkennung und Integration*, Vienna, 1988.

From Gaul to France

Anton, H. H., *Trier im frühen Mittelalter*, Paderborn, 1987.

Geary, P. J., *Before France and Germany: The Creation and Transformation of the Merovingian World*, New York, 1988.

Heinzelmann, M., 'Gallische Prosopographie 260–527', *Francia*, 10, 1982, 531–718.

Heinzelmann, M., and Poulin, J. C., *Les Vies anciennes de sainte Geneviève de Paris*, Paris/Geneva, 1986.

James, E., *The Franks*, Oxford, 1988.

Périn, P., 'A propos de publications étrangères récentes concernant le peuplement en Gaule à l'époque mérovingienne: la »question franque«', *Francia*, 8, 1980, 537–52.

Pietri, L., *La Ville de Tours du IVe au VIe siècle naissance d'une cité chrétienne*, Rome, 1983.

Werner, K. F., *Histoire de France*, I: *Les origines (avant l'an mille)*, Paris, 1984.

  'La «Conquête franque» de la Gaule Itinéraires: historiographiques d'une erreur', *Bibliothèque de l'École des chartes*, 154, 1996, 7–45.

Wood, Ian, *The Merovingian Kingdoms 450–751*, London, 1993.

From Britain to England

Bassett, S., ed., *The Origins of Anglo-Saxon Kingdoms*, Leicester, 1989.

Campbell, J., John, E., and Wormald, P., *The Anglo-Saxons*, Oxford, 1982.

Esmonde-Cleary, S., *The Ending of Roman Britain*, London, 1989.

Jones, M. E., *The End of Roman Britain*, Ithaca, NY, 1996.

Mayr-Harting, H., *The Coming of Christianity to Anglo-Saxon England*, 3rd edn, London, 1991.

Rutherford-Davis, K., *Britons and Saxons in the Chiltern Region 400–700*, Chichester, 1982.

Vince, A., *Saxon London: An Archaeological Investigation*, London, 1990.

Webster, L., and Backhouse, J., eds, *The Making of England: Anglo-Saxon Art and Culture, AD 600–900*, Toronto, 1991.

Western Mediterranean II
(beyond the works cited for Western Mediterranean I)

Bavant, B., 'Cadre de vie et habitat urbain en Italie centrale byzantine (VIᵉ–VIIᵉ siècles)', Mélanges de l'Ecole Française de Rome Moyen âge, 101, 1989, 465–532.

Brown, T. S., *Gentlemen and Officers: Imperial Administration and Aristocratic Power in Byzantine Italy, AD 554–800*, Rome, 1984.

Christie, Neil, *The Lombards: The Ancient Longobards*, Oxford, 1995.

Ferreiro, A., ed., *The Visigoths: Studies in Culture and Society*, Leiden, 1999.

Gasparri, S., and Cammarosano, P., eds, *Langobardia*, Udine, 1990.

Markus, R. A., *Gregory the Great and His World*, Cambridge, 1997.

Schiavone, A., ed., *Storia di Roma*, 3, Turin, 1993.

South of the Danube

Gyuzelev, V., *The Proto-Bulgarians*, Sophia, 1979.

Maenchen-Helfen, J. O., *The World of the Huns*, ed. Max Knight, Berkeley, CA, 1973.

Metcalf, D. M., 'Avar and Slav invasions into the Balkan peninsula (c.575–625): the nature of the numismatic evidence', *Journal of Roman Archaeology*, 4, 1991, 140–8.

Nystazopoulou-Pelekidon, M., 'Les Slavs dans l'empire byzantin', *Seventeenth International Byzantine Congress: Major Papers*, New York, 1986, 345–67.

Pohl, W., *Die Awaren: Ein Steppenvolk in Mitteleuropa 567–822 n. Chr*, Munich, 1988.

Urbanczyk, P., ed., *Origins of Central Europe*, Warsaw, 1997.

Villes et peuplement dans l'Illyricum protobyzantin, Rome, 1984.

Wiethmann, M. W., 'Strukturkontinuität und -Diskontinuität auf der greichischen Halbinsel im Gefolge der Slavischen Landnahme', *Müncher Zeitschrift für Balkankunde*, 2, 1979, 141–76.

East I

Brandes, W., *Die Städte Kleinasiens im 7. und 8. Jahrhundert*, Berlin, 1989.

'Die byzantinische Stadt Kleinasiens im 7. und 8. Jahrhundert – ein Forschungs-berichte', *Klio*, 70, 1988, 176–208.

Crone, P., and Cook, M., *Hagarism: The Making of the Islamic World*, Cambridge, 1977.

Haldon, J., *Byzantium in the Seventh Century*, Cambridge, 1990.

LaBianca, O. S., ed., *Sedentarization and Nomadisation: Food System Cycles at Hesban and Vicinity in Transjordan*, Herrien Springs, MI, 1990.

Shaban, M. A., *Islamic History: A New Interpretation*, 1: *AD 600–750 (AH 132)*, Cambridge, 1971.

Shahid, I., *Byzantium and the Arabs in the Sixth Century*, Washington, DC, 1995+.

Stein, E., *Histoire du bas-empire*, Paris, 1949.

Wittow, M., 'Ruling the late Roman and Byzantine city: a continuous history', *Past and Present*, 129, 1990, 3–29.

East II (beyond the works cited for East I)

Gervers, M., and Bikhazi, R. M., eds, *Conversion and Continuity: Indigenous Christian Communities in Islamic Lands, Eighth to Eighteenth Centuries*, Toronto, 1990.

Grabar, O., *The Formation of Islamic Art*, rev. edn, New Haven, CT, 1987.

Hillenbrand, R., '*La dolce vita* in early Islamic Syria: the evidence of later Islamic palaces', *Art History*, 5, 1982, 1–35.

  Islamic Architecture, Edinburgh, 1994.

MacCoull, L. S. B., 'The fate of Coptic', *Bulletin de la Société archéologique copte*, 27, 1985, 61–70.

Piccirillo, M., *The Mosaics of Jordan*, Amman, 1993.

Schick, R., 'Palestine in the early Islamic period: luxuriant legacy', *Near Eastern Archaeology*, 61, 1998, 74–108.

Taha, A., *The Muslim Conquest and Settlement of North Africa and Spain*, London, 1989.

Systems great and small

Claude, D., *Der Handel in westlichen Mittelmeer während des Frühmittelalters*, Göttingen, 1985.

Hodges, R., and Bowden, W., ed. *The Sixth Century: Production, Distribution and Demand*, Leiden, 1998.

Hodges, R., and Whitehouse, D., *Mohammed, Charlemagne and the Origins of Europe*, London, 1989.

Pirenne, H., *Mohammed and Charlemagne*, Engl. transl., London, 1939.

INDEX